Faulk's Basic Forensic Psychiatry

Faulk's Basic Forensic Psychiatry

Third edition

Revised by

J.H. Stone, M. Roberts, J. O'Grady & A.V. Taylor
with K. O'Shea

Blackwell
Science

Editorial offices:
Blackwell Science Ltd, 9600 Garsington Road, Oxford OX4 2DQ, UK
   Tel: +44 (0) 1865 776868
Blackwell Publishing Inc., 350 Main Street, Malden, MA 02148-5020, USA
   Tel: +1 781 388 8250
Blackwell Science Asia Pty Ltd, 550 Swanston Street, Carlton, Victoria 3053, Australia
   Tel : +61 (0)3 8359 1011

First edition published 1994
Second edition published 1995
Third edition published 2000
Reprinted 2003, 2005, 2006

ISBN-10: 0-632-05019-5
ISBN-13: 978-0-632-05019-2

Library of Congress Cataloging-in-Publication Data

Faulk's basic forensic psychiatry. – 3rd ed./
revised by J.H. Stone ... [et al.]
   p. cm.
  Rev. ed. of: Basic forensic psychiatry/
Malcolm Faulk. 2nd ed. 1994.
    Includes bibliographical references and
      index.
      ISBN 0–632–05019–5
     1. Forensic psychiatry. I. Stone, J.H.
     II. Faulk, Malcolm. Basic forensic
psychiatry. III. Title: Basic forensic
psychiatry.
    [DNLM: 1. Forensic Psychiatry. W 740
F2631 1999]
RA1151.F36   1999
614'.1–dc21
DNLM/DLC
for Library of Congress   99-34502
                        CIP

A catalogue record for this title is available from the British Library

Set in 10/12pt Times
by DP Photosetting, Aylesbury, Bucks
Printed and bound in India
by Gopsons Papers, Noida

The publisher's policy is to use permanent paper from mills that operate a sustainable forestry
policy, and which has been manufactured from pulp processed using acid-free and elementary
chlorine-free practices. Furthermore, the publisher ensures that the text paper and cover board used
have met acceptable environmental accreditation standards.

For further information on Blackwell Publishing, visit our website:
www.blackwellpublishing.com

Contents

Preface to Third Edition

In 1971, Dr Malcolm Faulk became one of the first jointly appointed Consultant Forensic Psychiatrists. He later wrote the first and, for some time, the only text book of Forensic Psychiatry in this country. This is the third edition of that text book to be published. Although larger text books have since been published, we believe that this book remains one of the most accessible and practical books on the subject. It should be useful to all practitioners in both the Mental Health Services, Criminal Justice Agencies and others who work with mentally abnormal offenders.

Although it is only six years since the second edition, it has been comprehensively revised and updated to take account of changes in forensic psychiatry practice and recent legislation. The latter include the Crime Sentences Act (1997), the Sex Offender Act (1997) and the Crime and Disorder Act (1998). In addition, the concepts of risk assessment and risk management, the treatment of sex offenders and the relationship of mental disorder to violence have all been introduced into this edition. However, the basic format of the first two editions of the text book, which has proved to be so successful, has been retained.

It is a well-known fact that any text book becomes out of date almost as soon as it is published. In our case, we are aware that the current review of the Mental Health Act which may lead to comprehensive changes in that legislation within the next few years and the current debate on the treatment of people with severe personality disorder, have both occurred since this edition was completed.

As editors, we hope that we have produced a book that lives up to the high standards of the first two editions written by Dr Faulk.

Finally, we would like to thank the contribution of all of our colleagues at Ravenswood House and our families, who have helped us in the preparation of this edition. In particular, we acknowledge the hard work undertaken by Dr Jane Ewbank who has compiled the index.

Huw Stone, Mark Roberts, John O'Grady, Amanda Taylor
Ravenswood House
Fareham, Hampshire

Chapter 1

The Forensic Psychiatry Services

Introduction

This chapter gives an outline of the areas in which forensic psychiatry is practised and covers the penal system, special hospitals, regional secure units, low secure units within local psychiatric hospitals, diversion schemes and community facilities.

Definition

'Forensic' means pertaining to, or connected with, or used in courts of law. A forensic psychiatrist's work may be said to start with the preparation of psychiatric reports for the court on the mental state of offenders suspected of having a mental abnormality. The psychiatrist will then be expected to provide or arrange treatment for the mentally abnormal offender where appropriate. Other psychiatrists and other professionals seeing the sort of patient the forensic psychiatrist is looking after will refer similar patients who may not actually have reached the court or broken the law. In practice all psychiatrists may, at some time or another, have to prepare psychiatric reports on their own patients.

The penal system

The large majority of the prisons are run by the Prison Service (an agency service to the Home Office) though there are increasing moves to contract out the running of the prisons to private companies answerable directly to the Director General of the Prison Service. The penal system is divided into facilities for prisoners on remand (awaiting trial) and facilities for convicted offenders.

There are prisons for adults over 21, convicted or remanded, and young offenders' institutions (which may be part of an existing prison or a separate institution) and remand centres for young people aged 17–21. The system is largely segregated into female prisons and male prisons but in some high security prisons the sexes are kept in separate wings of the same institution. Remand facilities for adults are generally centred in old prisons in the centre of county towns. Remand centres for young people are often separate new buildings. Whilst on remand the inmate has many rights (which are lost after conviction); own clothes may be worn, and frequent visitors are permitted, etc. Once convicted, the imprisoned offender is placed with other convicted offenders, prison clothes must be worn (though this rule is being relaxed), visitors are restricted and prison rules apply governing discipline and management. The adult convicted prisoner will subsequently be allocated to a prison with security appropriate to the case. The young adult (17–21) will be allocated to a young offenders' institution. All prisoners on ordinary custodial sentence serve only a proportion of their sentence in prison with a proportion in the community (the longer sentenced offenders on supervision). After a certain time, people on long sentences and life sentences have their case reviewed at set intervals by the parole board.

Advice on policy, standards and staffing relating to health care of prisoners within the Prison Service is currently the responsibility of the Health Care Service for Prisoners, a department (or directorate) of the Prison Service with its own medical director. This will change in 1999 through a formal partnership between the Prison Service and NHS. Each prison governor is responsible for seeing that there is proper health care for the inmates in his establishment. Each prison has a health care centre (varying from the equivalent of a general practice office in the smaller establishments to a building and service for in-patients' beds in the larger establishments) staffed by doctors and nursing staff responsible to the governor of the prison. Inmates with physical or mental illness will have to be cared for there until such time as they recover or can be transferred to the National Health Service (NHS). From a psychiatric point of view it is important to realise that the Health Care Centre is not recognised as a hospital within the meaning of the Mental Health Act and the doctors are therefore unable to treat any patient against his will except in certain emergencies. Floridly psychotic patients may have to remain untreated until they can be transferred to the NHS unless they are willing to cooperate or their condition deteriorates so that treatment becomes imperative.

The prison medical staff is made up of some 130 doctors who have been employed directly by the Home Office to work full time in the penal system. They are complemented by a similar number of practitioners employed to work sessions within the prisons. The present prison medical officers come from a varied background, some will have higher degrees in psychiatry while others will have acquired the bulk of their experience in psychiatry whilst in post. The history of medical services in prisons is described by Chiswick and Dooley.[1]

One of the lessons of history is that the plight of mentally disordered offenders is not a new problem, but can be traced historically through the eighteenth, nineteenth and twentieth centuries. This runs counter to the accepted wisdom that the plight of mentally disordered offenders is a modern problem caused by the demise of the mental hospital. The opening of Broadmoor Hospital in 1863 was in part prompted by public and governmental concern at the reluctance of county asylums to accept mentally disordered offenders. The medical service for the prisons began in the eighteenth century to preserve the health of prisoners. Legislation in 1808, 1816 and 1840 allowed the transfer of insane prisoners to a county asylum. Other arrangements within the prisons had to be made for mental defectives (housing them in particular prisons) until legislation in 1867 permitted their transfer to the county asylums. Later legislation (Mental Deficiency Acts 1913 and 1927) set up special institutions for the defective. An attempt was made to deal with inebriates by the Inebriates Act (1898) which enabled courts to send them to reformatories. This system was abandoned by the 1920s.

In the 1920s there was increasing interest in the possibility of using psychotherapy within the prisons to treat some offenders whose offending could be understood to have a neurotic basis. In 1939, Dr Norwood East (prison medical officer) and Dr W. de Hubert (visiting psychiatrist) recommended the setting up of a penal institution for (a) medical investigation and criminological research into treatment for selected prisoners and (b) a colony for offenders who could not adapt to ordinary life. This recommendation eventually resulted in the setting up of Grendon Prison (opened 1962), a prison with a psychiatrist as governor and using psychotherapeutic methods with psychopathic offenders.

Health Services and Prisons

The prison medical service is the oldest civilian medical service. Its origins can be traced to public concern about the spread of typhus from prisons to the surrounding communities. Prisoners are separated from society and their health care has also become separated from mainstream NHS provision. Smith,[2] reviewing the prison health service in 1984, was highly critical of its isolation and inability to deliver care to the same standard as that found in the NHS. Most recently the Chief Inspector of Prisons[3] concluded that 'The overall service provided does not match up to National Health standards or satisfy the provisions of the Patients Charter'. The report, *Patient or Prisoner*[3] concluded 'It is no longer sensible to maintain a Health Service for prisoners separate from the National Health Service'. The inadequacies and difficulties in care of prisoners are well described by Reed and Lynn.[4] Many of the problems of health care in prisons can however, be traced to inadequacies within the National Health Service. Long waiting lists for admission to medium secure units and special hospitals inevitably means that seriously mentally ill people are left in prison to be treated within facilities that are neither designed nor staffed to cope with their complex needs. The Mental Health Act does not apply in prisons and hence, compulsory treatment is not possible except within the very narrow limits laid down by common law. Prisons have no choice in whom they accept and health services in prisons have to cope with patients deemed untreatable within the National Health Service.

The principal aim of prisons is to keep in custody those committed by the courts.[5] It is not difficult therefore, for there to be conflicts of interest between security and treatment. There does not need however to be any incompatibility between health care and security, a principle supported by the United Kingdom Central Council for Nursing Midwifery and Health Visiting (UKCC). Special hospitals and regional secure units have been able to develop care in a secure environment.

The Health Advisory Committee for the Prison Service[6] advocates equivalence of care as the guiding principle in the development of health care within prisons. Equivalence should exist from the application of National Health policies to prisoners, provision of care at least equal to that in the NHS, equality of access to services and equivalent standards and training of those delivering health care within prisons. In practice, that should mean that prisoners have full access to community mental health teams, and their needs met within the framework on the care programme approach and enjoy seamless integration between their care in prisons and aftercare in the community upon release. Such an approach to health care within prisons will only work if the fundamental principle laid down by the Reed Committee is adhered to, namely that those inmates requiring in-patient care should receive that care through transfer to an NHS hospital.[7] Continuing long waiting lists for admission to medium secure units and special hospital place intolerable burdens on the prison health service, and this in turn could destroy any gains made in a future reform of the service. In the USA, Roth[8] expressed concern about moves to transform prisons into places of treatment and such moves might have the unforeseen consequence of allowing services outside prisons to divest themselves of any responsibility to the care of prisoners ultimately leading to deprivation of their right to receive care within a National Health Service hospital when they require it.

Concerns about the state of health care in prisons brought into sharp focus by the Chief Inspector of Prisons' report *Patient or Prisoner*[3] resulted in a Home Office/NHS working group on the future of health care in prisons. The report, accepted by government, recommends a formal part-nership between the prison service and the National Health Service to ensure equivalence of care, best use of resources inside and outside prisons and continuity of care between prison and community. This will be delivered though a policy board within the NHS, developing systems and standards for health care within prisons backed up by a task force to improve standards and with an ultimate aim of ensuring that the delivery of health care within prisons will eventually be by NHS staff and services.

Equivalence of care is central to the report's conclusions and will be reflected in primary care physicians within prisons being eligible to be a principal within general practice and secondary mental health care being delivered by doctors eligible for a GMC Specialist Register (Psychiatry). Historically, attempts to improve the health care of the prisoners have foundered and it remains to be seen whether a formal partnership between prisons and the NHS will deliver high standards of care to prisoners.

Psychiatric disorder amongst prisoners

The last decade has seen a sustained effort to understand the epidemiology of mental disorder in prisons. Gunn and colleagues have systematically surveyed convicted[9] and unconvicted[10] prisoners to describe the pattern of disorder among prisoners. The Office of National Statistics[11] using different methodology and definitions of disorder also systematically described the distribution of mental disorder in prisoners. This study is particularly important as exactly the same methodology and definitions of disorder were used to describe the pattern of disorder in the general population, thus allowing a direct comparison to be made between prisoners and the general population. Together these surveys provide evidence of a startlingly high incidence of mental disorder amongst prisoners. Because of the ability to compare figures directly with the general population, only the ONS study will be described in detail.

Only one in ten prisoners showed no evidence of any mental disorder and no more than two out of ten had only one disorder. Co-morbidity was the norm. High rates of neurotic disorder were found with rates of between 39% and 75% found in different sample groups (sentenced to unsentenced, male and female) compared to 14% in the ONS survey of adults living in the community. Women had generally higher scores on the neurotic scale than men. Using a standard instrument for screening for personality disorder (the structured clinical interview for DSM IV, SCID-11) the ONS study came to the startling conclusion that prevalence of any personality disorder among prisoners was 78%, with anti-social personality disorder having the highest prevalence of any category of personality disorder. Paranoid personality disorder was the second most prevalent personality disorder whilst borderline personality disorder was more common in female prisoners. The high incidence of anti-social personality disorder is perhaps not surprising, given the prominence of criminal and anti-social acts in the definition of that disorder, but even allowing for that, the incidence of other personality disorders was markedly high in the prison population. There was considerable overlap between those with various forms of personality disorder and evidence of functional psychosis, drug dependence and neurotic symptoms. The prevalence of functional psychosis was 7% for male sentenced, 10% for male remand and 40% for female prisoners. This compares to the ONS figures for the community sample of 0.4%. This study has interesting findings on intellectual functioning, social functioning and risk factors and mental disorder. Their findings point to prisoners as a group who are disadvantaged across a wide range of intellectual, social and personal functioning measures.

Alcohol misuse and drug dependence were found to be particularly high in the prison population. The majority of prisoners had used illicit drugs at some point in their life and many continued their drug use in prison. A high percentage of prisoners reported a degree of dependence on drugs, over 50% of remand prisoners reporting such dependence. National policy for the delivery of health services should be delivered on a basis of need. If equivalence of care is to be applied to the prison population, this may mean that prisons should receive an enhanced level of psychiatric care compared to the general population on the basis of the demonstrably greater prevalence of mental disorder amongst prisoners.

Substance misuse emerges as a particularly important issue in prisons. Co-morbidity between substance misuse and other disorders has serious implications for treatment. In the NHS, treatment services for the mentally ill and substance misuse are often separate with the ever present danger of the mentally ill substance misuser fitting the criteria for neither service. In the prison system, there has been a laudable effort to apply the UK government's strategy for tackling drugs[12] but the development of this service is not yet integrated with developments and provision of health care within prisons. Johns[13] reviews substance misuse and offending and discusses attempts to integrate mental health services and substance misuse services into systems that can cope with people with co-morbid conditions. This has particular relevance for prisoners.

Special problems in prison

The combination of committing a dreadful offence or being arrested and charged, separated from normal surroundings, imprisoned and facing the uncertainties of a trial and sentencing, naturally increases tension and feelings of dysphoria and depression. A good prison regime (based on human decency, consideration for the individual, sensible surroundings and interesting occupation) will do a lot to counteract these baleful effects.[13] In all prisons, but especially where the regimes are poor (inconsiderate staff with corresponding inmate hostility, lack of occupation, poor surroundings) it is more likely that the prisoner will show some adverse psychological reaction e.g. depression/anxiety/tension. There are also behaviours which seem particularly associated with imprisonment which the doctor may be asked to deal with. These include:

(1) suicide attempts;
(2) food refusal;

(3) self-mutilation;
(4) sleep disturbance.

Suicide attempts
Suicide rates have been increasing in prison (121% over 15 years) and are estimated to be higher than in the community as a whole[15] though there are methodological difficulties in assessing this (getting a proper control group). Higher rates in prison are especially associated with the first few stressful weeks on remand, long-term imprisonment and committing violent or destructive offences. The suicides seem associated with isolation, guilt, remorse, depression and despair, though a proportion are associated with psychosis. One-third will have had previous psychiatric contact. Unfortunately, there are no control studies to confirm whether these associations are solely a reaction to the stress of prison and loss of family, etc. or a feature of unstable prisoners. A ten year follow-up study of conscripts to the Swedish Army, for example, found a suicide rate more than three times normal amongst those with some features of anti-social personality.[16]

The increased death rate from suicide in prisoners is mirrored by the increased death rate in ex-prisoners (five times normal) and violent offenders where the principal causes of death are poisoning from drug abuse and violence.[17]

Prisons have responded by developing specific policies for identification and management of risk but there is no true evidence that such policies lead to reduction in the incidence of suicide amongst prisoners. Prisoners who are deemed to be at risk of suicide have characteristics indistinguishable from other prisoners, making it difficult to determine if the right people are being targeted in risk minimisation programmes. The 'listener scheme' is a particular innovation in British prison approaches to suicide prevention. In this system, prisoners offer support to vulnerable prisoners at times of crisis and are available to do what their title suggests, namely listen.

Food refusal
Inmates may refuse food and sometimes drink. Two forms may be recognised.[18]

(i) A minority who are seriously mentally ill. Their food refusal may well be coupled with fluid refusal. They are characterised by generally (though not always) being unable or unwilling to give a reason. They require urgent transfer to a psychiatric hospital.
(ii) A majority who use the food refusal in an argument with authority. 'I will refuse to eat until . . .' will not have serious psychiatric disorder. Some will have a severe personality disorder and one or two may also be psychotic or depressed. Prisons have a routine of having all food refusers psychiatrically assessed so that those who are psychiatrically ill can be identified and treated. Those who are normal usually respond to

counselling and support. Rarely, a determined psychiatrically normal inmate will starve to death to make a political point. Particular problems may arise in those prisoners with severe personality disorder for whom food refusal is one of a number of maladapted behaviours. Though clearly disordered, such prisoners may be deemed 'untreatable' by NHS facilities and pose particularly difficult ethical and treatment dilemmas for the prison health service.

Self-mutilation

Here inmates cut or burn themselves (superficial repeated cuts to the arms, burns, with cigarette ends) in reaction to feelings of tension and despair. Where the levels of tension are high in a prison, self-mutilation can acquire an almost infectious quality as the behaviour spreads in the institution. Emotional instability and immaturity are frequent features of these inmates. Some believe, on clinical grounds, that a high proportion of female self-mutilators have also been victims of serious sexual abuse.[19]

Sleep disturbance

Increased levels of tension and alleged sleep disturbance lead to requests for sedation. Prison doctors are likely to find themselves being pressed by inmates, especially by the personality disordered or those with a history of drug abuse, for sedatives and hypnotics. It requires considerable judgement to get the right balance between over and under prescribing. It may be useful for the doctors to agree a guidance policy for this situation, perhaps in consultation with an outside psychiatrist experienced in these matters.

Psychiatric treatment in prisons

The legal and ethical difficulties and the administrative constraints on practising psychiatry in prison are discussed in Chapter 16. Despite all the difficulties arising from both the ethical and administrative problems the medical staff see it as their task to provide medical care to the same personal standard as within the health service outside prison.[6]

The core team within a prison consists of the prison medical officer assisted by health care officers (discipline officers who have had special training in basic nursing but with very little psychiatric training) and, increasingly, trained nurses employed either as nurses or as health care workers. There are also visiting psychiatrists who will have the task of assessing and treating inmates both by psychotherapy and medication if the patient will accept these voluntarily. Some personality disordered and neurotic prisoners clinically appear to benefit (though effective long-term scientific evidence is lacking) from psychological treatments such as social skills training and drama therapy conducted by probation or education officers attached to the prison. Psychologists may be involved directly or as supervisors. Some workers have developed particular interests in particular groups, e.g. sex offenders. The extent of these services depends on the size of prison, with some prisons or youth custody centres taking a particular interest in psychiatrically disturbed prisoners and some in sex offenders. What has also become clear is that a humane regime, of which these therapies may be part, leads to a much better prison atmosphere which must be beneficial to all involved. The pattern of health care within prisons should change with the implementation of the recommendations made by the Home Office/NHS working group on the future of prison health care.

Special hospitals

The *special hospitals* are those hospitals in England and Wales which provide treatment of psychiatric patients who need to be nursed in high security because of their potential risk to others. The three special hospitals in England are Broadmoor Hospital in Berkshire, Rampton Hospital in Nottinghamshire and Ashworth Hospital in Merseyside. Carstairs Hospital in Perthshire is the equivalent hospital in Scotland and Dundrum Hospital in Dublin is the equivalent for Southern Ireland. The purpose of special hospitals is stated in Section 4 of the National Health Service Act 1977. This requires the Secretary of State to help to provide special hospitals for patients subject to detention who require treatment under conditions of special security on account of their dangerous, violent or criminal propensities. This is interpreted by the Department of Health as being of a nature such that the patient is an immediate grave danger to others, either to the public outside the hospital because of persistent, determined absconding associated with dangerous behaviour or to patients or staff within the hospital. In both cases the severity of the behaviour disorder must be such that it requires the security of a special hospital.

The development of forensic psychiatric services, including special hospitals, has been reviewed by Parker[20] and Forshaw and Rollin.[21] In 1800, following the attempted murder of George III by James Hadfield, the Criminal Lunatic Act was passed to allow for the detention in safe custody of insane persons charged with offences of treason, murder or felony and acquitted on the grounds of insanity or found insane on arraignment. But as no specific accommodation was available, it had to be built at the Bethlem Hospital, which opened a criminal asylum with both male and female wings in 1816. However, this could only take a proportion of the criminal lunatics and therefore it was agreed that a number of the mentally ill prisoners could be transferred to county asylums before or after sentence.

The counties complained that their facilities were inadequate to look after the criminal lunatic, and in 1860 the Criminal Lunatics Act made possible the building of the first separate special asylum, namely Broadmoor Hospital, to be run by the Home Office. Broadmoor Hospital, which took both male and female patients, became full despite enlargements. Special temporary arrangements had to be made for insane prisoners within prisons and a part of Parkhurst Prison was set aside as the Parkhurst Criminal Lunatic Asylum in 1900. In 1912 Rampton Hospital was opened as a second criminal lunatic asylum, also run by the Home Office.

In 1913 the Mental Deficiency Act allowed for the care of mental defectives. Moss Side Hospital (now part of Ashworth Hospital) opened in 1919 for dangerous male and female defectives admitted under the Deficiency Act. In 1948 after the National Health Service was set up, ownership of the three institutions passed to the Ministry of Health (now the Department of Health). The control of admissions and discharges of Broadmoor patients remained in the hands of the Home Office. Following the introduction of the 1959 Mental Health Act the Department of Health became the managers of the hospital and controlled admissions to them. The Home Office retained control of discharge in the case of restricted patients. In 1984 due to gross overcrowding at Broadmoor Hospital, Park Lane Hospital was built in the grounds next door to Moss Side. In 1989 Moss Side and Park Lane Hospitals were amalgamated into one, Ashworth Hospital, under the newly formed Special Hospitals Service Authority. The Special Hospitals Service Authority was set up to manage all three of the special hospitals with the aim of linking them more closely with other areas of the National Health Service. On 1 April 1996, the SHSA was dismantled and the individual hospitals became independently managed provider units with their own Special Hospital Authority board. In line with the purchaser/ provider model in the NHS, a complementary role was filled by the High Security Psychiatric Services Commissioning Board (HSPSCB) from the same date. Special hospital management is due to change again in April 2000 when they will become part of established mental health trusts. The purchasing for maximum security will be by regional specialised commissioning groups.

The special hospitals are sectorised and therefore take patients from specific areas of the country. Broadmoor provides maximum secure care for the South and West, South Wales and South London, Ashworth provides care for the West Midlands, the North West and North West London along with North Wales and Rampton provides maximum secure care for the North East of England, the East Midlands, East Anglia and North East London. The total population of special hospital patients is approximately 1500. Admission to special hospital is controlled by each hospital's admission panel to which psychiatric reports about the patient must be submitted with a request. The patients must be detained under the Mental Health Act 1983 and must be of sufficient risk to require conditions of special security. The Home Secretary can direct a patient for treatment in a special hospital even if the patient has been previously turned down by the admissions panel. However, this is a very rare occurrence.

Approximately, one-sixth of the patients are female and are mostly managed in separate all female wards. The majority of patient have a diagnosis of mental illness, though 25% of patients are detained under the legal category of psychopathic disorder. Approximately 9% are detained under the legal categories of mental impairment and severe mental impairment. The majority of admissions are from prison and court. The average length of stay is approximately 7–8 years. The treatment offered to patients in a special hospital is on the same lines as any other psychiatric hospital, given the limitations which the need for security imposes. Special hospitals have developed specialist units including personality disorder units and rehabilitation units. The most disturbed patients tend to be placed in a high dependency or intensive care unit.

Special hospitals have to by nature give a great deal of attention to the level of their security in order to prevent patients from absconding. This usually involves a perimeter fence or wall, well established routines of locking and checking movements of patients. The nursing staffing levels tend to be high and overall the nurse to patient ratio is about one to one.

Overall, approximately 26% of those patients released from special hospitals re-offend within five years though the majority of the offences will be trivial. Approximately 60% of the patients will be in the community, 20% recalled to special hospital and the rest divided between prison and ordinary psychiatric hospital. Conditionally discharged patients, particularly the mentally ill, do better than those who are absolutely discharged.[22]

The age of the patient, legal category of psychopathic disorder and a history of criminal conditions are risk factors for future offending.[23] All three of the special hospitals have been subject to major inquiries, the most recent being the enquiry into the personality disorder unit at Ashworth Hospital.[24] In 1980 Sir John Boynton chaired an inquiry into Rampton which pointed to a number of serious problems including the professional, geographical and cultural isolation of the special hospitals and lack of medical and nursing leadership, recruitment difficulties and focus on containment rather than therapy. In 1988 the Health Advisory Service visited Broadmoor and their report made similar criticisms. In 1992 Sir Louis Blom-Cooper QC reported on Ashworth.[25] Following this, a working group on high secure and related psychiatric provision was set up under the chairmanship of Dr John Reed which recommended that high secure services should become more dispersed with units catering for no more than 200 patients each.[26] They also recommended that NHS purchasing contracts should aim to meet the needs of patients requiring long-term medium security. There have also been surveys which suggest that up to 50% of the patients in special hospitals do not actually require to be there but could be managed in lesser security if long-stay beds in medium security were provided within the region.

Regional secure units

As local psychiatric hospitals abandoned physical security and became increasingly open from the 1950s onwards, so it was felt that there would be a need for a special regional arrangement to look after those patients who were too difficult or dangerous to be coped with in an open setting but not so disturbed as to require a special hospital.

The first official suggestion came from the Royal Commission in 1957[27] and this was made more explicit in 1961 by the working party on special hospitals.[28] That working party recommended regional secure units which would become centres for the care of difficult and dangerous patients, both psychopathic and otherwise, a centre for forensic psychiatry, education and research. The recommendation was taken up by the then Department of Health and Social Security (DHSS) and the regional health authorities were asked to provide them. Only two attempted to do so but neither survived as such. The Northgate Clinic in North-West Thames region became an adolescent unit and the secure unit at South Ockenden Hospital was abandoned after a hospital enquiry revealed bad practice. No further attempts to construct a regional secure unit occurred despite continuing DHSS circulars.

In 1974 the interim report of the Committee on Mentally Abnormal Offenders (the Butler Committee) was published[29] and the report from the Working Party on Security in the National Health Service (NHS) (the Glancy Report) was circulated.[30] Both had studied the increasing problems arising from patients being refused treatment by psychiatric hospitals because of the lack of proper facilities to cope with difficult or dangerous patients. Such patients were therefore being sent to prison, held too long in special hospitals or simply not cared for. Both reports concluded that regional secure units would be the answer though they differed radically about the number of beds required. Butler recommended 2,000 while Glancy recommended 1,000. The DHSS accepted the lower recommendation and urged the regional health authorities to provide them. When it became clear that the regional health authorities were not going to hurry, the DHSS made funds available to promote the scheme asking that interim arrangements be made quickly whilst designs for definitive units were drawn up.

Regional Forensic Psychiatry Services, based on regional secure units, developed in some regions before others. A quick method of providing medium secure beds was to convert an existing ward to an interim secure unit (ISU). This allowed plans to be drawn up for a purpose built regional secure unit later. Three interim secure units were opened in the late 1970s. Regional Forensic Psychiatry Services were developed in most regions during the 1980s. By 1989 there were 655 NHS medium secure unit beds in twelve out of the fourteen regions of England. Often the lessons that were learnt from the operation of interim secure units in that region were used to inform the development of the regional secure units. In 1985, Treasenden[31] described the operation of four interim secure units. He found that a quarter of the patients had been admitted from local psychiatric hospitals who were unable to manage them because of their aggressive behaviour. Two-thirds of patients had been transferred from prison or special hospitals. The most common diagnosis was of a functional psychosis and the usual reason for admission was violence to others. The treatment regimes in these units usually included rehabilitation in addition to conventional psychiatric treatment. Most patients were either discharged to the community or to an open psychiatric ward. However, there were critics of the development of regional secure units. Most notably, Scott[32] in 1974 predicted that the following might occur:

(1) They would not relieve overcrowding in special hospitals.
(2) They would not help long-term prison inmates who were mentally abnormal.
(3) They could prevent therapeutic developments in prison.
(4) They would be expensive to construct and run.
(5) It would be difficult to find enough skilled nurses.
(6) They could be too selective in the patients that they would admit.

Scott suggested that instead, psychiatric facilities in prison should be improved.

In 1991 a review of services for mentally disordered offenders and others requiring similar services (the Reed Committee[7]) began. This review included regional secure units and forensic psychiatry services. The Reed Committee identified that there were nearly 600 places in NHS regional secure units in 1991. This was still some way short of the original DHSS target of 1,000 beds. The Reed Committee identified a number of groups for whom medium secure services were not adequately provided. These included:

(1) Patients with learning disabilities.
(2) Patients with acquired brain damage.
(3) Children and adolescents.
(4) Personality disordered patients.
(5) Women.
(6) Long-stay patients, primarily with a diagnosis of mental illness.

The Reed Committee[7] believed that there was an unmet need which arose from special hospitals, prisons (remand and sentenced), private secure units and court diversion schemes. They recommended an increase in numbers of regional secure unit beds to 1,500 in England and Wales. The exact distribution of the extra beds would be determined after a local needs assessment had been carried out. The committee noted the role of the independent sector in providing services where those in the NHS were insufficiently developed. However, this often led to patients being treated far from their homes. The Reed Committee concluded that a much greater diversity of secure beds was required to treat this group of patients.

In 1992, the Department of Health carried out a good practice exercise of medium secure units.[33] This had been one of the recommendations of the Reed Committee.[7] As a result of that, the following conclusions were drawn.

(1) In order to provide a therapeutic environment there should be a balance between nursing observations and the ward security.
(2) Ward security depended primarily on the doors, windows and ceilings. There was no evidence that other security measures, including air locks and fences around units, increased security.
(3) Over-concern with security leads to anti-therapeutic regimes.
(4) The vast majority of absconding from medium secure units was by patients who had been granted unescorted ground leave.
(5) In order to manage all types of patients that the regional secure unit could expect to admit there should be an intensive care ward or area, an admission/assessment ward and rehabilitation wards which would include a flat. In this way, varying levels of security could be provided within a unit.

Medium secure units vary in size from some 30 beds to over 100 beds. They have the function of caring for those patients who are too difficult or dangerous for the ordinary hospitals but not so disturbed as to require care in a special hospital. They are said to provide medium security, by which is meant that they have the capacity to prevent patients absconding as necessary, but at the same time run a treatment programme which as the patient improves, will include leave outside the unit. Thus, on such a unit some patients will be virtually as secure as in a special hospital whilst others will have unescorted freedom of movement into the local community. All regional secure units have an area which is physically secure and all aim to provide a good range of therapeutic facilities within their campus. They are highly staffed on the assumption that this will produce greater therapeutic efficacy and greater security.

The only survey of all patients occupying NHS medium secure unit beds on one day was conducted by Murray[34] in 1991. He found that just over half had been admitted from prison and nearly 18% from special hospitals; this latter group included most of those patients detained under psychopathic disorder. Since only 12% of patients had been in-patients for greater than two years, Murray concluded that as a whole, the medium secure units did not have a significant number of patients who were difficult to discharge. He was concerned that the medium secure units were taking patients from prison, perhaps at the expense of transfers from special hospital. He suggested that the medium secure units had primarily become facilities for the assessment and treatment of mentally ill remand prisoners who had committed serious offences.

In 1994, Reed[35] conducted a survey of all NHS (785 beds) and independent sector (478 beds) medium secure units. It was concluded that 190 of these 1,263 patients (15%) were judged to require long-term medium security based on the views of their current consultant psychiatrist. A further 270 patients (21%) were thought to require long-term low secure care. After surveying patients in special hospital and potential transfers from prison, Reed concluded that in England and Wales, 740 long-term medium secure beds were required.

In 1990 the Home Office and Department of Health produced the widely quoted circular 66/90 *Provision for Mentally Disordered Offenders*.[36] This promoted the diversion of mentally disordered offenders from the criminal justice system to the NHS. At about the same time, the Mental Health Unit of the Home Office (at that time called C3 Division) also clarified the use of Section 48 of the Mental Health Act. This section allows for the transfer of inmates on remand who are suffering from mental illness or severe mental impairment, if they are in 'urgent need of treatment'. The Home Office made it clear to prison medical officers that any mentally ill inmate on remand should be considered in urgent need of treatment. The effect of these changes is evident from the Home Office's own statistics.[37] In 1989, 98 inmates were transferred under Section 48 to hospital. The following year, this had nearly doubled to 180 per year. The numbers have continued to increase, reaching a peak of 536 transfers under Section 48 in 1994, since when there have been about 500 transfers each year. In addition, over the same period, the transfer of convicted inmates under Section 47 of the Mental Health Act has also increased. In 1989 there were 120 such transfers which increased to a peak of 284 in 1993 and remained at that level each year since. Over 95% of the transfers under Sections 48 and 47 of the Mental Health Act are to regional secure units. Therefore, ever since 1993, there have been over 750 patients transferred from prison to regional secure units each year. This has had the effect of saturating the NHS provision for medium secure beds, despite the fact that the numbers of beds have increased over the same period of time.

Originally the regional secure units were directly financed and protected by the Regional Health Authorities with money top-sliced from the regional budget. The NHS and Community Care Act 1990 which followed the 1989 White Paper, *Working for Patients*, fundamentally changed the way in which the Health Service, including regional forensic psychiatry services, was funded. The funding was devolved from regional health authorities to local, district based purchasing health authorities. In 1997, the NHS White Paper, *The New NHS*, recommended that a number of specialised services should be purchased at a regional level by regional specialised commissioning groups (RSCG). Included in the specialised services were medium secure unit beds. In 1998, the Department of Health stated that as from April 2000, all maximum and medium secure services would be purchased by the RSCGs.

Local low secure services

The Reed report[7] highlighted the fact that although in 1986 there were 1,163 locked beds for patients with mental illness, by 1991 there were only 639 such beds. Since these deficiencies were highlighted, there has been increased interest in the provision of local low secure beds. One problem has been the different terminology which has developed to describe these beds. Examples include, low secure, challenging behaviour, psychiatric intensive care, and close supervision units. However, a pattern does appear to have emerged between two different types of provision.

The first is the psychiatric intensive care unit (PICU). These are usually part of a local general psychiatry service and provide care for a short period of time such as 4–5 days with rapid transfer back to the general psychiatry wards.[38] These units are not usually seen as part of the local services for mentally disordered offenders and therefore, rarely accept patients directly from the criminal justice system.

In contrast, there is now a second type of service which is similar to that proposed by Grounds.[39] This is often described as a District Forensic Psychiatry Service. Grounds suggested that the components of such a service would include:

(1) A focus on community care backed up by local beds, some open and some secure.
(2) These services would work with the local general psychiatry service to minimise the need for transfer of patients to medium and high security.
(3) The services would be flexible and have several functions including intensive outreach, assertive follow up, and out of hours service and a rapid assessment service for the criminal justice system.
(4) The service would include a range of residential facilities including highly staffed hostels in the community which would be able to provide beds for crisis admissions and also be able to act as a psychiatric bail hostel.
(5) The services would also be expected to work closely with the local social services department, probation service and other criminal justice system agencies.

A model of how forensic psychiatry services could work with community mental health teams has been described by Whittle and Scally.[40] They reported on the problems that were encountered in co-working with local mental health services and how they were managed. The advantages of this type of working included: reducing stigma, providing support and education to staff and enabling forensic psychiatry services to reach a wider group of patients.

The review by Reed[35] in 1994 of the security needs of patients in all levels of secure care, concluded that 640 long-term low secure beds for mentally disordered offenders were required. A further 1,400 long-term low secure beds which would operate as part of general psychiatry services were also needed.

Diversion schemes and outpatient and community services

It has now been recognised that there are several levels within the criminal justice system at which a patient might be diverted to the health system. This has led to a number of different models of diversion schemes. But they all have in common the aim of providing a service to the police and the courts which rapidly identifies and transfers those offenders who require psychiatric treatment. In certain cases the Crown Prosecution Service may then choose not to proceed with the prosecution (lesser offences with clear psychiatric illness and good psychiatric care). Encouraged by the Department of Health and the Home Office various schemes have been developed.[41] Early schemes such as those described by Joseph,[42] involved two psychiatrists regularly attending a magistrates' court. Since then other model of schemes have been developed based on the local needs.[43]

In large metropolitan areas, a psychiatrist or community psychiatric nurse might regularly attend or make himself available to a busy court or police station for an immediate consultation on an offender suspected of being mentally disordered. Arrangements can then be made for immediate transfer to hospital if required. In some places the emphasis has been on developing a multidisciplinary panel to consider the placement and after-care of problematical cases which might involve probation, social services, housing and a variable psychiatric input. Overall the results seem very encouraging with a reduction in the time taken to get the mentally abnormal offender into proper care.[44] Joseph and Potter[45] point out, however, that to do the job properly for the 25% most difficult patients there must be secure hospital facilities.

Patients who have broken the law may be remanded on bail and a report be sought from local psychiatric facilities. People on probation may require psychiatric assessment and they too will be referred to local psychiatric facilities. Arrangements vary from region to region. In some, the forensic psychiatrists attached to the regional secure unit have outpatient clinics, based in probation offices, which cope with the majority of these cases. This arrangement is particularly suitable for densely populated metropolitan areas. Huckle *et al.* have described such a service and 100 referrals over a three year period.[46] The commonest diagnosis was of a personality disorder in one third, 11% had a substance misuse problem and 10% had schizophrenia. They concluded that a probation order with a condition of psychiatric treatment could be a useful alternative to a prison sentence in the mentally disordered. In other regions, where the workload is more evenly distributed, this work is shared with the local psychiatrists, although the regional secure unit psychiatrist may have an outpatient clinic to serve local courts.

Hostels and probation officers may find themselves with an offender who is beginning to show a mental abnormality. Easy access to a psychiatric service considerably facilitates the work of these services. Some local psychiatrists, particularly those with a special interest in the problems of the mentally abnormal offender, may become a consultant to a local probation hostel or voluntary hostel. Their function will be to give advice and guidance to the staff of the hostel as well as psychiatric opinions on residents.

All local psychiatrists will find themselves at the beginning or end of a chain in the management of the potentially dangerous patient in that as the patient improves, so transfer is expected. This transfer, using the 'care programme approach' should be in conjunction with the local authority services as part of the community health services generally. There will need to be, especially in the case of the restricted patient, continued supervision on an out-patient basis so that treatment will be continued and re-entry to hospital will be facilitated if necessary. It is essential that the community workers are fully briefed and aware of the clinical facts. As the community workers change (social workers leaving etc.) so a dangerous loss of awareness can occur. A formal regular link between the original team and the community workers is essential.

Interconnection of the services

Reed[7] enunciated five principles which should govern the care of the mentally abnormal offender:

(1) Care should be based on individual need.
(2) Care should, as far as possible, be in the community.
(3) Care should be near the patient's home.
(4) Care should only be at the level of security justified by the patient's dangerousness.
(5) Care should be aimed at maximising rehabilitation and the prospect of independent living.

Psychiatric services for the mentally abnormal offender can only work if all the above institutions are in place and working together so there can be a continual flow of patients through the system according to their psychiatric needs.

The total numbers are relatively small (approximately 700 patients per annum are sent by the courts to hospital for treatment under Section 37 and a further 200 under Sections 37/41 of the Mental Health Act). The majority will be sent to ordinary psychiatric hospital, a minority to regional secure units and a smaller number still to a special hospital. Nevertheless there have been considerable difficulties. Special hospitals and regional secure units often have problems in getting their patients accepted by catchment area hospitals. Prisons, including remand prisons, can experience similar difficulties. Coid[47,48] found that one in five mentally abnormal offenders remanded in prison were rejected by local psychiatric services. Local mental hospitals did best and district general hospitals and academic units worst. In a comparison of two similar regions, he found that the one with a regional secure unit provided the better service. What evidence there is suggests that the problems reflect a shortage of resources and negative professional attitudes to difficult, sometimes dangerous and uncooperative patients.

References

(1) Chiswick, D. and Dooley, E. (1995). Psychiatry in prisons. In: *Seminars in Practical Forensic Psychiatry* (eds D. Chiswick and R. Cope). Gaskell: London.
(2) Smith, R. (1984) *Prison Health Care*. British Medical Association: London.
(3) Her Majesty's Inspectorate of Prisons for England and Wales (1996) *Patient or Prisoner: A New Strategy for Health Care in Prison*. Home Office: London.
(4) Reed, J. and Lynn, M. (1997) The quality of health care in prison. *British Medical Journal* **7120**, 1420–1424.
(5) Her Majesty's Prison Service Health Care (1996) *Health Care Standards for Prisons in England and Wales*. Home Office: London.
(6) Health Advisory Committee for the Prison Service (1997) *The Provision of Mental Health Care in Prisons*. Home Office: London.
(7) Department of Health and Home Office (1992) *Review of Health and Social Services for Mentally Disordered Offenders and Others Requiring Similar Services* (Reed Committee) Final Summary Report. CM 2088. HMSO: London.
(8) Roth, L. (1980) Correctional psychiatry. In: *Modern Legal Medicine, Psychiatry and Forensic Sciences* (eds W.D. Curran, A.L. McGarry and C.S. Petty). Davies: Philadelphia.
(9) Gunn, J., Maden, A. and Swinton, M. (1991) Treatment needs of prisoners with psychiatric disorders. *British Medical Journal* **303**, 338–341.
(10) Brooke, D., Taylor, C., Gunn, J. and Maden, A. (1996) The point prevalence of mental disorder in unconvicted male prisoners in England and Wales. *British Medical Journal* **313**, 1524–1527.
(11) Singleton, N., Meltzer, H. and Gatward, R. (1998) *Psychiatric Morbidity among Prisoners*. Office of National Statistics. The Stationery Office: London.
(12) Home Office (1998) *Tackling Drugs to Build a Better Britain*. Cnd. 3945. The Stationery Office: London.
(13) Johns, A. (1998) Substance Misuse and Offending. *Current Opinion in Psychiatry*, **11**, 669–673.
(14) Grapendaal, M. (1990) The Inmate Culture in Dutch Prisons. *British Journal of Criminology* **30**, 341–357.
(15) Dooley, E. (1990) Prison Suicide in England and Wales. 1972–1987. *British Journal of Psychiatry* **156**, 40–45.
(16) Allebeck, P., Allgulander, C. and Fisher, L.D. (1988) Predictors of completed

suicide in a cohort of 50,465 young men: role of personality and deviant behaviour. *British Medical Journal* **297**, 176–178.

(17) Harding-Pink, D. (1990) Mortality following release from prison. *Medicine, Science and the Law* **30**, 12–16.

(18) Larkin, E.P. (1991) Food refusal in prison. *Medicine, Science and the Law* **31**, 41–44.

(19) Wilkins, J. and Coid, J. (1991) Self mutilation in female remand prisoners. 1. An indication of severe psycho-pathology. *Criminal Behaviour and Mental Health* **1**, 245–267.

(20) Parker, E. (1985) The development of secure provision. In: *Secure Provision* (ed. L. Gostin) Tavistock Publications: London & New York.

(21) Forshaw, D. and Rollin, H. In: The history of forensic psychiatry in England. *Principles and Practice of Forensic Psychiatry* (eds R. Bluglass and P. Bowden). Churchill Livingstone: Edinburgh.

(22) Buchanan, A. (1998) Criminal conviction after discharge from special (high security) hospital. Incidence in the first 10 years. *British Journal of Psychiatry* **172**, 472–477.

(23) Bowden, P. (1985) Psychiatry and Dangerousness: A Counter Renaissance. In: *Secure Provision* (ed. L. Gostin) Tavistock Publications: London & New York.

(24) Department of Health (1999) *Report of the Committee of Inquiry into the Personality Disorder Unit, Ashworth Special Hospital*. CMND 4194. Stationery Office: London.

(25) *Report of the Committee of Inquiry into Complaints about Ashworth Hospital*. (1992) CMND. 2028. HMSO: London.

(26) Reed, J. and Department of Health (1994) *Report of the Working Group on High Security and Related Psychiatric Provision* (Chairman Dr John Reed). Department of Health: London.

(27) *Report of the Royal Commission on the Law Relating to Mental Illness and Mental Deficiency 1954–57*. Cmnd. 169. HMSO: London.

(28) Ministry of Health (1961) *Special Hospitals. Report of Working Party*. HMSO: London.

(29) Home Office and Department of Health & Social Security (1974) *Interim Report of the Committee on Mentally Abnormal Offenders*. Cmnd. 5698. HMSO: London.

(30) Department of Health & Social Security (1974) *Revised Report of the Working Party on Security in NHS Psychiatric Hospitals* (Glancy Report). DHSS: London.

(31) Treasaden, I. (1985) Current practice in regional interim secure units. In: *Secure Provision* (ed L. Gostin). Tavistock: London. pp 176–207.

(32) Scott, P.D. (1974) Solutions to the Problem of the Dangerous Offender. *British Medical Journal* **4**, 640–641.

(33) Department of Health (1992) *Medium Secure Units: Good practice exercise*. Department of Health: London.

(34) Murray, K. (1996) The use of beds in NHS medium secure units in England. *Journal of Forensic Psychiatry* **7**, 504–24.

(35) Reed, J. (1997) The need for longer term psychiatric care in medium or low security. *Criminal Behaviour and Mental Health* **7**, 201–212.

(36) Home Office (1990) *Provision for Mentally Disordered Offenders*. Circular 66/90. Home Office: London.

(37) Home Office (1998) *Statistics of Mentally Disordered Offenders, England and Wales, 1997.* Statistical Bulletin 19/98. Home Office: London.

(38) Hyde, C.E. and Harrower-Wilson, C. (1994) Psychiatric intensive care: principles and problems. *Hospital Update* 287–295.

(39) Grounds, A. (1996) Forensic psychiatry for the millennium. *Journal of Forensic Psychiatry* **7**, 221–227.

(40) Whittle, M. and Scally, M. (1998) Model of forensic psychiatric community care. *Psychiatric Bulletin* **22**, 748–750.

(41) Blumenthal, S. and Wessely, S. (1992) National survey of current arrangements for diversion from custody in England and Wales'. *British Medical Journal* **305**, 1322–1325.

(42) Joseph, P. (1992) *Psychiatric Assessment at the Magistrates' Court.* Home Office and Department of Health: London.

(43) Mendelson, E.F. and Frost, C. (1994) An alternative to the panel scheme for the diversion of mentally disordered offenders. *Psychiatric Bulletin* **18**, 39–40.

(44) Exworthy, T. and Parrott, J. (1997) Comparative evaluation of a diversion from custody scheme. *Journal of Forensic Psychiatry* **8**, 406–16.

(45) Joseph, P.L.A. and Potter, M. (1993) Diversion from custody. II: Effect on hospital and prison resources. *British Journal of Psychiatry* **162**, 330–334.

(46) Huckle, P. Tavier and Scarf, S. (1996). Psychiatric clinics in probation offices in South Wales. *Psychiatric Bulletin* **20**, 205–206.

(47) Coid, J.W. (1988) Mentally abnormal prisoners on remand: 1 – Rejected or accepted by the NHS? *British Medical Journal* **296**, 1779–1782.

(48) Coid, J.W. (1988) Mentally abnormal prisoners on remand II – Comparison of services providing Oxford and Wessex Regions. *British Medical Journal* **296**, 1783–785.

Chapter 2

Legal Aspects: The Courts and their Sentences

Introduction

The courts of law in this country are divided according to function. The forensic psychiatrist is primarily concerned with the criminal courts (adult and juvenile) but may also be involved, from time to time, with the civil courts, the appellate courts and the coroner's court. The courts, in sentencing, have to consider the safety of the public, retribution for the offence, the general deterrent effect of the sentence on the offender and on others and, finally, the interests of the offender. This chapter introduces the types of offences and the concept of responsibility in law. The structure of the courts and an outline of the sentences available to them is described as is the probation service and its relationship to psychiatry.

The Crown Prosecution Service

The police are responsible for investigating crime and referring the case to the Crown Prosecution Service. This service (set up by the Prosecution of Offences Act 1985) then takes over the conduct of criminal proceedings including the decision to prosecute. The Director of Public Prosecutions heads the service and deals with the most difficult cases. England and Wales are divided into geographical areas, each with a chief crown prosecutor. The Crown Prosecution Service may contact a psychiatrist to prepare a psychiatric report on an offender either to rebut a defence report or because an offender's mental state is in doubt. In general, under the Code for Crown Prosecutors, there is a presumption against prosecuting a person who was mentally disordered at the time of the offence unless over-ridden by public interest as in serious cases. This is particularly so where the psychiatrist can offer appropriate care. Where a prosecution has been started the Crown Prosecutor will pay serious attention to any report which says that continuing the prosecution will worsen the mental condition. This will be balanced by the knowledge that some mental conditions may have been brought on by the fact of prosecution.

It is also possible for individuals or organisations to make private prosecutions. An example would be where department stores prosecute shoplifting offences. Other organisations that can undertake prosecutions include the Inland Revenue, Customs and Excise, certain local authority departments and the RSPCA.

Offences and the court

The offences which bring an offender before the criminal court are divided into three types:

(1) Minor offences which can be dealt with in a magistrates' court ('summary offences'), such as minor criminal damage, common assault, minor motoring offences, begging, drunkenness and breaching civil orders.
(2) Offences which are triable in either a magistrates' court or in a Crown Court, for instance theft, burglary, indecent assault. The decision as to which court rests both with the magistrates and with the accused
(3) More serious offences are known as indictable offences (for example murder, rape, robbery) because the offender has to be indicted (accused) before a jury in a Crown Court.

Concepts of responsibility and mental disorder

In all offences it must be proven that the accused physically did the act (known as the '*actus reus*'). In most offences it must also be proven that the defendant's intention or attitude of mind was as required for the crime in question (known as having the necessary '*mens rea*'). For a crime to have been committed, therefore, it is not only necessary for the accused to have done the act but there must have been intent to do it or negligence about the consequences of the behaviour. A plea of not guilty may be based on an absence of *mens rea*, e.g. the act may have been carried out in a state of distraction, at which time the person may not have formed the necessary intent. There are a few crimes which require no proof of *mens rea* where the act itself is sufficient for an offence to have been committed. These are known as offences of strict liability and include certain statutory offences such as driving through a red traffic light.

The concept of responsibility in law concerns the degree to which the accused is held accountable for the act committed. To be found guilty means to have done the act and deserve punishment. Full responsibility goes hand in hand with full rationality and consciousness (or will). Impairment of either is taken to alter responsibility. Automatism (see Chapter 3) implies the absence of conscious control and therefore there is no guilt. Rationality may be so impaired by mental disorder that the offender is not held responsible for his acts resulting in the finding of not guilty by reason of insanity (see Chapter 3). Less severe mental disorder will often mitigate the sentence of the court, which will, generally, seek to give a more merciful sentence aimed at assisting the offender rather than providing punishment and deterrence. In infanticide (see Chapter 3) a disturbed balance of mind reduces responsibility.

The term 'diminished responsibility' is a technical term in law specifically related to a defence against the charge of murder (see Chapter 3). In such cases the defendant admits the act and the intent but claims that his mind at the time was so disturbed by an abnormality of mind that his mental responsibility for his act was substantially impaired. If the court is convinced of the defendant's claim then the defendant will be found guilty of manslaughter rather than murder. Apart from this very specific example of deciding to what extent responsibility is diminished, with all other charges the psychiatrist is generally not asked to comment on 'responsibility' and to use the term may lead to confusion. The court is very much more pragmatic and requires simply an account of the patient's mental abnormality, its effect on the patient, its prognosis and the treatment arrangements which can be made. Without mentioning the word 'responsibility' the legal representatives of the offender will hope to use the psychiatric report as mitigation, in any particular case.

The accusatorial system

In criminal and civil courts in England the accusatorial system is adopted in which first the evidence of the prosecution or the plaintiff is heard and then the evidence of the defence. On the strength of this evidence the decision about guilt or, in the civil courts, responsibility, is made. Similarly, a psychiatrist will be asked by one side to prepare a report. It may be found that the other side is represented by a psychiatrist taking a different point of view. The court has to decide which of the psychiatric views it will accept, if any, and will also decide whether or not to take up the suggestions made by the psychiatrists. The court may agree, for example, with the psychiatrist that the defendant is mentally disordered, but disagree about the disposal, believing that the protection of the public overrides the defendant's needs for treatment.

Magistrates' courts

There are two sorts of magistrates. The commonest is a lay person who has been accepted as a Justice of the Peace, to sit, generally with two others, in a magistrates' court. Their task is to hear the evidence, in the case of summary offences, decide the question of guilt and sentence the offender when guilty. The magistrates will be guided on the legal aspects of the case by the clerk of the court. The other sort of magistrate is the paid professional lawyer who may sit alone and is known as a stipendiary magistrate (he receives a salary as opposed to the non-stipendiary magistrate who works voluntarily). Stipendiary magistrates are only employed in metropolitan areas. The defendant is usually represented by a solicitor in a magistrates' court. The magistrates' courts deal with some 2 million offenders annually whilst the Crown Courts deal with some 100,000 offenders.

At the first appearance in court, if the matter is minor it may be dealt with there and then, but in most cases it will be set back to allow the accused to prepare a defence with his legal advisers. Similarly, time will be required by the prosecution to prepare their evidence.

The accused will then be remanded for up to three weeks when the accused, or his representatives, will have to appear again and the position is reviewed. These remands continue until both parties are ready to present their evidence. The magistrates' court will then deal with those cases within its powers. In the case of indictable offences the magistrates' court will decide whether there is a case to answer against the accused. The magistrate can dismiss the case at that point but if there is a case to be answered then it is 'committed' to a Crown Court to be heard by a judge and jury. The accused will be remanded again, in custody or on bail, and there may be a wait of some months until the Crown Court case can be heard. The sentencing powers of a magistrates' court are severely limited. The maximum fine they can order is £5,000. They may only give a maximum of six months imprisonment for any one offence with a total sentence up to one year. There are certain offences which may require a longer or more severe sentence than this, in which case the magistrates, having found the defendant guilty, may refer the case to the Crown Courts.

Crown Courts

In the Crown Court the case for the prosecution and the defence is argued by barristers (although suitably qualified solicitors also have a right of audience). The decision about guilt, if contested, is made by a jury and the judge ensures that the rule of law is followed during the trial. The judge also has the task of summing up the evidence for the jury and finally has the task of sentencing the defendant if he is found guilty. Crown Courts are ranked into three levels according to the seriousness of the offences which they try. The most serious offences, e.g. murder, go to Tier 1 courts. The judges are High Court judges, circuit judges or recorders, depending on the seriousness of the offence.

The Crown Court also acts as a court of appeal on decisions made in the magistrates' court. The accused may appeal against conviction, sentence or both. In the case of an appeal the judge sits with magistrates but without a jury. The judge, at the end of an appeal, if the accused is still found guilty, has the power to increase or decrease the original sentence within the limits available to magistrates.

Court of Appeal (Criminal Division)

The Court of Appeal (Criminal Division) sits in London. Hearings on appeals against Crown Court decisions occur before three judges (known as Lords Justices of Appeal) and including a senior Lord Justice of Appeal. There is an automatic right of appeal on a point of law, however before an accused can have an appeal against sentence heard in the Court of Appeal he must present his reasons to that court who will decide whether there are sufficient grounds to hear the appeal. Psychiatrists may be involved where the defendant claims that the Crown Court sentence did not give proper weight to psychiatric opinion at the time.

The House of Lords

This is the court of appeal against the decisions of the Court of Appeal. The House of Lords will only hear cases after giving consent to do so based on a study of the case put forward by the defendant. An appeal to the House of Lords will generally be on a point of law and will not affect the sentence directly.

Juveniles and responsibility

Juveniles are defined by the Criminal Justice Act 1991 as young people below the age of 18 years. They are divided into 'young persons' (14–17 inclusive) and 'children' (under 14). Children are considered criminally responsible from the age of 10. The age at which children are regarded as responsible for their actions in law varies across Europe. In Ireland and Switzerland it is 7 and in Scandinavian countries it is 15. Children and young offenders are tried in Youth Courts except in rare cases. This occurs

(1) when the charge is homicide;
(2) when the offence which carries a maximum sentence of 14 years in an adult;
(3) when the offence was carried out with an adult and they are charged jointly with an offence of sufficient seriousness that the adult has to go to Crown Court; and

(4) possibly when the charge arises as a result of circumstances connected with an adult being charged. In these cases they must be tried and sentenced in a crown court.

Youth courts

The youth court arises from the Criminal Justice Act 1991. The courts are held by three magistrates from a special youth court panel. They deal with all 'children' (aged 10 to 13 years) and 'young persons' (aged 14 to 17 years. inclusive) who have broken the law except for certain very serious cases. The 1991 Act extends 'young person' to include 17 year olds.

The youth court has special rules to protect young people from publicity and contact with older defendants. The general public have no access to these courts. The Criminal Justice Act 1991 holds parents responsible for their children's behaviour. They must attend court with their child unless the court considers it unreasonable. If the offender is 16 or over, the court may require the parents to attend. If the child is in care then the local authority with parental responsibility must send a representative.

Coroners' courts

The coroner is always a doctor or lawyer. The functions of the court include enquiring into the cause of death when someone dies in prison or dies from violent or unnatural causes or where the cause of death is unknown. A jury is empanelled to give a verdict on the facts. Psychiatrists may have to give evidence about their own patients who have died in such circumstances.

Sentences of the court

The 1991 Criminal Justice Act is the principal Act governing the court's powers in criminal cases. It is designed to reduce the number of minor offenders placed in custody and places the emphasis on non-custodial sentences for this group. Very good reasons have to be given to justify custodial sentences.

It is important to know the range of sentences that a criminal court can impose.

They can be divided into:

(1) discharges
(2) fines
(3) community sentences
(4) custodial sentences.

There are other sentences for specific circumstances such as disqualification from driving or the making of exclusion orders from licensed premises. The death sentence, originally abolished for murder in 1957, was abolished for treason in 1998.

Three age groups have to be considered, 'adult' (21 years and older), 'young adult' (18–21), and offenders under 18 years. Below 10 years a child is not considered criminally responsible and cannot be prosecuted.

Mentally abnormal offenders will be considered separately.

Adults

Discharges

There are two main types of discharge, *absolute* and *conditional*. An absolute discharge means the defendant has been found guilty but the court has decided not to punish him at all, either because of the triviality of the offence or the circumstances of it. A conditional discharge means that if a defendant is not found guilty of any other offence in a specified period (up to three years), they will receive no punishment. If during the discharge period they are convicted of a further offence they may be sentenced for the offence for which they were originally discharged. In the case of an offender being *bound over to keep the peace*, the court chooses not to punish them but requires them to comply with certain conditions or otherwise forfeit a stipulated sum of money and have the original offence dealt with. The offender can be brought back to court if there is any breach of the conditions, which may include keeping the peace and being of good behaviour.

Fines

This is the most common penalty, particularly in the magistrates' court. Fines are imposed according to the seriousness of the offence and the offender's means. Compensation must be considered by the court when there has been loss, damage or personal injury. The order may be the only sentence or it may be combined with any other. A criminal bankruptcy order gives the court the power to make the offender bankrupt and turn his assets over to the court. It is a way of dealing with offenders who have made substantial financial gains from their offending. Costs are also frequently ordered against offenders but rank after compensation and fines in order of payment.

Community sentences

These include probation orders, community service orders and curfew orders. In appropriate cases for 16 year olds and older (where supervision in the community is desirable for rehabilitation or prevention of offending or harm to others) the court may choose to place the offender on *probation* from six months to three years. The offender must be willing to comply with the order before it can be made and a probation officer consulted. Failure to comply once the order is made may constitute a breach of probation which may lead to resentencing for the offence. However a new offence in itself does not constitute a breach to any community sentence. The court will deal with it on its merits.

The order can be reviewed (and terminated for good behaviour) at the request of the supervising officer or the offender.

Various requirements can be attached to the order, such as:

(1) to live in a particular place, e.g. a probation hostel;
(2) to attend a probation centre where there may be groups (e.g. sex offender groups, anger management groups) or other therapies aimed at dealing with the offender's behaviour;
(3) to attend at a specified place to take part in various schemes or activities organised by the probation service;
(4) to attend for treatment for substance abuse (residential or non-residential);
(5) to refrain from doing particular things during a particular time;
(6) to have psychiatric treatment (see below).

A probation order may be combined with a fine or other community sentence.

In the case of a *community service order* the offender (who must be 16 or older), who has been convicted of an imprisonable offence, is required to complete a period (40 to 240 hours over 12 months) doing a job organised by the probation service for the benefit of the community. The offender has to be accepted by the probation community service organiser, who will write a report to the court on the suitability of the offender for such an order (the offender must consent). If the offender fails to complete his community service then he can be taken back to court and resentenced. The order may be combined with a fine for the same offence. Although community service orders are frequently denigrated as a 'soft option', they are only made when the alternative sentence is a custodial one.

A probation order and community service order can be put together to form a combination order for offenders of 16 or older and who have committed an imprisonable offence. The conditions for the order are the same as for a probation and community service order.

A *curfew order* is a sentence which can be imposed in association with another sentence or alone. It requires the offender to remain at a specified place for 2 to 12 hours a day for up to six months. The court must consider information about the place and the effect on others of the enforced presence of the offender. The curfew may be reinforced by electronic monitoring (tagging). The curfew must not interfere with religious beliefs or work or school. Someone must be responsible for monitoring the curfew. The offender must be willing to comply with the order.

Custodial sentences

Custodial sentences are restricted to those cases in which nothing less than imprisonment will do either because the offence is so serious or where (in the case of a violent or sexual offence) it is needed to protect the public from serious harm. Reasons must be given in court as to why the sentence is being given. What is to be regarded as serious tends to be defined by the Court of Appeal judgements. Serious harm is defined as 'death or serious personal injury, whether physical or psychological'. Seriousness should be balanced by any mitigating factors. In considering the seriousness of any offence the court may take into account any previous convictions of the offender or any failure to respond to previous sentences.

Having decided that a custodial sentence is required, the length of sentence will reflect the circumstances of the offence and the number of offences. In the case of violent or sexual offences the length of the sentence will reflect any need to protect the public. Custodial sentences may be divided into three categories

- determinate sentences
- suspended sentences
- life sentences.

Determinate sentences have a fixed length. All prisoners serve at least half their sentence in custody. After that the rules controlling release reflect length of sentence. Misbehaviour in prison may lead to up to 14 additional days being spent in prison before final release. The Criminal Justice Act 1991 set the rules that govern when the offender is released.

(1) Those serving a sentence of less than 12 months will spend half in custody then receive an automatic unconditional release in the community. Further offending in this period may lead the court to require the outstanding term to be served in prison in addition to any new sentence.

(2) Those serving sentences of 12 months to up to 4 years will spend half in custody then receive an automatic conditional release on licence (supervision by a probation officer) for the next quarter with the possibility of serving the outstanding term in prison for further offending in addition to any new sentence.

(3) Those serving four years or more must spend half in custody but then have the possibility of discretionary conditional release on parole between half and two-thirds of sentence. At two-thirds there will be automatic conditional release on licence (supervision by a probation officer) until three-quarters of the sentence.

Re-offending may lead to the offender having to spend the outstanding term in prison as well as any new sentence. In the case of sex offenders, the sentencing court may order that supervision be continued to the end of the sentence.

A *suspended sentence* is a custodial sentence of up to two years which may be suspended for between one and two years but only if there are exceptional grounds to do so. In this case the court sentences the offender to a period of imprisonment but chooses not to impose the sentence at once but let the offender go back to the community on condition that there are no further offences within a stated period of up to two years. Should there be a further offence in that period then the original sentence will be served plus further time for the new offence. It may be combined with supervision, compensation order or a fine.

A life sentence means that the offender is held in prison for an 'indeterminate' length of time. There are three sorts of life sentences:

(1) the *mandatory* life sentence where the sentence is mandatory for the offence (i.e. murder);
(2) the *discretionary* life sentence (one given for an offence other than murder including offences such as manslaughter, arson and rape where the court has discretion as to what sentence was passed).
(3) The *automatic* life sentence is a mandatory sentence for an offender aged 18 committing a second offence of a very serious nature as defined in the Crime Sentences Act 1997. The court does not have to impose the automatic life sentence if there are exceptional circumstances relating either to the offences or to the offender which justifies its not doing so.

The trial judge may recommend, in the case of the mandatory life sentence, a minimum period to be spent in custody to satisfy the requirements of retribution and deterrence (the tariff). The prisoner has a right to know what this is and the reasons for it so a representation can be made to the Home Secretary if it is felt to be unjust. The Home Secretary (after consultation) lays down a minimum tariff period to be served in each case which may be longer than that of the trial judge.

In the case of the mandatory life sentence, release is at the discretion of the Home Secretary following a favourable review by the Mandatory Lifer Panel of the Parole Board in consultation with the Lord Chief Justice and, if possible, the trial judge. The offender is then released into the community on licence to a probation officer. Recall to prison may occur at any time during this period of licence if the offender's behaviour demands it. The condition of seeing a probation officer will continue for some years. However, even after that the offender remains liable to recall for life.

In the case of the discretionary and automatic life sentence (for very serious offences such as rape, arson etc.) the sentencing judge states in open court a tariff period. The European Court of Human Rights has ruled that the prisoner on a discretionary life sentence is entitled to have his detention reviewed by an independent body with the status of a court and that the matter should not just be left to the Home Secretary. The Discretionary Lifer Panel (a judge, a psychiatrist and an independent member) of the Parole Board reviews the case at the prison in an open tribunal-like setting with the prisoner having legal representation. The Board can, when appropriate, direct the Home Secretary to release the offender which has to occur within seven days. Automatic life sentences will be dealt with in the same way.

The first review by the Parole Board of either type of lifer occurs three years before the tariff date and thereafter at regular intervals.

Young adults (18–21 years)

Non-custodial sentences
Non-custodial sentences for young adults are the same as for adults with the addition of an attendance centre order for 16 to 20 year olds. In this case the offender is required to attend a Senior Attendance Centre for three hours at a time (usually Saturdays) to a maximum of 36 hours as a punishment. The 'centre' may be based at a school or youth club where the offender is expected to take part in organised activities e.g. physical exercise, carpentry etc.

Custodial sentences
The law asks courts to avoid, if possible, the use of custody for this age group as well as for juveniles. Since the Criminal Justice Act 1988, custody must only be used for this group if:

(1) the offender has repeatedly failed to respond to non-custodial penalties or is unable or unwilling to do so;
(2) it is necessary to protect the public from serious harm; or
(3) the offence is of such seriousness that it would lead to imprisonment if the offender was over 21 years and a non-custodial sentence cannot be justified. The court must also specify what criteria justify the sentence if custody is used.

Young adults (aged 18–20 years inclusive) can be sent to an ordinary prison during this period of their life but as far as possible they are placed in a young offenders' institution where they can stay until 21 years when they must move to an adult prison. Young offenders' institutions are designed with an emphasis on training and education. The custodial sentences are the same as those received by adults and follow the same rules. However, all young offenders are subject to at least three months supervision after a custodial sentence whatever the length. Custody for life for those found guilty of murder is treated in practice as if it were a discretionary life sentence.

Offenders under 18 years

Sentencing in this group has changed over the years, and this may reflect the difficulties that agencies have had in dealing with young offenders and the changes in attitudes to young offenders. This section will describe the present legislation and the changes that are due to come into force in 1999. Offenders under 18 years (young offenders) are divided into 'young persons' (14–17) and 'children' (under 14). Some of the powers of the courts are derived from the Children and Young Persons Acts 1933 and 1969 and the Criminal Justice Act 1991. The Crime and Disorder Act 1998 has made significant changes to the management of young offenders. The organisations and institutions used in the sentencing of young offenders are described in Chapter 13.

Discharges and fines

The types of sentences for both young persons and children are similar to those used for adult offenders but with some variation. Like an adult, a young offender can receive absolute or conditional discharges. The maximum fine for an offender aged less than 14 years is £250 and for an offender aged 14 to 17 years is £1000. If the offender is less than 16 a compensation order is paid by the parent or guardian. In addition to these sentences a Youth Court may, with the consent of the parent or guardian, order them to enter into a 'recognisance' to take and exercise proper control of an offender aged less than 16. The parent then promises to pay a specified sum if they fail to do so.

Community sentences

A sentence introduced by the Crime and Disorder Act 1998 is the *reparation order* which the courts will have to consider if they are not ordering a compensation order. The reparation must be made to either the community or the victim and may include some form of community work.

Young offenders can also receive an *attendance centre order*, similar to those given to offenders aged 18 years to 21 years. This sentence is available for offences that would be punishable by imprisonment in an adult. The maximum attendance is 12 hours if the offender is less than 14 years, up to 24 hours for offenders aged less than 16 years and 36 hours for 16 and 17 year olds. The centre is usually based at a school or youth club.

The equivalent of a probation order for a young offender is a *supervision order*. The supervisor is either a probation officer or a social worker. The maximum length is three years and it can carry similar conditions to an adult probation order, although many of these would have time limits. These conditions can include attendance at a probation centre or attendance at school. A night restriction order can also be imposed ordering the young offender to stay in a specified place for up to 10 hours a night. The restrictions cannot be imposed for more than 30 days within a 3 month period. Young offenders aged over 16 years can also receive community service orders which can also be part of a combination order with a supervision order.

A further sentence introduced by the Crime and Disorder Act 1998 is the *action plan order*. This is designed for 10 to 17 year olds in order to provide supervision by a social worker, a probation officer or a member of the youth offending team for three months. A detailed plan of action will be provided for the court which will include ways in which the offending behaviour will be addressed. This may include some form of reparation to the victim of the offence.

A *curfew order* requires the offender to remain in a specified place for a specified period (up to six months) It applies to those of 10 years or more who consent. It is meant to keep the offender indoors and away from sites of trouble. Where the facilities are available it may be combined with electronic monitoring arrangements ('tagging').

Custodial sentences

Short sentences

At the time of writing, offenders aged between 15 years and 17 years inclusive can receive a sentence of *detention in a young offenders' institution*. Persistent young offenders aged 12 years to 14 years inclusive with previous convictions may be sentenced to a *secure training order*, which was introduced under the Criminal Justice and Public Order Act 1994, and came into effect in March 1998. The offender spends half the sentence in a secure training centre and the second half supervised in the community. The length of the sentence is between six months and two years. These two forms of sentences are due to be replaced by the *detention and training order* which is described in the Crime and Disorder Act 1998. The detention and training order is a generic custodial sentence for 10 to 17 year olds which will only be used for serious offences. In the 10 and 11 year old group it will be primarily for the protection of the public, for the 12 to 14 year old group it will be used for persistent offenders and for 15 to 17 year olds it will be used for serious offences. This will replace the secure training order and detention in a young offenders' institution. It is likely to be implemented in late 1999. Offenders will be detained for half the sentence and will spend the rest supervised in the community. They can be detained in a variety of institutions including young offenders' institution, youth treatment centre or local authority secure unit.

Long sentences

Young offenders aged 10 years to 17 years charged with a grave crime (defined as one that for an adult carries a maximum term of imprisonment of 14 years or indecent assault or dangerous driving) is dealt with in the Crown Courts. The Crown Court will also sentence if the offence would have incurred a sentence of two or more years imprisonment for an adult. These sentences are dealt with under the 1991 Act and the Children and Young Persons Act 1933. Section 53(2) deals with prolonged detention for serious offences. The young offender may not be detained longer than an adult would have been. The sentence may begin in a local authority home or youth treatment centre (see Chapter 13) and go on to a penal institution (young offenders' institution and later adult prison). Young offenders charged with homicide (murder or manslaughter) are automatically committed for trial in a Crown Court. If convicted of murder, they are dealt with by Section 53(1) of the Children and Young Persons Act 1933 (otherwise known as being detained at Her Majesty's's Pleasure (HMP)) which is the equivalent to a life sentence. They are detained in the same way as those under Section 53(2).

Young people and children: remands in custody

Where bail for juveniles is refused, the rules vary by age: 17 year olds may be remanded in a remand centre or prison; those under 17 years are remanded to local authority accommodation. The court may add conditions, e.g. a curfew order or that the accommodation is secure. At present, however, until suitable alternatives are provided, the courts may for very violent or serious offences or persistent absconding, remand 15 and 16 year olds to a remand centre or prison if nothing else will do to protect the public from serious harm. The offender must be legally represented and there must be proper consultation.

The arrangements for children depend on local authority observation and assessment centres being available. Some because of the risk of dangerousness or persistent absconding, will need to be held in a secure unit within the centre. For this an order from the court is required for other than brief emergency admission.

Mentally abnormal offenders

The court will require a psychiatric report where the offender appears mentally disordered. If a custodial sentence is being considered then the court must consider its likely effect on the offender's mental condition. The court will be anxious not to imprison someone whose mental state indicates that psychiatric care is needed. The court is assisted in this by diversion schemes (see Chapter 1). The sentences involving a psychiatric disposal include treatment in the community or treatment or hospital.

Psychiatric treatment as a condition of probation
The Powers of Criminal Courts Act 1973, Section 3 and the Criminal Justice Act 1991 allow the court to attach to a probation order a condition or requirement that the offender receives psychiatric treatment. This treatment may be as an out-patient, as an in-patient or 'at the direction of' the psychiatrist. If the offender fails to attend the psychiatrist or refuses treatment then he can be taken back for the court to reconsider the case.

Binding over to keep the peace
The conditions attached to this disposal can include accepting psychiatric treatment.

Guardianship order
Attendance for treatment may be a condition of this order (see Chapter 3).

Hospital orders
Treatment in hospital using various **orders under the Mental Health Act 1983** (see Chapter 3) is another widely used option.

The probation service

The origins of the probation service stem from voluntary workers in the late nineteenth century offering to supervise offenders who had been bound over. From this there grew a national service of probation officers, who are servants of the court, to befriend, advise and assist offenders. The service is organised in England on a county basis, and its activities cover many areas, some of which are listed below.

- Provision of social enquiry reports to the courts on the background of offenders. In cases of offenders being considered for a custodial sentence the report will help the court in reaching its decision as to whether custody is required. It will also provide detailed information about community alternatives for the court to consider.
- Provision of probation supervision to offenders placed on probation by a court. This may also include intensive probation programmes aimed at controlling offending behaviour.
- Secondment to penal institutions to offer resettlement plans as well as counselling, group work and welfare provision.
- The running and manning of probation hostels in which people on probation can be placed.
- The running and staffing of bail hostels in which accused persons can be given accommodation whilst on bail as an alternative to being remanded in custody.
- The provision and manning of day probation centres for people on probation. This will include activities such as woodwork, job training, social skills and job finding.
- The development and supervision of community service orders.
- The provision of statutory supervision for licensed and paroled prisoners, prisoners on life sentence, and some mentally disordered offenders on conditional discharge to the community under Sections 37/41 of the Mental Health Act.
- The provision of aftercare to those prisoners who seek help.

- Running bail information services for the court.
- Playing a part in court diversion schemes.
- Supervision of juveniles in the community and playing a part in the youth justice service.

The forensic psychiatrist will find that probation officers will often provide invaluable information on the background of offenders on whom a psychiatric report is being prepared. The psychiatrist will often 'share' the care of offenders with the probation service, either seeing an offender as a condition of probation, or working with a probation officer to supervise a conditionally discharged restricted patient in the community. The probation service will value any help the forensic psychiatrist can give in the care of disturbed inmates in probation or bail hostels. The forensic psychiatrist is also likely to be involved in reporting to the court on any mentally abnormal offenders who find their way into a bail hostel. Psychiatrc clinics have been run in probation offices, as described by Huckle *et al.*[5]

Civil courts

The civil law deals with citizens' rights. A more detailed account of civil matters can be found in Cope and Humphreys.[6] It involves seeking redress for injury, wrongdoing or fraud. It also deals with settling disputes and claims between people in a variety of circumstances such as matters of boundaries, contracts, negligence or family disputes following divorce or inheritance. It can also involve injunctions or sex offender orders (see Chapter 12).

   Civil cases are disposed of mostly by county courts but also magistrates' courts and more serious cases in the High Court. Cases in the county courts and High Court are generally heard by one judge. The High Court is also the first court of appeal for the Mental Health Review Tribunals and Mental Health Act Commission. The High Court is divided into three divisions. These are:

(1) Queen's Bench Division: the majority of common law cases concerning contracts and personal injury are dealt with here.
(2) Chancery Division: deals with trusts, wills, companies and tax and other financial matters.
(3) Family Division: deals with adoption, wardships and divorces.

Appeals from these courts are heard at the Court of Appeal. The House of Lords acts as the final UK court of appeal.

The role of the psychiatrist in civil law

Psychiatrists become involved in civil law on an occasional basis. Their main role is in the following situations:

(1) *Where the mental fitness of a subject, suspected of having a mental disorder is being questioned.* The psychiatrist may be asked to comment on the state of mind of a patient or individual in relation to a contract or statement, e.g. to show whether the patient could reasonably enter into a contract, including marriage, have the ability to make a will (testamentary capacity), manage their financial affairs or be responsible for a libel. On the other hand the involvement may be in an appeal against a decision by a Mental Health Tribunal.

(2) *Where the psychiatric damage caused to a subject is being considered.* The psychiatrist may be asked to consider whether a particular act or omission committed by a defendant has caused a psychiatric disorder in the complainant sufficient to justify the payment of compensation.

(3) *Where the psychiatrist's practice is being questioned.*

(4) *Child care proceedings.* Child psychiatrists are mostly involved in these cases. However, general and forensic psychiatrists may become involved if the parents have mental disorder, have histories of offending against children or if the child has been the victim of abuse.

References

(1) *Criminal Justice Act 1991. Sentencing: The New Framework.* NACRO: London.

(2) *Criminal Justice Act 1991. Defendants and Offenders Under 18:* NACRO. London.

(3) *The Crime and Disorder Act 1998.* Draft guidance document, the Home Office: London.

(4) Davies, M., Croall, H. and Tyrer, J. (1998) *Criminal Justice: An Introduction to the Criminal Justice System in England and Wales.* Longman Press: Harlow.

(5) Huckle, P. Tavier and Scarf, S. (1996) Psychiatric clinics in probation offices in South Wales. *Psychiatric Bulletin* **20**, 205–206.

(6) Cope, R. and Humphreys, M. (1995) Civil matters. In: *Practical Forensic Psychiatry* (eds D. Chiswick and R. Cope) Gaskell Books: London.

Chapter 3

Legal Aspects: The Law and the Mentally Abnormal Offender

Introduction

This chapter deals with the way the mentally abnormal offender is helped by the Mental Health Act 1983, the Criminal Procedures (Insanity and Unfitness to Plead) Act 1991, the Crime (Sentences) Act 1997, and the acts in relation to probation. The chapter goes on to describe the various legal definitions of mental abnormality as used in legal proceedings. Mental abnormality may be grounds for mitigation, a reason to be excused trial, a reason for diminished responsibility or grounds to be excused guilt. The medicolegal problems of amnesia, intoxication, muteness and false confessions are considered next. Mental abnormality and the civil law are dealt with in Chapter 2. This chapter does not give details of all the relevant laws. The reader is directed to the standard sources, which for case law is Archbold[1] and for the Mental Health Act is Jones.[2]

Definition of terms

It is imperative, in dealing with the legal profession, to realise that the various definitions referring to mental disorder used in the different acts are technical terms. The careless use of terms like 'mentally ill', 'psychiatrically disordered' leads to confusion and misunderstanding in the courts. Particular care should be taking in using exact legal terminology in court reports. The Homicide Act 1957 and the Mental Health Act 1983 both use terms which must be used precisely in their proper context and not confused.

Mental abnormality (used in the Homicide Act 1957) is a generic term meaning any abnormality of the mind and certainly encompassing illness, all mental impairment and psychopathic disorder.

Mental disorder (used in the Mental Health Act 1983) is a generic term meant to encompass all mental disorder. It is divided into *mental illness*, *arrested or incomplete development of mind*, *psychopathic disorder* and any *other disorder or disability of mind*.

(1) *Mental illness* (Mental Health Act 1983): The term is undefined in the Act and is a matter for clinical judgement. In practice it is used by psychiatrists to cover a range of psychiatric disorders, including psychosis, psychoneurosis and organic states. Whether the illness is of sufficient severity to warrant detention in hospital will be a matter of judgement depending on the severity of the illness, the risk to self or others and the likelihood of co-operation with the doctor if the subject is not detained.

(2) *Arrested or incomplete development of the mind* (Mental Health Act 1983): This may be grounds for detention only if associated with certain conditions, which are laid down in the Act. It is sub-divided into:

    (i) *Severe mental impairment*: This is 'a state of arrested or incomplete development of mind, which includes severe impairment of intelligence and social functioning, and is associated with abnormally aggressive or seriously irresponsible conduct on the part of the person concerned'. This definition clearly refers to people of a very low intelligence (level undefined) but is not applied legally to people unless there is also impaired social functioning and associated abnormally aggressive or seriously irresponsible conduct. In practice the IQ level tends to be below 50. There is no comment on what is meant by impaired social functioning, abnormally aggressive or seriously irresponsible conduct, this is left to the clinician to define. Clearly a person (of low intelligence) whose behaviour was dangerous to others (e.g. fire setting) or to himself (wandering in front of cars) would come within the definition. Persistent minor offending may well be classed as seriously irresponsible in this context.

    (ii) *Mental impairment*: This is 'a state of arrested or incomplete development of mind (not amounting to severe mental impairment) which includes significant impairment of intelligence and social functioning and is associated with abnormally aggressive or seriously irresponsible conduct on the part of the person concerned'. This definition again does not utilise an IQ level but in practice covers an IQ level between 50 and 70 (though there is no strict cut-off point). There has to be impairment of social functioning and associated abnormally aggressive or seriously irresponsible conduct to bring the person within this legal definition. Even if the person fits this part of the definition it will be seen later that orders for the detention of those with simple mental impairment (unlike severe mental impairment) cannot be made unless it is also the case that treatment would be likely to alleviate or prevent a deterioration in their condition.

(3) *Psychopathic disorder* (Mental Health Act 1983): This definition is not identical with that of psychopathic personality or anti-social personality or any other personality disorder. It is a legal definition covering a group of disorders. The definition is 'a persistent disorder or disability of the mind (whether or not including significant impairment of intelligence) which results in abnormally aggressive or seriously irresponsible conduct on the part of the person concerned'. Again 'abnormally aggressive or seriously irresponsible' are not defined and neither is 'persistent'. Section 1(3) of the Mental Health Act makes it clear that 'a person may not be dealt with under the Act as suffering from a mental disorder by reason only of promiscuity or other immoral conduct, sexual deviancy or dependence on alcohol or drugs'. It will be seen from further discussion that subjects within this definition cannot be detained in hospital on an order unless 'treatment is likely to alleviate or prevent a deterioration in their condition'.

(4) *Any other disorder or disability of mind* (Mental Health Act 1983): As Jones[2] points out, the conditions in this residual category will depend on how broad a view is taken of mental illness. However, it has been said to include some neuroses, personality disorders, sexual deviation, alcohol or drug dependence, the behaviour disorders of children, certain specific disorders of learning, disability after head injury or encephalitis or mental enfeeblement as an aftermath of mental illness as well as other minor psychiatric disorders. The common feature of the group, from a legal point of view, is that they cannot be the basis of an order for detention in hospital under the Mental Health Act. They may be considered in mitigation by the court, which may be happy to accept recommendations for the subject to receive treatment for them, perhaps as a condition of probation or on a voluntary basis.

The legal framework for diversion from the legal system for mentally abnormal offenders

Systems for the diversion of the mentally abnormal offender from the legal system – particularly from custody – have been discussed in Chapter 1. It is government policy that an offender needing specialist care and treatment should where possible receive that treatment in hospital rather than in custody. The precise advice on this policy is contained in Home Office circulars 66/1990 and 12/1995. Courts, when sentencing, are bound by Section 4 of the Criminal Justice Act 1991 to consider any information before it which relates to the defendant's mental condition and except where the penalty is fixed by law (mandatory life sentence), courts are required to consider the effect of a custodial sentence on the offender's mental condition before passing sentence.

Magistrates' and Crown Courts have the power, in certain circumstances, to commit mentally disturbed people to a hospital before or during the trial, as well as after conviction. The power to do this lies principally in the Mental Health Act 1983 but also in the Criminal Procedure (Insanity and Unfitness to Plead) Act 1991 and the Crime (Sentences) Act 1997. Disordered people may also be treated by a psychiatrist as a condition of probation, made possible by the Powers of Criminal Courts Act 1973 and the Criminal Justice Acts 1982 and 1991.

The legal basis for diversion of the seriously mentally ill depends on where the subject is when the diversion occurs and at what stage in the legal process:

After arrest

After arrest, police may bring the subject to the hospital for 72 hours detention and observation, under Section 136 of the Mental Health Act 1983. In the police station, admission may be arranged voluntarily or by using Section 2, 3 or 4 of the Mental Health Act 1983. Neither of these situations or the relevant sections of the Mental Health Act will be discussed further in this textbook. Useful annotations on these sections are provided by Jones.[2]

In court, before or during trial

Before trial, if the subject consents, he may be bailed to a hospital (Bail Act 1976) by the court. Psychiatric reports may be requested. Two reports (one by a doctor approved under Section 12 of the Mental Health Act 1983) are mandatory under the Bail Act if the subject is charged with murder.

Before, or during trial, Section 35 of the Mental Health Act 1983 may be used to admit the accused to hospital for reports, and the Crown Court may remand the accused to hospital, rather than in custody under Section 35. For defendants found unfit to plead or not guilty by reason of insanity, various disposals are available to the court under the Criminal Procedure (Insanity and Unfitness to Plead) Act 1991.

Whilst on remand in prison

A prison governor's order can be used to move someone to hospital in an emergency if immediate transfer is required. A Section 48 (Mental Health Act 1983) transfer direction can also be arranged with the Home Office very quickly using fax and telephone.

During remand in prison

Section 48 of the Mental Halth Act 1983 allows for the transfer to a hospital of men in prison who are on remand (or civil prisoners during their sentence or those detained under the Immigration Act 1971) if they are suffering from mental illness or severe mental impairment only. It was formerly used only for the most severely mentally ill patients or severely mentally impaired where urgent psychiatric treatment in hospital was required. It is now used more liberally as a way of quickly getting the mentally ill into hospital. This section requires that:

(1) Two doctors (one approved) recommend to the Home Secretary that such a transfer be effected on the basis of the severity of the mental illness or severe mental impairment of the prisoner.
(2) The Home Secretary considers that the transfer is expedient.
(3) A hospital is willing to accept the patient.
(4) The patient is moved within 14 days of the transfer direction having been provided.

The patient may stay in the hospital until he is well enough to return to prison to continue his remand. In the case of patients who have been remanded by a magistrates' court, they can only be detained for the length of that remand. However, that remand can be renewed by the magistrates' court to allow the patient to stay in hospital. In the case of patients remanded to await trial in a Crown Court the date of appearance at the Crown Court will be altered to suit the case. If the patient does not improve the question of fitness to plead or a hospital order through Section 51 may have to be considered (see below).

After conviction

The court can dispose of the defendant by means of an order to detain a person in hospital for medical treatment under Section 37 of the Mental Health Act 1983. Before deciding on disposal the court can order the detention in hospital of a person to determine if a hospital order under this section is appropriate (sometimes referred to as a 'trial of treatment', Section 38 Mental Health Act 1983).

Courts have the option of imposing a custodial sentence but directing that the prisoner be first admitted to hospital for treatment. This is called a hospital direction and is usually accompanied by a restriction order (to be described below) called a limitation direction. This power was introduced by means of an amendment to the Mental Health Act 1983, Section 45A, introduced in the Crime (Sentences) Act 1997.

Following a custodial sentence

After a custodial sentence: a transfer to hospital under Section 47 of the Mental Health Act 1983 can be made but the prisoner remains subject to the custodial sentence imposed by the court.

Details of relevant acts governing diversion from the criminal justice system

The details of the various acts governing diversion of the mentally disordered are discussed in order of the stage of proceedings, i.e. before or during trial, during remand in prison, after conviction or whilst serving a custodial sentence.

Before or during trial

Section 35 of the Mental Health Act 1983 provides for a remand to hospital so that a report on the accused's mental condition may be compiled. It is applicable for any offence punishable by imprisonment, except if the subject has been convicted of murder, in which case the assessment must be in prison. It should be noted that the section does not allow the patient to be treated against his will.

This section can be effected by the Crown Court for people awaiting trial or during or after the trial but before sentence where the offence is punishable by imprisonment, or by a magistrates' court for defendants in the following circumstances:

(1) after conviction for an offence punishable by imprisonment but before sentence;
(2) before conviction for such an offence if the court is satisfied the person did the act;
(3) before conviction and the person agrees.

In order to effect this section there must also be a report from a doctor approved under Section 12 of the Mental Health Act 1983 to convince the court (oral or written evidence) that there is reason to suspect mental illness, severe mental impairment, mental impairment or psychopathic disorder, and a recognition by the court that a report on bail is impractical: There must also be a hospital willing and able to provide a bed within seven days (there must be written or oral evidence from a doctor or manager of the hospital on this point). The defendant must be held in a place of safety (usually the prison) until the hospital bed is available.

The defendant can arrange his own private psychiatric report or appeal against the remand. The Mental Health Review Tribunal has no power to discharge such a subject. The court has to decide if the security in the hospital is appropriate for the case. The court cannot order the subject to a hospital without the hospital's agreement. Treatment may be required during this period but consent refused. In these circumstances the Code of Practice for the Mental Health Act advises that the patient should be promptly referred back to court with an appropriate recommendation. If this would entail undue delay then consideration should be given to whether the patient fulfils criteria for detention under Section 3 of the Mental Health Act 1983 (Section 17.3, Code of Practice, Mental Health Act).

Section 36 of the 1983 Act provides for remand of an accused person to hospital for treatment, and is used for mental illness or severe mental impairment. This section applies to any defendant whose offence is punishable by imprisonment except those charged with murder (they can be transferred under Section 48, Mental Health Act 1983). The purpose of the section is to allow the court to remand a defendant to hospital for treatment. In practice, Section 48 of the Mental Health Act is more usually employed. The section can be effected by the Crown Court only and is an alternative to prison remand. It may be done in the pre-trial period (in which case it may get a defendant well enough to be tried) or during the trial.

The order requires two doctors, one approved under Section 12 of the Mental Health Act 1983, to say that the patient is suffering from mental illness or severe mental impairment of a degree requiring hospital treatment. (Both doctors may come from the same hospital.) Note that the order cannot be applied to those with psychopathic disorder or mental impairment alone, presumably because these disorders would never be thought to require emergency treatment in their own right. There must also be evidence from the doctor who will be in charge of the patient or a hospital manager that a bed will be available within seven days.

The patient will then be remanded in prison for up to seven days until the bed becomes available. The patient is subject to 'consent to treatment regulations' and therefore may be treated against his will. The Mental Health Review Tribunal has no powers to discharge the patient.

Under the Criminal Procedure (Insanity and Unfitness to Plead) Act 1991 the courts have powers to deal with persons found not guilty by reason of insanity or unfitness to plead (see below). These are, in a case of murder, an admission order to a hospital specified by the Secretary of State (effectively a hospital order with a restriction order unlimited in time); or in other cases the possibilities are an absolute discharge, a guardianship order (under Section 37 Mental Health Act 1983), or a supervision and treatment order. This is an order leading to supervision by a social worker for a period of up to two years with a requirement to submit to treatment by a registered medical practitioner. The order specifies whether the treatment be in a hospital, out-patient, or as the doctor directs. Medical advice must be given that compulsory detention for treatment is not needed, and the court must be satisfied that release into the community will not pose an unacceptable risk. The court has to be satisfied that social work supervision is available. Continuing care may be needed after the order is over. The order is designed for relatively minor offences where the offender is likely to co-operate.

The court has to be satisfied that social work supervision is available. Continuing care may be needed after the order is over.

The other possibility is an admission order to a hospital specified by the Secretary of State. This works like a Section 37 from the date of the order. The court has the option of adding a restriction order. If the jury is unconvinced of the disability then the accused is found fit to plead. The trial proper then begins and a new jury empanelled.

Under the old Act someone found under disability was automatically detained as though under a hospital order with a restriction order unlimited in time. This dissuaded seriously ill people from this plea when the offence was a minor one. The present Act with its wide range of disposals will encourage more people to plead that they are under disability and may, for the same reasons, lead to more insanity defences.

After conviction

Section 37 hospital orders

Once a mentally disordered defendant has been convicted, a common disposal is the use of a Section 37 'hospital order'. This is the principal section within Part 3 of the Mental Health Act, and allows the magistrates' court and the Crown Court to order a convicted offender suffering from the appropriate mental disorder to go to hospital for treatment. Before making this order the court has to have certain conditions satisfied:

(1) The offence is one that can lead to imprisonment.
(2) Two doctors must offer reports and one of the doctors must be approved under Section 12 of the Mental Health Act as having special experience. Both doctors may come from the same hospital.
(3) The two doctors must agree on the main diagnostic group, which must be mental illness, severe mental impairment, mental impairment or psychopathic disorder. Two doctors must also agree in the case of psychopathy or mental impairment that treatment is likely to alleviate or prevent a deterioration in his condition.
(4) The hospital must be willing and able to take the patient within 28 days of the order being made. The doctor who will be in charge of the treatment or a hospital manager must give oral or written evidence of this. Pending the move to hospital the court will direct the patient to a place of safety, in general this will be back to the remand prison. If at the end of the 28 days the arrangements for transfer break down, the subject must be released. To prevent this the Secretary of State can direct the subject to another more appropriate hospital within the 28 days and the order will continue there, or alternatively the patient can be taken back to court and re-sentenced (Section 11(2) Crown Court Act 1971 and Section 142 Magistrates Courts Act 1980). This new sentence can be a renewal of the hospital order to allow time for a bed to become available. The Crime Sentencing Act 1997 empowered courts and the Home Secretary to specify a hospital unit within a

hospital when an order is made under Sections 37, 45A, 47 and Schedule 1 of the Criminal Procedure (Insanity and Unfitness to Plead) Act 1991.

(5) Before making the order the court must be agreed that this is the most suitable way of dealing with the offender. If this disposal is used then other sentences cannot also be used for that offence such as a fine or probation. In some cases the court may feel that the suggestions by the doctor are not appropriate to the particular prisoner and the offender may be sent to prison instead. Sometimes a court may ask the doctors to find a place in a more secure hospital than the one suggested. The doctors may investigate this possibility but at the end of the day if a bed in a more secure hospital is unavailable, or the doctors feel it entirely inappropriate, then the disagreement between the doctors and the court may be resolved by the court sending the offender to prison, rather than accepting what it regards as an unsatisfactory recommendation.

The juvenile court has similar powers to make a hospital order in the case of mentally disturbed children. Magistrates' courts can make a hospital order (Section 37(3)) without convicting the accused if the accused is suffering from mental illness or severe mental impairment. The court has to be satisfied that the accused did the act. This is rarely used but is a way of dealing with a defendant who is so ill as to be unable to take part in the proceedings, and it seems to the court the best way of dealing with the matter. In a Crown Court if the accused was that disturbed then the formal question of fitness to plead (see below) must be considered.

The District Health Authority and local social services have a duty to provide after-care services to hospital order patients (Section 117, Mental Health Act 1983).

Guardianship orders

The purpose of this order under Section 37 is to provide social worker control in the community for appropriate subjects. It is applied only to those offenders who have attained 16 years (before that control would probably be provided through childcare legislation) and order can only be made if certain conditions are met. These are that two doctors (one approved under Section 12) must offer reports that the mental disorder is of a nature or degree which warrants reception into guardianship; the doctors must agree on the main category; and the local social services, or any other person has to be willing to receive the offender.

A guardianship order has the following effects:

(1) It can be used in cases where the offender does not consent (unlike a probation order, which is an agreement between the offender and the court).
(2) The subject may be required to live where directed.

(3) Access to the subject must be allowed for the approved social worker, registered medical practitioner, or other person specified.
(4) The subject must present himself for medical treatment, occupation, education or training if required to do so.

The disadvantage of the order is that there is no sanction available to the guardian if the subject refuses to co-operate, although he can be re-arrested if he fails to live where directed. The guardian has to rely on the moral position given to him by the order to gain the client's co-operation. The order tends to be used mostly to look after mentally impaired patients in the community, although it could be used for any diagnosis where supervision and control is desirable.

Section 38: interim hospital order
The order is designed to facilitate trials of treatment with difficult to place patients, particularly those with psychopathic disorder or mental impairment. However the Act does allow it to be used for mental illness and severe impairment as well. In order to effect this section the following conditions must be satisfied:

(1) The offence must be an imprisonable one.
(2) Two doctors, including an approved one, must agree on the main diagnosis and make the recommendation. One of the doctors must be from the hospital accepting the patient.
(3) It can apply to mental illness, psychopathic disorder, severe mental impairment and mental impairment.
(4) There must be reason to suppose that the disorder may be appropriate for a hospital order.
(5) A hospital bed should be available within 28 days of the order being made and evidence of this must be given in to the court by the potential responsible medical officer or a manager of the hospital.

An interim hospital order means that the patient can be detained in a hospital for a trial of treatment for up to 12 weeks initially, the order being renewed every 28 days up to 12 months' total (as amended by the Crime (Sentences) Act 1997). At the end of the trial of treatment the court converts the order into a hospital order or re-sentences the subject. Renewals and conversions to a hospital order can be done in the patient's absence if he is legally represented and medical evidence is available. The effect of the order in terms of treatment is the same as a hospital order. There is no appeal to the Mental Health Review Tribunal.

Section 41: restriction order
The purpose of this section is to protect the public by ordering that a patient detained on a hospital order will not be allowed to leave the hospital without the Home Secretary's permission. The order can be made for a

stated period of time (several years) or unlimited in point of time (i.e. potentially to last for the rest of the patient's life). This interference with the patient's liberty is so great that only a judge in a higher court can make the order. Judges are recommended only to make the order where there is a risk of the patient causing serious harm to others if set at large. In making this order the court must consider 'the nature of the offence, the antecedents of the offender and the risk of him committing further offences if set at large'. The requirements for a judge to make this order are:

(1) All the recommendations of a Section 37 order.
(2) The restrictions are necessary to protect the public from serious harm.
(3) The judge has heard oral evidence from one of the doctors writing the reports for the court about the patient. The doctor will be asked whether or not he feels the restriction order is required. The doctor will give his mind to the dangerousness of the patient, the chances of his absconding, responding to treatment, and complying with treatment when he has left hospital. However, whatever the doctor's opinion, the judge may impose the restriction order if it seems to him appropriate.

If a restriction order under Section 41 is made, the patient comes directly under the Secretary of State for Home Affairs, though he would generally delegate this to a minister under him. The freedom of the patient within the hospital grounds is left to the doctor's discretion. All questions of movement from the hospital and the management of the patient after discharge have to be referred to the Home Office. Thus permission is required for the patient to have leave outside the hospital grounds with an escort (e.g. for a shopping trip); or the patient to have leave outside the hospital without an escort. Permission is further required for leave of absence overnight from the hospital; transfer of the patient to other hospitals; or a discharge or conditional discharge. Unlike a simple Section 37, detention is continuous without renewals. Regular reports on patients subject to Section 41 orders are requested by the Secretary of State.

When the patient is discharged the Home Secretary will generally impose conditions which the patient must fulfil, otherwise the Home Secretary may issue a warrant for his recall to hospital (see below). The conditions are, usually, to be subject to social work supervision and psychiatric care. These conditions will generally, in practice, last five years but may in certain circumstances be extended or shortened. The Home Secretary does have the power to discharge someone absolutely, which he will do when he is satisfied that the patient is no longer a danger to others. Recall by the Home Secretary may be exercised even without medical advice when the Home Secretary has reason to believe that the patient has a mental disorder such that he is liable to be detained and there is a risk to his own health or safety or a risk to others.

The patient cannot obtain his discharge by absconding. No matter how long he stays away from the hospital he is liable to be recalled if found.

The patient under a Section 41 order can apply to the Mental Health Review Tribunal after six months. The Tribunal does have the power to discharge the patient either conditionally or absolutely but other powers are limited (see below).

Permission for increased freedom for the patient is obtained by writing letters to the Home Secretary's Department describing the improvements in the patient's mental state, the reduction in risk, the new proposals and the lack of danger involved in the proposal (see Chapter 15). The Home Office provides the clinician with guidelines, which are periodically revised, on the type of information required to allow the Home Office to assess risk. These guidelines should be obtained from and consulted before proposals are put to the Home Office.

It should be noted that a restriction order does not necessarily imply that a hospital must have security. The restriction order may be placed on the patient largely in order to enforce treatment after discharge. The initial treatment may, in appropriate cases, be carried out in open conditions. Similarly the patient who may require secure conditions at the beginning of his treatment may improve sufficiently to move to open conditions for rehabilitation.

If the patient is conditionally discharged and has a relapse he can be readmitted to a hospital by the doctor without a formal Home Office recall simply by admitting informally or by admitting under Part II of the Mental Health Act. The Home Office may however exercise its discretion formally to recall the patient to hospital. The hospital need not be the original hospital but any suitable to the case. The clinician should discuss with the Home Office the best approach to ensuring the patient is safely dealt with.

A magistrates' court, wishing to make a hospital order on a mentally disordered offender, may have enough evidence before them to regard the offender as sufficiently dangerous to require a restriction order. In that case the court would have to refer the offender (see below) to a Crown Court, which would review the case before deciding whether or not to make a restriction order with the hospital order. Sections 43 and 44 lay down procedures for magistrates' courts to follow for this situation.

The problems of a restriction order include:

(1) Interference in the clinical management of the case by legal controls. The clinician may find that he has to detain the patient in hospital for much longer than he might consider necessary on clinical grounds in order to satisfy the Home Secretary's anxieties about dangerousness.
(2) The difficulty of deciding if someone is still a risk to others. Patients, for example, with psychopathic disorder and sadistic offences, or psychotic patients not fully under control may be detained far longer in hospital than they would have been had they received a simple prison sentence for the same offence.

Section 42 of the 1983 Act allows the Home Secretary to order a conditional or absolute discharge, or withdraw the restriction order. It also allows the Home Secretary to recall a conditionally discharged patient, by issuing a warrant, usually to the police, to arrest the patient and take him to an appropriate hospital. This would be prompted by a report from the patient's social worker, or responsible medical officer, that the patient was breaking the conditions of his conditional discharge or that his behaviour suggested that he was becoming dangerous again. Health Service Guidelines (HSG (93) 20) recommend that the patient has to be informed immediately that he is being recalled and given the reasons (orally and in writing) within 72 hours by the responsible medical officer, an approved social worker or administrator. The patient has then the right to appeal to the Mental Health Review Tribunal, within one month, against the recall. This protects the patient against arbitrary recall.

The Crime (Sentences) Act 1997

The Reed Committee on Psychopathic Disorder[3] recommended the introduction of a 'hybrid order' combining a prison sentence and a transfer direction equivalent to a Section 47 direction. The Reed Committee did not envisage this being used for mental illness, nor that those found to be successfully treated should be returned to the prison system to complete their sentence but both are included in the Act.

The Crime (Sentences) Act 1997 initially applies to those suffering from psychopathic disorder but the Home Secretary can, by order, extend the Act to those suffering from other forms of mental disorder, including mental illness. The Act introduces a new section to the Mental Health Act, Section 45a. This section of the Mental Health Act is intended for serious cases where the court is not satisfied that merely dealing with the mental disorder will prevent further serious offences. The court can under this new power both impose a custodial sentence whilst simultaneously directing a defendant to hospital. When treatment in hospital is no longer indicated the prisoner then returns to prison to complete their sentence. This new section is not intended to interfere with existing powers; the court is obliged to first consider and then reject the making of a hospital order under Section 37. This is meant to be a safeguard to prevent improper use where treatment is appropriate.

Significant concerns have been expressed about these new powers.[4] The hybrid order combining treatment and punishment fundamentally alters the law's traditional attitude that those suffering from mental disorder should receive treatment not punishment. Psychiatrists are likely to have reservations about returning to prison patients who have completed successful treatment but have a further portion of their sentence to serve. If these successfully treated patients do not return to prison, then the hospital in effect becomes a place for detention rather than treatment.

Under the new powers the court can give a direction that, instead of being removed and detained in the prison, the offender be removed and detained in such hospital as may be specified in the direction, in this Act referred to as a 'hospital direction', or give a direction that the offender be subject to the special restrictions set out in Section 41(of the Mental Health Act 1983), in this Act referred to as the 'limitation direction'.

Section 45a applies in the case of any person convicted before the Crown Court of an imprisonable offence which is not fixed by law and which does not fall to be imposed under Section 2 of the Crime (Sentences) Act 1997 (mandatory life sentences for second serious offences). Section 45a (2) requires the court to be satisfied on the written or oral evidence of two registered medical practitioners that the offender is suffering from psychopathic disorder; that the mental disorder from which the offender is suffering is of a nature or degree which makes it appropriate for him to be detained in hospital for medical treatment; and that such treatment is likely to alleviate or prevent the deterioration of his condition.

The position in respect of a hospital bed being made available is the same as for other transfer directions. The court has powers to make an order under Section 38 of the Mental Health Act in order to determine whether the making of a hospital direction under Section 45a is appropriate.

Mentally disordered offenders and probation

Where someone convicted is mentally disordered, but not to such an extent that admission to hospital is necessary, it may be appropriate for them to receive psychiatric treatment as an outpatient as a condition of probation. It can be a very useful disposal for patients for whom out-patient care is the most appropriate. It can also be applied to those mentally disordered people who fall outside the categories which permit detention, e.g. inadequate personalities with minor depressive swings, personality disorders accompanied by sexual deviations, alcoholics, etc. Treatment as a condition of probation can be required to last for up to three years and may be residential, non-residential, and under the direction of a specified doctor.

To make such an order the court requires oral or written evidence from a doctor approved under Section 12 that such treatment would be appropriate; evidence that a named doctor is available to provide such treatment; and the offender's agreement to comply with the order. A probation officer has to have been consulted about the order.

The effect of the order under this section is that the patient is expected to accept the treatment as prescribed, however, the doctor can discharge the patient from treatment when the patient no longer needs it. If the patient breaches the conditions of the order (e.g. fails to attend) then the doctor should inform the probation officer, who may choose to take the patient back to court for breach of probation. The court may then choose, depending on the circumstances, to leave the matter or to re-sentence the offender.

Under the same act the court has the power to remand an offender in custody or on bail after conviction in order to obtain social and psychiatric reports to aid them in their sentencing. If the patient is remanded in custody, the request for a psychiatric report from the court will be sent to the prison doctors. If the patient is remanded on bail then the request will be sent to a local psychiatrist.

Whilst serving a prison sentence

The Mental Health Act allows for the transfer of mentally disordered people (remanded or convicted) from prison to hospital (Sections 47 and 48). The doctors involved usually find the bed and then apply to the Home Office to make the recommendation for transfer. This is done without the courts being involved. If a bed has not been found then the Home Office pass on the prison doctor's recommendation to the appropriate Health Authority who has a duty to find a bed.

Section 47 (transfer direction for convicted prisoners)
This section allows movement of mentally disordered convicted prisoners from prison to a hospital. Once recovered in hospital the patient can be returned to the prison to finish their sentence. If, however, it is more appropriate to stay in hospital, this may be allowed. If the illness is not relieved by the date the patient was due to be released from prison then the patient can still be detained in the hospital. The transfer direction is treated as though it was a Section 37 (called notional 37) from the date the patient was admitted to the hospital (see also Section 49 below). The requirements for Section 47 are that two doctors, one approved, recommend to the Secretary of State that the patient is suffering from mental illness, psychopathy, mental impairment or severe mental impairment, which warrants attention in a psychiatric hospital. The doctors state what sort of hospital would be most appropriate. The Secretary of State must judge that it is expedient to remove and direct the offender to a suitable hospital, and a hospital must have accepted the patient. The transfer must be enacted within 14 days; otherwise a further transfer direction would have to be sought.

The effect of Section 47 is that the patient is detained in hospital as though on a hospital order though without the same relationship to the Mental Health Review Tribunal. In practice the Section 47 is accompanied by a restriction direction under Section 49 of the Mental Health Act (see below).

Section 49 restriction directions
This section allows the Home Secretary to place restrictions (as in Section 41) on a transferred convicted prisoner (known as a restriction direction) and makes mandatory that restrictions be placed on transferred remand

prisoners. The restriction direction lasts, in the case of convicted prisoners, until the earliest date of release from prison when the order effectively becomes a simple Section 37. Should the doctor then continue the detention it would be without the restrictions. In the case of remanded prisoners the restriction direction lasts until the court deals with the case, or until the subject is returned to remand prison.

Sections 50–53 transfer directions
These sections deal with the management by the Home Secretary (or courts as well in remand cases) of transferred prisoners once they are declared well again, or it is found that no effective treatment can be given. This allows the transfer back to prison from hospital. Section 51(v) and (vi) allows the making of a hospital order on the mentally ill, or severely mentally impaired who are on a transfer direction whilst on remand, in their absence and without convicting them. This section is used when a prisoner has been moved from remand prison to hospital (Section 48) and there is little likelihood of recovery sufficient to stand trial. Two doctors must give oral or written evidence about his mental state, and then the court can make a Section 37 order in the patient's absence but without registering a conviction.

Mental abnormality as a defence in court

In the majority of cases an accused person with a mental abnormality will stand trial. Normally it will only be after a guilty plea or a finding of guilt that medical evidence will be presented in order to mitigate the sentence of the court. The offender is saying, 'At the time of the offence I was suffering from a mental disorder which I would like you to take into consideration in sentencing and if possible send me for treatment rather than punishment'.

In certain uncommon cases the accused, suffering from a mental disorder, says, as it were, to the court that:

He is not fit enough to appear in court (not fit to stand trial); or although fit enough to appear in the courtroom he is not fit enough to take part in the trial. The phrases used to describe this are 'not fit to plead' or 'under disability in relation to the trial'; or although the offender agrees that he did the act, he claims that he was not fully responsible at the time. He may claim that because of severe mental disorder he had

(1) no responsibility for his acts and therefore should not be found guilty (but insane); or that
(2) (in the case of homicide) he had diminished responsibility for his acts; or that
(3) he was behaving automatically and therefore no crime was committed; or

(4) in the case of a mother accused of killing her baby, that the balance of her mind was so disturbed that she should be found not guilty of murder but guilty of the lesser offence, infanticide.

Thus in these cases the psychiatric evidence is heard before the trial or as part of the trial. These various pleas are described below.

Not fit to stand trial

An accused may not be fit to stand trial (to appear in court) on medical grounds, either because of severe physical illness or severe mental disorder, such as a state of mania. In such a case, if the accused has been remanded in custody, it is quite likely that the prison doctor will already have initiated arrangements for a transfer direction under Section 48 to have the accused treated in a local hospital. The consultants at the local hospital will then keep in contact with the clerk of the court over the weeks to keep the court acquainted with the accused's state of mind. When the accused is fit enough he or she can then be produced in court. In the case of the magistrates' court the patient has to be remanded regularly. This can be done in the patient's absence if they are legally represented and there is a report from the doctor. In the case of a Crown Court the date of appearance in court can be simply put off until the patient is well enough to appear. If the offence is trivial and the patient is going to be treated anyway, the court or prosecution may choose not to proceed with the charge but allow the patient to stay in hospital to receive treatment. In a more serious case, on a transfer direction, Section 51(vi) of the Mental Health Act allows a court to make a hospital order in the patient's absence (see above).

Not fit to plead (under disability)

The question of the accused being unfit may be raised by the defence, the prosecution or the judge and is a matter that has to be tried in a Crown Court. The question may be raised at the very start of the trial or the judge may allow it to be postponed until the prosecution case is heard, for if the case is weak then the accused may have no case to answer. The plea must be proven, on the balance of probabilities (if raised by the defence), or, beyond reasonable doubt (if raised by the prosecution). A new jury is empanelled just to decide the question. If the matter is not proven then the original trial goes on.

The test of unfitness to plead is derived from case law that preceded the Criminal Procedure (Insanity and Unfitness to Plead) Act 1991, the relevant case being that of *R* v. *Pritchard* (1836). The tests enunciated in that case were whether the accused was able:

(1) To plead to the indictment.
(2) To comprehend the course of the proceedings of the trial so as to make a proper defence.

(3) To know that he might challenge a juror.
(4) To comprehend the details of the evidence.

Archbold (1998) lists the questions to be put to juries following the tests of *R* v. *Pritchard* as 'whether the defendant has sufficient intellect to instruct his solicitors and council, to plead to the indictment, to challenge jurors, to understand the evidence and to give evidence'.[1] The essential issue is whether the defendant will get a fair trial and to be able properly to make a defence to the charges against him. Archbold defines it as 'the ability to participate to the requisite extent in any necessary trial process that is important and to this extent the expression "fitness to plead" may be misleading'.[1] The 'requisite extent' is determined also by the relevant issues in court such that somebody may be fit to plead in cases where a guilty plea is entered but not in a fully contested trial. Intellectual impairment of any kind might make someone fall within these rules. Mental illness without gross intellectual impairment may so interfere with communication, understanding, ability to follow proceedings or ability to give evidence that the defendant is found to be unable to participate to 'the requisite extent' and is therefore unfit to plead. It is not enough simply that the accused might act against his own interests (e.g. in paranoia) or that he conducts his defence unwisely; the disorder must involve such disability that the defendant is unable to properly make a defence to the charges against him.

In order to 'prove' the disability in the case of mental illness two psychiatrists (one approved under Section 12, Mental Health Act 1983) are asked to give reports before a jury empanelled for the purpose. If the jury is convinced of the disability then the court deals with the case under the Criminal Procedure (Insanity and Unfitness to Plead) Act 1991.

Following a verdict of unfit to plead, proceedings move to a 'trial of the facts', where a jury hearing evidence determine if the accused 'did the act or made the omission against him'. The important issue to grasp is that this does not amount to a finding of guilt. If not satisfied on this issue, they return a verdict of acquittal. If they are convinced, a finding that the defendant did the act is recorded.

The judge then has a number of possible disposals available under this new Act.

Not guilty by reason of insanity

This plea is of historic interest and has been discussed in detail by West and Walk.[5] It has for centuries been a principle in English law that a gravely mentally ill person is not responsible for his actions. The Criminal Lunatics Act of 1800 allowed the acquittal of an accused if he was found not guilty on the grounds of insanity, though this finding was always followed by detention in custody pending His Majesty's pleasure. This custody came to mean incarceration in institutions for the psychiatrically ill.

In 1843 a Scotsman named McNaughten attempted to kill the Prime

Minister, Sir Robert Peel, and in error killed the Prime Minister's secretary. McNaughten was under the delusion that his life was in danger from the Prime Minister's political party. He was found not guilty by reason of insanity. The finding was unpopular and there was a demand for clear guidelines to the court on such cases. In response to this the Law Lords laid down the criteria known as the *McNaughten Rules*.

In such cases it is argued that the defendant cannot be held responsible for his actions because of the severity of the mental illness. The accused has to prove in a higher court on the balance of probabilities that at the time of the offence he laboured under such defect of the mind that he met the *McNaughten Rules*, i.e.

(1) That by reason of such defect from disease of the mind he did not know the nature or quality of his act (this means that he did not realise what he was physically doing at the time); or
(2) by reason of such defect from disease of the mind that he did not know what he was doing was wrong (i.e. that he did not know that what he was doing was forbidden by law or that the act was morally wrong according to the standards of ordinary people); or
(3) where a person is under an insane delusion that prevents the true appreciation of the nature and quality of his act, he is under the same degree of responsibility as if the facts were as he imagined them to be. If for example whilst deluded he believes his life to be in grave danger and acts in self-defence, he would be treated as thought acting in self-defence. However if whilst deluded he acts to gain revenge, then he is punishable.

A finding of not guilty by reason of insanity is known as the *special verdict*. To prove the case evidence must be presented by two or more medical practitioners one of whom is approved under the Mental Health Act 1983. The Criminal Procedure (Insanity and Unfitness to Plead) Act 1991 allows the judge to make use of a range of options for the care of the defendant. Under the previous 1964 Act the special verdict was followed automatically by detention in hospital as though on Section 37, Mental Health Act 1983 with a restriction order unlimited in time. In consequence only offenders who had committed serious offences used the plea. Offenders who met the McNaughten criteria but whose offence was minor lacked, at Crown Court level, a sensible disposal. The disposals now available are the same as for those defendants found to be "under disability".

The McNaughten Rules became particularly important for mentally abnormal offenders charged with murder, because, until the abolition of the death sentence, a successful plea avoided execution. The rules have, however, been subject to criticism. They are said to be based on a misunderstanding of mental illness and its effect on the patient. The rules assume that mental illness is a disorder of reason only and do not recognise that mental illness may affect very severely aspects of mental life other than reason. The rules are very strict and many severely mentally disordered people strictly speaking fall outside them, particularly those with disorders of emotion.

Diminished responsibility

The 1957 Homicide Act introduced, in the case of murder, the defence of *diminished responsibility*. This Act allows a person charged with murder to plead that his mental abnormality, while not sufficiently severe to meet the strict criteria of the McNaughten Rules, is sufficient substantially to diminish his responsibility. It has to be shown, on the balance of probabilities, that at the time of the offence the accused suffered from

'such abnormality of mind, (whether arising from a condition of arrested or retarded development of mind or inherent causes or induced by disease or injury), as substantially impaired his mental responsibilities for his acts or omissions in doing or being party to the killing'. Section 2 Homicide Act 1957.

There are therefore three limbs to the defence of diminished responsibility. These are, first, whether the defendant has an abnormality of mind. Abnormality of Mind has been ruled by the Court of Criminal Appeal (*R* v. *Byrne*, 1960, 2 QB 396; 44 CrAppR, 246) to mean

'a state of mind so different from that of ordinary human beings that the reasonable man would term it abnormal. It appears to us to be wide enough to cover the mind's activities in all its aspects, not only the perception of physical acts and matters, and the ability to form a rational judgement as to whether the act was right or wrong, but also the ability to exercise willpower to control physical acts in accordance with that rational judgement'.

It is solely a matter for the jury to determine if an abnormality of mind exists taking into account not only medical evidence but also all evidence put before them.

Having established that there is an abnormality of mind it is necessary to determine whether it arises from arrested or incomplete development of mind, or any inherent causes or whether it is induced by disease or injury. This is properly a matter for expert medical opinion. 'Any inherent cause' has been held (*R* v. *Sanderson*, (1994) Cr98AppR, 325) to include 'functional mental illness as well as organic or physical injury or disease of body including the brain'. In practice a wide range of conditions have been held to fall within this section including gross mental retardation, psychotic disorders, chronic reactive depression, battered women's syndrome, premenstrual tension, severe personality disorder, alcoholism and mercy killings associated with depression.

If the jury is satisfied on the balance of probabilities that the defendant is suffering from an abnormality of mind arising from one of the three causes above, then they go on to determine if the abnormality 'substantially impaired his mental responsibility for his acts'. The jury will take into account medical evidence on this limb of the defence but this is a matter for the jury alone as enunciated in *R* v. *Byrne* 'whether such impairment can properly be called substantial [is] a matter upon which juries may quite legitimately differ from doctors'. The meaning of 'mental responsibility' is unclear but is taken to refer to culpability. 'Substantially' is also undefined and is left for the jury to decide, although the doctor will be asked his opinion. The Judicial Studies Board gives guidance as follows: 'substantially impaired means just that. You (the jury) must conclude that his abnormality of mind was a real cause of the defendant's conduct. The defendant does not have to prove that his condition was the sole cause of it but he must show that it was more than merely a trivial one.'

Homicide is frequently associated with intoxication with alcohol or drugs. The defendant's state of mind may then arise partly from intoxication and partly from an abnormality of mind. Successive judgements in court have concluded that juries must disregard what in their opinion the effect of drink or drugs on the defendant was, as an abnormality of mind induced by drugs or alcohol alone is not regarded as arising from inherent causes. Two tests have been formulated to put to juries in these circumstances: "first have the defence satisfied you on the balance of probabilities that if the defendant had not taken drink he would have killed as he did and second, that he would have been under diminished responsibility when he did so (i.e. with alcohol or drugs disregarded)". Where the alcoholism has led to gross brain disease then the defendant's abnormality of mind may fall within the phrase 'induced by disease or injury'.

If medical experts are in agreement then the jury can only bring in a verdict of murder if there were facts that entitled the jury to reject or differ from the medical evidence. The effect of a successful plea is to reduce the charge from murder to manslaughter. Murder carried a statutory sentence of execution in the days of capital punishment though nowadays it carries the statutory sentence of life imprisonment. If the charge is reduced to manslaughter then the court is free to make any sentence including hospital orders and probation.

The Act has been criticised because of the lack of definitions and the stretching of the meanings of the words that occur. Nevertheless because of its flexibility the plea of diminished responsibility has largely replaced the plea of not guilty by reason of insanity. In the case of the severely mentally ill the outcome of both pleas, if successful, is much the same, i.e. committal to a hospital for treatment with a restriction order attached. However, in the case of a successful plea of diminished responsibility, more choices are available to the judge, for instance, if the offender's mental state does not require admission to a psychiatric hospital, the judge is free to make treatment a condition of probation. If the psychiatric condition is such that treatment in a hospital is unlikely to be helpful (in the case of psychopathic disorder) the judge may choose to sentence the offender to imprisonment, indeed to life imprisonment in appropriate cases.

It is important to note that the defence of diminished responsibility is specific to the 1957 Homicide Act and use of the term should be restricted to this defence against a charge of murder.

Automatism

This is a rare plea in which the defendant claims that at the time of the offence he was behaving 'automatically' and therefore is not guilty of a crime. In law this term means a state where the mind is not ruling the body. Fenwick[6] provides a clinical definition of automatism:

> An automatism is an involuntary piece of behaviour over which an individual has no control. The behaviour itself is usually inappropriate to the circumstances, and may be out of character for the individual. It can be complex, co-ordinated, and apparently purposeful and directed, though lacking in judgement. Afterwards, the individual may have no recollection, or a partial or confused memory, for his actions. In organic automatism, there must be some disturbance of brain function, sufficient to give rise to the above features. In psychogenic automatism, the behaviour is complex, co-ordinated and appropriate to some aspect of the patient's psychopathology. The sensorium is usually clear, but there will be severe or complete amnesia for the episode.

The law is more succinct in its definition, defining automatism, as 'unconscious involuntary action and it is therefore a defence because the mind does not go with what is being done' (*Bratty* v. *AG for Northern Ireland*, [1963] AC 386 401). Case law[1] has concerned itself with organic automatism but there is no reason, following Fenwick's definition, why psychogenic automatism should not come within the legal definition of automatism. However it is difficult to prove that in psychogenic automatism there is complete lack of conscious awareness of action (the mind not going with what is being done). In dissociative states there remains partial awareness of action and therefore complete lack of conscious awareness will be difficult to prove. In such cases the legal definition of automatism will not be fulfilled.

Two forms of automatism are recognised. *Sane automatism* is due to external causes, (e.g. behaviour in a state of concussion after a blow on the head or behaviour in a confusional state after an anaesthetic). The plea has even been successful with absent-minded behaviour at a time of stress or being in a hypoglycaemic state from a large insulin injection. It is argued that in automatism there is no conscious capacity to control one's actions and therefore no possibility of *mens rea*. A successful plea of sane automatism leads therefore to a total acquittal.

Insane automatism is an automatism due to an 'internal' cause of behaviour without voluntary control such as epilepsy or insulinoma degenerative brain disease and would include psychogenic automatism. Such behaviour may, the law argues, recur until the illness is controlled. It is argued that the disease so affects the mind that the subject at the time of the incident does not know what he is doing. The subject thus falls into the McNaughten Rules. A successful plea of insane automatism leads the subject being found not guilty by reason of insanity. The defendant is then sentenced according to the Criminal Procedure (Insanity and Unfitness to Plead) Act 1991 (see Not fit to plead above). This allows considerable latitude in disposal that can be adjusted to the particular case.

Historically, people who have offended whilst their consciousness was affected by sleep (in sleep walking, night terrors or awaking from deep sleep) have been regarded as having sane automatism (despite the fact that sleep is an internal cause). They have been acquitted and advised to sleep alone with the bedroom door locked (see Chapter 9). The illogicality of regarding all sleep disorders as having an external cause has been pointed out in court.[8] As a result, in the case of a man who behaved violently whilst sleepwalking, the court ruled (supported by the Court of Appeal) that a finding of insane automatism was appropriate just as it would have been if he were in fact in an hysterical fugue.

Infanticide

This is a plea that can be offered under the Infanticide Act 1938, as a defence when a woman is accused of the murder of her child. For the defence to succeed, the child must have been less than 12 months old, and it must be shown that the balance of the mother's mind was disturbed by reason of her not having fully recovered from the effects of giving birth to the child, or by reason of the effects of lactation, consequent upon the birth of the child. The effect of a successful plea is to reduce the charge of murder to one of manslaughter, the same effect as a successful plea of diminished responsibility. It would clearly be the proper plea in a case occurring during puerperal psychosis but it is also used successfully where the degree of mental disturbance is less than would be required for a plea of diminished responsibility. It is not necessary to argue that the woman had a mental illness or abnormality – it is only necessary to show that the balance of the mother's mind was disturbed.

Other problems

Amnesia

Amnesia may arise from organic causes (see Chapter 9) or psychological ones.[7,8] The latter occurs in the absence of detectable brain pathology. Psychological causes are suspected clinically when there is evidence of new information being retained normally or when there appears to be inability to retain any memory for even a few seconds. It may be caused by

(1) a failure to lay down memory (in organic brain disease, severe depression, extreme emotional arousal or severe psychotic arousal);
(2) the motivated forgetting of unpleasant memories;
(3) impaired ability to recall due to a disturbed mood, e.g. in severe depression.

Amnesia for the offence has been found in 40% of men remanded for homicide and 10% overall in remanded men mostly due to psychogenic causes. Deciding whether an amnesia is feigned or a genuine psychogenic amnesia is extremely difficult if not impossible.

Amnesia (loss of memory) for the offence, or the period around it, is not in itself a defence. The trial will proceed regardless of whether the accused can remember the events or not. However, if it can be shown that the amnesia is due to a mental disorder then, clearly, that mental disorder may be a defence e.g. if an offence is committed whilst consciousness is disturbed following a fit, or during a state of extreme excitability during an acute psychotic breakdown, then those disturbed mental states would form the basis of the defence, not the associated amnesia.

Drugs and alcohol

The relation of substance induced disorders and the law is discussed in Chapter 9. In law a person is held to be fully responsible for anything done after knowingly taking drugs or alcohol. The only possible exceptions to this are:

(1) where substances have induced psychosis or a reaction which could not have been anticipated; and
(2) where the drugs and alcohol have removed the ability to form a specific intent there may be some defence. This is discussed in Chapter 9.

Mute defendants

If a defendant is mute the court has to decide whether he is mute by 'malice or by visitation of God'. The doctor may be asked to assist in this. If the defendant is mute through some illness, whatever it is, then the question of fitness to plead is raised. The final outcome may then be a disposal under The Criminal Procedure (Insanity and Unfitness to Plead) Act 1991. If he is mute by malice then there is no bar to his trial.

False confessions

Attention has recently been drawn to the problem of people who come to deny the confession of guilt that they made to the police. Psychologists or psychiatrists may be asked to comment on the chances of a confession being false. For a detailed review of this subject and associated subject of suggestibility of defendants see Gudjonsson.[9]

Clearly when the original confession was truly false it may have been given because of undue pressure in interrogation or in attempt to escape the pressures of custody which may include the effects of hunger, lack of sleep, fear etc. It may also be due to suggestibility, undue compliance or acquiescence. Gudjonsson[10] reported on 100 cases of people who had retracted their confessions. He found they were characterised by lower intelligence and increased scores on a suggestibility and compliance test. However this does not imply that such features necessarily indicate lack of guilt. They are the features of people who retract their confessions.

Three types of proven false confessions were described by Gudjonsson and McKeith.[11]

(1) *Voluntary false confession* (person comes forward voluntarily to 'confess': this may be due to a delusional state, a morbid depression, or perhaps for attention or notoriety).
(2) *Coerced confession* (the person confesses in the hope of stopping what is experienced as unbearable pressure either from style of questioning or the stress of the situation, perhaps exacerbated by hunger, fatigue or fear).
(3) *Coerced – internalised* (the person seems to become confused and appears temporarily convinced of his guilt during interrogation perhaps due to the combination of the subject's suggestibility and tendency to compliance and methods of questioning).

Interviews in the Police Station

Where the defendant is known to be vulnerable then the Police and Criminal Evidence Act 1984 (PACE) requires that an independent person, known as an appropriate adult, be present in the interview to help protect the interviewee who is deemed vulnerable. Norfolk[12] reviews the doctor's role in police station interviews. There are two factors to be considered in assessing fitness to be interviewed in police custody: first, is the detainee fit both physically and mentally to be interviewed and second should the detainee have benefit of an appropriate adult. Where the detained person is known to suffer from mental illness or mental handicap then an appropriate adult should be always present. Section 78 (1) of PACE allows courts to exclude evidence

If it appears to the court having regard to the circumstances, including the circumstances in which the evidence was obtained, the admission of the evidence would have such an adverse effect on the fairness of the proceedings that the court ought no to admit it.

Self-induced intoxication with alcohol or drugs would appear to be excluded from this. Norfolk[12] and Rix[13] provide conceptual frameworks for examinations for fitness to be interviewed. Rix,[13] in a thorough overview of fitness to be interviewed, lists psychiatric disorders, which might lead to unfitness to be interviewed. These include organic mental states, mental handicap, and severe functional psychotic conditions. Both authorities suggest a systematic approach to recording the results of physical and mental state examinations carried out together with a record of any advice given to the police prior to interview.

References

(1) Archbold (1998) *Criminal Pleading, Evidence and Practice*. Sweet and Maxwell: London.
(2) Jones, R.M. (1996) *Mental Health Act Manual*. Fifth edition. Sweet and Maxwell: London.
(3) Reed, J. (1994) *Report of the Department of Health and the Home Office Working Group on Psychopathic Disorder*. Department of Health/Home Office: London.
(4) Ward, R. (1997) *Criminal Sentencing. The New Law*. Jordans: Bristol.
(5) West, D.J. and Walk, A. (1977) *Daniel McNaghten: His Trial and the Aftermath*. Gaskell Books (for the Royal College of Psychiatrists): Ashford.
(6) Fenwick, P. (1990) Automatism. In: *Principles and Practice of Forensic Psychiatry* (eds R. Bluglass and P. Bowden). Churchill Livingstone: Edinburgh
(7) Stone, J.H. (1992) 'Memory disorder in offenders and victims'. *Criminal Behaviour and Mental Health*. **2**, 342–56.
(8) Lishman, W.A. (1987) *Organic Psychiatry*. Blackwell Scientific Publications: Oxford.
(9) Gudjonsson,G.H. (1996) *Psychology of Interrogations, Confessions, and Testimony*. John Wiley: London.
(10) Gudjonsson, G.H. (1990) 'One hundred alleged false confession cases: some normative data'. *British Journal of Clinical Psychology*. **29**, 249–50.
(11) Gudjonsson, G.H. and McKeith, J.A.C. (1990) 'A proven case of false confession: psychological aspects of the coerced compliant type'. *Medicine, Science and the Law*. **30**, 329–35.
(12) Norfolk, G. (1997) 'Fitness to be interviewed' – a proposed definition and scheme of examination. *Medicine, Science and the Law*. **37**, 228–34.
(13) Rix, K.J.B. (1997) Fit to be interviewed by the Police? *Advances in Psychiatric Treatment*. **3**, 33–40.

Chapter 4

Legal Aspects: Appeals and Protection

Introduction

Patients have protection against the activities of courts, doctors, the Home Secretary (responsible for restricted patients), and the managers of the hospital (responsible for detaining them). This protection comes from appellate courts, the Mental Health Act Commission, the Mental Health Review Tribunal, and the duties placed on the managers. Each of these will be considered in turn. The duties of the Home Office Advisory Board which is responsible for assessing certain dangerous restricted patients in order to protect the public are described next. This is followed by a note on the role of the European Commission on Human Rights.

Appealing against court decisions

The appeal system

Appeals are made to the court above the one which gave the sentence. Thus an appeal about the verdict or sentence of a magistrates' court is made to the Crown Court and appeals from the Crown Court go to the Court of Appeal, which is situated in the Royal Courts of Justice in London and consists of a Criminal Division and a Civil Division. The president of the Criminal Division is the Lord Chief Justice and he is assisted by 21 full time Lords Justices of Appeal. Three judges sit at each Court of Appeal hearing.

On points of law one can then appeal to the Lords of Appeal in Ordinary (the Law Lords) in the House of Lords. It is also possible to appeal to the European Court of Justice if it is felt that English law conflicts with the European Treaties.

The European Court of Human Rights, a separate body established by the European Commission of Human Rights, may also have jurisdiction where an individual complains of violation of their rights as established under the 1950 European Convention on Human Rights.

Whenever someone wishes to appeal he usually has to obtain permission from the court for the appeal to be considered. This permission will be given on the basis of there being good grounds for appeal.

Who may appeal?

There are various methods by which an appeal may be brought.

(1) In the case of someone found not fit to plead or someone found not guilty by reason of insanity the Home Secretary can appeal on their behalf if requested to do so.
(2) The convicted offender may appeal.
(3) The Attorney General may appeal against too small a sentence in certain serious cases (Criminal Justice Act 1988) and a new sentence may be set. The Attorney General, after an acquittal, may refer the case on points of law to the Court of Appeal, but the effects of this appeal will not affect the acquitted defendant; however, the court's advice may affect future practice.

Subjects of appeal

An appeal may be brought

(1) against conviction;
(2) against sentence;
(3) against conviction and sentence;
(4) against a verdict of not guilty by reason of insanity;
(5) against a finding of being unfit to be tried.

Grounds for appeal

The appeal may be founded in a number of ways.

(1) That the verdict of the jury was unsafe or unsatisfactory because:
    (a) inadmissible evidence was used;
    (b) proper evidence was excluded;
    (c) uncorroborated evidence was used or no warning was given to a jury of the dangers of convicting or uncorroborrated evidence alone;
    (d) there was misdirection of the jury by the judge on technical matters.
(2) The judgement of the court was wrong on a question of law.

(3) There were irregularities in the course of the trial.
(4) The sentence did not fall within the normal tariff for the offence as being either too severe (or too lenient in the limited cases where the prosecution has the right to appeal).

The effect of the appeal

At Crown Court level
The Crown Court hears appeals against the judgment of the magistrates' court. The court may grant the appeal and change the finding or sentence of the magistrates' court. However, it may also increase the sentence if it believes the magistrates have been too lenient, though it must keep within the limits of the magistrates' court's sentencing powers.

In the Court of Appeal, Criminal Division
The Court of Appeal deals with cases which come from the Crown Court. The Court of Appeal may quash the conviction or reduce, change or increase the sentence if they feel that it is not within the normal tariff.

The House of Lords
This deals only with points of law.

Mental Health Review Tribunal

Definition

A tribunal is effectively a court under the Lord Chancellor's jurisdiction with the specialist function of dealing with disputes in which the weak are pitted against the powerful. The function of the Mental Health Review Tribunal is to deal with disputes between the detained patient and his detainer.

Structure

There are 14 regional services (matching the old regional health authorities) covering England and Wales. A regional chairman has responsibility for the tribunals which consist of a lawyer as president sitting with a psychiatrist and a layman of appropriate experience. When the tribunal is dealing with a restricted case then the president must be a circuit judge or a recorder, otherwise the president is frequently a solicitor. Five administrative offices provide the support for the tribunals.

Legal aspects

Mental Health Review Tribunals have powers under the Mental Health Act 1983[1] and their practice is governed by guidelines issued in association with that Act. In all cases (except the restricted) even though illness may still be present, they have the discretionary power to discharge if they believe it appropriate without any special conditions being met. They must discharge under certain conditions (see below). In non-restricted cases the tribunal may recommend transfer or trial leave. In restricted cases, the tribunal can recommend a conditional or absolute discharge. Their decision may be deferred to allow further investigation or arrangements to be made. These have to then be confirmed with the tribunal before the final decision is made. They may also direct that a patient's condition be reclassified e.g. 'mental illness' to 'psychopathic disorder'.

Procedures of the tribunals

It is now normal practice for the patient to be represented by a solicitor (for which legal aid is available). The patient and his legal representative, the responsible medical officer, the social worker and relatives will come together before the tribunal which will sit usually in a room provided by the hospital in which the patient is detained. The patient and his representative will give their case, possibly supported by the former's relatives, and then the doctor and social worker will give theirs. Other people who may have relevant information may be called, such as a nurse or psychologist.

The tribunals normally expect that the patient should hear the reasons for his detention although the tribunal also recognises that there may be instances where the responsible medical officer may wish to say something which would be damaging for the patient to hear. However, even in this case, the patient's representative will be present, though it is understood that he will not divulge the damaging material. Similarly the patient's relatives may wish to see the tribunal without the patient being present, and they have an opportunity to write to the tribunal and ask for this before the tribunal sits. It may be that they feel unable at that time to support the patient's application but fear that if the knowledge came to the patient's ears it would permanently ruin their relationship with the patient. When all the evidence is heard the tribunal considers the case and conveys its decision to the patient and the responsible medical officer within seven days.

Tribunals are normally private and the proceedings may not be published unless the applicant applies for a public hearing (perhaps to publicise his case).

Preparation for a tribunal

Before the tribunal meets the responsible medical officer and social workers will be asked to supply a detailed account of the case including a view about the continued need for detention. The social worker should also obtain a description of the community resources in the patient's home area so that the tribunal has this information in case they wish to discharge. In the case of a restricted patient the Home Office will also be asked their view about the need for further detention. The patient will require a solicitor to represent him (a list of local solicitors willing to provide this service is normally kept by the hospital or the Law Society). The solicitor must be given access to the patient and the opportunity to discuss the case with the responsible medical officer. The solicitor may instruct another psychiatrist to supply him with an independent report. It is proper to give this psychiatrist every facility to assess the case, including access to the notes. The psychiatrist on the tribunal will also visit the patient before the hearing. He also must have every facility to investigate the case, including the opportunity to see the medical notes and the chance to discuss the case with staff who look after the patient.

A patient's right to a tribunal

The Mental Health Act 1983 (Sections 65–79) substantially increased the power of tribunals and the access of patients to them. The situation is complex, however, for the rights of the patient depend on his section as do the powers of the tribunal. They are discussed in detail by Jones.[1] The principal features are described below.

Patients detained under Part II of the Mental Health Act
Tribunals may be requested in the following situations.

After a patient has been detained for assessment (Section 2): The patient may apply for a tribunal in order to obtain his discharge within 14 days of the section being activated. The tribunal must discharge immediately or at a future date if:

(1) the patient does not meet the criteria of any or sufficient mental disorder to merit assessment in hospital; or
(2) the patient's detention is not justified in the interests of his health and safety or protection of others.

Leave of absence or transfer may also be recommended in appropriate cases.

After a patient has been detained for treatment (Section 3): The patient may apply within six months of the section being activated, as can his relatives. Patients can then apply for a tribunal after every renewal of detention.

After 6 months the managers of the hospital have a statutory duty to have a tribunal which must, under statute, be repeated every three years. The tribunal must discharge if they find the patient does not fulfil the criteria for detention.

If the patient is not fit for discharge he may be sufficiently well for the tribunal to recommend leave of absence or transfer. Such a recommendation, although not a mandatory order, does carry considerable weight. If this recommendation is not complied with, the tribunal may further consider the case at a later date. When making these recommendations or exercising discretionary discharge powers, the tribunal has to consider the likely effects of further treatment and also the ability of the mentally ill and severely impaired patients to care for themselves or guard themselves against serious exploitation. Tribunals must satisfy themselves on a balance of probabilities.

After a patient has been detained under Section 3 in guardianship: The patient may apply, as may his relatives, within the first six months and thereafter as in the case of Section 3 treatment orders. The tribunal must discharge if they find the patient is not mentally disordered or if they find it is unnecessary to be in guardianship.

After a responsible medical officer has reclassified the patient under Section 16 (changed the category of mental disorder): The patient or his nearest relative may apply for a tribunal in the first 28 days.

After the issue of a certificate of dangerousness: If a responsible medical officer (under Section 25) has issued a statement to the managers that the patient is dangerous in order to prevent relatives discharging a patient, then the nearest relative can apply to the Mental Health Review Tribunal within 28 days.

After the County Court directs someone to take over the function of the nearest relative: After a County Court has directed (under Section 29) that the function of the nearest relative (in terms of application or discharge) be taken over by another relative or social worker, then the nearest relative can apply to the Mental Health Review Tribunal within 12 months and any subsequent period of 12 months.

Patients detained under Part III of the Mental Health Act

After a patient has been detained on a hospital order: The patient or his relative may apply but only after six months have elapsed and then once during each time the section is renewed. The hospital managers otherwise have a duty to arrange a tribunal every three years. The powers of the tribunal are as for patients detained under Section 3 (see above).

After the patient has been placed on a guardianship order by the court: The patient may apply within six months and the nearest relative within 12 months. The powers of the tribunal are the same as for a Section 3 guardianship order (see above).

After a patient has been detained on a hospital order with a restriction order: The patient may apply to the tribunal after six months and then subsequently annually. The Secretary of State otherwise has a duty to arrange a tribunal every three years beginning from the day the order was made. In the case of restricted patients the tribunal's powers are limited. However, the tribunal must discharge absolutely if they find that the patient is:

(1) not now mentally disordered or the disorder is not such as to need detention in hospital, or the patient is disordered but that it is not necessary for the health and safety of the patient or the protection of others that he should receive treatment; and
(2) it is also not appropriate that he is liable to recall.

On the other hand the tribunal must discharge conditionally if:

(3) It is felt that it is appropriate that he be liable to recall but now is:
   (a) not suffering from mental disorder; or
   (b) his mental disorder is such as not to need detention in hospital for treatment; or
   (c) that it is no longer necessary for the health or safety of the patient or protection of others that he should receive treatment.

The tribunal can delay its final direction whilst arrangements are made for the conditional discharge so that the plans for aftercare can be approved by the tribunal.

In cases subject to a restriction order the tribunal has, however, no discretionary powers of discharge or powers of recommending to recommend transfer to another hospital or leave of absence from the hospital. They can merely offer these as suggestions to the Home Office.

After a conditionally discharged restricted patient has been recalled to hospital: The Secretary of State has a statutory duty to arrange a tribunal within 28 days of the patient's return to hospital. This arrangement came about because there have been complaints to the European Court of Human Rights, under the old Act, that a man might be recalled without any form of appeal. Thus the tribunal now acts as an appeal against the Home Secretary's judgment that the patient should be recalled.

After a patient has been transferred from prison to hospital for treatment under Sections 47 and 48: The patient may apply for a tribunal within six months and there must be a statutory tribunal held every three years. The tribunal's powers are severely limited in these cases. The tribunal notifies the Home Secretary of their opinion about suitability for discharge, detention in hospital or return to prison. If the only alternative to detention in hospital is prison the Mental Health Review Tribunal can suggest further detention in hospital. The Home Secretary then decides within 90 days whether he will accept the suggestion for discharge (absolute or conditional as the case may be). If he does not agree to discharge, then the patient returns to prison or stays in hospital depending on the tribunal's suggestion. In the case of life sentenced prisoners, if they are post tariff, the tribunal can recommend that their case should be referred to the parole board while they are still in hospital if release through the hospital system is seen as appropriate. Otherwise the tribunal can recommend a return to prison if the patient no longer fullfils the criteria for detention under the Mental Health Act.

After a restricted patient has been conditionally discharged: The patient may apply to a tribunal for absolute discharge after 12 months and then every 2 years. The powers of the tribunal are the same as for restricted patients.

Patients detained under the Criminal Procedures (Insanity) Act 1964, Section 5(i) (not guilty by reason of insanity or found not fit to plead)

The patient may apply within six months and thereafter in the next six months and then annually. The Secretary of State will otherwise refer the patient for a tribunal after the first six months and then every three years. The tribunal's powers are the same as for restricted patients.

Patients who have no right to a tribunal

Some patients detained in hospital have no right or access to a tribunal. These include patients detained for 72 hours (Sections 4, 135 and 136), those detained under Section 35 (remand to hospital for report), Section 36 (detained by the court for treatment before sentence), Section 38 (detained for a trial of treatment), Section 44 (detained in hospital awaiting sentence for a restriction order from a Crown Court having been found guilty in a magistrates' court) and Section 5(ii) and 5(iv) (detentions of voluntary patients already in hospital).

Criticism of tribunals

Peay[2] studied the workings of tribunals in various settings and regions. A lack of consistency was the principal finding. Some regions discharge many more than others and different presidents vary in their 'results', some seeming to have more discharges than others. Tribunals tend on the whole to be very cautious about discharging and are heavily influenced by medical opinion and rarely disagreed with the responsible medical officer. The tribunal system has also been criticised for being slow to respond to requests for a tribunal for people detained on the longer sections. It may take several weeks or months to set up such a tribunal due in part to the pressure of work on the tribunals.

Managers of the hospital and detained patients

Definition

The Mental Health Act defines managers as members of the Hospital Trust Board, District Health Authority or the Special Hospital Authority responsible for the administration of the hospital. Managers may 'authorise' officers to act on their behalf.

Duties of the managers in relation to detained patients

The duties and responsibilities of managers are clearly defined.

(1) The managers have a duty to nominate officers to receive the reception papers (which are legal documents), to check the documents and their contents, and to ensure that all procedures are followed, as laid down in the Mental Health Act, including the duty to inform the patient and his relatives of their rights.

(2) The managers have a responsibility to ensure that the patients' condition meets the criteria defined in the Mental Health Act (Section 20) necessary for them to be detained. They have, in fact, the powers to review and discharge a patient at any time if these criteria are not met.

(3) When a detention order is being renewed, three managers of the hospital must first review the renewal. In the past this has been a procedure which tended to rubber stamp the doctors' recommendations. The renewal should be a thorough affair[3] with the three managers reviewing the case thoroughly (with a full history before them) by interviewing the patient and considering the relatives' views.

(4) Apart from assessing the case when the order for detention is renewed, they must review the case if (a) a patient requests it; (b) the doctor makes a report to the managers to override (usually because of the patient's dangerousness) a nearest relative's application to discharge the patient detained under Part 2 of the Act.

(5) The managers have a variety of other roles and duties relating to detained in-patients including monitoring of complaints, monitoring the use of seclusion, withholding patients' outgoing mail if the addressee has requested it and being responsible for managing the supervision register. In the case of special hospital patients they have the powers to withhold outgoing and incoming mail in certain circumstances.

Mental Health Act Commission

Definition

This body was set up as a result of the Mental Health (Amendment) Act 1982 with the express purpose of guarding the rights of detained patients following a general feeling that these rights may have been abused.

Functions of the Mental Health Act Commission

These are given in the Act and include the following duties and responsibilities.

(1) The appointment of medical practitioners and others for the purposes of supervising the consent to treatment procedures.
(2) To receive reports on treatment given under the consent to treatment procedures.
(3) To keep the Mental Health Act under review, to visit patients and investigate complaints. This is done by the commissioners making regular visits to hospitals to see detained patients.
(4) To submit proposals for the Code of Practice[3] for the care of detained patients.

Rules in regard to consent to treatment and detained patients

Three categories of treatment for detained patients require special consideration (Sections 57 and 58 of the Mental Health Act). Other treatments for mental disorder outside these categories (for example occupational therapy) can be given without consent.

Treatments which do not initially require consent

The first group are those treatments which can be given without the patient's consent for three months from the date the treatment starts. If the patient, after three months, does consent after proper explanation, the consent is recorded on Form 38 and the treatment continues. On the other hand, if the patient refuses to consent, withdraws consent or is unable to give real consent because of the effects of mental disorder (see below), then a second opinion is required from a doctor appointed by the Commission for this purpose. This doctor will give consideration to the treatment plan put forward by the responsible medical officer after interviewing the patient, assessing the case, and discussing it with at least two members of the multi-disciplinary team, only one of whom may be a nurse. He will also check that the legal documents are in order. The appointed doctor will record his agreement to the treatment on Form 39. Such approval lasts until the section is renewed. The responsible medical officer then furnishes a report to the Commission who decide if the approval shall continue or if a further visit is required. Treatment which can be given under this category includes medication by oral or parenteral routes and includes any vene-section needed for blood tests (as with lithium or clozapine therapy).

Treatments which do require the patient's consent

The second group includes treatment which can only be given with the patient's consent or, failing this, after support has been obtained from an appointed doctor who will consider the case as above. This category of treatment includes only ECT at the present time (Section 58, Mental Health Act 1983).

Treatments causing irreversible changes

The third category applies to informal as well as detained patients. It includes treatments which cause irreversible changes. The Commission must send a doctor and two other Commission members to review the case to confirm the patient's general understanding and consent and the appropriateness of the treatment. Without the Commission's agreement, an informal patient may not receive the treatment even if the patient consents. At present this group includes only psychosurgical operations and hormonal implants (Section 57, Mental Health Act 1983).

Who comes under the consent rules?

The 'consent rules' do not apply to every detained patient. Some sections do not allow patients to be treated against their will. These sections are the ones which hold people for 72 hours or less (Sections 4, 5(ii), 5(iv), 135 and 136) and a remand to hospital for psychiatric reports (Section 35). In the former cases, if treatment is required then the section should be re-graded. In the latter case the Code of Practice (3) allows the use of Section 2 or 3 (in conjunction with Section 35) to detain the patient for treatment. This might occur in the case of a patient referred for a report who turns out to be so severely ill that treatment is required at once.

Conditionally discharged patients do not fall within the rules – they may refuse the medication though this may mean that recall has to be considered.

Consent and mental capacity

A patient, to give consent must have the capacity to do so.[3] The patient must understand what the treatment is, and that someone says he needs it and why. The nature, benefits and risks must be understood in general terms and the consequences of not receiving the treatment. The patient's capacity is a matter for clinical judgement subject to the above guidance and current professional practice. Clearly the consent must be voluntary and can be withdrawn at any time. A record in the notes must be kept of the patient's capacity to consent.

Young people over 16 years are treated as adults (Family Law Reform Act 1969). Children under 16 are governed by a House of Lords decision (*Gillick* v. *West Norfolk and Wisbech Area Health Authority and Another* [1986] AC 112). Those with sufficient intelligence and understanding of the proposed treatment are treated like adults. For a full review of this subject see the BMA Guidance.[4]

Treatment in an emergency

The Mental Health Act allows the doctor to treat without consent in an emergency under Section 62 in order to:

(1) save the patient's life;
(2) prevent a serious deterioration;
(3) alleviate serious suffering;
(4) prevent the patient from behaving violently or being a danger to himself or others.

The Aarvold Committee and the Advisory Board to the Home Office

Graham Young, who had a history of poisoning others at the age of 14 years, was released from Broadmoor after nine years and a short time later, in 1971, killed workmates by poisoning. The ensuing outcry led to the setting up of a working party in 1972 under the chairmanship of Sir Carl Aarvold.[5] The purpose of the working party was to examine the way dangerous offenders were assessed before discharge from special hospitals. The recommendation for a three man advisory board (a judge, a psychiatrist and a senior social worker or probation officer) was adopted (though it is now expanded). Patients in special hospital on restriction orders who are identified by the responsible medical officer as representing a special risk are referred to the Board by the Home Secretary for an opinion on dangerousness as are any other patients causing concern to the Home Secretary. The Board's report to the Home Secretary is a further source of advice when the Home Secretary considers discharging or transferring a restricted patient.

The forensic psychiatrist will come across the work of the Board when looking after a patient who has been so identified. The Home Secretary may delay a decision about the psychiatrist's recommendations on such a patient in order to obtain the Board's advice. The Board makes its judgement by sending one of its members to assess the case and interview the patient and staff. The Board then discusses the case in the light of the findings and all previous reports in order to prepare a report for the Home Office. Where there is a conflict between the advice from the responsible medical officer and the Board the Home Secretary will necessarily have to choose between them. He does not automatically give precedence to the Board.

Inquiries after homicide

In the early 1990s, as a result of public concern following well publicised homicides by psychiatric patients, the Confidential Inquiry into Homicides and Suicides by Mentally Ill People was set up by the Department of Health in cooperation with the Royal College of Psychiatrists. The objectives were to inquire into the homicides and suicides committed by people under the care of or recently discharged by the mental health services. The first full report was published in 1996. Reccomendations from this report included the need for better risk assessment, better communication between professionals and better liaison with carers. The now named Confidential Inquiry into Suicides and Homicides by People with Mental Illness is based in Manchester.[6]

In 1994 the NHS Executive published their *Guidance on the Discharge of Mentally Disorderd People and their Care in the Community*.[7] Within the section entitled 'If things go wrong' it states that 'in the cases of homicide it will always be necessary to hold an inquiry which is independent of the providers involved'. Since then there have been at least 40 inquiry reports published and others are continuing. For a more detailed review of these inquiries see Peay,[8] Muidjen,[9] and Grounds.[10]

References

(1) Jones, R.M. (ed) (1991) *Mental Health Act Manual*. Sweet and Maxwell: London.
(2) Peay, J. (1989) *Tribunals on Trial: a Study of Decision Making under the Mental Health Act 1983*. Clarendon Press: London.
(3) Department of Health and Welsh Office (1990) *Code of Practice. Mental Health Act 1983*. HMSO: London.
(4) *Assessment of Mental Capacity: Guidance for Doctors and Lawyers* (1995) A Report by the British Medical Association and the Law Society: London.
(5) Home Office and Department of Health and Social Security (1973) *Report on*

the Review of Procedures for the Discharge and Supervision of Psychiatric Patients Subject to Special Restriction* (Aarvold Report). Cmnd. 5191. HMSO: London.

 (6) Appleby, L., Shaw, J. and Amos, T. (1997) National Confidential Inquiry into Suicide and Homicide by People with Mental Illness. *British Journal of Psychiatry* **170**, 101–2.

 (7) Department of Health (NHSE) (1994) *Guidance on the Discharge of Mentally Disordered People and their Care in the Community*. HSG/94/27. DoH: London.

 (8) Peay, J. (1996) (ed) *Inquiries after Homicide*. Duckworth: London.

 (9) Muidjen, M. (1997) Inquiries: Who needs them? *Psychiatric Bulletin*. **21**, 132–3.

(10) Grounds, A. (1997) Commentary on 'Inquiries: Who needs them?'. *Psychiatric Bulletin* **21**, 134–5.

Chapter 5

Criminologial Facts and Theories

Introduction

Studies show that the bulk of the population will break the law in some way at some time, though only a minority will be apprehended. A still smaller number will go on to become persistent serious offenders. This chapter touches on the facts and figures of offending, and goes on to discuss the factors which are believed to affect the chances of an individual behaving in a delinquent way. A disorder of personality is the commonest psychiatric condition associated with persistent offending, and it is not surprising therefore that the factors believed to be contributory to persistent delinquency are the same as those believed to lead to those personality disorders encompassed by the legal term 'psychopathic disorder'. The chapter finishes with a consideration of the effects of crime on the victim. Later chapters discuss the way mental disorder may lead to crime.

Definitions

A crime has been defined as an 'act that is capable of being followed by criminal proceedings'. Some acts may be criminalised or decriminalised as the law changes, the classic example being homosexual acts between consenting adults in private which ceased to be a crime after the Sexual Offences Act 1967. Similarly, children used to be regarded as being criminally responsible from the age of 8 until the Children and Young Person's Act 1963 changed the age of criminal responsibility to 10 years. Children under 10 who commit 'criminal acts' cannot be charged with an offence but are dealt with using civil procedures such as care proceedings. Between the ages of 10 and 14 children are presumed not to have responsibility unless the evidence rebuts this. Full criminal responsibility is reached at the age of 14 years.

The role of intent in the definition of crime and the nature of criminal responsibility are discussed in Chapter 2.

Crime rates

Introduction

A crime may be committed but not noticed by others, e.g. theft from a shop. The theft may be noticed but not reported to official bodies. If the theft is reported it may not be recorded by the police and therefore will not show up in police statistics. The offender however may or may not be detected and, if detected, he may or may not be arrested (if the offence is very minor there may be a simple warning). If arrested he may not be prosecuted but simply cautioned or the prosecution may not proceed if the evidence is not strong enough. Prosecution may be unsuccessful. Clearly there is an enormous gap between the number of crimes committed and the number of offenders found guilty. Indeed, there are gaps between all the levels in the above system. Crime which is not reported is known as *hidden crime*, other crime may be *undetected crime, reported crime* or *detected crime*.

Criminologists discuss at considerable length whether crime rates are truly rising. The increase in convictions which has accompanied an increase in reported crime may reflect a decrease in tolerance of criminal behaviour by the population as well as an actual increase in crime. Historical studies indicate that the rate of crime does seem to swing from being at a peak in the late 18th century, falling in parts in the 19th century, being fairly stable at the beginning of this century, steadily rising after the First World War until the 1930s when it remained stable again until the 1950s. Since the 1950s crime rates appear to have risen once more.

A guide to the total amount of certain sorts of crime can be obtained by house to house surveys to find out how much crime the householders have been subject to. Seven (from 1982 to 1998) have been completed by the British Crime Survey (BCS).[1] They showed the considerable gap between the crime experienced by householders and the amount appearing in police statistics as well as the rise in crime over these years experienced by the public. Although the percentage of crimes reported to the police has risen year by year, many crimes are left unreported. They are felt to be too trivial or it is felt that the police had little chance of solving them, for instance minor burglaries, minor thefts, minor assaults. It has been said that some crimes, e.g. rape, domestic violence, are not reported because of the embarrassment of the victim or fear of further violence.

The British Crime Survey found that in 1997 only 44% of offences were reported to the police. In turn, only 50% of the crimes reported to the police are recorded by them and appear in the criminal statistics. Therefore the official crime statistics only records a quarter of all crimes committed. Another way of trying to estimate the amount of hidden crime is to do self-reporting surveys to find out how many offences have been committed by different groups of people. Such surveys[2] also show that there is considerably more crime committed than is recorded, though the biggest gap, naturally, is in the minor offences.

It is apparent therefore, that if the reporting behaviour of the public increased then the police statistics would also show an increase without there actually being a change in the real crime rate. Similarly if the police record all offences reported to them then again there would be an apparent increase in the crime rate.

Criminal statistics for England and Wales record 500,000 indictable offences per year in the 1950s rising to 1 million in the 1960s, 2 million in the 1970s and reaching a peak of 5.6 million in 1993. Since then, there has been a drop in each successive year. In 1997 there were 4.6 million notifiable crimes recorded by the police.[3] This was mainly as a result of a decrease in acquisitive offences. Over the same period, violent offences reported to the police rose by 21%. For the first time the BCS[1] reported a decrease in all crime from 1995 to 1997 of 14%. The total number of homicides have risen from 350 per year in 1946 to 711 in 1997 though this includes all forms of homicide including death by terrorism. It is often believed, particularly by the press, that crimes such as the killing of a child by a stranger have greatly increased in recent years. However the criminal statistics over a 20 year period from 1976 to 1996 show that children are far more likely to be killed by someone known to them. The number of these crimes has averaged 6 or 7 each year.

Rates of offending

Studies of offenders rather than offences show that to some extent, delinquent acts are normal. Only a tiny minority of delinquent acts lead to a court appearance; but the more substantial the offence the more the likelihood of being caught. Thus only 8% of shoplifters may be caught compared to 60% of those who break and enter. Offending is an activity of the young reaching its peak at around 17 years and declining rapidly by the late 20s. In 1997, 83% of offenders convicted or cautioned for indictable offences were male and 11% were under 17 years of age. Of people born in 1953, 34% of males and 18% of females had been convicted of a criminal offence by the age of 34 years.[3]

Females offend much less than males. Self-report studies show that the difference is not as great as has seemed from official statistics but it may be that this is because the majority of female offending is very minor. However, there was a substantial increase between the 1950s and 1970s in female offending, as though they were trying to catch up on the males. The male to female ratio for offences in 1957 was 11 to 1. This had altered to 5 males to 1 female by 1977 and has remained the same ratio since then. Similarly, there has been a 379% increase in convictions of females under 17 in the same periods as the males increased by 148%. These ages and sex associations are reviewed in detail by Rutter and Giller.[4] The peak age for offending in females rose to 18 years in 1997, which for the first time was the same as for males.[3]

Patterns of crime

By far the commonest offence is simple theft. The British Crime Survey[1] found that of the 16.5 million crimes in 1997, 62% were acquisitive and 21% were violent offences, the majority of which were trivial common assaults. Of all crimes, 4% were serious assaults involving significant injury. Sexual offences were not measured by the survey but have been given as less than 1% of recorded crime and 9% of recorded violent crime.

The prognosis of offending

In 1996, 21% of males and 9% of females who had been convicted of an indictable offence, had 10 or more previous convictions. However, the majority of offenders are not re-convicted after the first offence, though the younger the offender the greater the likelihood he will be re-convicted. For children under 14 the re-conviction rate after the first offence is 60%,[5] whereas for 17–19 years the rate is 35%, and for first offenders over 40, re-conviction is only 9%. Similarly the chances of re-conviction are greater for those who have been previously convicted, for example, among juvenile offenders with four previous convictions the re-conviction rate is nearly 80%. However, there appears to be a trend towards social conformity as the young offender matures. Only a minority of people are going to become persistent adult offenders. In Camberwell, a working class area of London, West and Farrington[2] showed that perhaps 80% of the boys would have committed an act which was criminal by the time they were 17, though only 20% would have been caught. Of those 20%, half went on to be convicted of a second crime and of these a small proportion would go on to become chronic recidivists. Each year after 17 years there would be some new first time offenders but the number of first time offenders and re-offenders falls with each year of life. There is a similar fall in the crime rate for females from the late teens, except in their case the fall is interrupted by a small increase in the rates around the late 40s and early 50s.

Factors associated with delinquency

Introduction

Why one person and not another should become persistently delinquent has promoted considerable theorising and study. These have been reviewed in detail by Garland.[6] Historically, there was a desire to find 'the cause' of delinquency and, as a result, a number of rival 'monolithic' theories were developed from criminology, sociology and psychiatry to explain delinquency. Professor Lombroso (the 'father of criminology') in nineteenth century Italy proposed the idea that criminals were born and that they had a particular primitive constitution and physique associated with primitive impulsiveness, cruelty, etc. He believed, from his study of prisoners, that there were physical stigmata of criminality, e.g. absence of ear lobes, low foreheads, etc.

This theory held the forefront of thinking until it was toppled in 1913, by a careful statistically controlled study of criminals in Parkhurst Prison, when it was demonstrated that the so-called stigmata were, in fact, equally common in non-criminal populations. Attention after Lombroso moved to the idea of there being a deficiency of the 'moral faculty' in a similar way to there being a deficiency in some people of the intellectual faculty. The Mental Deficiency Acts of 1913 and 1927 encapsulated these concepts, covering both intellectual and moral deficiency. A moral defective was defined as 'a person in whose case mental defectiveness was coupled with strongly vicious and criminal propensities and who required care and supervision and control for the protection of others'. This permitted the detention in hospital of people labelled as 'moral defectives'.

Sociological theories developed in the 1920s and 1930s. They have been comprehensively reviewed by Rock.[7] These theories denied that criminality arose from some individual disturbance. Criminal behaviour was seen to be the result of social factors or pressures acting on normal people. Sutherland proposed that crime was learned, like anything else, and that the main factor leading someone into crime was due to the association and imitation of criminals. Merton saw criminal behaviour as one of the possible ways a disadvantaged person might obtain the goals of society (i.e. money and success), when unable to gain them by legitimate means or being unable to simply accept the *status quo*. Similar theories referring to social inequalities were developed to explain the phenomenon of delinquent gangs.

However, the social theories, whilst adding to our understanding, failed to allay the clinical suspicion that individual personal experiences were of outstanding importance. Contemporaneous with the social theories was a growing body of evidence supporting the idea that there was a clear association between the individual's early family experience and crime.

The more recent realisation of the ubiquitousness of criminal behaviour has led to a different view. It now seems clear that delinquent behaviour is best understood on a multifactorial basis, the sum of many factors in a person's life. This view and the evidence have been reviewed in detail by Rutter and Giller.[4] The next section will discuss these factors which can be considered under the headings of inherited and acquired factors.

Inheritance and criminality

It has long been known that delinquency and anti-social behaviour often run in families. The question arises about the extent that inherited traits contribute to these family histories. Twin studies have, in the past, given rather conflicting results. More recent studies of criminality in twins show a greater concordance for monozygotic than for dizygotic pairs (35% to 13%) though the differences between them are reduced when the pairs are controlled for similarity in environment.[4]

Further support for the idea of a genetic factor is derived from adoption studies. Mednick and Finello[8] studied in Denmark over 14,000 adoptees. They divided the biological and adoptive parents into criminal and non-criminal groups and looked at delinquency patterns in the adopted children. The rate of delinquency in children born to non-criminal biological parents and given to non-criminal adoptive parents was very similar (13.5%) to the delinquency rate for children as a whole in Denmark. Children of criminal biological parents given to criminal adoptive parents had a 24.5% official delinquency rate. The important finding, however, was that a higher rate of delinquency was found in the children of criminal biological parents given to non-criminal adoptive parents (20%) compared to the 14.7% in children of non-criminal biological parents given to criminal adoptive parents. Clearly from this study it would seem that both upbringing and inheritance contribute towards delinquency but that biological weighting seems more important. Other (though not all) adoptee studies have found similar results though there is evidence that part of the predisposition to crime arises from an inherited tendency to abuse alcohol.[9]

Inherited and constitutional factors

What biological factors might be inherited is unclear. Current thought looks towards neurophysiological factors as well as intelligence. Chromosomal abnormalities are another factor which has attracted attention.

Neurophysiological factors

Disturbance of brain function – EEG studies
A number of workers have claimed to find a variety of abnormal EEG activity in particular types of offenders. However, for each study which appears to show some correlation of abnormal EEG records with criminality, there is another which fails to demonstrate any link. For a review of this topic, see Blackburn.[10] One particular type of EEG, the contingent negative variation has shown some difference between individuals with a personality disorder compared to normals.[11] Contingent negative variation

is a slow negative potential change seen on the EEG recording when the subject is preparing to respond to a stimulus. It has been suggested that it could be used to predict risk of violence in a special hospital population.[12]

Disturbance of the autonomic nervous system and conditioning

It has been argued that delinquency may be associated with an inability to condition normally due to abnormalities within the autonomic nervous system or to defects in cortical arousal. However, there has not been a clear demonstration of physiological abnormality in any group of offenders. One of the methodological problems in this type of work is the definition of psychopathy. Nevertheless there is some evidence that the hypothesis that delinquency may be a failure of 'passive avoidance learning' is correct.[10, 13] That is to say the subject fails to learn to avoid certain behaviour (e.g. stealing) due to his inability to condition (learn) normally.

Attention deficit disorder with hyperactivity

This condition of children is recognised in the ICD-10[14] as the hyperkinetic conduct disorder (ICD-10, F90.1). It has been asserted that the condition is due to minimal brain damage and can persist into adult life and result in impulsive character disorders, irritability, lability, explosiveness and violence. A study of 94 subjects and 78 controls suggests that 32% with the disorder will develop antisocial disorders as young adults compared to 8% in the controls.[15]

Raine *et al.*[16] have tried to bring these various findings together. They tested 101 randomly selected English schoolboys at 15 years for heart rate, skin conductance and EEG wave form. Their criminality was examined at 24 years. Of those surveyed, 17 serious offenders were identified from criminal records. These 17 had lower heart rates, lower skin conductance and greater theta activity in the EEG at 15. These variables predicted 74% of the criminals in the group. Nevertheless it is not clear if these features were the result of personality rather than the basis of it.

Abnormalities of brain chemistry

It has been postulated, based on levels in the cerebrospinal fluid, that habitually violent, alcohol abusing men are deficient in the neuro-transmitter, 5-hydroxytryptamine (see Chapter 7). It is not known whether this condition (if it proves to be a real one) is inherited or acquired.

Intelligence

It seems likely from many studies that low intelligence is a factor in delinquency. West and Farrington in the Cambridge study (see below) found that intelligence was one of the principal factors associated with persistent delinquency, a finding which is now generally supported. To the extent that this faculty is biologically based and inherited, so it is an inherited factor which plays a significant part in behaviour.

Chromosomal abnormalities

The chromosomal abnormalities which have been associated with anti-social behaviour include some of the disorders with an extra sex chromosome, i.e. the XYY, XXY (Klinefelter) and XXX (superfemale) karyotypes.[17,18] The incidence of XYY and XXY in the population is just over 0.1% per 1,000 liveborn male infants. In the 1960s XYY men were found to make up 3% of patients at Carstairs, the Scottish state hospital. A series of papers followed confirming a raised incidence of XYY and XXY males in special hospitals though as the true national incidence became apparent it also became clear that only a small proportion of such cases were in institutions. Rates in subnormality hospitals and penal institutions for delinquent youths were normal. Are XYY youths easily identified and transferred to hospital?

The initial description of XYY males as tall, aggressive, impulsive and of dull intelligence has had to be modified. Only 50% are taller than 6 feet and behavioural disorder is probably not present in the majority and when present can take any form. The behaviourally disturbed cannot be distinguished on physical grounds. Their intelligence has been found to vary from the superior level to the subnormal although the mean is said to be below normal.

XXY males are characterised by very poor testicular development, eunuchoid habits, tallness, feminine breast development, intellectual deficit, and small head. XXX females are characterised by tallness, long legs, intellectual defect and small head. Behavioural problems have been described in both XXY and XXX patients. The present view appears to be that these chromosomal abnormalities are not direct causes of criminal behaviour. Where they are associated with such behaviour they may exert their influence through the effects on intelligence or temperamental characteristics, the situation is unclear. Nevertheless it is calculated that an XYY male has a 1:100 chance of being sent to a special hospital.[19] A case report of a sexually abusive adolescent boy with XXYY karyotype stated that there was no specific association between this syndrome and this type of offending described in the literature.[20]

Medicolegally, in England, (though not in all countries) chromosomal abnormalities themselves are not regarded as relevant to the question of responsibility. When the patient also has a mental disorder (e.g. personality disorder) the knowledge that there is also a chromosomal defect may alter the perception of the court or professionals involved in the case who may be more ready to see it as a 'medical' problem.

Acquired factors associated with delinquency

The Cambridge study

There have been innumerable cross sectional studies concerning delinquents and non-delinquents to identify individual differences, but good longitudinal studies are rare. From a methodological point of view the best approach might be to study a random group of children from an early age and follow them through into adulthood.

One such study was the Cambridge study[21] which was carried out by West and Farrington. Some 400 boys were identified at the age of 8 years from a working class neighbourhood in London and followed up to the age of 32, by which time 37% of the group had acquired a criminal record. The aim of the study was to assess 'the relative importance of social pressures (such as low income), individual style of upbringing (manifest in parental attitude and discipline), personal attributes (such as intelligence, physique and aggressiveness) and extraneous events (mischance of being found out)'; i.e. to examine the influence of both acquired and inherited features. It was also hoped that it would be possible to identify criteria present at an early age which could be used to predict which individuals would be more likely to become persistent delinquents. The study was designed to encompass a wide range of items. Assessments were made by psychologists, experienced social workers and experienced research workers. Full assessments were made at the age of 8 and then every 2 years after that up to the age of 18. After that, they were interviewed at 21, 25 and 32 years. The persistence of the interviewers was such that information was obtained on 94% of the subjects at the age of 32.

For a comprehensive review of the Cambridge study see Farrington.[21] From 200 items which were investigated the following six groups of factors which were identified at age 8 to 10 years predicted later delinquent behaviour.

(1) *Anti-social behaviour by the child*. 45% of boys rated as 'troublesome' at school were later delinquents compared with 14% of non-delinquents.
(2) *Hyperactivity – impulsivity – attention deficit*. Hyperactivity at age 8 to 10 years predicted juvenile convictions independently of conduct disorder at that age.
(3) *Low intelligence and poor school attainment*. It was not possible to distinguish further between these factors, since they are obviously related to one another.
(4) *Family criminality*. This finding has also been shown in studies from New Zealand and the USA.
(5) *Family poverty*. In particular, those from larger families with low income and in poor housing, were later delinquent.

(6) *Poor parental child rearing*. This could be harsh or erratic discipline, cruel, passive or neglectful attitude and included parental conflict. These boys were often poorly supervised by parents who failed to enforce rules of behaviour.

A prediction score based on these six factors was able to predict two thirds of the boys who would later be identified as chronic offenders by the age of 25 years. Men who committed first offences after the age of 21 years tended to be unemployed at the age of 18 years in addition to possessing some of the above factors.

The best single predictor of juvenile delinquency was found to be a measure of 'troublesomeness' derived from teachers and classmates at primary school. This assessment covers areas such as application to work, scholastic performance, concentration, cleanliness, obedience, attendance and relations with other children. Of the 92 boys categorised as the most troublesome at primary school, half became juvenile delinquents whereas only 3.5% of the 143 boys in the least troublesome group became a delinquent.

Other acquired factors contributing to delinquent behaviour

These are reviewed by Rutter and Giller[4] and include:

Racial background

In England the arrest rate amongst Asian juveniles has been lower than in the equivalent white groups, whereas, on the other hand, it was higher among Afro-Caribbeans. The difference may, to some extent, represent distortions due to differences in reporting rates, detection rates and policing methods. There have also been studies to indicate that the higher rate of crime amongst black youths may be accounted for by greater socio-economic deprivations. The situation is unclear and further research is required.

Physical characteristics

Studies in the past have suggested that extreme physical characteristics are associated with delinquency, i.e. muscularity or being undersized. However, more recent evidence shows that these associations disappear once relevant social factors are taken into account. No connection between body build and delinquency was identified in the Cambridge study. Some workers have claimed an association between delinquency, ill health and multiple biological impairments such as those which might be obtained around the neonatal period due to bad maternal care, resulting perhaps in impaired growth or minimal brain damage. However, no such relationship occurred in the Cambridge study.

Living in large towns

Comparative studies indicate lower delinquency rates in rural areas, compared to metropolitan areas. West and Farrington[2] found that the delinquent behaviour of their subjects dropped if they moved from London to rural areas.

Different crime rates also occur in different parts of a city. It has long been known that the crime rates are highest in the most run down areas. Even within such areas there are high risk communities and low risk communities. The possible causes for this include the policy of local authorities to group problem families together and the drift of delinquent people into areas of high delinquency. The extent to which such areas influence the behaviour of people moving into them is unclear. Experimental initiatives which have tried to improve social cohesiveness and awareness, such as crime reduction schemes on large estates or community policing hold out hope of reducing delinquency.

The effect of 'bad' schools

Power[22] showed that different schools serving similar areas had substantial differences in delinquency rates. Most of the school variation could be explained in terms of differences in intake and in terms of behaviourally different children. Nevertheless, Rutter[4] was able to show that a school could influence, for good or bad, the development of the potentially delinquent boy. By giving a predictive score to children on factors similar to those found by West and Farrington,[2] he was able to show statistically that some schools persistently improved the chances of boys leaving their delinquent behaviour behind whilst other schools increase the chances of a boy becoming delinquent. The effect seemed due to the mix of pupils (the higher the intellectual ability and social status the less the delinquency) and the styles of management by the teachers which influenced the climate of the school. Styles which encouraged a positive atmosphere were the more successful.

Being labelled a delinquent

There has long been a social theory that 'labelling' (i.e. identifying and processing) a child as a delinquent will increase his chances of continuing to be one. This labelling could alter the child's perception of himself and therefore his behaviour. West and Farrington[2] found evidence in support of this theory. They were able to match a small group of boys who had been caught by the police with a group of boys who were similar in all other respects except they had not been caught. The group who were caught were found to alter their view of the police from a positive to a negative one. Furthermore, the group who were caught went on to commit more offences (to judge by self-report and official records) than the group who were not caught. It remains possible that the group who were caught were in some way more incompetent as criminals or more anti-social than those who were not. West and Farrington were unable to find evidence for this.

Exposure to violent films and television

There has been a great deal of debate, particularly in regard to violence, as to the effect of films and television on offending rates. There are many laboratory studies which show that children will play at violence and appear more aggressive immediately after seeing a violent film though such studies are criticised as being too artificial. It is suggested that exposure to violence on TV or in films may affect behaviour in the following ways:

(1) Imitation of violence seen on films.
(2) Triggering aggressive impulses in individuals predisposed to this.
(3) Reducing empathy towards victims of crime.

A more realistic study, from the Home Office,[23] looked at the effect of video violence on young offenders. Three groups were interviewed, violent offenders, non-violent offenders and a control group of non-offenders. Information on their viewing habits and family background was collected. They were shown a violent video and questioned on it immediately afterwards, 4 months and 10 months later. Both of the offender groups preferred watching violent videos and identified with the violent characters more than the non-offender group. However there were no significant differences between the two offender groups. When the backgrounds of the groups were compared and subjected to multivariant analysis, it showed that personality and social background discriminated those who commit offences more than factors associated with violent videos. It appears that while watching violent videos may reinforce existing distorted perceptions, the well established link between poor social background and delinquency is more significant.

What factors protect a person against delinquency?

In the Cambridge study[2] it was found that some people might have all the factors associated with delinquency and not show up as a recorded delinquent. When this was examined more closely it was found that many of the non-recorded delinquents had in fact avoided detection. Some boys however did not become delinquent but developed marked neurotic symptoms instead. Nevertheless, there were still some boys who seemed to survive, developing neither persistent delinquency nor neurotic symptoms.

Factors which may protect the child include:

(1) *Personality:* Werner[24] studied the development of 689 infants born in 1955 in Hawaii. Children who survived adversity seemed to have, even as babies, more equable temperamental characteristics with greater competence socially, at school and at play. This may be the reverse of a disposition to criminality but may also be due to their being more advantaged as babies (more first born, less sibling pressure). Rutter[25] argues that inherited temperamental traits (emotionality, activity levels, sociability) influence interactions with parents and others (for good or bad) and thus contribute to the final personality and view of the world.

(2) *A good peer group:* the Cambridge study[2] showed that those who moved away from a delinquent career abandoned their delinquent friends. However, what is not clear is whether it is the change of associates which led to a change in the subject's behaviour or vice versa.

(3) *Successful employment:* It is clear that delinquency and unemployment are strongly associated. Whether the experience of unemployment increases the chances of a subject becoming delinquent is uncertain, though social studies have claimed that there is a rising crime rate in periods of high unemployment. The Cambridge study showed that unemployment has most effect on the criminality of those who already have a delinquent history. The non-delinquent is not easily precipitated into offending by unemployment.

(4) *Marriage:* It is not clear whether marriage is a protective factor or not. The Cambridge study[2] and others have shown that an enduring marriage does reduce the risk of further offending.

(5) Other factors include any improvement in life circumstances, good relationships with one parent and good life experiences outside the home.

These factors demonstrate something that other research has also shown, that is, that changes in environment are more likely to produce beneficial effects than changes in the individual.[26]

Offender profiling

Criminology research has shifted over the last 40 years from work on individuals, which had led to theories on the 'causes of crime', to research on offences. It has been suggested that this change followed the lead given by the Home Office's own research department.[27] One area of recent study which most contemporary criminologists would not necessarily see as relevant to them, has been on offender profiling. In this country, it has mainly been developed by psychologists and perhaps represents a shift back to offender based work.

Although it is primarily a police investigative technique, offender profiling relies on data drawn from the analysis of other similar offenders. It was first developed by the FBI in their behavioural sciences unit. In this country, one of the leading workers has been Professor David Canter. For a detailed description of his work, see Canter and Heritage.[28] In summary, a profile is drawn up of an offender, usually a serial murderer or rapist. This is taken up from evidence from the scene of the crime, the victim and the offender's known behaviour. A hypothesis is then proposed regarding the motives for the offences and perhaps the characteristics of the offender which the police would then hope to use to apprehend him.

Despite its claims for success, there is no clear evidence that profiling contributes directly to the arrest of offenders. In one high profile murder case, the use of an offender profile to attempt to convict a suspect, caused considerable public disquiet when the case collapsed.[29] It has been suggested that this was caused by the fact that a knowledge base does not yet exist to support this type of work.[30]

The effects of crime on the victims

Since the late 1970s there has been an increased awareness that the victim not only suffers from the immediate effect of the crime (loss, injury) but may also suffer psychological after effects (see Chapter 7 Aftermath of homicide). These range from immediate shock to short- and long-term symptoms such as anxiety, depression, sleep disturbance, fear, anger, inability to perform ordinary tasks, nightmares, intrusive thoughts, the symptoms of post traumatic stress disorder. People emotionally close to the victim or offender may also be affected especially in the case of homicide. Black[31] has drawn attention to the effects of a murder in the family on children and the need they have for specialised help. Counselling for victims[32] may be helpful both for practical matters (insurance, security) and for psychological ones.

Various studies have shown that approximately one quarter of the victims of violent crime (excluding sexual offences) require some psychological support afterwards. It is believed that criminal victimisation produces greater pathology than other types of trauma. Mezey[33] describes six predisposing factors which increase the risk of post traumatic stress disorder occurring in victims of all types of violent crime. These are:

(1) if the crime was a sexual assault;
(2) if the victim was female;
(3) if the victim was from an ethnic minority;
(4) a younger victim;

(5) if there was experience of separation and anxiety during childhood;
(6) previous anxiety and traumatic experiences.

The most traumatic of offences appears to be rape. Studies have shown that 90% of rape victims suffer symptoms of post traumatic stress disorder after the offence.

References

(1) Mirlees-Black, C., Budd, T., Partridge, S. and Mayhew, P. (1998) *The 1998 British Crime Survey*. Home Office Statistical Bulletin 21/98.
(2) West, D.J. and Farrington, D.P. (1977) *The Delinquent Way of Life*. Heinemann Educational: London.
(3) Home Office (1998) *Criminal Statistics for England and Wales 1997*. Cmd. 4162. The Stationery Office: London.
(4) Rutter, M. and Giller, H. (1983) *Juvenile Delinquency. Trends and Perspectives*. Penguin: Harmondsworth.
(5) West, D.J. (1982) *Delinquency: Its Roots, Careers and Prospects*. Heinemann: London.
(6) Garland, D. (1997) Of Crimes and Criminals: The Development of Criminology in Britain. In: *Oxford Handbook of Criminology*, pp 11–56 (eds: M. Maguire, R. Morgan and R. Reiner.) Oxford: Clarendon Press.
(7) Rock, P. (1997) Sociological Theories of Crime. In *Oxford Handbook of Criminology* pp 233–64 (eds: M. Maguire, R. Morgan and R. Reiner). Clarendon Press: Oxford.
(8) Mednick, S.A. and Finello, K.M. (1983) Biological Factors and Crime: Implications for Forensic Psychiatry. *International Journal of Law and Psychiatry* **6**, 1–15.
(9) Bohman, M., Cloninger, C.R., Sigvardsson, S. and Van Knorring, A.L. (1983) Gene–environment Interaction in the Psychopathology of Adoptees: Some Recent Studies in the Origin of Alcoholism and Criminality. In *Human Development: An Interactional Perspective* (eds D. Magnusson and V. Allen). Academic Press: New York and London.
(10) Blackburn, R. (1993) *The Psychology of Criminal Conduct*. Wiley: Chichester.
(11) Howard, R.C., Fenton, G.W. and Fenwick, P.B.C. (1984) Contingent Negative Variation, Personality and Antisocial Behaviour. *British Journal of Psychiatry* **144**, 463–74.
(12) Howard, R. and Lumsden, J. (1997) CNV predicts violent outcomes in patients released from special hospital. *Criminal Behaviour and Mental Health*, **7**(3), 237–40.
(13) Trasler, G.B. (1973). Criminal Behaviour. In *Handbook of Abnormal Psychology*, second edition (ed H.J. Eysenk). Pitman Medical: London.
(14) World Health Organization (1992) *ICD-10 Classification of Mental and Behavioural Disorder*. WHO: Geneva.
(15) Mannuzza, S., Klein, R.G., Bonagura, N., Malloy, P., Giampino, T. and Addalli, K.A. (1991) Hyperactive children almost grown up. *Archives of General Psychiatry* **48**, 77–83.

(16) Raine, A., Venables, P.H., and Williams, M. (1990) Relationship between central and autonomic measures of arousal at age 15 years and criminality at age 24 years. *Archives of General Psychiatry* **47**, 1003–7.

(17) Pitcher, D.C.R. (1971) Criminological implications of chromosome abnormalities. *New Law Journal* **121**, 1078–9.

(18) Pitcher, D.C.R. (1982) Sex chromosome disorders. In *Recent Advances in Clinical Psychiatry*. Number Four (ed. K. Granville-Grossman). Churchill-Livingstone: Edinburgh.

(19) Editorial (1974) What becomes of the XYY male? *Lancet* Nov. 1297–8.

(20) Epps, K.J. (1996) Sexually abusive behaviour in an adolescent boy with the 48XXY syndrome: a case study. *Criminal Behaviour and Mental Health*, **6**(2), 137–46.

(21) Farrington, D.P. (1995) The development of offending and anti-social behaviour from childhood: key findings from the Cambridge Study in delinquent behaviour. *Journal of Child Psychology and Psychiatry* **360**(6), 929–64.

(22) Power, M.J., Benn, R.T. and Morris, J.N. (1972) Neighbourhood, school and juveniles before the courts. *British Journal of Criminology* **12**, 111–132.

(23) Browne, K. and Pennell, A. (1998) *The Effects of Video Violence on Young Offenders*. Home Office Research Findings No. 65.

(24) Werner, E.E. (1989) High risk children in young adulthood. *American Journal of Orthopsychiatry* **59**, 72–81.

(25) Rutter, M. (1987) Temperament, personality and personality disorder. *British Journal of Psychiatry* **150**, 443–468.

(26) Clarke, R.V.G. (1985) Delinquency, environment and intervention. *Journal of Child Psychology and Psychiatry* **26**, 505–523.

(27) Maguire, M. (1997) Crime statistics, patterns and trends: changing perceptions and their implications. In: *Oxford Handbook of Criminology*, pp 135–188 (eds: M. Maguire, R. Morgan and R. Reiner). Clarendon Press, Oxford.

(28) Canter, D. and Heritage, R. (1990) A multivariate model of sexual offence behaviour: developments in offender profiling I. *Journal of Forensic Psychiatry* **1**(2) 185–212.

(29) Ormerod, D (1996) Psychological profiling. *Journal of Forensic Psychiatry* **7**(2), 341–52.

(30) Grubin, D. (1995) Offender profiling. *Journal of Forensic Psychiatry* **6**(2), 259–63.

(31) Black, D. and Caplan, T. (1988) Father kill mother. *British Journal of Psychiatry* **153**, 624–30.

(32) Shepherd J. (1988) Supporting victims of violent crime. *British Medical Journal* **297**, 1353.

(33) Mezey, G. (1997) Psychological responses to interpersonal violence. A: Adults. In: *Psychological Trauma* pp 178–83 (eds. D. Black, M. Newman, J. Harris-Hendriks and G. Mezey). Gaskell Books: London.

Chapter 6

Offences against Property and Forensic Psychiatry

Introduction

This chapter defines property offences (acquisitive and destructive). The different 'motives' (including psychiatric disorder) for acquisitive offending are discussed using shoplifting as an example. Similarly, the motivations for destructive offending are discussed with particular attention to arson as an example of a destructive offence.

The normal human motives for property offences (greed, envy, anger, jealousy, resentment, etc.) occur also as motives in the mentally disordered. The presence of a mental disorder does not preclude the patient from experiencing such feelings. The disorder, by intensifying emotional reactions or distorting perception, may engender similar feelings which precipitate an offence.

Definitions

The term 'property offence' covers a variety of offences including:

(1) *Theft:* Dishonestly appropriating property belonging to another with the intention of permanently depriving the other of it.
(2) *Taking a conveyance without authority:* Taking and driving away a conveyance without the consent of the owner or other lawful authority (but *without* the intention to permanently deprive the owner of it). If the act is associated with injury, dangerous driving or damage to property then it makes the offender liable to a charge of *aggravated vehicle taking.*
(3) *Robbery:* Using force or seeking to put a person in fear of being subjected to force at the same time as or immediately before stealing.
(4) *Blackmail:* Making unwarranted demands with menaces with intent to gain for oneself and to cause loss to another.
(5) *Burglary:* Entering a building as a trespasser with intent to steal. The

charge may also be with intent to inflict grievous bodily harm, rape or to do unlawful damage to the building; if force or a weapon are involved, the charge is one of *aggravated burglary.*

(6) *Going equipped:* Having an article for use for stealing, cheating or committing a burglary.

(7) *Fraud:* Dishonestly obtaining by deception, of which there are several varieties, e.g.
   (a) obtaining property by deception;
   (b) obtaining pecuniary advantage by deception;
   (c) false accounting and false statements by company directors;
   (d) obtaining services by deception;
   (e) evasion of liability by deception.

(8) *Handling stolen goods:* The receiving of goods or assisting in their retention, removal or disposal, knowing or believing the goods to be stolen goods.

(9) *Forgery:* Making of a false document in order that it may be used as genuine.

(10) *Criminal damage to property:* The destruction or damaging of property without lawful excuse. The offender must have intended the effect or have been reckless as to the effects of his action. A more serious charge is *criminal damage with intent to endanger life* or being reckless as to whether life was endangered.

(11) *Arson:* The destruction or damaging of property by fire (without lawful excuse). A more serious charge is *arson with intent to danger life* or being reckless as to whether life was endangered. For arson to have occurred the arsonist must have intended to set the fire and intended its effects, or to have been careless of its effects.

It will be seen that there are two forms of property offences:

(1) the *acquisitive offences* which cover the various forms of theft, robbery, burglary and fraud; and
(2) *destructive offences* which include arson and malicious damage to property. From a psychiatric point of view the acquisitive often have a different psychopathology from destructive offences.

Acquisitive offences

In 1997, 91% of offences recorded by the police in the UK were against property;[1] thefts accounted for 50% of the total number. However, not all crimes are reported to the police and not all those that are, are recorded by them. Victim surveys[2,3] give further information on crime and from these, it has been estimated that the amount of certain crimes committed is perhaps underestimated by up to seven times.

In these offences the question of specific intent (*mens rea*) has to be examined as its presence is legally necessary for an offence to have been committed. The absence of the intent will form a defence to the charge, e.g. if a person absent-mindedly carried goods out of a shop, it would not be a crime as there would be no intent to permanently deprive.

An understanding of the variety of patterns and motives for theft has been derived both from clinical practice and from various studies, the principal English study being on shoplifting.[4] The findings from that study have application to other acquisitive offences. Most acquisitive offending is carried out by people with no psychiatric problems. Offenders with psychiatric illness may have a variety of motives for offending, including those totally unrelated to their mental health problems.

Patterns of offending not associated with psychiatric disorder

There are many reasons for the commission of acquisitive offences, which do not necessarily demonstrate any mental disorder.

(1) *Avarice:* offences such as fraud, credit card fraud, theft from financial institutions may fall into this category. Examples also include stealing from places of work where such thefts are accepted as normal 'perks' by staff. Studies of the 'wastage' from shops have shown that a substantial proportion of the goods are taken by the people who work in the shop.

(2) *Poverty:* the shoplifting study identified a very small group of offenders who were stealing through poverty or deprivation. The motives included a need to provide for the family, to maintain appearances, or to fund a substance misuse problem.

(3) *Excitement:* excitement appears to be the principal motivation in certain groups, such as children or adolescents. Amongst young foreign women caught shoplifting in London, excitement appeared to be an important factor in the motivation. Excitement may be part of the motive when groups of youths urge each other on to commit offences of stealing, taking and driving cars, or even breaking and entering. Boredom can be a factor in these offences.

(4) *Antisocial families:* a group of shoplifters from antisocial families was identified where the whole family took part in the shoplifting, accepting it as normal behaviour. Such families tended to be involved in other forms of acquisitive offence.

(5) *Professional theft:* in the shoplifting study a gang drove from one town to another where they systematically deceived the shop assistants and took the goods back to the first town for distribution. The desire for gain often appeared associated with resentment and bitterness towards society and was part of the cultural lifestyle adopted by this group.

Similar groups may organise themselves to take part in other property offences. There are also groups who steal to order items such as cars and, more recently, food stuffs.

(6) *Pre-occupation and absent mindedness:* Accusations of theft often arise when people remove goods from shops without intent to deprive, and if it can be proved that there was no intention to deprive, no crime has in fact been committed.

Acquisitive offending and psychiatric disorder

The incidence of psychiatric disorder amongst adult acquisitive offenders is unknown, though serious disorder only occurs in a small proportion. In 1959 Gibbens[5] thought that 10–15% of shoplifters fell into the disordered group though in 1981[6] he thought it might be only 5%, an expression of the increase in shoplifting amongst those without disorder. In a study of 1,649 shoplifting convictions in Montreal, only 3.2% of cases involved mentally ill patients. It reported that the most common diagnoses were affective disorders, alcohol and substance misuse disorders.[7] Gibbens and Prince[4] analysed the psychiatric disorders amongst shoplifters and these give an insight into the types of disorder one might see amongst other acquisitive offenders. The following expansion of their findings is based on clinical practice and relates offending to different disorders.

Acquisitive offending and neurosis

Depression

Depression is perhaps the commonest symptom amongst mentally ill offenders convicted of theft. It is often appropriately treated on an outpatient basis, perhaps as a condition of probation. Four groups can be identified based on the study of shoplifters, as detailed below

Isolated young adults under stress
In the shoplifting study a group of young women with children was identified. Characteristically they lived in multistorey blocks of flats, separated from parents, looking after children on their own with a husband out at work and without support from neighbours. Depressive symptoms appeared and then after some months an offence occurred. The theft could be understood as a cry for help and the acquisition may have been comforting.

Older people with a chronic depression
The study identified a group of women in late middle age with a chronic depression, isolated within their families with children having left home,

and the husband having become rather neglectful. This depression occurred at the menopausal period which, of course, coincides with these other 'losses'. Characteristically the woman would have attended her doctor for some weeks with vague symptoms. After a time she would sense his loss of interest and would then stop going. A month or so later she would be convicted of shoplifting. The motivation was similar to that in the first group.

Subjects with depression associated with acute loss such as a death in the family

In a study of 24 shoplifters,[8] a number of the subjects had experienced a very significant loss or were about to do so. The reasons can be preoccupation with problems or comfort stealing an object that may have symbolic meaning.

Personality disordered subjects experiencing a depressive swing

Such people often have aggressive feelings of resentment. The offending can be understood as a sudden impulse to give themselves a treat, or an attempt to embarrass and therefore punish their family by bringing disgrace on themselves, or attempt to gain the family's sympathy by drawing attention to their plight.

Shoplifting to manipulate

Subjects with depression may use shoplifting to manipulate. These subjects find themselves in very unhappy situations (e.g. the newly emigrated young woman who hates her new country) and consciously or unconsciously use shoplifting to draw attention to their plight or force a change of circumstances.

Anxiety

Anxiety states may cause a state of distraction and in this state it is possible that a subject may 'absent-mindedly' take goods from a shop without paying. Panic disorder can lead to individuals needing to leave a shop rapidly which would lead to stealing.

Eating disorders

The stealing of food, usually from shops, has been reported in anorexic patients.[9] Those patients with eating disorders who have been sexually abused may be more likely to shoplift.[10]

Compulsive states and kleptomania

Phobias and obsessional states with unwanted intrusive thoughts are rarely associated with theft. However some persistent offenders appear or claim to experience a compulsion to steal and fit the DSM IV and ICD-10 description of kleptomania. The compulsion is characterised by a feeling of tension associated with a particular urge to steal, excitement during the theft (which in a minority of occasions may be sexual) and relief after committing the act. At the same time the urge is recognised as senseless and wrong and the act is followed by guilt. The stealing is not an expression of anger or vengeance nor part of a conduct disorder or antisocial personality. The goods are usually worth little and often not required. They may be hidden, hoarded or given away. Such a compulsion seems associated with other neurotic symptoms such as:

(1) depression;
(2) anxiety perhaps associated with other compulsive behaviours (hand washing, checking);
(3) bulimia nervosa;
(4) sexual dysfunction (promiscuity or frigidity);
(5) fetishistic stealing (e.g. women's underwear).

The literature suggests that the condition occurs at any age and is commoner (77%) in females.[11] Behavioural therapy, psychotherapy and antidepressants have all been used with clinical evidence of success in relieving the compulsion in some cases. Overlapping with this disorder are those with chronic feelings of sadness, tension and depression whose dysphoria is relieved by theft.[12]

Another example of compulsive behaviour is that of youths who persistently drive and take away vehicles on their own at times of despondency. Once behind the wheel they feel a sense of wellbeing and a return of self-esteem. After driving around they then abandon the car. They become very skilled at taking cars and carry keys for this purpose. It is basically a neurotic behaviour said to occur particularly in association with dominating mothers.

Such offenders have to be distinguished from people with antisocial personalities who show opportunistic and impulsive behaviour in many areas but without a neurotic cause. They must also be distinguished from those where psychosis or brain damage underlies the repetitive behaviour.

Acquisitive offending and psychosis

Schizophrenia

There are a number of reasons why someone with a schizophrenic illness may steal. It may be as a direct response to symptoms of their illness such as delusions or hallucinations.

Schizophrenia may lead to a deteriorated vagrant state leading to theft. Without sustenance or money and handicapped by severe mental illness the subject may well steal in order to obtain food. The theft may be a simple one from a shop or a doorstep, or may be more complicated, involving a burglary.

Affective psychosis

Offending may occur in association with mania, either due to an expansive grandiose mood or due to associated delusions. When a manic person offends in this way typically it might be by writing cheques which cannot be met, ordering goods which cannot be paid for, or taking articles believing that 'all is in order'. These offences all arise from an exaggerated grandiosity and elevation of mood, possibly associated with delusional beliefs. In severe depression the 'theft' may be due to an absent-minded state, a desire to comfort, an attempt to draw attention to the subject's plight or arising from an associated delusion.

Acquisitive offences and organic states

Dementia

Stealing may occur either because of a state of confusion where a person might walk out with goods without paying, or because the dementia undermines the subject's resistance to temptation. A fronto-temporal dementia is more likely to cause antisocial behaviour than Alzheimer's disease.[13] A careful examination and history from the subject and relatives will reveal the diagnosis.

Brain damage

Some subjects following brain damage show a marked deterioration in personality and develop anti-social behaviour which may well include theft. It may also cause memory difficulties which may lead to absent-minded theft.

Epilepsy

The epileptic attack may be followed by a state of confusion in which, theoretically at least, a person might leave a shop with goods without remembering to pay, though this must be extremely rare.

Substance abuse

Alcohol or drugs may be associated with theft or burglary in a number of ways though substance abuse is not a defence (see Chapter 9):

(1) the subject may steal to maintain the habit or to provide sustenance;
(2) the substance abuse may disinhibit the subject sufficiently for him to take part in a burglary or other offence such as stealing cars either by himself or with others.

Acquisitive offending and mental impairment

Stealing may occur in subjects with mental retardation due to there being:

(1) less resistance to temptation;
(2) an associated personality disturbance;
(3) resentments which are due in part to recent or chronic difficulties and frustrations experienced by the handicapped person as a result of the effect of low intelligence.

Acquisitive offending and personality disorder

The shoplifting study[4] revealed a group of young people with lifelong chaotic, disturbed lives who stole impulsively and had other offences. Their backgrounds were likely to be severely disordered and their adjustment to life unsuccessful. Their ability to sustain relationships, maintain themselves in work and manage their own affairs was poor.

Acquisitive offending and other 'disorders'

'Absent-minded' taking of goods

Patients may take things from stores in an 'absent-minded' state[12] without intent to deprive, in which case they should be found not guilty. Absent-minded behaviour may occur in a number of conditions including depression, anxiety, dementia and post epileptic confusion.

Impaired concentration due to medication

This has been described[5] in association with excessive night sedation, antidepressants, anti-epileptic medication, steroids. Typically such people would be honest people who had offended whilst taking medication. There should, obviously, be no history from observers (e.g. the detective) of stealth or attempts to conceal the goods. It is most common in the elderly.

Clinical assessment of the case

A full history should give an indication of any psychiatric disturbance. Subjects may claim to be unable to recall the actual offence. Possible causes of such failure to remember include:

(1) malingering;
(2) hysterical denial;
(3) poor retention due to being:
    (a) distracted;
    (b) ill;
    (c) under the influence of medication;
    (d) under the influence of alcohol or drugs;
(4) dementia with poor memory;
(5) rare disturbances of consciousness, e.g. hypoglycaemia, postictal phenomena, etc.

In clinical practice malingering and hysterical denial appear to be by far the most common cause of failing to remember. It is very important to check as much of the history as possible from other sources. Relatives should be seen, if possible, or information obtained at second hand through a social report (probably prepared by the probation service). A detailed history of past offences should be obtained from the patient (and checked with the probation or police record). Ideally an objective account of the present offence should be obtained from statements or the police. This becomes particularly important where it is being asserted that there was no intent. The observations of others are essential to make a balanced appraisal of the case.

If, of course, one feels certain on psychiatric grounds that there was no intent then this opinion should be given to the court. On the other hand, some subjects will not proceed with such a defence fearing that it will increase the chances of their case being publicised in the newspapers. They hope, by pleading guilty, to dispose of the matter quickly and anonymously.

Management and treatment of mentally disordered property offenders

The appropriate treatment is that of the underlying mental disorder. Whether or not this will require admission to hospital will depend on the severity of the disorder and the likelihood of the patient co-operating with treatment. Generally it will be the psychotic or severely organically disturbed who will need hospital treatment on a hospital order. The neurotic disorders (minor depression, anxiety states) may be managed on an out-patient basis, often as a condition of probation. All patients will benefit not just from medication, but also from supportive counselling and sound practical advice, e.g. leaving bags outside shops, shopping with others, getting rid of car keys, finding daytime activities etc. Cognitive behavioural therapy has been used successfully in depressed shoplifters.

The most difficult patients include those with severe personality disorders (who may not be amenable to treatment) and the 'compulsive' groups. Various attempts have been made with behavioural techniques in the latter group including[14] aversive conditioning, covert sensitisation, redirected activities, and mass practice. Of primary relevance is the motivation which may be dependent on mood (frustration, low self-esteem, depression).

Prosecution and the courts

There have been cases where a prosecution for shoplifting has led to the attempted and successful suicide of a vulnerable person. The Code for Crown Prosecutors gives guidelines to the prosecution which indicate that sympathetic consideration should be given to those with some form of psychiatric illness or impairment. The subjects may be cautioned or not prosecuted, or the prosecution abandoned particularly where the adverse effects of prosecution on the defendant's mental health outweigh the interests of justice.

However, where there is a successful prosecution, and psychiatric disorder is also present, then the disorder may be put forward in mitigation on behalf of the subject. The courts are usually very anxious to assist those who are clearly psychiatrically disordered and usually willing to go along with a psychiatric recommendation. It is the case, however, in shoplifting particularly, that the courts had become so disillusioned with the frequent plea that the shoplifter must have been depressed that there are signs of the courts having less sympathy when this plea is put forward. Nevertheless, they usually accept recommendations for out-patient treatment as a condition of probation, or in-patient hospital care on a hospital order in appropriate cases.

Destructive offences

Introduction

The literature in this area has principally been about arson which seems to have been of a particular interest to psychiatrists, though many of the findings apply to other destructive offences. It has always been recognised that arson could be due to mental illness as well as common motivations like jealousy, revenge or anger. This has been well reviewed by Barnett and Spitzer[15] and Barker.[16] The first descriptions go back to Esquirol in 1835[17] who described arsonists suffering from psychotic illness, dementia and subnormality etc. At that time repeated arson without other psychiatric disorder led to a diagnosis of pyromania (in keeping with the then fashionable diagnosis of monomania), though now repeated fire setting is seen as the end result of a number of problems.

Scientific surveys of arsonists began in the 1950s with the classical study by Lewis and Yarnell[18] of 1,100 arson cases which threw further light on the motives behind fire setting and resulted in a classification of fire setters. Whilst that study gave a view of a representative sample, other studies have been on very selected groups, e.g. arsonists in special hospital and arsonists in prison.

Rix carried out a prospective study of 153 arsonists referred for psychiatric reports which addressed both the psychiatric diagnoses as well as their motivations.[19] A further study by Puri *et al.*[20] reviewed the relationship between mental disorder and fire setting by describing the characteristics and motivation of 36 offenders referred to psychiatric services. They concluded that a multi-axial approach to classification should be adopted. Barker agrees with this but also suggests in her review that by studying in detail individual fire setters, 'syndromes' of arson may emerge which will enable psychiatrists to develop better methods of intervention and prevention.

The classification below is modified from that of Lewis and Yarnell. The classification might equally well be applied to other destructive behaviour such as malicious damage. Psychiatric abnormality can be associated with any of the subgroups.

Fire as a means to an end

In this heterogeneous group the fire is used to achieve an end such as the collection of insurance money, revenge, or self-protection.

Insurance fraud
In this group the fire is set in order to claim insurance money. It is unlikely that a psychiatrist will be asked to see such a case except where the accused has a history of mental illness or there is a suspicion of illness.

Desire to earn money
Cases have been described where part-time firemen have deliberately created work for themselves by setting fires in order that they will be called out and thus earn extra money. Such cases are unlikely to come the way of

the psychiatrist and are usually dealt with by prison or other penal sentences.

Covering up the evidence of a crime

The fire is set to hide a crime or destroy clues. Such cases are unlikely to be referred for a psychiatric report but may be if the situation is sufficiently bizarre. The psychiatrist must ensure that he has seen all the relevant statements which were made to the court. These may throw light on what appears to be an otherwise perplexing event. Sometimes the excuse of covering up a crime may be offered by a defendant who wishes to hide more pathological motives, such as a repetitive urge to set fires, and sometimes the original crime may spring from a mental illness.

Political motives

The fire is set to achieve a political goal. It is unlikely that a psychiatrist will be asked to see a person who has set fire for this purpose (except for the rare psychotic subject) for such persons usually take great pains to point out that their actions are those of a sane and responsible man. Some may have a history of personality instability but generally a hospital disposal is inappropriate.

Gang activities for excitement

Immature people, particularly adolescents, may work themselves up into a state of excitement during which time they may commit various offences, including arson (for which there seems to be a very good prognosis from the re-offending point of view). This can be associated with boredom. One sometimes sees cases where there is one very disturbed member influencing a group of relatively normal boys to indulge in wild behaviour, or one sees a disturbed youth attempt to gain attention or status with other youths by behaving in a dangerous way. The relatively normal youths are unlikely to set other fires once the dominating or disturbed youth is separated from them.

Revenge, self protection, anger group

In this group the fire is the result of intense emotions of fear or anger often arising out of interactions with others. This is probably the most common motivation for fire setting even in psychiatric patients. Rix[19] reported that nearly one third of his sample had set fires with revenge in mind.

A cry for help state

In this group the fire is a way of drawing attention to the plight of the subject. In Rix's group[19] this was seen more commonly in women but was also associated with psychiatric morbidity. He also described a group with psychiatric diagnoses who set fires in order to be rehoused.

Desire to feel powerful
This group obtain satisfaction from the sense of power they feel by setting a fire, watching the commotion and reading about it the next day, whilst enjoying the feeling of being the cause of it. They are usually inadequate people of low self-esteem.

To be seen as a hero
This group tends to be subjects of rather inadequate personality with low self-esteem who construct a situation in which they appear to be a hero. They set a fire, call the fire brigade and rush to the rescue of people caught in the blaze in the hope of capturing the limelight. Long-term follow up studies do not clarify whether this motivation necessarily means a bad prognosis. One might expect supportive therapy to be helpful to such men.

Suicide
Studies have implied that the majority of suicides by fire have been in individuals with psychiatric histories and often a history of serious self destructive behaviour. There have been epidemics of suicide by fire such as between 1978 and 1979 when coroners recorded 82 cases compared to the previous average annual rate of 23.

A fire as a thing of interest

This category consists of a heterogeneous group in which there is fascination with the fire itself.

Irresistible impulse group
People in this group are aware of a repeated urge to set fires which they do not fully understand and when questioned about it are very inarticulate. They are often isolated, inadequate people. They overlap with the tension reducing group. They have a history, usually, of setting several fires and of being caught. They describe a build up of tension and then pleasure or release when the fire is under way. The fires may escalate in severity.

Sexual excitement group
Although fire as a fetish was thought in the 19th century to be a common cause of fire setting, in practice men who are directly sexually stimulated by fire seem to be rare (though there has been considerable psychiatric interest in the sexual symbolism in fire setting). The surveys of arsonists have described people who are sexually aroused by the fire which they have set though this is a very small proportion of all fire setters. Some receive prison sentences where they may receive psychotherapy, others find themselves admitted to special hospital. The motivation seems so bizarre in these cases that a psychiatric report is usually requested. It is usually believed (without much evidence) that the prognosis must be bad. Certainly the subject

should be regarded as dangerous as long as the fantasies of sexual arousal by fire setting persist.

Tension or depression reducing group
In this group the principal motivation arises from the discovery by the subject that the act relieves feelings of despondency or tension. This group overlaps with the 'irresistible impulse' group and the 'cry for help' group. Such fire setting may be associated with other tension reducing activity such as self mutilation and suicide. In women there are clinical grounds for suspecting an association with early sexual abuse. It has also been seen in women with post traumatic stress disorder. Management depends on how easily the symptoms of depression and anxiety can be reduced, perhaps by offering asylum in hospital or supportive therapy as an out-patient (with or without medication), or whether it is necessary to contain the patient in a more secure establishment until, through time and treatment, there is maturation and greater self-control.

This classification does not include those who set fires either through carelessness or reckless behaviour.

Risk of re-offending in fire setters

Lewis and Yarnell painted a picture of arsonists being a very handicapped group of people of whom 30% were likely to repeat fire setting. However, prediction in individual cases is often difficult.[21] A recent study showed an overall recidivism rate of only 4% for arson amongst convicted arsonists although many commit other types of offences.[22] Offenders on short sentences have a very low re-offending rate for arson over a five year period (2%) but 20% of arsonists who have served long terms of imprisonment committed further arson. Of the above offenders, 25% of the short termers and 50% of the long termers were found to have committed a destructive offence (arson, sexual, property damage or violence) in the follow up period. If all offences are taken into account then 43% of the short termers were reconvicted of some offence (including theft) and 80% of the long termers re-offended overall. Arson appears to be like all other crimes in that the risk is increased if the offender has a previous history of setting fires. Sapsford[23] also implied that those who receive longer sentences have an increased risk of re-offending. A German study described fire setters with mental illness as being more likely to re-offend than those without.[24] However arson is a notoriously difficult offence to detect and to gain a conviction for. It is therefore impossible to be accurate about re-offending rates or predict future behaviour.

In summary, whilst it may be difficult to tell whether a particular person may commit arson again, the statistical chances of a repeat after serving a period in prison or other institutions appears to be low overall. Further research is required in this area to improve the quality of risk assessment in these offenders.

Psychiatric diagnoses and arson

In Rix's study[19] 8% of the subjects had a diagnosis of psychosis, 11% had a manic depressive disorder, but personality disorder was the commonest diagnosis along with substance misuse. However the group Rix studied was biased in that the court had recommended that they have psychiatric reports prepared prior to sentencing which implies there had been some concern about their mental states. Approximately 2% of arsonists a year receive a hospital order. However considering the number of hospital orders made each year, arsonists do appear to be over represented. It may be that mentally ill arsonists are detected more easily than others. However the Court of Appeal in 1975 recommended that psychiatric reports should be requested as a matter of routine in cases of arson and therefore psychiatrists do have a role to play in the assessment of these offenders.

Clinical assessment of arsonists and other destructive offenders

As with all potentially dangerous offenders, the best chance of making a good assessment depends on getting the best objective information as well as taking a careful detailed history. Nothing can replace a painstakingly detailed examination of previous psychiatric records, social reports, lists of previous convictions (with details if possible) and statements relating to the current offence. There should be current information from people about the subject's background, best obtained by interviewing the relatives, and certainly by discussing the case with a social worker, or probation officer who knows the case.

The assessment will be aimed at elucidating whether there was a psychiatric abnormality either at the time of the offence or since and the motivation for the offence. The relationship with a psychiatric abnormality may be direct (acting on a delusion), or indirect (e.g. reflecting the stresses which occurred secondarily to the illness). An assessment of risk should also be made based on the history of previous fire setting and offending, understanding the precipitant to the fire setting and the likelihood of the precipitant recurring, and listening to the subject's own account and assessment of his potential for further fire setting, and his account of his fantasies and impulses.

Outcome in court

In cases of arson the court is, as usual, generally very anxious to help those with psychiatric disorders. The court will also be anxious to keep the protection of the public in mind. Recommendations for treatment should therefore take cognisance of this and be seen to be realistic in terms of safety. Whilst it is not necessary to recommend everyone for a special hospital or regional secure unit, recommendations for out-patient care for an actively psychotic man who has just set a fire would also clearly be inappropriate. Recommendations for a restriction order may be appropriate when it is advisable to have obligatory aftercare in the community or where absconding from hospital (with a risk to others) is likely.

References

(1) Povey, D., Prime, J. and Taylor, P. (1998) *Notifiable Offences: England and Wales 1997.* HMSO: London.
(2) Mirrlees-Black, C., Mayhew, P. and Percy, A. (1996) *The 1996 British Crime Survey.* Home Office Statistical Bulletin 19/96
(3) Office of Population Censuses and Surveys (1995) *The General Household Survey 1993.* HMSO: London.
(4) Gibbens, T.C.N. and Prince, J. (1962) *Shoplifting.* Institute for the Study and Treatment of Delinquency: London.
(5) Gibbens, T.C.N., Palmer, C. and Prince, J. (1971) Mental health aspects of shoplifting. *British Medical Journal* **3**, 612–15.
(6) Gibbens, T.C.N. (1981) Shoplifting. *British Journal of Psychiatry* **138**, 346–7.
(7) Lamontagne, Y., Carpentier, N., Hetu, C. and Lacerte-Lamontagne, C. (1994) Shoplifting and mental illness. *Canadian Journal of Psychiatry* **39**(5), 300–302.
(8) Cupchick, W. and Acherson, J.D. (1983) Shoplifting, an occasional crime of the moral majority. *Bulletin of the American Academy of Psychiatry and the Law.* **11**, 343–54.
(9) Crisp, H., Hsu, L. and Harding, B. (1980) The starving hoarder and voracious spender: stealing in anorexia nervosa. *Journal of Psychosomatic Research* **24**, 225–31.
(10) Fullerton, D.T., Wonderlich, S.A. and Gosnell, B.A. (1995) Clinical characteristics of eating disordered patients who report sexual or physical abuse. *International Journal of Eating Disorders* **17**(3), 243–9.
(11) McElroy, S.L., Hudson, J.I., Pope, H.G. and Keck, P.E. (1991) Kleptomania: clinical characteristics and associated psychopathology. *Psychological Medicine* **21**, 93–108.
(12) Editorial (1976) The Absent Minded 137 Shoplifter. *British Medical Journal* **1**, 675–6.
(13) Miller, B.L., Darby, A., Benson, D.F., Cummings, J.L. and Miller, M.H. (1997) Aggressive, socially disruptive and antisocial behaviour associated with fronto-temporal dementia'. *British Journal of Psychiatry* **170**, 150–4.
(14) Gudjonsson, G.H. (1990) Psychological and psychiatric aspects of shoplifting. *Medicine, Science and the Law* **30**, 45–51.
(15) Barnett, W. and Spitzer, D.M. (1994) Pathological fire setting 1951–1991: a review. *Medicine, Science and the Law* **34**(1), 4–20.
(16) Barker, A. (1994) *Arson: A Review of the Psychiatric Literature.* Maudsley Monograph, Oxford University Press: Oxford.

(17) Esquirol, J.E.D (1965) *Mental Maladies, Treatise on Insanity*. Hafner: London.
(18) Lewis, N.D.C. and Yarnell, H. (1951) *Pathological fire setting*. Nervous and Mental Disease Monograph. No 82; New York.
(19) Rix, K.J. (1994) A psychiatric study of adult arsonists. *Medicine, Science and the Law* **34**(1), 21–34.
(20) Puri, B.K., Baxter, R. and Cordess, C.C. (1995) Characteristics of fire setters. A study and proposed multi axial psychiatric classification *British Journal of Psychiatry* **166**(3), 393–6.
(21) Faulk, M. (1982) Assessing dangerousness in arsonists. In: *Dangerousness: Psychiatric Assessment and Management* (eds) J.R. Hamilton and H. Freeman. Gaskell (for the Royal College of Psychiatrists): London.
(22) Soothill, K.L. and Pope, P.J. (1973) Arson: a twenty-year cohort study. *Medical Science Law* **13**, 127–38.
(23) Sapsford, R.J., Banks, C. and Smith, D.D. (1978) Arsonists in prison. *Medical Science Law* **18**, 247–54.
(24) Barnett, W., Richter, P., Sigmund, D. and Spitzer, M. (1997) Recidivism and concomitant criminality in pathological fire setters. *Journal of Forensic Sciences* **42**(5), 879–83.

Chapter 7

Offences against the Person and Forensic Psychiatry

Introduction

This chapter defines offences against the person and discusses proposed changes in the law. Basic criminological data, the theories of violence, the relationship of mental abnormality to violence and the forensic aspects are discussed. This is followed by a description of the psychiatric assessment of violent offenders. Sexual offences are described in Chapter 12.

As in all offending, violence may be the end result of several different factors of which mental abnormality is but one. The task of the psychiatrist in any particular case must be to detect the presence, and demonstrate the influence, of any mental abnormality. The motive (anger, jealousy, etc.) which drives the 'normal' person to a violent offence may well be the final motive in the mentally abnormal. In the latter case, however, the motive will often be exaggerated by, or the result of, mental abnormality.

Definitions

An 'offence against the person' is a legal term and includes a variety of crimes which are considered below.

Homicide

This is the killing of a human being by another. It is subdivided into *lawful* and *unlawful homicide*.

Lawful homicide
This includes justifiable killing (e.g. capital punishment, where it is practised) and excusable homicide (e.g. death resulting from pure accident or as a result of honest and reasonable mistake).

Unlawful homicide

This is defined as the unlawful killing of any reasonable creature in being and under the Queen's peace. The previous rule that the death should have followed within a year and a day of the deed has now been abolished. It is subdivided into:

Murder: The offender must be of sound mind and discretion (i.e. sane , and over 10 years of age). It must be proven that there was malice aforethought (i.e. intent to cause death or grievous bodily harm), or that the death follows unlawful and voluntary intent to do serious injury. Courts have varied in their rulings but currently it seems that intent may be assumed if there was recklessness as to the effect of an action either when the offender appreciated that death or serious harm was a virtual certainty or had given no thought to an obvious risk. This is known as the *subjective test.* Previously (the *objective test*) it had been ruled that intent was assumed if an ordinary person (not necessarily the offender) would have realised that the death or serious harm was the natural result of the act. A person found guilty of murder is automatically sentenced to life imprisonment. The court has no discretion in this sentence.

Manslaughter: In this case the homicide follows an unlawful act or omission but the circumstances do not meet the full criteria of murder, or there are mitigating factors, i.e. there is

(1) an absence of intent to kill or cause grievous bodily harm;
(2) negligent behaviour without intent to kill;
(3) having a mental abnormality of such severity as to substantially diminish the responsibility of the accused;
(4) homicide as part of a suicide pact.

In the case of manslaughter the court has discretion to give any sentence ranging from a life sentence down to a conditional discharge including, in appropriate cases, hospital orders.

Infanticide: This crime is defined under the Infanticide Act 1938. A woman may be found guilty of infanticide instead of murder after she has killed her child if the child is under 12 months and, at the time of the act or omission, the balance of her mind was disturbed by reason of her not being fully recovered from the effects of giving birth to the child or the effects of lactation. If she is found guilty of infanticide and not murder then she is dealt with as in the case of manslaughter.

Death of infants

There are three offences connected with the death of infants:

Child destruction
The killing of a child capable of being born alive before it has an existence independent of its mother. The Abortion Act 1967 protects doctors from being charged with child destruction.

Concealment of birth
It is an offence to dispose of the dead body of a recently born child whether or not it was born alive.

An attempt to procure an abortion
It is an offence to attempt to procure an abortion except in the situation defined by the Abortion Act 1967. If a woman died as a consequence of an illegal abortion then the person attempting to procure the abortion would be indicted for manslaughter.

Assaults

An assault occurs when a person strikes another or does an action which makes the other fear immediate personal violence. A battery is the actual application of unlawful force through an 'assault' and is frequently used to cover both. In certain situations an assault or battery is justifiable, e.g. in the furtherance of public authority, reasonable self-defence or by consent. Relevant offences in this group include:

Wounding
Technically, to establish this offence the skin must be broken. The Offences Against the Person Act 1861 cites the causing of grievous bodily harm as an alternative. Wounding is subdivided into:

(1) *wounding with intent to cause grievous bodily harm* (i.e. serious bodily harm). The prosecution must prove intent.
(2) *Unlawful wounding*, where there is no intent to cause grievous bodily harm even though grievous bodily harm may be caused.

Assaults
Here there may be little or severe damage but the form of it is not that of wounding. It is divided into two offences.

(1) Assault occasioning actual bodily harm (a hurt or injury which interferes with the health or comfort of the injured but not such as to amount to grievous bodily harm).
(2) Common assault in which there is an attempt to offer violence or do harm but without wounding or actual bodily harm.

Proposed legislation

The definition of assault and battery and the various assault offences described above, derive from the Offences Against the Person Act 1861. In 1980, the Criminal Law Revision Committee made recommendations for the reform of this legislation. In February 1998 the Home Office published a consultation document which proposed reform of this Act of Parliament.[1] Included in it was a new Offences Against the Person Bill. This Bill introduces new offences of *injury and assault.*

The new offences are:

(1) Intentional serious injury
(2) Reckless serious injury
(3) Intentional or reckless injury
(4) Assault.

In addition, the previous offences relating to assaults against the police remain. These are:

(5) Assault on a constable
(6) Causing serious injury to resist arrest
(7) Assault to resist arrest

Included in this legislation are statutory definitions of intent and recklessness. The Bill states that:

A person acts intentionally with respect to a result if:
(a) it is his purpose to cause it, or
(b) although it is not his purpose to cause it, he knows that it would occur in the ordinary course of events if he were to succeed in his purpose of causing some other result.

A person acts recklessly with respect to a result if he is aware of a risk that it will occur and it is unreasonable to take that risk having regard to the circumstances as he knows or believes them to be.

However these definitions will only apply to non-fatal violence and will not affect murder or other homicide offences.

Assault is defined as:

A person is guilty of an offence if:
(a) he intentionally or recklessly applies force to or causes impact on the body of another, or
(b) he intentionally or recklessly causes the other to believe that any such force or impact is imminent.

The previous offence of making threats to kill is broadened to include threats to cause serious injury.

A person is guilty of an offence if he makes to another a threat to cause the death of, or serious injury to, that other or a third person intending that other to believe that it will be carried out.

Within the proposed legislation, the definition of injury includes both physical and mental injury. This latter type of injury is defined as 'any impairment of a person's mental health', but excludes disease. This concept of mental injury had already been introduced into case law following the conviction of a man for causing actual bodily harm to a woman whom he had stalked but not physically attacked (*R. v. Burstow* [1997] Crim L R 452–5).

The proposed Bill also includes clear statements on the effect of voluntary intoxication. This states that if a person was voluntarily intoxicated at the time of committing an offence against the person, then he would be treated the same as if he had not been intoxicated. Voluntary intoxication is defined:

> A person is voluntarily intoxicated if:
> (a) he takes an intoxicant otherwise than properly for a medicinal purpose,
> (b) he is aware that it is or may be an intoxicant,
> (c) he takes it in such a quantity as impairs his awareness or understanding.

The presumption will be that intoxication is voluntary unless there is evidence to the contrary.

When the Bill becomes law the common law offences of common assault and battery, referred to earlier, will be abolished.

Poisoning

Poisoning is the deliberate administering of a noxious substance intending to cause harm or death. It has been discussed by Cordess.[2]

Four situations can be recognised:

(1) Poisoning of children: some parents poison their children as
    (a) a form of non-accidental injury to punish, control or sedate the child;
    (b) as a form of Münchausen Syndrome by proxy presenting themselves as caring, worried parents with a mysteriously ill child and enjoying the attention of, and intimacy with, the hospital staff;
    (c) in order to claim the life insurance.
(2) Poisoning of sick parents by their carers. Often altruistic motives are professed ('to put them out of their misery') though sadistic motives or financial gain may be suspected.
(3) Poisoning to kill or get rid of people:
    (a) within relationships as in other forms of homicide;
    (b) for financial gain;
    (c) for sadistic reasons as in the case of Graham Young[3] who was fascinated by poisons and their effects and enjoyed observing the effects of poisons and the power poisons brought him.

(4) Threats and acts of mass poisoning:
   (a) to secure a ransom,
   (b) to achieve a political or terrorist goal ('do what we want or we will poison your products');
   (c) unknown motivation – manifested as the discovery of poisoned foods, the offender may perhaps enjoy the feelings of power accompanying the widespread concern and panic caused by the action.

Driving offences

The driving offences in this section are those which are dangerous to others and include:

(1) Careless driving (without due care or reasonable consideration);
(2) Driving or attempting to drive when unfit through drink or drugs or with excess alcohol in the blood.
(3) Being in charge of a motor vehicle when unfit through drink or drugs.
(4) Causing death by careless driving while under the influence of drink or drugs.
(5) Reckless driving – driving recklessly at speed or in a manner dangerous to the public (automatism, e.g. sudden unconsciousness, would be a defence).
(6) Causing injury or death by reckless driving.
(7) Dangerous driving and causing death by dangerous driving.
(8) Failure to provide a specimen of urine or blood for laboratory tests (a medical certificate to say that it would make the offender ill might be a defence).

Criminological details of offences against the person

There are two principal sources of data. The best source is derived from the British Crime Survey in which nearly 15,000 people were questioned about their experience as victims. The survey, in 1998 was the seventh one since 1981.[4] The traditional police statistics of reported crime are now known to be unreliable by comparison. They are an underestimate as people do not always report crime and the police do not always record it. They distort the true figures because people report some crimes more than others.

The number of recorded crimes of violence has risen in the last few decades. Total crimes of personal violence (severe and trivial) recorded by the police, rose from 89,599 in 1974 up to 350,698 in 1997.[5] Crimes of violence in 1997 amounted to 8% of all recorded offences. The British Crime Survey (BCS)[4] found that from 1995 to 1997, while recorded crime had shown an increase of 18% in wounding offences, there was a decrease of

17% according to BCS figures. They suggested that the apparent increase in the police figures was accounted for by changes in the recording of these offences by the police. This change in recording practice has particularly affected the figures for domestic violence. Common assault is not recorded by the police but is recorded by the BCS, the numbers of these offences having doubled since 1981. The type of the offence is relevant as to whether it is reported. Trivial assaults may not be worth reporting. Rape may be under-reported, on the other hand, because of the embarrassment of the victim. Serious violent assaults in the home may be under-reported, in part, due to the fear of the victim that reporting the offence will anger or alienate the attacker and provoke further violence.

Violence known to the police seems to be committed by a very small proportion of the population. Of the 31,436 males born in Denmark between 1944–47, 2.3% of them accounted for all the convictions of violence by the time they were 30 years of age. Of the violent convictions, 43% were committed by 0.6% of the cohort.[6]

Over 90% of violent offenders are male and over 50% aged between 17–24. The principal victim outside the home is another young male. The offences are often carried out in association with the abuse of alcohol. In serious wounding, male victims are six times more likely than female but only three times for less serious wounding. Two-thirds of the victims of robberies are male though older victims tend to be female. Violence is commoner in areas of social deprivation.

The amount of unreported homicide is unknown – there are a large number of missing people each year, some of whom may be homicide victims. The reported homicide rate in England and Wales has varied throughout the century with peaks in the first, third and present decades. Currently the rate has risen to 13 per million per annum (711 homicides in 1997) having been around 10 per million for a number of years. England and Wales have one of the lowest homicide rates in Western Europe. Rates in Eastern Europe are generally higher, e.g. 29 per million in Poland. Australia, New Zealand and Canada have similar rates of approximately 20 per million. The USA has one of the highest rates, 74 per million, which is over five times that of England and Wales.

In homicide cases, the offender is known to 50% of the male victims and 75% of female victims. Women are more likely to be asphyxiated, whereas men are most likely to be killed by a sharp instrument. The most likely victims of homicide are children under the age of 1 year (44 per million). These deaths commonly arise as baby battering but also from psychosis and the killing of unwanted babies.

Parricide (killing of parents) is rare (4% of homicides) and is committed by sons more often than daughters, with the father more at risk. Schizophrenia is said to be common in the adult sons convicted of this offence (75%). In childhood or adolescence, non-psychotic children who commit parricide do so as an explosive reaction to prolonged provocation or abuse, sometimes to the relief of the entire family. Female parricide is rare (4% of female homicides) and is usually matricide.[7] Matricide often arises in a setting of chronic discord, social isolation with a widowed daughter who has become mentally ill or alcoholic. Patricides by younger women occur in relation to long-term abuse and violence.

To give proportion to the figures it should be remembered that the number of people killed on the roads in the United Kingdom is around 5,000 per year, one-fifth of which are due to dangerous driving.

Causes of violence

There have been many attempts to find, as in delinquency, a single 'monolithic' theory of violence. These attempts have each been criticised as failing to explain the whole range of aggression and violence.[8, 9] Violence, like delinquency, has to be understood in a multifactorial way. It is useful, however, to be aware of these 'monolithic' hypotheses as each contributes to our understanding. The main hypotheses include

(1) the instinct hypothesis;
(2) the frustrated-drive hypothesis; and
(3) the social learning theory.

The instinct hypothesis

Lorenz,[10] from his studies on lower vertebrates came to the conclusion that aggression is a spontaneously generated force, a natural instinct, which has the biological functions of ensuring proper spacing of the animals, the maintenance of dominance hierarchies and therefore group stability and aiding natural selection. He observed that the release of aggression on members of the same species occurred when there were specific threats in these biological situations. He postulated that, despite our complex social situation, there is such a spontaneous, aggressive force in man. Normally, he argued, it is expressed and released in socially approved, aggressive activities, e.g. sport. Failure to find such expression leads to undesirable, aggressive acts. He linked this force to the instinctual forces postulated by Freud of *Eros*, the basic life instinct and *Thanatos*, the death instinct. The hypothesis has been criticised because of the failure to find support for the idea in man that aggression (as in lower animals) is released by specific aggression releasing stimuli and inhibited by other behaviour (e.g. gestures of submission) and because the theory is extrapolated from lower forms to man.

The frustrated-drive hypothesis

Dollard *et al.*[11] postulated that aggression arises as a result of the frustration of goal directed behaviour. Thus it was argued that frustration always leads to some form of aggression, and the occurrence of aggression always presupposes some form of frustration. The degree of frustration would reflect both the importance of the behaviour which had been frustrated and the number of times it occurred. It was argued that frustration may not immediately give way to aggression if inhibiting forces were present, such as an awareness of anticipated consequences of aggression. It was also noted that the aggression, when it occurs, could be displaced onto objects other than the frustrating agent. Whilst the frustration hypothesis may explain some aggression it cannot account for the whole picture. It has been pointed out that frustration may be followed by a variety of responses from dejection and resignation to positive active effort. It fails to explain various sorts of violence including sadistic acts or that done in defence of a reputation.

Social learning theory

Bandura[12] is a leading proponent of the hypothesis that aggressive responses are largely learned though they may be motivated by emotional arousal resulting from any aversive stimuli. Aversive stimuli lead to a variety of responses, from withdrawal, to escape and aggression. Learning to be aggressive (and learning to inhibit aggression) occurs in two principal ways:

(1) by learning from experience, aggressive behaviour being encouraged or not by others, rewarded or not by success or a rise in self-esteem, followed or not by unpleasant consequences. The pleasurable feelings achieved by the violent behaviour may come to have the features of an addictive experience.[13]
(2) by observation of the behaviour of others, particularly adults by children (i.e. by modelling). A 20 year follow up of children of violent parents, in fact, found an increased risk of violence in the children although the majority were not violent.[14]

Thus the occurrence of aggression depends both on conditioned responses (by shaping or by the classical conditioning) and by cognitive elements based on modelling and experience[15] as for example goal directed violence intended to sustain a subject's reputation and self-image, e.g. 'no-one walks over me'.

Environmental versus individual theories

All of these theories have one thing in common, they are based on individual characteristics. But the social setting in which violence occurs is also important. Situational studies have concentrated on the social setting but have ignored the interaction of the individual factors. It seems likely that whether an individual will be violent will be determined by the interaction of individual factors with environmental ones. It is unlikely that any theory that is based solely on individual factors will provide an explanation for all violent behaviour. A combination of individual and situational factors is likely to be more successful.[16]

Modifying factors on aggressive or violent responses

Whether or not any individual is aggressive or violent in any particular situation is modified by many factors.

(1) Personality
(2) The immediate social group
(3) The behaviour of the victim
(4) The presence of disinhibiting factors such as alcohol or drugs
(5) Environmental factors
(6) Physiological and biological factors
(7) The presence of mental abnormality.

Personality
Megargee[17] related the presence and extent of aggressive behaviour to the presence of either an over-controlled or under-controlled personality. Blackburn[18] extended this hypothesis by the cluster analysis of personality test data obtained from violent offenders. He identified four major groups using two factors. The first, anti-social aggression (impulsivity, aggression, hostility, low denial of anger), distinguished between the under-controlled (psychopathic) and the over-controlled group. The second factor, sociability (social anxiety and proneness to mood disorder), divided them into the following categories.

- Group 1: under-controlled, low social anxiety (primary psychopath),
- Group 2: under-controlled, high social anxiety (secondary psychopath),
- Group 3: over-controlled, low social anxiety ('controlled' group),
- Group 4: over-controlled, high social anxiety ('inhibited' group).

He had previously found that being under-controlled was associated with more frequent aggression whilst being over-controlled was associated with infrequent but extreme aggression. It seemed as though the under-controlled, used to aggressive outbursts following relatively little provocation, had learned, with practice, to control the extent of it. The over-controlled person, being unused to aggressive feeling and reactions, becomes overcome and loses control once the aggressive outburst begins, with excessive violence as the result. Comparison with other studies shows that group 3 is most like the general population in personality and may, therefore, be best called 'controlled' and not 'over-controlled'. This group contained the largest proportion of the mentally ill. Group 4 contained men with considerable interpersonal and emotional difficulties and included a high proportion of sex offenders. However, these personality types are not exclusive to violent offenders. The fact that studies of non-violent offenders have demonstrated the same personality types, questions the validity of this type of personality classification.

The immediate social group

The influence of the immediate social group can obviously be a big factor as seen in football hooliganism, groups of adolescents, angry crowds, etc. Care has to be taken to distinguish between true aggressive behaviour in terms of actual violence and mere aggressive posturing, the latter being more common than the former. Aggression exhibited by certain minority groups is perceived to be the result of the social frustrations and prejudices experienced by the group. Nevertheless the individual's behaviour in the group may owe more to the effect of group pressure than to his own experience.

The behaviour of the victim

Victims of aggressive attacks are often well known to the aggressor. There has been considerable interest in the role the victim plays in provoking and precipitating the violence. Wolfgang and Ferracuti[19] concluded that the victim played a substantial part in precipitating the violence by provoking the aggressor in a quarter of the homicides he studied. Bluglass[20] found half of spouse murder victims were alcoholic, psychotic or disabled and had played a significant part in their own death.

Studies of female victims of domestic violence have revealed a subgroup who within emotionally charged marital relationships were repeatedly assaulted by their explosive husbands.[21] A study of victims of assault found a correlation between the severity of the injury and the alcohol intake of the victims.[22]

Disinhibiting factors such as alcohol and drugs

There seems, clinically, to be a clear link between the abuse of alcohol and aggressive behaviour in individual cases. Certainly alcohol plays a significant part in dangerous driving and in association with serious offending.[23] Drugs seem related to aggression by the pattern of life of the user rather than the disinhibiting effect as in alcohol. The need to obtain drugs or money leads to violent crime, though in England drug abuse does not contribute significantly, as yet, to violent offending.

Environmental factors

The extent of the violence may be influenced by such simple matters as the availability of weapons and the attitudes of the group towards them. Other features in the environment may influence the level of arousal or instability of the subject. Overcrowding, temperature, noise, environmental or social pressures may all play a part at the time of the aggression. The influence of the social mores is much debated but presumably are extremely important. How much the general social standards influence behaviour and how much specific experiences do, such as exposure to violent films and television, is still debated. The latter may be merely a symptom of the former and not harmful in itself.

Physiological and biochemical factors

A disturbance of the physiology of the body may alter the subject's irritability or self-control. The more common influences are likely to be such things as fatigue, hunger and lack of sleep. Rarer medical conditions may occasionally be seen such as endocrine disorders (e.g. thyrotoxicosis, hypoglycaemia) and brain disorders (e.g. brain tumours, brain injury).

Impulsiveness and aggression may be linked to a decrease in brain 5-hydroxytryptamine turnover in the limbic system and cortex. Similarly, 5-hydroxytryptamine is thought to be a possible inhibitor of impulsiveness and aggression. Virkkunen[24] followed up impulsive fire setters and violent, alcohol abusing offenders after imprisonment and found a correlation between recidivism for violence and arson and lowered cerebrospinal fluid levels of 5-hydroxyindoleacetic acid (a metabolite of 5-hydroxytryptamine), homovanillic acid and a flattened glucose tolerance curve.

The presence of mental abnormality

It is the relationship of mental disorder to violence that is of particular interest to the forensic psychiatrist and will therefore be described in more detail.

The question 'Does mental illness make somebody more or less likely to be violent?' has been the subject of much debate for many years. The answer to this question has varied over the years according to the population that has been studied. Up to the 1960s it had been asserted that the rate of offending, including violent offences, was less amongst discharged psychiatric patients than amongst the general population, with the patients having offending rates 14 times lower than in the general population. One example is the often quoted Baxstrom case. Following a ruling by the US Supreme Court in 1966, Johnnie Baxstrom was released from a state hospital in New York along with 966 other patients. All of these patients had been detained because it was believed that there would be a risk of violence if they were released. A four year follow up of these 967 patients by Steadman and Cocozza[25] found that only 3% were in prison or secure hospital. Of the 246 patients in the community, only 9 of them had offended, the vast majority of which were minor offences. The conclusion from this study was that the risk of violence was lower in the mentally ill than in the general population. But as this was a population of former long stay patients it was not a valid sample to investigate. (There is further discussion of this case in Chapter 14.)

One of the most methodologically sound studies was conducted by Hafner and Boker[26] in the then Federal Republic of Germany during the 1950s and 1960s. Interestingly, their study was prompted by a public perception of greatly increased rates of violence in the mentally ill. This followed a number of high profile crimes of violence by mentally ill people. They studied all crimes of serious violence during a ten year period. They found that the mentally ill represented 3% of all violent offenders and concluded that the rate of violence by the mentally ill was no greater than the general population. One study from this country demonstrated that 20% of newly diagnosed schizophrenics had exhibited life threatening violence to other people prior to admission to hospital.[27] Violent behaviour seemed to be a function of the length of time the illness had been untreated.

However, more recent studies suggest that rates of violence are higher in the mentally ill. This has been found in studies with better methodology and using more representative populations. These include a number of birth cohort studies from Scandinavia, in which the criminal records of entire birth cohorts, born in a particular year, were studied over 20 years later.[28] The studies consistently showed that there was an increased rate of violent offending in those who also suffered a mental illness. Two types of mentally ill offenders have been described. In the first group, the offending occurred before the onset of symptoms of the illness and in the second group, the offending occurred after the illness had been diagnosed. These studies also demonstrated the significant effect that substance abuse has on violent offending. This was most marked if mental illness occurred with a history of substance abuse in childhood. There is also evidence that although the rate of violent offending is up to four times higher in the mentally ill, the rate of non-violent offending is no different.[29]

Monahan and Steadman[30] criticised many of the earlier studies into the relationship between violence and mental disorder for a number of reasons. First, the studies relied too heavily on a narrow range of markers of violent behaviour (particularly those studies which used arrest rates only), second, they had used populations that were not representative of the general population and last, they were often based on small samples. The Epidemiological Catchment Area study from the USA avoided some of these pitfalls.[31] Its strength was the fact that it used a whole community sample of over 10,000 people from three large cities in the USA, who were interviewed face to face rather than relying on official records. All subjects were interviewed using the Diagnostic Interview Schedule which generated a DSM III diagnosis of schizophrenia or schizophreniform disorder, major affective disorder, anxiety disorder, substance abuse or anti-social personality disorder. The subject's history of violence in the preceding year was also obtained. This study found that base rates for violence amongst those who did not have psychiatric diagnosis or a prior history of arrest or hospitalisation was nearly 2%. The presence of schizophrenia or a major affective disorder increased this risk by four times to nearly 8%. The addition of substance misuse to a diagnosis of schizophrenia or major affective disorder increased the risk of violence by 16 times to approximately 30%. In all these diagnostic groups, a past history of arrest or hospitalisation increased the risk of violence by between three and five times. The effect of co-morbidity of substance abuse with mental illness in increasing violence confirmed the earlier quoted studies from Scandinavia. However, it is not just the presence of substance misuse which makes people who are mentally ill more likely to be violent. A study by Link and colleagues[32] confirmed that those with active symptoms of psychosis showed higher rates of violence, independently of substance misuse. But, although the rates of violence are increased amongst the mentally ill, their contribution to levels of violence in the community, particularly serious violence, is still quite small.

Mulvey[33] concluded from all the available studies in 1994, that the following statements could be made regarding the association between mental disorder and violence.

(1) Mental illness appears to be a risk factor for violence in the community.
(2) The size of the association between mental illness and violence, whilst statistically significant, does not appear to be very large. Also the absolute risk of violence caused by mental illness is small.
(3) The combination of a serious mental illness and a substance abuse disorder probably significantly increases the risk of involvement in a violent act.
(4) The association between mental illness and violence is probably significant even when demographic characteristics are taken into account. There is no sizable body of evidence that indicates the relative strength of mental illness as a risk factor for violence compared with other characteristics such as socio-economic status or history of violence.
(5) Active symptoms are probably more important as a risk factor than simply the presence of an identifiable mental disorder.
(6) There is no evidence available that demonstrates the pathway between mental illness and violence.

Mulvey[33] concluded that an association between the two variables of mental disorder and violence existed, but how one led to the other was not clear from available evidence. Ongoing research[34,35,36] has increased the understanding of the important effects of the mental disorder, namely specific psychotic symptoms linked to violence and the role of substance misuse amongst the mentally disordered population.

Characteristic symptomatology has been found to be associated with violence in the mentally ill. The Hafner and Boker study[26] demonstrated that the types of delusions that a patient describes could predict whether they would be more likely to act on them. Those mentally ill patients who committed acts of violence were more likely to have delusions which were first systematised, second had themes of morbid jealousy or persecution and finally, they experienced an emotional response to these delusions which was often one of anger or fear. More recently, Link and Stueve[34] described the 'threat/control override' symptoms. Essentially these were thought insertion, passivity control and paranoia symptoms. They occur when a psychotic person experiences threatening delusions and their own internal controls are compromised. In this situation, it is suggested that a violent act is more understandable. Swanson *et al*.[35] using data from the ECA survey quoted earlier, replicated the study by Link and Stueve.[34] These authors used a clearer definition of the 'threat/control override' symptoms, which were:

(1) Belief that others are controlling how one moves and thinks against one's will.
(2) Belief that others are plotting against one, trying to hurt or poison one.
(3) Belief that others can insert thought directly into one's mind or steal thoughts out of one's mind.
(4) Believing that others are following one.

The results showed that if one or more of these symptoms were present then the risk of violence in the previous year was doubled. In contrast to Link and Stueve,[34] they found a much stronger effect on violence when these symptoms occurred when alcohol or other substances were used. Over a lifetime, threat/control override symptoms remained significantly related to violence even when controlling for the co-occurrence of substance misuse. They also found that the probability of violent behaviour was greatest amongst those subjects who had threat/control override symptoms and also met criteria for a major mental illness. The authors concluded that the assessment of risk of violence amongst people who are mentally ill would be enhanced if attention were paid to the occurrence of threat/control override symptoms, particularly when these occurred in those with a co-existing substance misuse disorder.

The criticism of previous studies of linkage between mental disorder and violent offending has led to the development of a second generation of studies examining this association. Steadman *et al*.[36] have reported on the first of a series of studies conducted by the Macarthur Foundation research network on mental health and the law. This study was a longitudinal prospective study of violence amongst a sample of people discharged from acute psychiatric facilities. They confirmed the conclusion of Mulvey,[33] quoted earlier, that the association between mental illness and violence was not very large. They found there was no significant difference between the prevalence of violence in patients without symptoms of substance abuse and the prevalence of violence in a matched sample living in the same area, who did not have any symptoms of substance misuse. Substance abuse symptoms significantly increased the rate of violence, in both the discharged patient group and the matched community sample. This study is important in that it demonstrates that mental illness *per se*, is not linked directly to violence in a discharged patient sample, except where substance misuse is a co-morbid condition. However, the prevalence of violence in the mentally ill who also abused substances was higher than in a matched sample of individuals without mental illness who reported substance misuse symptoms. One other finding of importance is that violence amongst the discharged patient population was largely directed towards family members and friends and that the pattern and characteristics of the violence were remarkably similar to those of the non-patient sample. Indiscriminate violence to strangers was not a feature of the patient population compared to their non-patient counterparts.

Mulvey[33] and Steadman *et al.*[36] urged caution in interpreting the findings of those studies that appear to demonstrate a causal link between mental illness and violence. The most direct evidence of a clear causal link comes from those studies which showed that the threat/control override symptoms are linked directly to violence. Though even here, the co-occurrence of substance misuse complicates the certainty of a causal link between these symptoms and violence. Mulvey[33] concludes, 'These phenomenon could simply co-exist. Violence and mental disorder [may be] part of a larger constellation of maladaptive outcomes rather than links in a clearly causal chain of events'.

However, there is not always a direct relationship between the particular symptoms of mental illness and violent offending. An indirect relationship may be said to occur when the illness causes a change in the social circumstances of the subject which then leads to offending. This is seen in severely ill people who may offend because the social decline they have experienced results in their being without money or social contacts. This may be further complicated by an excessive emotional reaction due to the effects of the mental disorder and may also be associated with the social and psychological deteriorations caused by alcoholism or drug abuse.

A coincidental relationship may be said to occur when a person with a violent history develops a mental disorder but continues to be violent. The disorder may increase the violent behaviour and may also be associated with a deterioration of functioning in other areas. Such a picture is seen particularly in violent men who sustain brain damage from a head injury and become more impulsive and violent.

The medicolegal aspects of mental abnormality and violence

The mental abnormality, if severe enough, may be a reason for being unfit to plead, for being regarded as not responsible (or, in the case of a charge of murder, for having diminished responsibility). Finally, it may be used in mitigation. Such defences are available even if the link between the offence and the abnormality is indirect or coincidental. It will be seen that the nature of the abnormality, its severity and (in the case of psychopathic disorder and mental impairment) its treatability, are the important factors. Subsequent chapters will deal with particular disorders and their relationship to the law.

Special cases of violence and the psychiatrist

The charge of murder

Murder has been of particular interest because of its association (in the past) with the death penalty and the dramatic effect psychiatric testimony could have on the outcome. It remains of special interest not only because of the serious nature of the charge and the mandatory sentence of life imprisonment but because of the special defences available and also as a paradigm for other violent offences.

Defences to murder

There are a number of possible defences to the charge of murder including a number of medical defences. The defences include:

(1) *Self-defence:* the accused had good reason to apprehend the immediate threat of death and/or serious harm to himself at the hands of the deceased, and acted to defend himself.
(2) *Lack of intent to kill or cause grievous bodily harm:* the deceased's death occurred by accident, and the accused was not negligent. In the latter case the offence is one of manslaughter.
(3) *Provocation:* here the jury must decide if the provocation was sufficient to provoke a reasonable man. Previously the provocation must have immediately been followed by the killing, but recent case law suggests that while there needs to be a 'sudden and temporary loss of control' the provocation does not have immediately to precede the killing. Such a defence applies only to the charge of murder and if successful may reduce it to a finding of manslaughter.
(4) That the death was in pursuance of a *suicide pact* between the offender and the victim. Section 4 of the Homicide Act 1957 states that in order for this defence to succeed there has to be evidence of 'common

agreement' between the persons involved and that it was the 'settled intention' of all of them to die in pursuance of the pact. A successful plea will lead to a conviction for manslaughter.

(5) *Diminished responsibility.* Section 2 of the Homicide Act 1957 requires that the defendant was suffering from such an 'abnormality of mind (whether arising from a condition of arrested or retarded development of mind or any inherent causes or induced by disease or injury) as substantially impaired his mental responsibility' for the killing. A successful plea will lead to a conviction for manslaughter.

(6) *Provocation and diminished responsibility:* it is now possible for a combined defence of provocation and diminished responsibility, the effect of which would be to allow a verdict of manslaughter if the defendant suffered an abnormality of mind *and* was provoked. This change in the law followed two notable cases of 'battered women syndrome'. The level of provocation required does not have to be sufficient to provoke a person of 'normal mentality' to kill.[37]

(7) *Insanity:* here the offender asserts that he was so mentally ill at the time of the offence that he was not responsible for his acts and therefore has not committed a crime. The McNaughten Rules state that the person should not know what they were doing or that it was wrong. Such a finding would lead to the special verdict, 'not guilty by reason of insanity'. One particular instance where this verdict can be used is in the case of automatism. Here the offender asserts that his state of consciousness was so disturbed at the time that he was behaving automatically and therefore has not committed any crime. Those defendants found to be legally insane are dealt with by the Criminal Procedure (Insanity and Unfitness to Plead) Act 1991.

(8) *Infanticide:* here a mother is claiming that at the time of the death of the child (which must be under the age of 12 months) the balance of her mind was disturbed because she had not fully recovered from the effects of giving birth or the effects of lactation consequent upon the birth of the child. If her plea is successful she will be treated as though guilty of manslaughter.

(9) *Not fit to plead:* here the offender is not really putting up a defence against the charge but simply saying that he is too mentally ill to be tried. If the plea is successful then the offender will be dealt with under the Criminal Procedure (Insanity and Unfitness to Plead) Act 1991 (see Chapter 3).

For a detailed and critical account of all these defences, see Mackay.[37]

Incidence of psychiatric abnormality in homicide

Figures vary from year to year but, in 1996, 704 people were suspected or charged with homicide in England and Wales of which 518 were convicted of an offence of homicide. This included 7% who were found guilty of manslaughter due to diminished responsibility; this figure has declined since 1989, when it was 13%. Only 55% of these received a hospital order with or without a restriction order and only one person received a probation order. In 1996 there were two cases where the accused was found to be unfit to plead, no one was found not guilty by reason of insanity and four women were convicted of infanticide. All of these numbers are typical of recent years.

A number of people (35 in 1996) who commit homicide also commit suicide and it may be assumed that some will have had a mental abnormality. A classic pattern, for example, is a man in a state of severe depression who feels that there is no future for himself or his family. He may kill his family and then himself. Therefore, in England and Wales in 1996, up to 17% of those who committed homicide were found to have some form of judicially determined mental abnormality covered by insanity, diminished responsibility, infanticide, being unfit to plead or having committed suicide. This is usually referred to as the rate of 'abnormal' homicide for a country. The incidence of abnormal homicide expressed as a percentage of the normal population seems remarkably constant in different countries,[38] with the rate between 0.1–0.2 per 100,000 of population. The difference in homicide rates between different countries seems to be accounted for by differences in normal rather than abnormal homicide and the fact that the former depends more on social norms and conditions and the availability of weapons. In countries where the overall homicide rate is relatively low, such as Great Britain, there is a danger that the risk of homicide by the mentally ill is wrongly viewed as too high. However in countries such as the USA where the overall rate is much higher, this risk may seem negligible.[39]

Contrary to reports in the media, it appears that the number of homicides by the mentally ill has steadily declined since the 1950s.[40] So, although the homicide rate in England and Wales has risen from 7 to 12 per million over the last 30 years, the contribution that mental disorder makes to that trend has decreased. However, perhaps in response to public concern, the Royal College of Psychiatrists launched the National Confidential Inquiry into Homicides and Suicides by Mentally Ill People. Its preliminary report[41] concluded that 5% of all homicides were committed by people with schizophrenia and that over 80% of the victims of the mentally ill offenders were family members.

The assessment of the offender

The assessment described below acts as a pattern for the assessment of any violent offender. A useful description of the assessment in homicide is given by Hamilton.[42]

Where is the assessment done?

The bulk of offenders charged with homicide will be remanded in custody because of the nature of the offence. There are a few, where the circumstances are appropriate, who remain on bail and may be seen as outpatients. The majority will therefore be assessed in prison where they are detained, usually in the prison hospital, for observation. In due course the court or prosecution will formally request a report from the prison doctors but the assessment begins from the day the offender enters the prison. Of the cases remanded on bail, the request for a report will be sent usually to a local psychiatrist.

Who makes the assessment?

The prison medical service begins the assessment on those in custody. Should they suspect a psychiatric disorder they may choose to call in a psychiatrist from outside the prison medical service for an independent opinion. If it is thought there is a psychiatric disorder which will require hospital treatment then a psychiatrist will be called in from an appropriate hospital (depending on the security needs of the offender) in order to consider whether treatment can be offered. The defendant, through his solicitor, may request a report from a psychiatrist of their choosing. When a report is being prepared on behalf of the defence it is sometimes helpful to communicate with the prison medical service or the independent psychiatrist (with the permission of the defence), especially where it is likely that all the doctors are going to agree in order that a well organised recommendation can be put to the court.

What is required in order to make an examination?

The doctor making the examination must take a full history from the offender and must obtain copies of prosecution statements, and forensic reports relevant to the case so that he can get a full account of what is said to have happened. It is always helpful to see relatives or have an account from them of the offender to try to get a clearer idea of his mental state at the time of the offence. It will also be helpful to find out from the prison staff how the offender has behaved whilst under observation. In cases of suspected subnormality or organic disorder, there should be a psychometric assessment and other investigations, including a CT or MRI scan. Other relevant documents which should be obtained include previous psychiatric records, a list of previous offences and a copy of any reports on the social background (probation or social worker).

What questions is the psychiatrist addressing?

The psychiatrist will have in his mind several questions for his report. All the matters discussed have been examined at greater length in Chapter 3.

Is the client fit to plead?

The illness which makes the person unfit to plead may have been present at the time of the offence or may have developed whilst in custody. Should the subject be considered unfit to plead then it is sensible to find out what the other doctors involved in the case think. If they are of like mind then the doctors can present their views to the lawyers and the case is put before the jury. If there is disagreement between doctors then the court or solicitors may choose to obtain a further psychiatric opinion. Where the defendant is thought to be unfit to plead the psychiatric report might conclude:

> 'Opinion:
> X is suffering from the severe mental illness of schizophrenia, an illness, which in his case, was not only present at the time of the offence but is also affecting him now. In this case the illness severely disrupts the defendant's ability to think logically or converse comprehensibly. So severe is the disruption that the defendant is unable to understand what is going on in court or give instruction to his legal advisers. He is therefore under disability within the meaning of the Criminal Procedure (Insanity and Unfitness to Plead) Act 1991. He requires treatment in a psychiatric hospital.'

Whether or not someone is fit to plead is a decision made by a special jury i.e. one empanelled to decide on this matter alone and not to try the case. At the court, before the plea or after the prosecution's case is heard, either the prosecution or the defence advise the court that they consider the accused unfit to plead. A special jury is empanelled and evidence about the accused's fitness is put before them. Sometimes there is disagreement between the doctors and both opinions must be put to the jury. If the jury finds the accused unfit to plead then the court deals with the case under the Criminal Procedure (Insanity and Unfitness to Plead) Act 1991. Recovery in hospital may be followed by a trial (see Chapter 3).

Was the patient mentally disordered at the time of the offence to the extent that he was without responsibility within the meaning of the McNaughten Rules?

In this case the disorder must have been present at the time of the offence.

> A middle aged man developed a paranoid illness from which he came to believe that his life was in immediate danger from his father and relatives. In a state of considerable agitation he killed his father in the night, immediately informing the neighbours of the deed and the 'reasons' for it. On remand in prison he accepted antipsychotic medication. By the time of the trial he had lost his delusion. Nevertheless he was able to successfully plead 'not guilty by reason of insanity'.

A typical wording at the end of a report of which the man is insane would read as follows:

'Opinion:
(1) The defendant is fit to plead and stand trial.
(2) At the time of the alleged offence he knew what he was doing and whether or not it was wrong. However, at the time he was suffering from the severe mental illness of schizophrenia, and he was under the delusion that the victim was about to kill him. He was therefore insane at the time of the offence within the terms of the third limb of the McNaughten Rules.
(3) Although he is much improved following treatment or remand, he will continue to require psychiatric treatment in hospital until his condition is stabilised.'

If the plea is successful then the judge informs the Home Secretary of the finding and a hospital place is sought, via the Department of Health under the powers of the Criminal Procedure (Insanity and Unfitness to Plead) Act 1991. In hospital the patient (in a case of murder) is detained as though on a hospital order (Section 37) with a restriction order unlimited in time (Section 41).

Was the defendant suffering from a mental abnormality which substantially diminished his responsibility at the time of the offence?

This can present the most difficulty to the psychiatrist. It is easy if there was a psychosis at the time. Less easy are cases with a past history of psychosis who become obviously psychotic shortly after the offence. It is possible that they have been suffering from a prepsychotic mental disturbance sufficient to substantially diminish their responsibility. Much more difficult are the cases of severe personality disorder, complicated by a neurotic disturbance at the time, such as a depressive reaction. Examples of mental states which have been found to be grounds for diminished responsibility include psychoses, endogenous depression, severe neurotic depression, severe psychopathy coupled with neurotic depressive episodes (psychopathy alone is usually insufficient), organic brain damage and subnormality. The finding of diminished responsibility does not rule out the possibility of the offender receiving a life sentence, particularly where the main diagnosis is psychopathy.

In the cases where treatment in hospital would be appropriate, the psychiatrist may reasonably contact the other doctors seeing the case. If they are all in agreement then one of the doctors can take responsibility for obtaining a place in an appropriate hospital. That doctor should also be sure that two reports will also go to the court recommending a hospital order. If the case is such that treatment as an out-patient is appropriate, the arrangements should be made beforehand so that the court can be informed of what would be available if the court wished to make use of it. Typical reports might conclude:

'Opinion:
(1) The defendant is fit to plead and stand trial.
(2) At the time of the alleged offence the defendant was not insane within the McNaughten Rules. He knew what he was doing and whether or not it was wrong.
(3) At the time of the offence the defendant was suffering from the mental illness of depression. The illness developed over the preceding 3 months and was characterised by excessive sadness, disturbed sleep, loss of weight, suicidal feelings and increased irritability. This illness constitutes an abnormality of mind (induced by disease) as defined by the Homicide Act 1957, which substantially diminished the defendant's mental responsibility.
(4) The defendant is still suffering from this mental illness and requires treatment in hospital. The court may feel that an order for treatment under Section 37 of the Mental Health Act 1983 would be appropriate in his case. A bed will be available at Barchester Hospital within 28 days of the order being made should the court feel that this would be an appropriate disposal.
(5) In this case, in view of the need to protect the public from the risk of serious harm, particularly when the patient is well enough to be in the community, the court may feel that a restriction order under Section 41 of the Mental Health Act 1983, unlimited in time, would be appropriate.'

The psychiatrist may well be expected to attend court to give his opinion as to whether or not a restriction order would be appropriate, though the court may make the restriction order whether or not the doctor recommends it. The court may also be interested in the degree of security the hospital can offer and may wish to assure itself that the security offered is sufficient for the case. If the court feels it is not adequate, it may request the psychiatrist to try to obtain a bed in a more secure institution, or refuse to send the offender to hospital.

Was the defendant so disordered at the time as to be able to plead the defence of automatism?

This defence is very rarely put forward. It has been successfully used in cases of homicide committed in association with epilepsy (see Chapter 9) and for people in stage 4 sleep (sleepwalking, night terrors, confused waking from stage 4 sleep) and REM sleep (waking from a dream).[43] It has also be successfully associated with degenerative brain disorder and might be successful after a head injury. The courts have accepted, in a lesser case, the mental confusion arising from hypoglycaemia as a basis for automatism (*R* v. *Quick*, [1973] QB 910).

A man was knocked unconscious by a blow to the head. He appeared to recover and sought out and killed his assailant. However, he had no memory of this act and in retrospect appears to have had a period of disturbed consciousness which lasted from the head injury until some hours later. It was during this period of disturbed consciousness, when he appeared to outsiders to be behaving normally, that he committed the offence. His plea of automatism was unsuccessful though he was successful with the alternative plea of diminished responsibility on the grounds that the head injury had caused a disturbance of consciousness which constituted an abnormality of mind (induced by injury) which substantially diminished his mental responsibility. He received a seven year prison sentence.

Is the woman charged with the murder of her baby sufficiently disturbed to be brought within the Infanticide Act?

The psychiatrist has to decide whether the balance of the accused's mind was disturbed and, if so, was it related to birth or lactation. Clearly this would be simple enough in the case of a puerperal illness but becomes less so afterwards. The problem is nowadays somewhat reduced because the alternative defence of diminished responsibility is available to cover cases where an illness supervenes with a less definite relationship to the birth or lactation.

A woman who had been suffering from schizophrenia for some years became pregnant. She feared understandably that her medication would be present in her own breast milk and therefore refused to accept it in the last month of her pregnancy. Within days of the child being born she became grossly psychotic and she came to believe the child was in terrible danger and, as a result, she killed it. In her case the choice of a defence under the Infanticide Act or the Homicide Act was available to her. She could have claimed that the balance of her mind had been disturbed from the effect of giving birth to the child as it could be argued that it lead to an exacerbation of her illness. On the other hand she could have claimed that she had diminished responsibility under the Homicide Act because of the mental abnormality (her mental illness) which substantially diminished her responsibility. Her plea of diminished responsibility was accepted and a hospital order was made.

A report putting forward an infanticide plea in this case might conclude:

'Opinion:
(1) The defendant is fit to plead and stand trial.
(2) Although mentally ill at the time of the offence the defendant was not insane within the McNaughten Rules.
(3) At the time of the offence the balance of the defendant's mind was disturbed (as described above) within the meaning of the Infanticide Act. The disturbance results from the effect of giving birth to the child.
(4) At the present time the defendant suffers from the mental illness of schizophrenia characterised in her case by delusional ideas. She requires treatment within a psychiatric hospital. The court may feel that a hospital order (under Section 37, Mental Health Act 1983) would be appropriate with a restriction order unlimited in time. A bed will be available at Barchester Hospital within 28 days of the order being made should the court feel this to be an appropriate disposal.'

Multiple homicide

There have been a number of cases over recent years, which have focused attention on murderers who have several victims. The newspaper reports of such dramatic cases suggest that the incidence may be increasing. Multiple 'murderers' may be classified into those with multiple victims from one event as in atrocities of war, terrorist or organised criminal activities, or the so-called 'mass murderer' in which, typically, a non-psychotic white male, aged 20–30 years, creates a dramatic scenario by going berserk with a firearm killing a number of strangers, often ending by being killed or taking his own life. The act is believed to represent a boiling up at deep felt resentments and anger at life's frustrations and personal difficulties. Sometimes the offence seems a 'copycat' of a similar dramatic offence committed elsewhere in the world. The last category of this classification involves the killing of a specific group e.g. the killing of the offender's family during a depressive or psychotic illness.

There are also murderers with a number of single victims killed separately over a period of time, such as criminal or terrorist assassinations, 'serial killers' – people who kill repeatedly, motivated by psychological needs. Of these, four main types can be recognised.

- Psychotically motivated killings, such as the repetitive killing of prostitutes in response to hallucinatory voices and delusional beliefs. The killings are usually (in the UK) by strangulation or battering.
- Sexually motivated, sadistic killings, where the victims may be tortured or bizarrely mutilated. The offenders, typically white, males aged 25–35 years, are normally reserved, quiet and conforming in appearance. They pick strangers as victims and plan the offence. Persistently escalating violent sexual fantasies underlie the behaviour.[44] The offences may be associated with deviant sexual behaviour (e.g. fetishism, cross-dressing, voyeurism).
- The killing of consecutive babies by psychopathic mothers as an expression of an unwillingness or inability to cope (see the section on neonaticide in Chapter 13).
- Psychopathic offenders who are preoccupied by and enjoy thoughts of killing or experimenting on others, e.g. by poisoning.

Aftermath of homicide and other serious offences

The psychological shock waves caused by the offence pass not only to the surviving victims (and offender) but also to the relatives of the victim, especially to any children of the victim or the offender (see Chapter 5 Effects of crime on victims).

Children

Black[45] has drawn attention to the disturbances which occur in the children of men who kill their wives. They may develop in reaction to the violence and double loss (death of mother, imprisonment of father) both a pathological grief reaction (repressed or extended) and a post-traumatic syndrome with intrusive thoughts, nightmares, fears, anxiety and increased arousal and sensitivity. Black recommends referring the child to a special child psychiatric team with experience in this field. The children should give, within 24 hours, a comprehensive account of the offence and their feelings. The child should be taken into wardship or social work care and great care taken with placement and future access. It is asserted that it should be generally assumed that contact with the father will be therapeutic.

The offender

The offender who has killed a friend or relative not only has to come to terms with his own behaviour, to understand it and digest it, he must also come to terms with his feelings of guilt and loss and feelings of ambivalence towards the victim. In those who were mentally ill at the time of the offence the process has to be integrated with knowledge of the illness.

After a psychotic killing, counselling will help the patient understand his illness and its effect on reducing his responsibility or even absolving him from responsibility for the act and give the patient an understanding of the need to monitor his illness in the future. A depressive illness may be exacerbated by the offence or mistaken for a grief reaction. On the other hand a grief reaction may be suppressed by enthusiastic treatment for a supposed depression.[46]

The victim

Of victims who survive a serious crime, 90% will have psychological after effects up to 30 months later to a greater or lesser extent.[47] Sexual assault victims are likely to be the most disturbed. Voluntary victim support agencies have sprung up to assist, both with material advice (insurance and security etc.) but also psychological support. Specialist support has been developed for rape victims, battered wives, and sexually assaulted females. The Criminal Injuries Compensation Scheme also gives, on application, financial compensation to injured victims.

Lesser (non-sexual) offences against the person and psychiatric assessment

Psychiatric assessment

The principles of the assessment are the same as for those accused of murder. The psychiatrist will require a full history from the defendant, a copy of the prosecution statements, a copy of previous convictions, social reports and an interview with relatives, if indicated. Information must be obtained of any previous psychiatric care, and contact should be made with the probation officer or social worker involved.

Where will the assessment be done?

The more serious the case the more likely the offender will be remanded in custody. A number of cases will be remanded on bail and can be assessed in outpatients.

Who will do the assessment?

A report will be requested only on a fraction of those charged with assault. Factors which will lead to the request of a report include any known mental disorder, bizarre behaviour in court, bizarreness of the offence, a recommendation of the probation officer, and the request of a solicitor. If the defendant is in custody, and the court requests the report, then the prison medical officers will be the doctors principally involved. A solicitor, on the other hand, may instruct a psychiatrist to go to the prison to prepare a report independently, whether or not the court has requested a report. If needed, a request for a remand to hospital (Section 35, Mental Health Act 1983) can be requested (see Chapter 4). When a psychiatric disorder requiring treatment is discovered then whoever is seeing the case will have to ensure that a second medical report is available if a recommendation for a hospital order or trial of treatment is required. It will also be necessary to ensure that a hospital bed can be made available in case the court wants to take up the recommendation to place the offender in a hospital. Offenders on bail may be assessed at the request of the court or the solicitors. Identical arrangements must be made as above if an order under the Mental Health Act is to be made.

What questions does the psychiatrist consider?

The defences of diminished responsibility and infanticide are limited to the charge of murder. The 'defences' of being unfit to plead or insanity are available to any offender though both are rarely used, particularly the latter. The insanity defence under the new Criminal Procedure (Insanity and Unfitness to Plead) Act 1991 may be used more than it was now that courts have wider powers (see Chapter 3). While automatism is a possible plea it is also very rare. Psychiatrists' reports, therefore, are used principally in mitigating the sentence. A psychiatrist will ask the following questions of the case.

(1) Is the defendant fit to plead or insane within the 1991 Act?
(2) Is the defendant suffering from a mental abnormality?
(3) Is enough known about the case to reach a diagnosis or is it necessary to recommend admission to hospital for observation under Section 35?
(4) Does the defendant suffer from a psychiatric disorder for which it would be appropriate to recommend a hospital order under Section 37 of the Mental Health Act? If so, should one also recommend a restriction order under Section 41?
(5) Is the disorder such that a trial of treatment would be indicated under Section 38 rather than making a recommendation immediately for a hospital order under Section 37? This might be most appropriate in cases of psychopathic disorder or mental impairment where it is unclear how the subject will respond to psychiatric treatment.
(6) Where should the treatment be given (taking the dangerousness of the patient and the safety of the public into account):
    (a) ordinary psychiatric hospital, which might include a low secure unit;
    (b) medium secure unit;
    (c) special hospital?
(7) Does the defendant suffer from a lesser degree of psychiatric disorder such that he does not fall within Mental Health Act definitions, or does not require to be in hospital for treatment? In this case treatment might be offered as a condition of probation or on a voluntary basis. The court may prefer to place the defendant on probation. If the patient then refuses to cooperate with treatment, or his behaviour gives cause for anxiety in other ways, then the probation officer will be able to bring the defendant before the court again for the case to be reconsidered. This approach can be very useful in the case of personality disordered people who benefit from support, and also some psychotic people who would benefit from support and continued medication whilst in the community. Although it is well recognised that the powers under guardianship orders are limited, they are used only with the agreement of the local social services department.
(8) If the defendant has no disorder requiring psychiatric intervention, are there psychological or social problems which may be assisted in other ways? The psychiatrist may feel, after discussion with the probation officer, that the defendant would benefit from a simple probation order or probation combined with placement in a probation hostel, or a

placement in a specialised hostel such as a therapeutic community run by a voluntary body.

(9) What is the prognosis of the case; what are the chances of violent behaviour continuing or getting worse? The psychiatrist will need to have a clear idea of the pattern of violence in the defendant's life, how easily violence occurs and the situations in which it does occur, in order to give his mind to this question. The court will want an estimate of the likelihood of the interventions proposed by the psychiatrist altering the chances of assaultive behaviour continuing.

Domestic violence

Since the late 1960s, there has been an increased appreciation of the extent and severity of violence within the home, much of which has been and still is, hidden away. Domestic violence encompasses the violence between man and wife (or cohabitant) and perhaps should include all violence to children within the home. Psychological abuse and severe intimidation may also be used to the same ends. All these behaviours are often coupled with excessive jealousy, restraints on movements and control of money. The literature has been extensively reviewed by Smith.[48]

Incidence

Few of the violent incidents are reported to the police. The victims are too fearful or ashamed to report the violence or they hope that matters will spontaneously improve. In studying the incidence there are problems in deciding how violent the acts should be to count as domestic violence. In the USA it was found that in 25% of marriages, at some point one partner would push, shove or grab the other but there was severe violence (punching, biting, kicking, hitting with an object, beating up, or threatening with a weapon) at some point in 13% of marriages. The most severe (beating up or using a weapon) would occur at some point in 5% of marriages.

Such surveys have also revealed that wives attack the husbands only slightly less frequently but it seems that this is less violent and generally a defence response to the husband's violence. The British Crime Survey[4] found that those at greatest risk of violence are young women (aged 16–24 years), of whom 2.3% were victims in 1997. The next highest group were young men (1.6% in 1997). The risk of domestic violence was greatest in those people who were separated but not divorced. One-third of offenders admitted being under the influence of alcohol at the time and 13% were intoxicated with drugs. The victims of domestic violence were kicked and/or punched in two-thirds of cases. Weapons were used in 11% of incidents. It was believed that there was a greater reluctance to disclose domestic violence than other types of violence. It was likely that less serious violence was not reported to the researchers.

Aetiology

This is best considered as the end product of a number of factors. Background factors in individual cases may include the offender being exposed to domestic violence as a child (occurs in approximately 50% of wife abusers) and belonging to a family or culture in which dominance of the wife and the use of violence in family discord are implicit. Additional factors will include stresses such as unemployment, poverty (the majority of wife abusing occurs in lower socio-economic groups) work problems and frustrations and the effects of alcohol (as demonstrated in the BCS). The attack may arise due to the disinhibiting effects of alcohol on the angry fulminating husband or the precipitating effects of minor or imagined slights, jealousy or 'insubordination'. Studies of the individuals who have killed or attacked their spouse reveal patterns of repetitive violence, alcohol abuse, neurotic and personality difficulties. Actual mental illness seemed to be rare. How much the victim precipitates the violence, encourages it or accepts it, is unresolved.

Management

In general terms attempts to reduce the violence include the following.

(1) *Offering refuge to the battered spouse:* this provision began on a voluntary basis and is now widespread.
(2) *Providing counselling and group work with the battering husbands* (with or without their wives): this has been offered extensively but the recruitment rate of husbands is low and the drop-out from counselling high. There is therefore very little evidence of overall success.
(3) *Encouraging the police to arrest and hold the offender in police cells* (usually after a call to the home). Studies from Canada and the USA suggest that this approach may be the most effective way of inhibiting the violence. Whether a court appearance and a heavy sentence would increase the inhibition is unknown. There is some evidence to suggest that a court order for mandatory attendance at the counselling group increases effectiveness but the work awaits confirmation by other studies.[48]
(4) Rehabilitating the victim and the children is also a problem. Anecdotal accounts suggest that a great deal seems to be gained by the victim from the support received by other victims, either in the refuge or from groups. Attention has to be given to the children to help put their experience into perspective and break the cycle of generational transmission of violence. The emotional disturbance and feelings which

follow domestic violence (nervousness, distress, guilt feelings) must also be dealt with in children.

Non-accidental injury to children

Non-accidental injury covers those injuries sustained by children through violence and is a concept which is a development of the battered baby syndrome.

Examination of the defendant

The conclusion that the child has suffered an injury will rest on medical findings. The decision to prosecute will rest with the police. In order to assess the defendant it is necessary to have available:

(1) descriptions of the injuries;
(2) interviews with, or statements from, people who can give a description of the children and their relationship with the defendants; and
(3) interviews with the defendants.

Oliver[49] has described how easy it is to be deceived and overlook child abuse in those chaotic families where abuse is transmitted through the generations. Abuse is associated with bigger, more mobile, poorer families. Unemployment, criminality, young motherhood and substitute fathers are other features associated with abuse.

Classification by motive

Scott[50] proposed the following classification of motives:

(1) a desire to rid the defendant of an encumbrance;
(2) a desire to relieve suffering (mercy killing);
(3) a motive arising directly from frank mental illness;
(4) a displacing onto the child of anger, frustration or retaliation arising from elsewhere ('He is not going to get away with it – if I cannot have the children then neither shall he');
(5) a desire to stop the immediate infuriating and frustrating behaviour of the child, e.g. persistent crying, screaming, soiling.

As in most offences, the motives can be seen to be numerous and to reflect all aspects of human emotion, anger, pity, jealousy and resentment, as well as possibly being due to mental disturbance.

Management of the situation

The prevention of the offence must be the first priority. In the special case of non-accidental injury recommendations for the early recognition of children at risk include an effective at-risk register, more health visitors, better nursery facilities, more links between school and primary care services and greater public and professional awareness. The legal aspects (Children Act 1989) involve steps to protect the child and promote its welfare through the use of various orders (emergency protection, child assessment, care orders). There may also be prosecution of the offenders. This subject is discussed in more detail in Chapter 13.

References

(1) Home Office (1998) *Violence: Reforming the Offences Against the Person Act 1861*. Home Office: London.

(2) Cordess, C. (1990) Criminal poisoning and the psychopathology of the poisoner. *Journal of Forensic Psychiatry* **1**, 213–26.

(3) Bowden, P. (1996) Graham Young (1947–90); the St Albans poisoner: his life and times. *Criminal Behaviour and Mental Health* (Supplement) 17–24.

(4) Mirrlees-Black, C., Budd, T., Partridge, S. and Mayhew, P. (1998) *The 1998 British Crime Survey*. Home Office Statistical Bulletin 21/98.

(5) Home Office (1998) *Criminal Statistics England and Wales 1997*. Cmnd 4162. The Stationery Office: London.

(6) Brizer, D.A. and Crowner, M. (1989) Predicting careers of criminal violence: Descriptive data and predispositional factors. In: *Current Approaches to the Prediction of Violence* (eds A. Brizer and M. Crown). American Psychiatric Press: Washington.

(7) d'Orban, P.J. and O'Connor, A. (1989) Women who kill parents. *British Journal of Psychiatry* **154**, 27–33.

(8) Bornstein, P.H., Hamilton, S.B., and McFall, M.E. (1981) Modification of adult aggression: a critical review of theory, research, and practice. *Progress in Behaviour Modification*, **12**, 299–350.

(9) Glynn Owens, R. and Bogshaw, M. (1985) First steps in the functional analysis of aggression. In: *Current Issues in Clinical Psychology*, Vol. II. (ed. E. Karas) Plenum Press: New York and London.

(10) Lorenz, K. (1966) *On Aggression*. Harcourt: New York.

(11) Dollard, J., Doob, L.W., Miller, N.E., Mowrer, O.H. and Sears, R.R. (1939) *Frustration and Aggression*. Yale University Press: New Haven, Connecticut.

(12) Bandura, A. (1977) *Social Learning Theory*. Prentice Hall: Englewood Cliffs, N.J.

(13) Hodge, J.E. (1992) Addiction to violence: a new model of psychopathy. *Criminal Behaviour and Mental Health* **2**, 212–23.

(14) Widon, C.S. (1989) The cycle of violence. *Science* **244**, 160–6.

(15) Toch, H. (1969) *Violent Men*. Aldine: Chicago.

(16) Howells, K. and Hollin, C.R. (1989) *Clinical Approaches to Violence*. Wiley: Chichester.

(17) Megargee, E.I. (1966) Undercontrolled and overcontrolled personality types in extreme anti-social aggression. *Psychological Monographs*, **80**. Whole no. 611.

(18) Blackburn, R. (1986) Patterns of personality deviation among violent offenders: replication and extension of an empirical taxonomy. *British Journal of Criminology* **26**, 254–69.

(19) Wolfgang, M.E. and Ferracuti (1967) *The Subculture of Violence*. Barnes and Noble: New York.

(20) Bluglass, R. (1979) The psychiatric assessment of homicide. *British Journal of Hospital Medicine* **22**, 366–77.

(21) Gayford, J.J. (1979) Battered wives. *British Journal of Hospital Medicine*. November 496–503.

(22) Shepherd, J., Irish, M. and Scully, C. (1988) Alcohol intoxication and severity of injury in victims of assault. *British Medical Journal* **296**, 1299.

(23) Walmsley, R. (1986) *Personal Violence*. Home Office Research Study 89. HMSO: London.

(24) Virkkunen, M. (1992) Brain serotonin and violent behaviour. *Journal of Forensic Psychiatry* **3**, 171–4.

(25) Steadman, H. and Cocozza, J. (1994) *Careers of the Criminally Insane*. Lexington Books: Lexington, Mass.

(26) Hafner, H. and Boker, W. (1973) *Crimes of Violence by Mentally Abnormal Offenders* (Translated H. Marshall 1984). Cambridge University Press: Cambridge.

(27) Humphreys, M.S., Johnstone, E.C., MacMillan, J.F. and Taylor, P.J. (1992) Dangerous behaviour preceding first admissions for schizophrenia. *British Journal of Psychiatry* **161**, 501–5.

(28) Hodgins, S. (1993) The criminality of mentally disordered persons. In: *Mental Disorder and Crime*. (ed S. Hodgins). Sage: Newbury Park.

(29) Lindquist, P. and Allebeck, P. (1990) Schizophrenia and crime. *British Journal of Psychiatry* **157**, 345–50.

(30) Monahan, J. and Steadman, H.J. (1994) *Violence and Mental Disorder*. University of Chicago Press: London.

(31) Swanson, J.W., Holzer, C.E., Ganju, V.K. and Jono, R.T. (1990) Violence and psychiatric disorder in the community: evidence from epidemiological catchment area surveys. *Hospital and Community Psychiatry* **41**, 761–70.

(32) Link, B.G., Andrews, H. and Cullen, F. (1992) The violent and illegal behaviour of mental patients reconsidered. *American Sociological Review* **57**, 275–92.

(33) Mulvey, E.P. (1994) Assessing the evidence of a link between mental illness and violence. *Hospital and Community Psychiatry* **45**(7), 663–8.

(34) Link, B.G. and Stueve, A. (1994) Psychotic symptoms and the violent/illegal behaviour of mental patients compared to community controls. In: *Violence and Mental Disorder* pp 137–159 (eds J. Monahan and H.J. Steadman). University of Chicago Press: London.

(35) Swanson, J., Borum, R., Swartz, M.S. and Monahan, J. (1996) Psychotic symptoms and disorders and the risk of violent behaviour in the community. *Criminal Behaviour and Mental Health* **6**, 309–29.

(36) Steadman, H.J., Mulvey, E.P., Monahan, J., Robbins, P.C., Appelbaum, P.S., Grisso, T., Roth, L.H. and Silver, E. (1998) Violence by people discharged from acute psychiatric in-patient facilities and others in the same neighbourhoods. *Archives of General Psychiatry* **55**, 393–401.

(37) Mackay, R.D. (1995) *Mental Condition Defences in the Criminal Law*. Clarendon Press: Oxford.

(38) Coid, J. (1983) The epidemiology of abnormal homicide and murder followed by suicide. *Psychological Medicine* **13**, 855–60.

(39) Coid, J. (1996) Dangerous patients with mental illness: increased risks warrant new policies, adequate resources and appropriate legislation. *British Medical Journal* **312**, 965–6.

(40) Taylor, P.J. and Gunn, J. (1999) Homicides by people with mental illness: myth and reality. *British Journal of Psychiatry* **174**, 9–14.

(41) Appleby, L. (1997) *National Confidential Inquiry into Suicide and Homicide by People with Mental Illness*. Department of Health: London.

(42) Hamilton, J. (1990) Manslaughter: assessment for court. In: *Principles and Practice of Forensic Psychiatry* pp 205–214 (eds R. Bluglass and P. Bowden). Churchill Livingstone: Edinburgh.

(43) Fenwick, P. (1990) Automatism, medicine and the law. *Psychological Medicine*, (Monograph Supplement) 17.

(44) Prenky, R.A., Burgess, A.W. *et al.* (1989) The presumptive role of fantasy in serial sexual homicide. *Americal Journal Of Psychiatry* **146**, 887–91.

(45) Black, D. and Caplan, T. (1988) Father kills mother. *British Journal of Psychiatry* **153**, 624–30.

(46) Fraser, K.A. (1988) Bereavement in those who have killed. *Medicine, Science and the Law* **28**, 127–30.

(47) Shapland, J., Willmore, J. and Duff P. (1985) *Victims in the Criminal Justice System*. Cambridge Studies in Criminology LIII, Gower: Aldershot.

(48) Smith, L.J.F. (1989) *Domestic Violence: An Overview of the Literature*. Home Office Research Study 107. HMSO: London.

(49) Oliver, J.E. (1988) Successive generations of child maltreatment. *British Journal of Psychiatry* **153**, 543–53.

(50) Scott, P.D. (1977) Non accidental injury in children: memorandum of evidence to the Parliamentary Select Committee on Violence in the Family. *British Journal of Psychiatry*, **131**, 366–80.

Chapter 8

Mental Illness and Forensic Psychiatry: The Functional Psychoses and Neuroses

Introduction

The legal term 'mental illness' as used in the Mental Health Act is undefined. It is used to cover the psychoses (organic and functional), neurotic disorders and various organic disorders. This chapter will deal with the functional psychoses and neuroses. The following chapter will deal with the organic brain syndromes. A particular weakness of classification and hence the arrangement of chapters in this textbook, is that it hides the considerable overlap between disorders. In forensic practice, particularly for prison psychiatry,[1] co-morbidity is the norm and it is this co-morbidity that leads to unsuccessful treatment before offending and to major difficulties in providing an effective service to mentally disordered offenders. Indeed co-morbidity may be a misleading term as these patients will have a complex mix of mental illness, abnormal personality traits and physical illness with attendant social problems from being 'difficult to place'.[2] People with personality disorder are particularly vulnerable to the development of affective, neurotic and paranoid disorders which will require treatment in their own right.[3] Co-morbidity of severe mental illness and substance misuse may be as high as 50% and the association of severe mental illness and violent offending is highest where there is co-morbid substance misuse.[4]

The organisation of mental health care is usually organised around particular patient groups and those with complex needs arising from co-morbidity may find themselves excluded from services. The need to integrate treatment services to account for patients with complex needs is one of the defining characteristics of forensic psychiatry.

The link between mental disorder (especially psychosis and substance misuse) and violence has been reviewed in Chapter 7. That section should be read in conjunction with this chapter. Chapter 5 reviews the general factors associated with criminal behaviour. Social and personal factors associated with crime will also make an individual vulnerable to mental disorder. Indirect evidence for this comes from the greatly increased prevalence of all forms of mental disorder amongst those in prison compared with the general population.[1]

When a mentally ill person commits a criminal act he may be 'excused' by those around him especially if he is already in psychiatric hands, and the case not then reported to the police. If the police become involved, they in turn may choose not to prosecute but simply ensure that the person receives appropriate health care. The decision whether or not to prosecute will depend in part on the readiness of the psychiatric services to take over the case. Where there is no help to be obtained from the services then the authorities may feel obliged to prosecute where otherwise they might wish not to. The more serious the case the more likely that prosecution will proceed. Clearly all these variables have to be born in mind when interpreting statistics.

Functional psychosis and crime: classification

The traditional division of psychotic and neurotic has not been used in ICD-10. Disorders are grouped into themes, such as mood disorders. ICD-10 recognises:

- schizophrenia (sub-divided into various forms), schizotypal and delusional disorders (F20–F29) which includes those delusional states which are not organic nor yet clearly schizophrenia;
- mood (affective) disorders (F30–F39).

Schizophrenia

ICD-10 refers to delusions (bizarre, grandiose or persecutory), disordered thinking (interrupted and illogical flow of thought or incomprehensible speech), disturbed perceptions (hallucinations, feelings of passivity, ideas of reference), disturbed mood, disturbance of movements (catatonia, excitement, stupor) and deterioration in personality and functioning. The ICD-10 requires that the major symptoms be present for one month.

The relationship of offending to the illness
Wessely *et al.*,[5] utilising the Camberwell case register, addressed the question 'is schizophrenia associated with an increased risk and rate of offending?'. Their study concluded that those suffering from schizophrenia, whilst not having an overall increased risk of any criminal behaviour, did have an increased risk compared to other mental disorders of being convicted for violent offences. The evidence for a link between mental disorder and violence has been reviewed in Chapter 7 which concluded that there is

an increased risk of violence and hence conviction for violence for people with a psychotic illness but that association is less clear cut when there is no co-morbid substance misuse. The Office for National Statistics survey of psychiatric morbidity within prisons,[1] found prevalence rates for any functional psychosis in the year under scrutiny were 7% for male sentences, 10% for male remand and 14% for female prisoners compared to an exactly comparative figure in the general population of 0.4%. The results of this survey may require a revision of the above findings as bias on the part of courts in sentencing mentally disordered people or a bias arising from higher conviction rates for mentally disordered people would be unlikely to account for the a difference in prevalence rates between the prison population and the general population of this magnitude. These findings do not of course point to any causal link between crime and psychosis but point to an association.

The relationship between schizophrenia and violent offending has been studied more than links with other crimes. Taylor,[6] reviewing studies of this link, concluded that for people with schizophrenia who are convicted for violent offences, the violent acts occur after the illness starts in the vast majority of cases. The Northwick Park study of first episodes of schizophrenia[7] reported that of first episode patients, over a third had behaved violently in the month before they were admitted, including behaviour potentially threatening to the life of others and bizarre sexual behaviour. The police were involved with many of these patients prior to admission but hospitalisation resulted in charges being brought in only a minority.[7] Taylor[8] examined the evidence of schizophrenia among a consecutive sample of remands to Brixton Prison. Nearly 9% of consecutive remands had some form of psychosis and nearly all had active symptoms; of those charged with homicide there was a diagnosis of schizophrenia in 8%. The National Confidential Inquiry report into homicides by people with mental illness found that 5% of those convicted of homicide had symptoms of psychosis.[9] Contrary to the public perception of psychotic people, the victim is less likely to be a stranger and more likely to be a family member (a finding found more generally for violence in a community sample by Steadman *et al.*).[4]

Certain specific symptoms of schizophrenia have been linked to violence. Virkkunen,[10] studying a group of Finnish schizophrenics guilty of serious violence and a group guilty of arson found that one-third offended directly as a result of their hallucinations or delusions; the remaining two-thirds offended because of problems arising from the stresses produced within the family. Threat/control override symptoms (described in detail in Chapter 7) have been linked directly to violence. When experiencing symptoms that take away their sense of personal autonomy and control, patients can believe that they are acting reasonably to counter a threat against them ('rationality within irrationality').

Psychotic patients with delusions who act violently on their beliefs have been distinguished from those who do not by their preoccupation with seeking evidence for their beliefs, a conviction that they had found evidence for that belief and affective changes, particularly depression, anger or fearfulness resulting from preoccupation with delusional beliefs.[11] In the Brixton studies of Taylor *et al.*,[12] passivity delusions, religious delusions and delusions of influence were significantly more likely to be associated with violent action.

The risk associated with active symptoms of schizophrenia, including threat/override symptoms, is increased considerably by substance misuse. The importance of this latter factor is highlighted by the finding by Steadman *et al.*[4] that when substance misuse is controlled for, violence amongst recently discharged psychiatric patients is no higher than that of the general population. Hallucinations, when part of the illness, are most commonly associated with violence where they are command hallucinations or where hallucinatory tastes or smells are interpreted as 'evidence' to support delusions of control. The contribution of abnormal personality development to offending in schizophrenic subjects (whether as a co-morbid condition or resulting from the illness itself) as a contributory factor to offending among schizophrenic patients is less well studied.

Medicolegal aspects of schizophrenia

Schizophrenia is clearly a condition where a psychiatric disposal is required. It is not necessary that there must be a direct link between the psychotic experiences and the offence. It is quite sufficient for the subject to be ill. Generally, in practice, if the crime is not linked to positive psychotic features it will be linked to the deterioration in the patient's personality caused by the illness. Whilst it is, of course, possible to come across subjects whose offence is part of a lifelong pattern of criminality and who have, incidentally, developed schizophrenia, it is proper to offer psychiatric treatment if the subject currently requires it. This does not always happen, especially where hospital facilities are unsatisfactory. If, on the other hand, the subject offends as part of his criminal career whilst in full remission, then he is held responsible for his actions. The schizophrenia may be so severe as to render a subject unfit to plead. The illness is regarded as a basis for diminished responsibility in cases of homicide and may even bring the subject within the McNaughten Rules.

Delusional (paranoid) disorders

ICD-10 provides diagnostic guidelines for delusional disorder, which has replaced the older term paranoid disorder. These disorders include persecutory subtypes, litigious paranoia, and what Mullen[13] terms disorders of passion (erotomania and pathological jealousy). Individuals with these disorders do not often seek psychiatric help, but come to the attention of forensic services where offending leads to court referral for assessment in custody. The beliefs that are termed delusional exist in continuum with normally occurring emotions and beliefs. Particularly in relationship to morbid jealousy, overvalued ideas merge imperceptibly with delusions. Delusional disorders can arise as primary disorder or as a symptom complex within another disorder such as schizophrenia.

Paranoid states and the incidence of crime
In the literature on the relationship between mental disorder and crime, particularly violence, delusional disorders are often considered together with schizophrenia and therefore findings in relation to schizophrenia may apply to the delusional disorders. In particular the findings, concerning delusions described above[10, 11] are particularly important.

Disorders of passion: pathological jealousy and erotomania
Mullen[13] comprehensively reviews this group of disorders. The central belief in morbid jealousy centres on being a victim of infidelity, which dominates the thinking and action to a pathological degree. Jealousy is a normal phenomenon and the degree to which it is tolerated has a cultural dimension. Mullen[13] proposes that there is a continuum from deeply held convictions of normal individuals to overvalued ideas to delusional ideas in both morbid jealousy and erotomania. Jealousy has been found to be an important cause of violence in battered/abused wives studied. Partners are the usual victims of assault, whilst perceived rivals are infrequently victims. As well as actual assault, it is now recognised that partners of pathologically jealous people can experience intense psychological distress, including post traumatic stress disorder.[14]

Erotomania is characterised by a morbid belief in being loved. Mullen[13] proposes that there are three essential criteria:

(1) The convictions of being loved, despite the supposed lover having done nothing to encourage it.
(2) A propensity to reinterpret the words and actions of the object of their attention to maintain the belief.
(3) Preoccupation with the supposed love which comes to form a central part of the subject's existence.

It is not necessary for the individual to believe that their love is reciprocated (morbid infatuation). As with morbid jealousy, erotomania can occur as part of another disorder, usually schizophrenia or mood disorder. Schizophrenic subjects differ from pure erotomania in that the object of their love or infatuation can change over time and have a greater sexual element.[15] The objects for attention for erotomanic subjects are usually drawn from the patient's immediate environment although media coverage concentrates on cases where a prominent public figure is involved. Health professionals, who would presumably include psychiatrists, who encounter and help vulnerable people, are particularly susceptible to be the victims of the erotomanic.[13]

Mullen[13] considers stalking to be an almost inevitable accompaniment of erotomanic disorders. Stalking involves a determined effort to make contact or communicate with the object of the stalker's attention. When approaches are rebuffed, threatening, abusive or intimidating behaviour occur either face to face or through other modes of communication. Menzies *et al*.[16] report frank sexual intimidation or attack occurring in their series of male erotomanics. Both Mullen and Pathé[15] and Menzies *et al*.[16] found high levels of threatening and assaultive behaviour in their series of stalkers, though both series were drawn from the forensic population, therefore over-estimating the risk of actual assault. Nevertheless, the victims of stalking can be seriously traumatised through the repeated and unpredictable intrusions by the stalker. Many curtail their social lives, change or abandon their employment and in more extreme cases, change country to escape the unwanted attention.[14]

Medicolegal aspects of delusional disorder

The comments above on the medicolegal aspects of schizophrenia can be equally applied to patients with delusional disorder. For that group of patients with delusional disorder manifesting in morbid jealousy or erotomania, special considerations apply.

Where the cause of the jealousy rests in the delusional state, the underlying mental illness can form the basis of a recommendation for psychiatric treatment or the basis for a defence of diminished responsibility in cases of homicide. Where the jealousy is not delusional but has a neurotic cause then the medicolegal aspects are much less clear. There may be an associated personality disorder that falls into the 'psychopathic disorder' group. There may be other disturbance that may be classifiable as mental illness. Excessive jealousy would not, without underlying illness, be grounds for a medical defence.

In delusional jealousy very careful consideration has to be given to the security aspect of psychiatric care. The persistence of the disorder and its potential dangerousness is well known. The patient must be carefully assessed for co-operativeness and the risk of absconding and committing a violent offence. When the subject is known to be uncooperative, to have made violent attacks on the spouse, and to have absconded, he should be treated initially in some degree of security. Treatment may be difficult. Medication (antipsychotic or antidepressant) and cognitive therapy[10] may offer the best chance of improvement.

The medicolegal aspects of stalking are receiving increasing attention. Psychiatrists may be involved in providing evidence to court on the damage done to the victim in the same way as a physician may be involved in describing the injuries to a victim in physical assault. This gives rise to the charge of psychological GBH in stalking cases. The psychiatrist may also be involved with the perpetrator. As with morbid jealousy, the treatment of morbid love or infatuation is difficult and the results unpredictable. Given the persistence and tenacity with which such beliefs are adhered to, treatment and support through mental health services may be the only means available to provide victims with a degree of protection from the stalker. It is likely that psychiatric services, particularly forensic services will be increasingly called upon to provide advice to the courts and potential treatment to the perpetrator in these cases.

Mood disorders (affective psychoses)

The serious mood disorders are characterised by a severe disturbance of mood (depression and anxiety or elation and excitement) possibly accompanied by any of the following: delusions, perplexity, disturbed attitude to self, disorders of perception and behaviour, all in keeping with the subject's prevailing mood. Predominantly depressed, or manic or mixed (circular) forms are recognised.

Incidence of mood disorders and crime
The relationship between mood disorders and crime is not so well studied as that between schizophrenia and crime. In the Office of National Statistics survey of mental disorder in prison,[1] schizophrenic or delusional disorders were more common than affective disorder.

Relation of offending to mood disorders
Depressive and manic states can lead directly to offending. Whilst any offence may be committed because of an affective disorder, several well known associations are recognised:

(1) *Depression and homicide:* Severe depression can lead the subject to the view that everything is hopeless and that there is no further purpose in living and that death is the only solution. In some cases the homicide will be followed by suicide. The rate of suicide after homicide has varied in different studies.[18] West[19] found that a high proportion of the suicides were associated with a mental abnormality of which depression was a prominent condition.

(2) *Depression and infanticide:* In such a case the killing of the child may arise directly from delusions or hallucinations. On the other hand, the violent act may arise from the irritability associated with the disturbed affective state.

(3) *Depression and theft:* In severe depression there are several possible associations with theft:
  (a) the theft may represent a regressive, comforting act;
  (b) the theft may be an attempt to draw attention to the plight of the subject;

    (c) the act may not be a true theft but an absent-minded act in the distracted state of depression.
(4) *Depression and arson:* In this association the arson may be an attempt to destroy something due to feelings of hopelessness and despair, or the arson may, through its destructive effects, reduce the subject's feeling of tension and dysphoria.
(5) *Depression, alcoholism and offending:* Prolonged alcohol abuse may induce feelings of depression or depression may lead to alcohol abuse. The disinhibiting combination of alcohol and depression may then lead to offending, including sexual offending.
(6) *Depression and the explosive personality:* Personality disordered people often seem less able to cope with depressive feelings. The tension engendered by the discomfort of the depression may be followed by outbursts of violence or destructive behaviour.
(7) *Depression and the adolescent offender:* In this association the depression may be masked. Acting out histrionic behaviour may be seen, as may conduct disorder such as persistent stealing. There is usually a history of normal behaviour and personality in the past.
(8) *Depression relieved by the offence:* A number of writers have drawn attention to the phenomena of depression and tension appearing to be relieved by a violent act. A history of depression is obtained up to the act but afterwards the subject appears free of it. This, clinically, is seen most in personality disordered subjects.
(9) *Manic states and offending:* In mania the patient may be subject to elation with hallucinations or grandiose delusions which may lead to offending. The combination of poor judgement and substance misuse in mania may lead to socially offensive behaviour.

Medicolegal aspects of mood disorder

The major mood disorders are grounds for a psychiatric defence and should lead to a psychiatric recommendation. In severe cases, particularly in mania, the disorder may be so severe as to make the subject unfit to plead. In homicide cases a plea of diminished responsibility would normally be appropriate and where delusions or hallucinatory experiences have been present the subject may fall within the McNaughten Rules. Which hospital takes the patient depends on whether the patient is violent, uncooperative and determined to repeat the behaviour or not.

Other non-organic psychoses

This category includes a small group of psychoses (mood or delusional disorders) generally of an acute and transient nature and often appearing clinically to be largely, or wholly, attributable to a recent life experience (a reactive psychosis).

Medicolegal aspects
The relation of the illness to the offending is the same as with other psychotic illness. Despite the reactive nature of these illnesses they are such as to form the basis of a psychiatric defence.

The neuroses and crime
The ICD-10 brings together neurotic, stress-related and somatoform disorders in one large group (F40–49) though depression of a neurotic type is classified with the mood disorders (F32). The ICD-10 recognises a variety of categories:

(1) *Phobic anxiety disorders* (F40) including agoraphobia, social phobias, and specific phobias.
(2) *Other anxiety disorders* (e.g. panic, mixed states) (F41) including panic disorders, generalised anxiety, mixed anxiety and depression.
(3) *Obsessive–compulsive disorder* (F42).
(4) *Reactions to severe stress and adjustment disorders* (F43) including acute stress reaction, post-traumatic stress disorder (PTSD), adjustment disorder.
(5) *Dissociative (conversion) disorders* (F44) including dissociative amnesia, dissociative fugue, dissociative stupor, trance and possession states, and dissociative disorders of movement and sensation. This group also includes 'Ganser syndrome' (see below) and 'multiple personality disorder'. The ICD-10 reports that controversy exists about the extent to which multiple personality is iatrogenic or culture specific. The diagnosis is rarely made in England[20] though it is used in the USA even as a psychiatric defence.[21] In England it is likely to be perceived as a dissociative reaction, possibly iatrogenic, to deal with dysphoria arising in a person with substantial personality difficulties.[22]
(6) *Somatoform disorders* (F45) including somatisation syndrome, hypochondriacal syndrome, and other somatoform syndromes.
(7) *Other neurotic disorders* (F48) including neurasthenia, depersonalisation–derealisation syndrome and various specific neurotic disorders such as *Koro and Dhat's syndrome*.

Incidence of crime in neuroses
The incidence is unknown. In a study of shoplifters[23] some 10% were found to be neurotic but there was no control study. The Office of National Statistics to the Prison Service[1] found that 59% of remand, 40% of sentenced male prisoners, 76% of female remand prisoners and 40% of sentenced female prisoners had a neurotic disorder. These figures are far higher than that found in the corresponding samples studied in the community. Co-morbidity with personality disorder and substance misuse is commonly found in those with neurotic disorders. Post traumatic stress was present in 5% of male remand, 3% of male sentence, 9% of female remand and 5% of female sentence prisoners.[1]

The relation of neuroses to crime

Clinically the most common neurotic conditions seen amongst offenders are anxiety states and neurotic depressions. Phobic and compulsive states seem the least common.

Demonstrating a high level of neurotic symptoms among offenders does not necessarily imply that there is a causal relationship between such symptoms and offending. Offending behaviour and neurotic symptoms are associated with similar social and personal circumstances so that they arise in the same individual without necessarily directly interacting. Studies of neurotic symptoms among prisoners[1] report significantly higher scores for neurotic symptoms among those with personality disorder. Significant substance misuse is associated with neurotic symptoms and personality disorder. Given the interaction between these disorders, it is exceedingly difficult to tease out the precise contribution of neurotic disorders to offending.

Neuroses and homicide

A reactive neurotic state (depression and/or anxiety) may be so severe that the concomitant tension leads to a homicidal outburst even where there is no evidence of personality disorder. Chronic reactive depression and moderately severe depression have both been accepted by the courts as grounds for a defence of diminished responsibility.

The neurotic condition may have considerable impact when combined with personality disorders, e.g. a neurotic depressive reaction in a person of explosive or antisocial personality. It may disinhibit the subject in a tense situation so that a homicidal outburst occurs, either to destroy the source of the frustration or to displace the tension onto an innocent person.

Neuroses and theft

Stealing may certainly be associated with neurotic depressive states (as has been shown in shoplifting) when the stealing is committed, perhaps to draw attention to the subject's plight or as a comforting activity. Such motivation is also seen in stealing by unhappy and disturbed children. The tension associated with the neurotic state may lead to stealing as a psychologically destructive act. The subject may reveal a history of depression though in some the associated behaviour disorder may be so gross as to divert attention from the underlying mental state.

Neuroses and arson

An association between neurotic states and arson is well recognised, particularly with states of tension. The fire may be a way of getting rid of tension, relieving depressive feelings or symbolically destroying the source of pain. The known co-morbidity of neurotic disorder with substance misuse and personality disorder may be particularly important in cases of arson.

Neuroses and alcohol related offences

Alcohol may induce a melancholic state. Alternatively neurotic conditions (e.g. depression or anxiety) may precipitate, in the susceptible, a bout of alcohol abuse. This combination may lead to offending, the alcohol serving to disinhibit the subject.

Post traumatic stress disorder

Research interest in post traumatic stress disorder (PTSD) is relatively new and is likely to be of increasing importance in forensic psychiatry. Reference has already been made to post traumatic stress disorder being used as the 'psychological damage of a crime of psychological GBH' in stalking cases. Trauma in childhood, physical abuse and more particularly sexual abuse is strongly linked to the abused person becoming a perpetrator or victimiser in adult life.[24, 25] A model of borderline personality disorder proposes that it arises directly as a result of prolonged repetitive trauma at the hands of primary carers in childhood.[25, 26] Such prolonged repetitive trauma may severely affect normal personality development. In adult life the resultant disorder of personality can be linked with repetitive maladaptive or violent behaviours which re-enact elements of the trauma experienced in childhood. Such individuals are often to be found in prison populations.

Certain features of PTSD can be linked to offending.[27] Sensation seeking ('addiction to trauma'), seeking punishment to reduce a sense of guilt and the development of co-morbid substance abuse may be linked with offending. During 'flashbacks' (intrusive experiences) an individual may react in an uncharacteristically violent fashion to environmental reminders of the original traumatic event. This phenomenon has been reported in Vietnam veterans and police officers who may find they react violently to trigger events that mirror the combat situation.[27]

Neuroses and imprisonment

Being imprisoned, either on remand or after conviction, may produce neurotic symptoms in the offender, such as anxiety or depression. It is therefore very important to separate the symptoms that occur after arrest, with any disorder that preceded and was relevant to the offence. Imprisonment is a frightening experience involving loss of autonomy, separation from family and friends and exposure to the direct stress of the institution. The ONS prison study[1] reported four problems: worry, fatigue, depression and irritability as the most common neurotic symptoms amongst prisoners. Prisoners have a significantly higher consultation rate with doctors compared with the general population.

There is one particular syndrome, *Ganser Syndrome*, which has been described as a reaction to imprisonment, classified in ICD-10 as a form of dissociative disorder (F44.8).

Ganser in 1897[28] described three prisoners who had become mentally disturbed with:

(1) an inability to answer correctly the simplest questions even though their reply indicated some understanding of the question, (Q. 'How many legs has a horse?' A. 'Three'; Q. 'An elephant?' A. 'Five'.);

(2) clouding of consciousness, (i.e. disorientated in place and time, distracted, perplexed, slow to respond and vacant as if lost in dreams);

(3) hysterical conversion syndromes, (e.g. widespread loss of pain over the entire body or areas hypersensitive to pain);

(4) hallucinations, (visual and/or auditory);

(5) a temporary abrupt end to the disturbance with a loss of all symptoms and a return of total clarity to be followed by a deep depression and a recurrence of symptoms.

Ganser was certain that the condition was not malingering but a genuine illness which he believed was hysterical in nature. He notes that his three cases had been preceded by an illness (typhus and two cases of head injury). The exact nature of the condition has been debated ever since. It is a rare condition in its full-blown syndrome and occurs in people other than prisoners though individual features may occur with any mental disorder.[29] It has been said to be a true transient psychosis or even malingering but probably the most commonly accepted English view is that it is a hysterical reaction resulting from a state of depression.[30] It is to be distinguished from malingering, pseudo-dementia, schizophrenia, and drug induced states.

Medicolegal aspects of neurotic illness

Where there is a clear-cut neurotic illness underlying the offending which is uncomplicated by any antisocial personality disorder, the courts may consider a recommendation for psychiatric treatment. Such consideration may even extend to the most serious of crimes, as in the young depressed man charged with the murder of his wife. Where the neurotic condition complicates a psychopathic disorder then the court's anxiety for the safety of the public or the court's lack of sympathy may lead, in serious cases, to a prison sentence. In cases where the public is not at risk (e.g. the depressed shoplifter) and where hospital is not required, then out-patient treatment as a condition of probation is commonly used.

Dissociative phenomena (including dissociative phenomena associated with post traumatic stress disorder) may be cited as grounds for a defence of automatism. Chapter 3 points out that the legal grounds for a defence of automatism are stringent and in dissociative state there will usually be partial awareness and partial memory making it difficult to sustain a defence of automatism. Post traumatic stress disorder may, in certain conditions of repetitive trauma of which 'battered women syndrome'[31] is the best known, may so sensitise the victim that relatively little provocation may lead to violence, the traumatised person reacting to subtle environmental cues that have previously indicated imminent violence. Particularly in the USA such syndromal evidence has successfully resulted in a defence of provocation, including homicide as 'self defence'.

Substance misuse, mental disorder and crime

Substance misuse can be linked to crime in a variety of ways.[32] The illegality of drugs makes their possession or supply a criminal offence. Acquisitive offending has an obvious link to crime, as it is the means to obtain funds for drugs. Estimates of the scale of such offending indicate that crack cocaine users and heroin users may annually need £20,000 or £10,000 respectively to finance their dependence.[32] Direct causal links between crime and substance misuse are difficult to prove as association with delinquent subcultures, premorbid personality characteristics and risk taking lifestyles confounds the misuse.[32] Both criminality and alcohol misuse have their peak at the same age and tend to reduce during the life cycle.[32]

There is a substantial body of evidence that violence is linked to substance misuse. This can arise through direct toxic effects of the drug or from the pharmacological effects of the substance taken, the linkage between substance misuse and subcultures of crime, psychiatric disorder associated with substance misuse, brain damage resulting from dependence and the deliberate use of drugs or alcohol to induce a state of mind that promotes violence.[2] Alcohol is the drug most clearly associated with violent crimes including domestic violence. Alcohol is an important situational factor in both perpetrators and victims of violent offences[33] but for homicide, alcohol may be more often a factor in male perpetrators than female.[34]

Violence amongst mentally ill people is of considerable public and medical concern. Recent research has shown that people with major mental disorder without substance misuse problems are no more likely to commit acts of violence in the community than a matched sample of people in the community not abusing substances.[4] The risk of violence amongst the mentally ill is substantially increased when there is a co-morbid substance misuse problem. Dependence upon drugs or alcohol is the single most important factor in determining which mentally ill people will react violently. Rates of substance misuse amongst patients with severe mental illness seem to be increasing.[2] Severely mentally ill people may use substances to promote social interaction, to belong to peer groups, to self-medicate for the dysphoric mood states of severe psychosis or indeed the positive symptoms particularly where side effects of neuroleptics lead to non-compliance, to counteract negative symptoms or deal with unpleasant drug side effects.[2]

The incidence of and response to substance misuse in prisons is considered in Chapter 1.

Medicolegal aspects of substance misuse.

The particular medicolegal aspects of substance misuse are dealt with in Chapter 3. Probation orders may facilitate offenders in seeking out community treatment for substance misuse and where substance misuse and mental illness co-exist then a probation order with a condition of treatment may be appropriate. Dual diagnosis patients will present particular problems for the courts and psychiatrists, there being a danger of such patients being rejected by all agencies. Specialist dual diagnosis services have been advocated for this group.[2] The development of district forensic psychiatry services may be a way forward in the UK.[36]

References

(1) Singleton, N., Meltzer, H. and Gatward, R. (1998) *Psychiatric morbidity among prisoners in England and Wales*. Office of National Statistics, The Stationery Office: London.

(2) Marshall, J. (1998) Dual diagnosis: co-morbidity of severe mental illness and substance misuse. *Journal of Forensic Psychiatry* **9** (1), 9–15.

(3) Vize, C. and Tyrer P. (1994) The relationship between personality and other psychiatric conditions. *Current Opinion in Psychiatry* **7**, 123–8.

(4) Steadman, H.J., Mulvey, E.P., Monahan, J., Robbins, P.C., Applebaum, P.S., Grisso, T., Roth, L.H. and Silver, E. (1998) Violence by people discharged from acute psychiatric in-patient facilities and by others in the same neighbourhoods. *Archives of General Psychiatry* **55**, 393–401.

(5) Wessely, S., Castle, D., Douglas, A. *et al.* (1994) The criminal careers of incident cases of schizophrenia. *Psychological Medicine* **24**, 483–502.

(6) Taylor, P.J. (1997) Damage disease and danger. *Criminal Behaviour and Mental Health* **7**, 19–48.

(7) Johnson, E.C., Crow, T.J., Johnson, A.L. and McMillan, J.F. (1986) The Northwick Park study of first episodes of schizophrenia. I: Presentation of the illness and problems relating to admission. *British Journal of Psychiatry* **148**, 115–20.

(8) Taylor, P.J. and Gunn, J. (1984) Violence and psychosis. I: Risk of violence among psychotic men. *British Medical Journal* **288**, 1945–9.

(9) *National Confidential Inquiry into Suicide and Homicide by People with Mental Illness* (1997) Progress report 1997. Department of Health: London.

(10) Virkkunen, M. (1974) Observation on violence in schizophrenia. *Acta Psychiatrica Scandinavica* **50**, 145–51.

(11) Buchanan, A. (1997) The investigation of acting on delusions as a tool for risk assessment in the mentally disordered. *British Journal of Psychiatry* **170** (suppl. 32), 12–16.

(12) Taylor, P.J. (1985) Motives for offending among violent and psychotic men. *British Journal of Psychiatry* **147**, 491–8.

(13) Mullen, P.E. (1997) Disorders of Passion. In: *Troublesome Disguises. Underdiagnosed Psychiatric Syndromes* (eds D. Bruga and A. Munro), Blackwell Science: Oxford.

(14) Pathé, M. and Mullen, P.E. (1997) The impact of stalkers on their victims. *British Journal of Psychiatry* **170**, 12–17.

(15) Mullen, P.E. and Pathé, M. (1994) The pathological extension of love. *British Journal of Psychiatry* **165**, 614–23.

(16) Menzies, R.P.D., Fedoroff, J.P., Green, C.M. and Isaacson, K. (1995) Prediction of dangerous behaviour in male erotomanics. *British Journal of Psychiatry* **166**, 529–36.

(17) Tarrier, N., Beckett, R., Harwood, S. and Bishay, N. (1990) Morbid jealousy: a review and cognitive–behavioural formulation. *British Journal of Psychiatry* **157**, 319–26.

(18) Coid, J. (1983) The epidemiology of abnormal homicide and murder followed by suicide. *Psychological Medicine* **13**, 855–60.

(19) West, D.J. (1965) *Murder followed by Suicide.* Heinemann: London.

(20) Mersky, H. (1992) The manufacture of personalities. *British Journal of Psychiatry* **160**, 327–40.

(21) James, D. and Schramm, M. (1998) Multiple personality disorder presenting to the English courts. *Journal of Forensic Psychiatry* **9** (3), 615–28.

(22) Fahy, T.A., Abas, M. and Brown, J.C. (1989) Multiple personality. *British Journal of Psychiatry* **154**, 99–101.

(23) Gibbens, T.C.N. and Prince, J. (1962) *Shoplifting.* The Institute for the Study and Treatment of Delinquency: London.

(24) Mezey, G. and King, M. (1989) The effects of sexual assault on men: a study of 22 victims. *Psychological Medicine* **19**, 205–9.

(25) Burgess, A.W., Hartman, C.R. and McCormick, A. (1987) Abused to abuser: antecedents of socially deviant behaviour. *American Journal of Psychiatry* **144**, 1431–6.

(26) Herman, J.L. and van der Kolk, B.A. (1987) Traumatic origins of borderline personality disorder. In: *Psychological Trauma* (ed. B.A. van der Kolk). American Psychiatric Press: Washington.

(27) Pitman, R.K., Sparr, L.F., Saunders, L.S. and McFarlane, A.G. (1996) Legal issues in post traumatic stress disorder. In: *Traumatic Stress* (eds. B.A. van der Kolk, A.G. McFarlane and L. Weisaeth) Guilford Press: New York.

(28) Ganser, S.J.M. (1897) A peculiar hysterical state. Reproduced in translation in *British Journal of Criminology* (1963) **5**, 120–6.

(29) Whitlock, F.A. (1967) The Ganser Syndrome. *British Journal of Psychiatry* **113**, 19–29.

(30) Trethowan, W.H. (1979) Some rarer psychiatric disorders. In: *Current Themes in Psychiatry* (eds R.N. Gaind and B.L. Hudson). Macmillan Press Ltd: London and Basingstoke.

(31) Goodstein, R.K. and Page, A.W. (1981) Battered wife syndrome: overview of dynamics and treatment. *American Journal of Psychiatry* **138**, 1036–44.

(32) South, N. (1997) Drugs: use, crime and control. In: *Oxford Handbook of Criminality* (eds M. Maguire, R. Morgan and R. Reiner) Clarendon Press: Oxford.

(33) Kerner, H-J., Weitkamp, E.G.M., Stelly, W. and Thomas, J. (1997) Patterns of criminality and alcohol abuse: results of Tuebingen criminal behaviour development study. *Criminal Behaviour and Mental Health* **7**, 401–20.

(34) Wolfgang, M.E. and Strohm, R.B. (1956) The relationship between alcohol and criminal homicide. *Quarterly Journal of Studies in Alcohol* **17**, 411–25.

(35) Mitchell, B. (1997) Diminished responsibility manslaughter. *Journal of Forensic Psychiatry* **8**, 101–117.

(36) Grounds, A. (1996) Forensic psychiatry for the millennium. *Journal of Forensic Psychiatry* **7**, 221–7.

Chapter 9

Mental Illness and Forensic Psychiatry: Organic Brain Syndromes

Introduction

Brain damage or dysfunction may be caused by a multitude of factors including difficulties during birth, infections, trauma, tumour, cerebro-vascular disorders, neurological disease, endocrine and metabolic disorders, vitamin deficiencies and toxic disorders. These various disorders, depending on their extent and site of action, may cause a number of organic brain syndromes including:

(1) dementia
(2) delirium (confusional state)
(3) epilepsy and its associated psychiatric conditions
(4) organic personality syndrome
(5) psychological sequelae of head injury
(6) organic psychoses
    (a) organic delusional syndrome
    (b) organic hallucinosis
    (c) organic mood disorder
(7) substance induced organic disorders
(8) amnesic syndrome.

This chapter will deal with some aspects of organic disorder in order to illustrate the working of forensic psychiatry in this field.

Dementia and forensic psychiatry

Dementia in ICD-10[1] is defined as a syndrome caused by disease of the brain, which is usually chronic or progressive. There are characteristic deficits of a number of higher cortical functions including memory, thinking, orientation, comprehension, calculation, capacity to learn, language and judgement. These occur in clear consciousness. There is often an accompanying deterioration in social behaviour and emotional control. The decline in cognitive abilities usually leads to significant problems with activities of daily living, including washing, dressing, eating, personal hygiene and toilet activities. The classification of the types of disorder is based on the underlying disease process. The main two are Alzheimer's disease and cerebro-vascular disease. Others include Pick's disease, Creutzfeld Jacob disease, Huntington's disease, Parkinson's disease and HIV disease. Lishman[2] defines dementia as 'an acquired global impairment of intellect, memory and personality but without impairment of consciousness'. To differentiate it from delirium or intoxication, the state of consciousness should not be clouded. There must be evidence of a specific organic factor which is aetiologically related to the disturbance or an organic factor can be presumed.

Dementia and the law

The effect of the dementia may be to increase the subject's irritability, aggressiveness or suspiciousness (which may lead to violence), or it may lead to disinhibition (leading to offences such as unwanted sexual behaviour) or forgetfulness (leading to behaviour such as absent-minded shoplifting). Dementia clearly falls under the definition of mental illness as defined in the Mental Health Act 1983. Dementia, therefore, can be used as a basis of a recommendation for treatment under the appropriate section of the Mental Health Act. The court is interested in the extent of the dementia and how it affects the offender's judgement and behaviour. The severity would be of relevance to the degree of mitigation or responsibility.

Delirium and forensic psychiatry

This is a state, due to many organic causes, of clouded consciousness coupled with confusion, disorientation, possibly with delusions, vivid hallucinations or illusions. It is this state of mind, not the underlying cause, which forms the basis of a medical defence. Offending in a state of organic delirium must be very rare. The appropriate disposal would depend on the clinical need. What defence was adopted would depend on the situation. It might be appropriate to plead not guilty because of lack of intent, or to ask for a hospital order (or some other form of treatment) on the grounds of mental illness, or to plead, in a very serious case, insanity under the McNaughten Rules.

Epilepsy, associated psychiatric conditions and forensic psychiatry

Epilepsy is classified in the ICD-10[1] as a disease of the nervous system and is not a mental disorder but it becomes important because of its effects on the mental state of the subject. Epilepsy is divided[2] into *generalised* and *focal* (or *partial*) epilepsy.

Generalised epilepsy is sub-divided into primary generalised epilepsy, of which there are two differing forms, a grand mal and petit mal; and secondary generalised epilepsy, which occurs when a focal epileptic seizure spreads to involve thalamo-cortical pathways causing a generalised seizure. This may lead to a grand mal attack with a preceding aura.

The grand mal attack is associated with a tonic phase followed by a clonic phase and a period of unconsciousness lasting several minutes. In the petit mal attack there are only momentary lapses of consciousness, the patient immediately resuming normal activity. An absence is evident to the observer only by transient blankness of facial expression and perhaps a slight twitching of limbs or eyelids, an akinetic seizure by a sudden fall and a myoclonic jerk by a flung out limb.

In focal (partial) epilepsy, such seizures begin in part of the cortex of the brain. The symptoms produced will therefore depend on the area of the brain that is affected. Whilst they involve only part of the brain then there may be a conscious sensation (aura). The nature of the sensation gives a clue to where the discharge is coming from. Focal epilepsy is divided in its turn into simple partial (focal) seizures without impairment of consciousness, and complex partial (focal) seizures with complex movements and impairment of consciousness (generally arising in the temporal lobe).

Epilepsy and behaviour

Epilepsy becomes of importance to the forensic psychiatrist because of its effects on consciousness (which may be associated with offending) and its possible aetiological association with behavioural disturbance (including offending) between fits.

Disturbance of consciousness associated with a fit

The following alterations of consciousness have been described by Fenton[3] and Lishman.[2]

The aura
This represents the initial focus of the seizure, which occurs prior to the loss of consciousness. The subject is aware of various experiences depending on

the part of the brain discharging and is able to recall it afterwards. Typically auras include involuntary movements of limbs, discrete sensations, emotions, various hallucinations and intrusive thoughts. The aura may or may not progress to a fully developed seizure.

Total unconsciousness
This may be extremely brief as in petit mal or last several minutes as in a grand mal fit. A state of stupor has been described in petit mal due to rapidly repeated fits.

Epileptic automatism
Complex and semipurposive activity may accompany an abnormal disturbance of brain electrical activity – commonly from the temporal lobe (a variety of complex partial seizure). The activity occurs in a state of clouded consciousness, though the individual retains control of posture and muscle tone. The automatism lasts usually a few seconds or minutes, mostly less than five minutes, though rarely it can be prolonged (psychomotor status). The subject appears to the observer to be dazed or the behaviour is inappropriate to the situation in some way. The episode may culminate in a grand mal fit. The subject usually has an impaired memory of the automatism. Theoretically an 'offence' could be committed in this state if, for example, the subject had a knife in his hand at the start of the automatism and continued to make cutting movements.

Fugues
This is disturbed behaviour resembling complex epileptic automatism but lasting much longer (hours or days) in which journeys may be accomplished, purchases may be made, etc. Nevertheless the behaviour usually appears abnormal in some way. The subject has no memory of the event. Differentiating epileptic fugues from psychogenic fugues may be very difficult and indeed there may be overlap. A history of fits, an abnormal EEG, and a previous history of fugues will assist in diagnosis.

Twilight states
Lishman[2] recommends that this term be reserved for episodes of prolonged abnormal subjective experiences lasting up to several hours with impaired consciousness. There is dream-like absent-minded behaviour, and slowness of reaction. The degree of reaction to the environment is very variable. The subject experiences strong feelings of panic, terror, anger or ecstasy, and may sit quietly through the attack or show sudden outbursts of aggressive or destructive behaviour. Subjects may be very irritable and react with an outburst of rage to any interference. This could result in an 'offence'. The experience is accompanied by disturbed brain electrical activity often with a temporal lobe focus. The state may terminate with a grand mal fit.

Post ictal states
After the fit (ictus) proper there may be a failure to regain full consciousness. The subject appears confused and clumsy. The subject is in an irritable state and aggressive behaviour (which could lead to an offence) can occur, in which case it is usually a reaction to unwanted interference by others. Sometimes a post ictal twilight state may occur, lasting hours or days with retardation, hallucinations and affective disturbance or a post ictal paranoid psychosis.

Disturbance of behaviour between fits

There is a complex relation between epilepsy and disturbed behaviour between fits.[4] This may be due to the changes in the brain which caused the epilepsy or changes in the brain following severe epilepsy or the medication; it may also be the result of the psychological effects of suffering the disease of epilepsy. Any associated mental impairment, or associated mental illness have also been implicated as possible causes of disturbed behaviour between onsets of epilepsy.

As a result of the above factors the subject may experience

- changes in emotional state or personality;
- mental illness-like states;
- a degree of mental retardation; or
- disturbed sexual behaviour.

Changes in emotional state, behaviour and personality
Prodromata of fits: Some subjects (most commonly with temporal lobe epilepsy) are aware of an altered emotional state in the hours or days before a grand mal attack. This state is usually disagreeable with heightened irritability, tension and sullenness. This emotional state may be associated with difficult behaviour. It is possible that an assault might occur in such a state.

Behaviour disorder in epileptic children: It has been shown that children with some types of epilepsy (particularly temporal lobe epilepsy) are more likely than normal to show anti-social behaviour.[4] Such behaviour is not directly linked with seizures but is likely to be due to the complex interaction of multiple factors such as brain injury, adverse family influences, type of fit, the psychological reaction of the child to the illness, the effects of medication, and the effects of hospitalisation or placement in institutions. Children with petit mal epilepsy show less aggression than those with grand mal epilepsy.

Personality disorder in epileptics: It is now accepted that there is no specific epileptic personality disorder. The behaviours which were previously thought to be as a result of an epileptic personality disorder are now understood to be caused by co-existing brain damage, institutionalisation and the effects of older anti-convulsant drugs. Personality traits such as aggression may be commoner in temporal lobe epilepsy. In the small proportion of epileptics who do show personality disorder, the aetiology is likely to be multifactorial. The factors involved include psychosocial effects, effects due to brain injury, abnormal electrical activity occurring between seizures and the effects of anti-convulsants.[2]

Mental illness-like states

There are many clinical pictures and classifications but these are still unsatisfactory. Schizophrenia in particular has now been shown to be more prevalent in patients with epilepsy compared to patients with other chronic neurological disorders such as migraine. All, theoretically, could be associated with offending. The following have been described.[2]

(1) Hallucinations and/or grossly disordered emotional states occurring in association with the seizure, either during the aura or in one of the other disturbances of consciousness.
(2) Paranoid hallucinatory states following grand mal seizures lasting two to three weeks and accompanied by clouding of consciousness.
(3) Transient schizophrenia-like episodes which are self-limiting and occur between fits. They present a very variable picture: some patients remain fully alert whilst others have a clouded consciousness. Some are followed by amnesia and others by normal recall. Some are related to abnormal EEGs and others to normalisation of the EEG (which becomes abnormal when the psychosis stops). Some are related to medication.
(4) Chronic schizophrenia-like psychoses identical to paranoid schizophrenia. This has been described in association with a history of epilepsy (usually temporal lobe epilepsy) of longer than 14 years.
(5) Affective disorders. These seem to be more common in those with temporal lobe epilepsy. They are often short lived and self limiting. Affective and schizo-affective psychoses also occur. However, it must not be forgotten that there is a raised suicide rate amongst epileptics.

Mental handicap and epilepsy

Epilepsy is much more common amongst subjects with mental handicap. This reflects the underlying brain disorder which has caused both conditions. Severe fits may, of course, lead to brain damage which may worsen the mental handicap. Among severely mentally handicapped subjects 50% have had an epileptic fit. However when brain damage has been excluded, the intelligence of children with epilepsy has been shown to be within the normal range.

Sexual dysfunction and epilepsy

A number of studies have consistently described a lower libido and impotence in epileptics. However, apart from a suggestion that male sex hormones are reduced, it is not thought that there is a direct association with epilepsy. Hypersexuality is rare. Fetishism and transvestism have been shown to be associated with temporal lobe epilepsy in certain rare cases. Case reports have claimed that operative removal of a temporal lobe focus has cured a fetishism.[6] Whether there was any true direct link with the temporal lobe lesion or whether the sexual disorder was due to distorted human relationships because of the subject suffering from epilepsy is uncertain.

Epilepsy, the law and the Mental Health Act

Whilst epilepsy itself is not regarded as a mental disorder, clearly it can, as described above, be intimately associated with mental disorder. The mental disorder forms the basis of any defence or mitigation, and for any recommendations for treatment under the Mental Health Act.

However, the courts have insisted in the past that severe disturbance of consciousness associated with epilepsy should be regarded as a disease of the mind. This was highlighted in the case of Sullivan.[7] Sullivan committed an act of serious violence in a confusional state following a seizure. A plea of non-insane automatism was submitted. However, it was ruled (supported by the Court of Appeal and later by the House of Lords) that this was insane automatism which would result in a verdict of not guilty by reason of insanity. At that time the court would have had no option but to detain Sullivan under Sections 37/41 of the Mental Health Act 1983 as though he were insane under the Criminal Justice (Insanity) Act 1964. This was one of the cases that led to the change in the law, resulting in the present Criminal Procedure (Insanity and Unfitness to Plead) Act 1991 which gives the judge discretion in disposal after a finding of insanity (see Chapter 3).

One result of the change in the law may be that the distinction between sane and insane automatism may become less important, now that there are other sentences available to the courts. Therefore, under the Criminal Procedure (Insanity and Unfitness to Plead) Act 1991 a plea of insane automatism could be safely made in the expectation of being sent for treatment to an appropriate establishment under supervision. The legal defence of automatism is discussed in more detail in Chapter 3.

Epilepsy and crime

In the nineteenth century it was believed that epilepsy or a tendency to epilepsy was a feature of many criminals. Crimes committed in blind fury were particularly thought to represent an epileptic process. Modern studies refute this view. A number of studies of epileptics attending out-patient clinics have failed to demonstrate excessive criminality in the patients. However, a more complete study by Gudmundsson[8] of all the epileptics in Iceland showed a small excess of criminality amongst the male epileptics. Gunn[9] has shown that the incidence of epilepsy in English prisons is higher than in the general population: 7–8 prisoners per thousand had epilepsy compared to 4–5 people per thousand of the general population. In a study[10] of 158 epileptic prisoners there was no convincing evidence of offending in a state of automatism though nine offended just before or just after a fit. In a study of 32 epileptics in special hospitals,[10] two were probably in a post confusional state at the time of the offence. In short, whilst epilepsy may well be a factor leading to anti-social behaviour in some cases, the association is not common among epileptics and it is rare to offend at the time of the fit. The association of offending and epilepsy is summarised by Gunn.[9]

(1) The offence may occur in a disturbed state induced directly by a fit. This appears to be rare.
(2) The offence and the fit may be coincidental.
(3) The brain damage which caused the epilepsy may have led to personality problems resulting in anti-social behaviour.
(4) The subject may have developed strong anti-social attitudes as a result of the difficulties he has experienced in life as a result of his illness.
(5) An early deprived childhood environment may have both engendered anti-social attitudes and exposed the subject to epileptogenic features.
(6) Anti-social subjects may expose themselves to dangerous situations and sustain more head injuries than normal which may cause epilepsy.

EEG changes, epilepsy and crimes of violence

Violence is probably unusual in direct association with an epileptic fit.[11] Usually any violence associated with the fit occurs in the post confusional state and involves attacks on people who may be interfering. Violence can also occur (very rarely) in an epileptic automatism.[12] It has also been described associated with amygdaloid discharges (responding to amygdaloid ablation). Most violence committed by epileptics, however, seems to occur between fits. There is argument whether there is a raised incidence and surveys give varying results In a study[11] of 31 subjects with temporal lobe epilepsy referred to an epileptic clinic, 14 were found to have a history of aggression. The violence was generally mild and did not correlate with EEG or CAT scan findings. The behaviour did correlate with maleness, behavioural disturbance since childhood (often leading to residential schooling), adult personality problems, and dull intelligence. Violence may occur, of course, where there is an associated psychosis.

It has been asserted that electroencephalographic (EEG) changes are commoner amongst violent offenders. Evidence for this is based on a classical study which found that the incidence of EEG abnormalities were greater if the murder was impulsive or lacked motive.[13, 14] William[15] claimed that impulsive violent men had an increased incidence of temporal lobe abnormalities. Nevertheless, caution has been expressed about these findings as they are not supported by all studies. Gunn and Bonn,[16] for example, did not find that temporal lobe epilepsy was associated with violence. Lishman's study of head injury subjects[17] found that frontal lobe lesions were the commonest lesion to be associated with aggression. Driver *et al.*[18] failed to find any significant difference between the EEGs of murderers and the EEGs of non-violent subjects when the examiner of the EEGs had no knowledge of the subjects.

Assessing the offending epileptic

Fenwick[19] has suggested the following six criteria, to help psychiatrists determine whether a claim by a subject that his offence occurred in a disturbed state due to an epileptic phenomenon, is likely to be true.

(1) The patient should be known to be an epileptic, i.e. it should not be their first seizure.
(2) The act should be out of character and inappropriate for the circumstances.
(3) There should be no evidence of premeditation or any attempts to conceal the offence.
(4) Any witnesses to the offence should describe disturbed consciousness including a description of the subject becoming suddenly aware of their surroundings and confusion as the automatism ends.
(5) There should be amnesia for the whole of the period of the automatism. There should not be any memory disturbance preceding the automatism.
(6) The diagnosis of epilepsy and epileptic automatism are clinical ones. Although special investigation including MRI, CT and EEGs may be useful, they are unable to prove or exclude an automatism.

Organic personality disorder

This disorder occurs following some form of trauma to the brain. This could be a head injury, an infection such as encephalitis or as a result of brain disease, for example multiple sclerosis. There is a significant change in the person's behaviour. Emotions and impulse control are often affected.

Although it can occur following damage to any part of the brain, frontal lobe damage is of particular importance to forensic psychiatrists.

ICD-10[1] requires that in addition to evidence of brain disease, damage or dysfunction two of the following criteria are necessary for a diagnosis of organic personality disorder:

(1) reduced ability to persevere with goal directed activities;
(2) affective instability;
(3) impaired social judgement;
(4) suspiciousness or paranoid ideation;
(5) alterations in rate and flow of language;
(6) altered sexual behaviour.

Organic personality disorder and behaviour

The reasons for this condition coming to the attention of the forensic psychiatrist arise from the loss of normal controls, increased egocentricity and loss of normal social sensitivity. People of previously good personality will present with an out of character offence. The history will show the development of an organic cerebral state. Frontal lobe damage is most likely to be associated with such a picture. It is suggested that the finding most relevant to forensic issues in frontal lobe damage is executive control. This is defined as the ability to plan and anticipate consequences of behaviour.[20] The behaviour of the subjects reflects their previous personality and their emotional reaction to their loss of ability as well as the loss of brain function.

Organic personality disorder and the law

The organic personality disorder will be accepted by the court as a mental illness. The illness may then be used in mitigation and perhaps as the basis of a treatment order. Problems arise in knowing how to deal with the person of somewhat anti-social personality who sustains brain damage which exacerbates his anti-social attitudes and behaviour. The subject may be very difficult to manage in ordinary psychiatric hospitals due to the longstanding anti-social attitudes, increased impulsiveness and lack of concern. The case may be complicated by the anger and depression the subject feels about the illness. There is a temptation to describe such a patient as having a psychopathic disorder which is not amenable to treatment in order to pass his care over to the penal system. Whilst this may be appropriate in milder cases it really reflects a lack of specialised psychiatric units with the ability to take on the problem. It should not be forgotten that Section 37 of the Mental Health Act allows for a guardianship order to be made. Such an order may be appropriate if the offender is compliant with supervision and outpatient treatment is available from a specialist unit.

Case Study 1:

A 40 year old man who had previously held a responsible job in the civil service developed multiple sclerosis in his early 30s. The disease, which was primarily a cerebral form, progressed steadily with only short periods of remission. MRI scans demonstrated that both frontal lobes were affected by plaques of demyelination. As a result, his personality changed dramatically and he became sexually disinhibited and made offensive remarks to female colleagues. He was retired on medical grounds. He became promiscuous and approached women in the street and made inappropriate sexual suggestions. On several occasions when he was refused by these women, he indecently assaulted them. He also became more irritable and aggressive. Following conviction for several indecent assaults he was admitted to a medium secure unit under Sections 37/41 of the Mental Health Act 1983. His illness continued to progress over the following two years, during which the frequency of his assaults on female staff and patients increased. Therefore, he was eventually admitted to a special hospital.

The term *episodic dyscontrol syndrome* was coined in the early 1970s by several authors.[2] It was suggested that there is a group of individuals who do not have epilepsy, brain damage or psychosis but who act aggressively as a result of an underlying organic disorder. Their aggressive behaviour is the only symptom of this disorder. The majority of individuals who acquire this diagnosis are male. They have a long history of aggression dating back to their childhood and frequently have disturbed family backgrounds. The main supporting evidence for such a syndrome is the fact that these individuals frequently have abnormalities of their EEGs, particularly in the temporal lobe region. They also describe an aura, similar to that seen in temporal lobe epilepsy. It is suggested that there is a functional abnormality of the nervous system which leads to increased aggression. Lishman[2] believes that this syndrome stands on the borderline of aggressive personality disorder and temporal lobe epilepsy. Lucas[21] has described in detail the history of this disorder. He points out that in ICD-10 this constellation of behaviours is classified under adult personality disorder. There is insufficient evidence of underlying epilepsy and Lucas argues that it does not merit a separate classification as an organic brain disease.

A similar claim has been made for *attention deficit disorder with hyperactivity*. This condition is recognised in children as hyperkinetic disorder of childhood in ICD-10, where it is defined as a 'pervasive' condition. This requires that the hyperactivity is evident in all situations, for example, not just at school and not just at home. It has been asserted that the more severe form of the condition is due to minimal brain damage and can persist into adult life and present with impulsive character disorders, irritability, lability, explosiveness and violence. Evidence suggests that one-third will develop an anti-social disorder as a child and that the majority of these will become criminal adults.[22] As in children a therapeutic effect can be obtained with stimulant medication.[23]

Psychological sequelae of head injury

Psychiatric symptoms after head injury

The subject has been reviewed by Lishman[2] and McClelland.[24] Long-term psychiatric sequelae are common after severe head injury and can lead to a great deal of social and psychological impairment. Severe injuries will be associated with neurological symptoms which will tend to improve with time. Mild injuries may be associated with dizziness, transient disturbance or concussion with no later evidence of gross neurological damage.

Following a period of concussion, there will be a period of confusion from a few seconds to weeks depending on the severity of the injury and the physical condition of the subject (worse for the elderly, arteriosclerotic and alcoholics). In the confusional period there may be lethargy or irritability and perplexity, disturbed orientation, misinterpretations, depression or boisterous behaviour and there may be hysterical, aggressive or paranoid traits with delusions and hallucinations. Memory may be patchy or absent (post traumatic amnesia). Violent behaviour can occur. Crimes can be committed in this state and can appear, superficially at least, to be highly motivated just as sportsmen, following a blow to the head, can complete the game with no memory for it after the blow.

Post traumatic (anterograde) amnesia may be complete or patchy. The length of the post traumatic amnesia is a guide to the severity of the injury and the prognosis. Post traumatic amnesia lasting longer than one week indicates a poor prognosis with invalidism up to one year.

Retrograde amnesia is the amnesia which occurs before the blow and is generally very brief (seconds or minutes): 'I remember seeing the hammer fall but not the blow'. In very severe brain injury there may be a retrograde amnesia of days or weeks. The length of the retrograde amnesia may shrink with time. Long retrograde amnesia with minor head injuries suggests elaboration and deception.

Psychiatric symptoms following head injuries vary considerably and owe something to organic factors, mental constitution and something to psychogenic ones including those arising from environmental and legal problems. Symptoms include the following.

(1) Headaches, dizziness, fatigue, impaired concentration and irritability.
(2) Neurotic symptoms (phobias, anxiety states, depression) sometimes follow quite trivial injuries (as well as with serious ones). These are perhaps associated with other life difficulties and seem to be more psychogenic rather than organic. Careful history taking may reveal their presence before the injury.
(3) Major affective psychosis.
(4) Schizophrenic psychoses.

(5) Intellectual impairment and memory impairment (reflecting the severity of the injury).
(6) Wide ranging changes (deteriorations) in personality, commonly after severe head injuries and including frontal lobe syndrome, temporal lobe syndrome and basal syndrome.
(7) Sexual dysfunction,
(8) Epileptic phenomenon.

Prognosis will be worse the older the patient (perhaps due to the deteriorating ageing brain and any coexistent disease). Features of inadequacy and neurosis will worsen the prognosis as will emotional features arising from the incident (e.g. fear). The domestic and occupational problems which face the patient after the injury also influence recovery.

Post concussional syndrome

ICD-10[1] describes the syndrome as one following a head injury usually after concussion. It is characterised by headaches, dizziness, fatigue, irritability, difficulty with concentrating and performing menial tasks, impairment of memory, insomnia, and reduced tolerance to stress, emotional excitement or alcohol. Anxiety and depression are often present. Headaches and dizziness may persist in over half for some months but only 1% will have the symptoms at one year (and in the majority of those, examination will reveal no abnormality).

The evidence about the relative role of organic and psychogenic factors in the persistence of symptoms is contradictory.[25] It has been asserted that the symptoms merely reflect the desire for compensation. Some surveys in fact found the strongest association with previous constitution, social class, nature of the accident and litigation. Other surveys and follow ups suggest an association with early neurological symptoms (diplopia, anosmia, length of post traumatic amnesia). Lishman suggests that the symptoms begin organically and generally resolve but can be maintained by psychological factors. In a prospective study a mixture of causes (organic and social) was found for the persistence of symptoms but a desire for compensation was not a factor.[26]

Psychiatrists are often asked to prepare reports in relation to claims for compensation following head injuries. When preparing such reports for the civil courts, the following issues should be addressed:

(1) are the symptoms genuine;
(2) was the head injury a contributing cause of the symptoms;
(3) and if so, to what extent did the head injury contribute (would the symptoms have occurred anyway?);
(4) what is the prognosis?

The court will recognise the fact that a more vulnerable person will suffer more from an injury than will a robust person.

It is well recognised that increased irritability and aggression, which can particularly occur following a head injury, may lead to offending. The management of such patients is notoriously difficult and will usually necessitate a cognitive behavioural approach combined with appropriate pharmacotherapy.[27] Therefore, it has been argued that specific services are required for those who suffer head injury, particularly where there are neuropsychiatric sequelae. In 1992 the Department of Health set up twelve pilot sites for five years. Their future is not at all certain and evaluation of them is awaited.[28] If better services were available, then fewer people would be left in the least appropriate setting, often prison.

Accident neurosis (compensation neurosis) and malingering

Malt[29] followed up 107 adults who had been accidentally injured. Nearly a quarter had some psychiatric disorder in the two year follow-up period. At one year some 17% had non-organic symptoms (anxieties, affective disorder, adjustment disorder) and at two years only 9% had such symptoms. Litigants after injury may complain of such symptoms as well as having pain and weakness, headache, dizziness and fatigue, perhaps in conjunction with conversion hysteria. Such symptoms may seem organically unrelated to the precipitating trauma. The question of whether they have an unconscious psychological cause (eligible for compensation) or are due to deliberate malingering (not eligible) will arise. It has been said that such cases represent a spectrum with the majority of the complainants towards the malingering end. It was believed[30] that the desire for compensation sustained the symptoms which were said to disappear promptly when the case was settled. The situation seems more complex than this. In some studies the litigation group did not clear up after settlement.[31] The persistence of severe hysterical symptoms in those cases may owe something to the legal situation (desire for compensation) but also something to the role of the family in believing, supporting and adapting to the disabled complainant who would lose face if he 'recovered'. On the other hand, another group of litigants with psychiatric symptoms[32] involved in industrial and motor vehicle accidents showed a steady improvement both before and after the time that the compensation claims were settled and most eventually had substantial remission of psychological symptoms. Nevertheless there was a clear association between delay in getting the case settled and prolongation and exacerbation of the symptoms.

True malingering certainly occurs. Insurance companies have increasingly used detectives to demonstrate how allegedly handicapped people behave normally when they believe that they are not being observed. Complex frauds involving several families across the country were described in Australia with family members coaching each other to simulate illness (e.g. whiplash injury) after organised trivial car accidents. It can be almost impossible for an average physician or psychiatrist to detect such frauds especially when the differential diagnosis includes a conversion syndrome or neurotic condition. The best protection is a very careful history with probing of details and gathering of information from other sources, especially the notes of the general practitioner.

However, it should be remembered that it is not always possible to distinguish hysterical (psychogenic) symptoms from factitious symptoms which have been consciously manufactured. It is probable that there is a continuum from hysteria to malingering, with most patients lying somewhere between these two extremes. Several studies have shown that it is not possible to distinguish malingering from hysteria.[33]

Organic psychoses

Definition

These are included in other mental disorders due to brain damage and dysfunction and to physical disease in ICD-10.[1] The general criteria are that there should be:

(1) evidence of cerebral disease;
(2) a temporal relationship between the disease and the syndrome;
(3) recovery from the mental disorder when the underlying cause is effectively treated;
(4) no evidence of an alternative cause for the syndrome.

The types of disorder include, in addition to other neurotic types of disorders:

(1) organic hallucinosis;
(2) organic catatonic disorder;
(3) organic delusional (schizophrenia like) disorder;
(4) organic mood (affective) disorders.

The clinical picture is that of a severe psychotic condition arising from an organic cause. The behaviour of the subject simply reflects the psychosis and its content, e.g. paranoid state may lead to suspicious, hostile behaviour.

Organic psychoses and the law

The psychoses can clearly be accepted as a mental illness within the meaning of the Mental Health Act and thus can form the basis of a treatment order and can be considered as a factor in mitigation etc. Where the illness occurs after a head injury or other trauma there may also be grounds for compensation.

Substance induced organic disorders

Definition

These are disorders induced by any substance of which the most common is alcohol. Various drugs (sedatives, stimulants, hallucinogens, etc.) may be used illegally or legally and may induce various disorders of mental function, the most common of which are listed below.

(1) *Intoxication due to an excess of the drug* with altered mood, altered motor abilities and altered psychological functioning.
(2) *Idiosyncratic intoxication* where an apparent intoxication is induced by very small amounts due to an idiosyncratic reaction on the part of the subject. A variety of effects including delirium and autonomic changes may be observed.
(3) *Withdrawal effects:* a variety of effects may be induced by suddenly stopping a drug to which the subject has become addicted. These effects will include delirium, autonomic changes, depression, anxiety and tremors.
(4) *Mental illness:* this may be associated with drug use in several ways:
    (a) as a direct effect of the drug, e.g. amphetamines and their derivatives, cocaine, lysergic acid diethylamide or a medication such as steroids;
    (b) as an effect of a sudden withdrawal of a drug, e.g. paranoid psychosis after alcohol withdrawal;
    (c) due to the chronic effects of drug use, e.g. alcoholic dementia;
    (d) by precipitating relapse and worsening of symptoms in patients with schizophrenia, e.g. cannabis.

Substance induced disorders and the law

Intoxication

The Mental Health Act specifically excludes simple alcohol or drug abuse from the conditions which make a person subject to Mental Health Act orders. Generally speaking, if a person takes an illegal drug (including alcohol) he is held responsible for any actions he commits whilst intoxicated by the drug (see Chapter 7). The fact that it has disinhibited him or caused him to be amnesic for the occasion will be no excuse. Exceptions to this include (1) to (4) below. 'Involuntary intoxication' covers (1) to (3) and can lead to an acquittal.[34]

(1) The situation of a man being tricked into taking a substance without his knowledge (a difficult thing to prove).

(2) The situation where a person's reaction is quite idiosyncratic and could not be anticipated, e.g. gross intoxication following a very small amount of the substance. It has been claimed that some individuals show 'pathological intoxication' ('Mania a Poitu') on very small doses of alcohol particularly if there is some pre-existing brain damage. Following a small amount of alcohol there is a brief, severe aggressive outburst in a state of disorientation and even psychosis followed by sleep and amnesia. This claim has both supporters and detractors.[2] The situation is unresolved but the defence has been tried in court when the clinical picture justified it.

(3) The situation where the person had an untoward reaction to a medication prescribed by a doctor. For example, the sedative effects of a drug may make someone act out of character and without intent.

Edwards[35] has listed the necessary criteria to establish whether there is a genuine relationship between the drug intoxication and the crime. There must be a clear relationship between the medication and the act. The unwanted reaction should be authoritatively documented, the act should not be a manifestation of the illness the patient suffers from, no other substances which could have caused the reaction should have been taken, taking the medication and the reaction should be appropriately related in time and the reaction should disappear when the medication is stopped.

(4) The situation where the degree of intoxication was such that the subject became incapable of forming intent. Courts have been very sceptical of such a defence for fear that a successful plea would encourage similar pleas from any criminal who offended when in drink. It has now been ruled[36] that for crimes of basic intent (e.g. manslaughter, assault and unlawful wounding) the accused will not be acquitted if, having knowingly and willingly taken drink or drugs, he deprived himself of the ability to exercise self-control or became unconscious of what he was doing. In crimes of specific intent (e.g. murder or theft) there would still be a defence available of 'no intent'. In the case of murder the charge might then be reduced to manslaughter.

It is quite common for offenders who were heavily intoxicated at the time to claim that they had no memory of the offence and that it 'was all due to the drink'. A study of the relevant statements nearly always confirms that the subject's behaviour was perfectly understandable in terms of the situation even though intoxicated. In such a case it is no defence to plead the effects of the intoxication. Nevertheless, after conviction, courts will often take a sympathetic view of people anxious to rid themselves of dependence on alcohol or drugs and make probation orders with conditions of treatment for the dependency provided it seems appropriate in that particular case and the offence is not too serious.

Psychiatrists may be asked in a particular case what effect alcohol, taken perhaps on top of medication, may have had on the mental state or degree of intoxication. The blood level of alcohol varies with the subject's sex, the type of drink (fizzy drinks absorb more rapidly), food in the stomach, body build, and rate of gastric emptying (affected by some drugs). There is euphoria at 30 mg/100 ml, impaired driving at 50, dysarthria at 160 with loss of consciousness possible over this figure and death over 400. The risk of a road accident is more than double at 80 and is more than tenfold at 160. Alcohol is metabolised at about 15 mg/100 ml/hour but this varies considerably. Heavy drinkers metabolise more quickly unless there is liver damage, which slows the rate. Nevertheless, the Court of Appeal has allowed a back calculation to be made from a known blood level and given as evidence. The psychiatrist might be asked to comment on the factors which might have influenced this.

Withdrawal disorders

A court may accept, in mitigation, a disorder of mind induced by substance withdrawal, certainly where this disorder could not reasonably have been anticipated by the subject.

Mental illness associated with substance abuse

Where an offence has been committed whilst the subject is suffering from a substance-induced mental illness then the courts seem to be ready to consider accepting this in mitigation and to be willing to make a treatment order if recommended to do so by the doctors if it seems a fair and sensible disposal. On the other hand, psychiatrists are sometimes unwilling to accept as a patient someone who has had only a temporary disorder from substance abuse, especially where the patient is of anti-social inclination. The difficulty with this view is that some people seem to precipitate, with various drugs, a mental illness which does not rapidly clear up but which begins to take on all the features of a chronic psychosis (e.g. schizophrenia) for which hospital and after-care is needed.

Organic amnesia

Amnesia may be caused psychologically (see Chapter 3) or organically. Organic amnesia may be divided[2,37] into

(1) 'Amnesic' syndrome with focal pathological lesions. Pathological examination shows brain damage, particularly to the mamillary bodies, posterior hypothalamus, and the grey matter around the third and fourth ventricle and the aqueduct. Occasionally there are bilateral hippocampal lesions. The causes of this focal damage include tumours, thiamine deficiency (as in Wernicke's encephalopathy and Korsakoff's psychosis) and infarcts. There is an inability to lay down new memories from the time of the event (anterograde amnesia) and loss of old memories (retrograde amnesia) without confusion or loss of attention.

(2) Amnesia caused by diffuse brain damage as in dementia (e.g. Alzheimer's disease), toxic confusional state, head injury, or hypoglycaemia.

Amnesia and the law

The relationship of amnesia to violent offending is well recognised. It appears to be particularly related to intoxication with drugs and alcohol and the degree of violence involved. This latter fact is confirmed by the finding that victims of violent crime are more likely to have a memory loss for the events of the crime, than victims of non-violent crime.[37] It has been known for some time that the perpetrators of homicide crimes are more likely to have amnesia for their offences. In a number of studies of homicide, the frequency of amnesia has varied between 25–45%.[38] A frequent finding in such cases is that while the initial cause of the memory loss is organic, often alcohol intoxication, the amnesia is maintained by psychogenic factors, often as a result of an unconscious wish not to recall the offence, particularly where a spouse or other family member has been killed.

Taylor[38] has described the following factors which are known to be associated with amnesia for offending:

(1) the violence of the crime, particularly in homicide;
(2) extreme emotional arousal during the offence;
(3) alcohol abuse and intoxication;
(4) depressed mood in the perpetrator.

This latter finding was noted in a study of the prevalence of amnesia in a remand prison population.[39]

However, the presence of amnesia does not, in itself, make a defendant either unfit to plead or prove the absence of *mens rea* for an offence. In either of these situations, while the amnesia itself cannot constitute a defence, if it is a symptom of an underlying organic disease, such as dementia, brain injury or epileptic automatism, then amnesia may be a factor in making a defendant unfit to plead or show an absence of *mens rea*. This may be particularly true where there is an anterograde amnesia.

Case study 2

Mr M.B was a 50 year old man who was charged with the attempted murder of his estranged wife. They had been married for five years and part of the reason for the separation had been Mr B's violence towards his wife. Mr B had not seen a psychiatrist previously and did not have a criminal record. He had attempted to kill both himself and his wife by tying her up and locking both of them in his car with a hose attached to the exhaust with the engine running. Both were rendered unconscious but the engine cut out and they were discovered by neighbours. Mr B was unconscious on arrival at hospital and a CT scan showed hydrocephalous and cerebellar infarcts. He remained unconscious for two weeks. His wife recovered consciousness quickly and was not seriously affected by the carbon monoxide poisoning. Mr B spent eight months in a rehabilitation unit.

On psychometric testing, one year later, he had a severe deficit in short-term memory. He was only able to retain information for a few minutes. He also had a poor memory for the previous 10–15 years but could remember notable events prior to that time. He demonstrated clear abnormalities on frontal lobe testing with impairment of his executive skills, including his ability to plan, solve problems and carry out sequential activities. Mr B's personality had also changed, he was now apathetic, passive and emotionally blunted.

Mr B was found unfit to plead on the recommendation of two psychiatrists and a neuropsychologist. This was because he could not understand the evidence because he could not retain any information that he had heard or read for more than a few minutes. He would not be able to take part, to a requisite extent, in the trial process. He was found on the trial of the facts to have committed the acts. He was placed on a guardianship order under Section 37 of the Mental Health Act. He lived with friends who were his full time carers.

Mr B was unfit to plead because of an anterograde amnesia rather than his extensive retrograde amnesia. An anterograde amnesia of this severity affects a person's ability to comprehend what is said to him and therefore makes him unfit to plead. There was no doubt in this case, that the organic anterograde amnesia was genuine. This is despite the frequently stated view that an inability to retain new information is characteristic of a psychogenic amnesia. It is now recognised that the rigid distinction between psychogenic and organic amnesia which was previously held to be true, is an artificial distinction.[2]

Sleep disorders and the law

Offending can occur during sleep in which case a defence of automatism is appropriate. Following the case of Burgess (*R v. Burgess* (1991) 93 Cr App R 41), sleepwalking is now considered, by the courts, as arising from 'internal factors' and therefore is an insane automatism (see Chapter 3).

Sleepwalking occurs during stage 4 slow wave sleep, not REM (rapid eye movement) sleep where the body is normally paralysed.[2] There may be partial arousal in which complex actions are possible including violent attacks. Fenwick[19] had suggested that the following factors are necessary for a diagnosis of sleep walking, particularly when assessing crimes alleged to have occurred during sleep walking.

History

The following general factors are relevant:

(1) *Family history:* it is known that there is a genetic component to the aetiology of sleep walking;
(2) *Childhood onset:* sleep walking commonly begins in childhood, though a lower number of cases begin during adolescence;
(3) *Late onset of sleep walking is rare:* however, this could occur after a precipitant such as a head injury. If the first episode of sleep walking occurs at the time of an offence, this should be regarded with some suspicion.

Specific factors

One should then consider the episode more subjectively.

(1) Since sleep walking occurs in stages 3–4 of sleep, it should therefore occur within two hours of going to sleep.
(2) The person should be disorientated on awakening.
(3) Any witnesses should report inappropriate automatic behaviour and disorientation on awakening.
(4) There should be amnesia for the whole period of the sleep walking.
(5) Trigger factors may be present, these include drugs, alcohol, excessive fatigue and stress.
(6) If the crime is a sexual one, sexual arousal during sleep only occurs during REM sleep and would therefore not occur during sleep walking.
(7) Any memories from before the sleep walking, should be non-narrative and non-dreamlike.
(8) It is unusual for there to be any attempt to conceal a crime committed during sleep walking.
(9) There may have been similar behaviour during previous sleep walking.
(10) If the crime appears to be motiveless and out of character then this would give some support to it being committed during sleep walking.

Management and treatment is by advising the subject to sleep with doors and windows locked and prescribing drugs which suppress stage 3–4 sleep (such as Diazepam).

Two other sleep disorders are recognised:

- *Night terrors:* these also occur in stage 3–4 sleep. The subject wakes with intense fear and anxiety with autonomic arousal. The subject may run around screaming and may injure others.

- *Awaking from deep sleep:* a state similar to a night terror may be precipitated by being awakened suddenly from a deep sleep particularly in a threatening situation. The subject may then react violently.

References

(1) World Health Organization (1992) *ICD10 Classification of Mental and Behavioural Disorder*. WHO: Geneva.

(2) Lishman, W.A. (1998) *Organic Psychiatry, The Psychological Consequences of Cerebral Disorder*, Third Edition. Blackwell Scientific Publications: Oxford.

(3) Fenton, G.W. (1984) Epilepsy, mental abnormality and criminal behaviour. In: *Mentally Abnormal Offenders* (eds M. Craft and A. Craft). Ballière Tindall: Eastbourne.

(4) Gunn, J. (1977) *Epileptics in Prison*. Academic Press: London.

(5) Rutter, M., Graham, P.J. and Yule, W. (1970) *A Neuropsychiatric Study in Childhood*. Heinemann: London.

(6) Falconer, M.A. (1973) Reversibility by temporal lobe behavioural resection of the behavioural abnormalities of temporal lobe epilepsy. *New England Journal of Medicine* **289**, 450–5.

(7) Fenwick, P. and Fenwick, E. (1985) *Epilepsy and the law*. Royal Society of Medicine, International Congress and Symposium Series No. 81.

(8) Gudmundsson, G. (1966) Epilepsy in Iceland. A clinical and epidemiological investigation. *Acta Neurologica Scandinavica* (Supplement 25) 7–124.

(9) Gunn, J.C. (1969) The prevalence of epilepsy among prisoners. *Proceedings of the Royal Society of Medicine* **62**, 60–3.

(10) Gunn, J.C. and Fenton, G.W. (1971) Epilepsy, Automatism and Crime. *Lancet* **1**, 1173–6.

(11) Hertzberg, J.L. and Fenwick, P.B.C. (1988) The aetiology of aggression in temporal-lobe epilepsy. *British Journal of Psychiatry* **153**, 50–5.

(12) Hindler, C.G. (1989) Epilepsy and violence. *British Journal of Psychiatry* **155**, 246–9.

(13) Stafford-Clark, D. and Taylor, F.H. (1949) Clinical and electroencephalographic studies of prisoners charged with murder. *Journal of Neurology, Neurosurgery and Psychiatry* **12**, 325–30.

(14) Hill, D. and Pond, D.A. (1952) Reflections of one hundred capital cases submitted to electroencephalography. *Journal of Mental Science* **98**, 23–43.

(15) Williams, D. (1969) Neural factors related to habitual aggression. *Brain* **92**, 503–20.

(16) Gunn, J.C. and Bonn, J. (1971) Criminality and violence in epileptic prisoners. *British Journal of Psychiatry* **118**, 337–43.

(17) Lishman, W.A. (1968) Brain damage in relation to psychiatric disability after head injury. *British Journal of Psychiatry* **114**, 373–410.

(18) Driver, M.V., West, L.R. and Faulk, M. (1974) Clinical and EEG studies of prisoners charged with murder. *British Journal of Psychiatry* **125**, 583–7.

(19) Fenwick, P (1990) Automatism. In: *Principles and Practice of Forensic Psychiatry* pp 271–285 (eds R. Bluglass and P. Bowden) Churchill Livingstone: London.

(20) Restak, R.M. (1997) Forensic neuro-psychiatry. *Current Opinion in Psychiatry*, **10**, 63–8.

(21) Lucas, P. (1994) Episodic Dyscontrol: A look back at anger. *Journal of Forensic Psychiatry*, **5**, 371–407.

(22) Mannuzza, S., Klein, R.G., Bonagura, N., Malloy, P., Giampino, T. and Addalli, K.A. (1991) Hyperactive children almost grown up. *Archives of General Psychiatry* **48**, 77–83.

(23) Wender, P.H., Reimherr, F.W. and Wood, D.R. (1981) Attention deficit disorder (minimal brain dysfunction) in adults. *Archives of General Psychiatry* **38**, 449–56.

(24) McClelland, R.J. (1988) Psychosocial sequelae of head injury – anatomy of a relationship. *British Journal of Psychiatry* **153**, 141–6.

(25) Lishman, W.A. (1988) Physiogenesis and psychogenesis in the post concussion syndrome. *British Journal of Psychiatry* **153**, 460–80.

(26) Fenton, G., McClelland, R., Montgomery, A., MacFlynn, G. and Rutherford, W. (1993) The postconcussional syndrome: social antecedents and psychological sequelae. *British Journal of Psychiatry* **162**, 493–7.

(27) Jacobson, R.R. (1997) Commentary: aggression and impulsivity after head injury. *Advances in Psychiatric Treatment* **3**, 160–3.

(28) Perini, A. (1997) Commentary: head injury. *Advances in Psychiatric Treatment* **3**, 164–5.

(29) Malt, U. (1988) The long-term psychiatric consequences of accidental injury. *British Journal of Psychiatry* **153**, 810–8.

(30) Miller, H. (1961) Accident neurosis. *British Medical Journal* **i**, 919–5, 992–8.

(31) Tarsh, M.J. and Royston, C. (1985) A follow up of accident neurosis. *British Journal of Psychiatry* **146**, 18–25.

(32) Binder, R.L., Trimble, M.R., McNiel, D.E. (1991) The course of psychological symptoms after resolution of lawsuits. *American Journal of Psychiatry* **148**, 1073–5.

(33) Miller, E. (1998) Defining hysterical symptoms. *Psychological Medicine*, **18**, 275–7.

(34) d'Orban, P.T. (1989) Steroid induced psychosis. *Lancet* **ii**, 694.

(35) Edwards, J.G. (1992) Antidepressants and murder. *Psychiatric Bulletin* **16**, 537–9.

(36) Legal Correspondent (1976) Intoxication and crime. *British Medical Journal* **1**, 1286–7.

(37) Stone, J.H. (1992) Memory disorder In offenders and victims. *Criminal Behaviour and Mental Health* **2**, 342–56.

(38) Taylor, P.J. (1993) Organic Disorders, Mental Handicap and Offending. In: *Forensic Psychiatry: Clinical, Legal and Ethical Issues* pp 286–328 (eds. J. Gunn and P.J. Taylor). Butterworth Heinemann: Oxford.

(39) Taylor, P.J. and Kopelman, M.D. (1984) Amnesia for criminal offences. *Psychological Medicine* **14**, 581–8.

Chapter 10

Psychopathic Disorder and Forensic Psychiatry

Introduction

Since 1992 there have been significant developments in the area of psychopathic disorder. The 1990s have seen a new focus in psychiatry on all personality disorders resulting in a large literature with many excellent reviews. In 1994 the Department of Health–Home Office working party on Psychopathic Disorder chaired by Dr John Reed published its report.[1] The report has a very informative review of psychopathic disorder and 28 recommendations for the future, some of which have now resulted in legislative changes. In 1997 the Crime (Sentences) Act 1997 contained changes to the Mental Health Act 1983 specifically affecting the management of people detainable under the category of psychopathic disorder. At the time of writing the Fallon Inquiry[2] into the personality disorder unit at Ashworth Hospital has reported with 58 recommendations which are now being considered. Later in 1999 a Home Office–Department of Health working party on Psychopathic Disorder will report.

Definitions

Walker,[3] quoting Pinel shows how there has been a tradition for many years for psychiatrists to regard people with grossly disordered personalities, characterised by aggression and irresponsibility, as being subjects for psychiatric treatment. What has changed over time has been the understanding and the diagnostic titles. These have included *manie sans délire*, moral insanity, moral imbecility, psychopathy, degenerate constitution, congenital delinquency, constitutional inferiority, moral deficiency, and sociopathy as well as other terms.[4]

The term 'psychopathy' originated in the late nineteenth century in Germany[3,5] and was used originally (and still is on the continent) to embrace all disorders of personality. It was in the USA that the term first became restricted to those showing antisocial behaviour and it was with this meaning that it was imported into England. It became incorporated into statute in the Mental Health Act 1959 as 'psychopathic disorder'. This generic term replaced the older terms 'moral insanity' and 'moral defect' which had been used in the Mental Deficiency Acts. Despite the controversy about its value the term continues in the Mental Health Act 1983 (see Chapter 3). As highlighted in the Butler Report[5] the legal term 'psychopathic disorder' carries no implication that psychopathic disorder is a single entity, rather it is a generic term adopted for the purpose of legal categorisation covering a number of specific diagnoses. On the other hand reliable specific diagnoses in this area are still to be developed. In order to avoid confusion the term psychopathic disorder should now only be used for the legal concept; it should not be used to describe a clinical condition. Regrettably, however, confusion cannot be eliminated completely and it will be seen in the rest of this chapter that at times it is necessary to refer to psychopathic disorder as a clinical condition in order to discuss the literature on the subject.

The legal term encompasses a number of personality disorders in the ICD-10[6] and DSM IV[7,8]. Although the ICD-10 dissocial personality disorder (F60.2) and DSM IV anti-social personality disorder (301.7) equate most closely with the clinician's understanding of the term 'psychopathic disorder', the legal term psychopathic disorder is also used to cover some people with ICD-10 paranoid personality (F60.0), ICD-10 emotionally unstable personality disorder (including impulsive and borderline types F60.30, F60.31), DSM IV borderline personality disorder (301.83) and ICD-10 schizoid personality disorder (F60.1). In fact, as defined in the Mental Health Act, it includes any personality disorder which results in 'seriously irresponsible or abnormally aggressive behaviour'. Furthermore, some men with sexual deviations in conjunction with a disordered personality have been legally classified as psychopathic disorder although they may also fall, in psychiatric terms, into non-personality disorder DSM IV and ICD-10 groups such as sexual sadism/sadomasochism, paedophilia and exhibitionism.

Because of the problem of definition, the Butler Committee recommended the abandonment of the term psychopathic disorder. Nevertheless, the term was retained in the Mental Health Act 1983, despite these difficulties, though with two very important practical changes. First, that it is now clear in the 1983 Act that the diagnosis of psychopathic disorder is not in itself sufficient to lead to a hospital order. It is also necessary to show that medical treatment is likely to alleviate or prevent deterioration in the subject's condition before an order can be made; second, it is possible to use the 1983 Act to make a civil order for treatment in case of psychopathic disorder (provided the treatment conditions are met) at any age and not, as existed under the 1959 Act, just for those under the age of 21 years.

Treatability

Despite the laudable inclusion of 'treatability' in the criteria for admission to hospital, there is a lack of consensus amongst psychiatrists on what can and cannot be treated. This was demonstrated in a survey by Cope[9] of all forensic psychiatrists in England, Scotland and Wales. In this survey consultant forensic psychiatrists answered questions about three short vignettes considered to be classifiable as psychopathic disorder. Case A of the series (a male schizoid, possibly pre-psychotic patient) gave the least agreement with 27% of psychiatrists deciding the patient was untreatable and 73% considering the patient amenable to treatment. Case B (a female patient with a borderline personality disorder) gave the highest agreement – 5% of psychiatrists considered the patient untreatable and 95% treatable. In 1993 the results of this survey were considered by Dr John Reed's working group on Psychopathic Disorder for the Department of Health and Home Office.[1]

Despite this lack of consensus patients are admitted and treated under the category of psychopathic disorder. When considering admission to hospital under the Mental Health Act it is probably best to consider treatability similarly to beauty, i.e. as being in the eye of the beholder. It would be a mistake to declare a person treatable and admit them if you do not have the facilities to treat the person. For instance, if treatment will take several years with a large amount of psychotherapy input but your unit only provides short duration admissions with little psychotherapy then the person is not treatable there. The NHS arrangements allowing for out of area treatments (extra contractual referrals) cause ethical dilemmas here as it has to be decided how far to pursue possible appropriate placements elsewhere in the country if you do not have anything appropriate yourself.

Detention under psychopathic disorder only specifies that treatability is considered on admission, not on discharge, i.e. it is not possible for a patient who has become untreatable to be discharged on those grounds unless the tribunal were satisfied that there was no likelihood of the patient ever becoming treatable if the detention continued. This was rigorously tested in the case *R* v. *Canons Park Mental Health Tribunal, Ex parte A*.[10] in which an in-patient some way into her admission refused to accept the only treatment which it was now considered might help, this being psychotherapy. The patient's counsel argued that since the patient was no longer treatable (i.e. there were no treatments left as she was refusing to co-operate with psychotherapy) she should be discharged (despite the fact that she was dangerous and held in a secure unit). The tribunal refused to discharge the patient. The patient sought a judicial review which resulted in the Divisional Court (a part of the Court of Appeal) quashing the decision of the tribunal, thereby discharging the patient. The concluding comments of Mann LJ in the Divisional Court were 'I am however persuaded for the reasons given by Sedley J that parliament has enacted that an untreatable psychopath howsoever dangerous cannot be detained'.

This decision caused great concern because there are many highly dangerous 'untreatable' patients currently detained under psychopathic disorder in the high security hospitals – so were they now all to be released? The tribunal appealed and eventually the decision was reversed by a full sitting of the Court of Appeal. The Court of Appeal pointed out that the wording of the Mental Health Act is such that although the 'treatability test' has to be applied on admission it does not specifically have to be considered when the detention is being reviewed – at this stage what is required is for the tribunal to consider whether continuing detention is appropriate – the so called 'appropriateness test'. Therefore if it is considered that a person who is currently refusing treatment or has otherwise become untreatable, might through further detention eventually become treatable, the continuing detention is legal and appropriate. The *Canons Park* decision has been reviewed in a more recent case, *Hutchison Reid* v. *Secretary of State for Scotland and Another,*[11] but essentially the position appears unchanged.

Primary and secondary 'psychopaths'

In the past some practitioners have divided antisocial personalities into primary and secondary (neurotic) psychopaths. This is not to be found in ICD-10 or DSM IV but many psychiatrists still find the concept useful. The syndrome of a primary psychopath has been described by Cleckley.[12] At first sight the subject appears normal, charming, intelligent and articulate with low anxiety. The history, however, reveals extremely egocentric, impulsive and bizarre behaviour, which, in the long run, is against the subject's interest. Legal confrontation may be avoided indefinitely because of the subject's intelligence and charm, and prominent positions in society may be attained until the true picture emerges. The subject sometimes learns to give a history of early psychological trauma as this interests psychiatrists whereas, in fact, investigation fails to support this. The behaviour is not understandable in ordinary psychological terms. Cleckley postulates that such psychopaths have an inherent disorder of brain function by which emotions (e.g. guilt) and words are dissociated. Cleckley considered therefore that primary psychopathy is quite untreatable. The concept of a primary psychopath has been widely accepted in some research and psychological faculties but generally, in England, has not received much support from clinicians. Secondary psychopaths resemble the description of anti-social personalities with prominent anxiety. Their personality is understood largely in terms of psychological traumas experienced in early life. The clinical presentation of the secondary psychopath is usually much more noticeable with poor coping skills and frequently self harm.

Psychopathic disorder and psychotic symptoms

It is common experience in prisons and secure hospitals to observe relatively brief periods of psychotic symptoms in subjects categorised under psychopathic disorder.[8] They seem to occur in all the severe disorders of personality, usually at times of stress, but sometimes for no clear reason. Coid[13] studied 72 female patients with borderline personality disorder in special hospital. He described a cyclical pattern of affective disturbance (often seemingly endogenous in origin) with anxiety, anger, depression and tension as the principal features. After a build up of these symptoms (over hours or days) there was a compulsion to act out criminal (e.g. firesetting) or self-destructive behaviour. Acting out would be followed by a temporary relief of symptoms. The cycle would then be repeated.

The management of such disturbed periods can be difficult due to the difficulty of bringing the condition under control. In the psychotic periods there is usually a paranoid state with delusional and hallucinatory experiences. The subject may react to the psychotic experiences with tension, hostility and destructiveness as may occur in an affective disturbance. Similar difficulties in management, though recovery with antipsychotic medication tends to be good. A number of such subjects become more stable if they take antipsychotic medication regularly. Relatively small doses may be sufficient.

Psychopathic disorder, mental illness and substance misuse

Psychiatrists often see people with a history of longstanding disruptive behaviour and personality difficulties including poor impulse control, repeated deliberate self harm, violence against property and violence towards others. Often these people also abuse drugs and have episodes when they seem to have psychotic symptoms. They can present a serious management problem and a diagnostic dilemma because usually they are too disruptive for general psychiatric wards. They tend to move between psychiatric services and the criminal justice system and may also drift around the country homeless. There are no easy answers to helping such people, short of admission to a secure unit. These admissions are often via prison transfer or from police custody. It is a frequent finding of forensic psychiatrists that containing such patients in a secure and structured environment reveals a psychotic illness often with underlying personality problems. A lengthy admission can often result in significant functional improvement.

Medicolegal aspects of psychopathic disorder

An important legal issue raised by psychopathic disorder is the opportunity for a hospital disposal rather than a community or custodial sentence.

Occasionally a defence of diminished responsibility in murder cases has been allowed on the grounds of personality disorder but this is rare. Psychopathic disorder does not lead to findings of unfitness to plead or insanity. If a hospital disposal is not being recommended then a finding of psychopathic disorder can be a double edged sword for the defendant, since on the one hand it could be seen as a mitigating factor at sentence; however, on the other a judge faced with sentencing an 'untreatable psychopath' may give a longer sentence than usual on the grounds of protecting the public.

For many years psychiatrists have been cautious about recommending hospital treatment for 'psychopaths'. This has been largely because of uncertainty about treatability, a lack of appropriate resources and the experience of accepting a patient for treatment then finding that the patient is not treatable. After accepting a patient who is found to be or becomes untreatable the psychiatrist sometimes then encounters the dilemma of either being put under pressure to discharge a dangerous person who will be no less risky in the community after discharge or entering into long-term 'preventive' detention in hospital ('preventive' here is used to mean preventing harm to the public, i.e. psychiatric care becomes custodial care). The latter is particularly likely when a patient detained under Sections 37/41 of the Mental Health Act is found to be or becomes untreatable, as in these cases the Home Office and Mental Health Review Tribunals are unwilling to authorise discharge. To help prevent these problems the Reed Report[1] made a number of recommendations which have now been incorporated into practice and law.

The problem of accurately determining treatability has been assisted in two ways. First, the Reed Report has recommended that decisions about treatment should only be made after a multidisciplinary assessment. In the past decisions have sometimes been made by doctors alone, but good assessments now rightly always include other disciplines. Second, as a result of recommendations by the Reed Report, the Crime (Sentences) Act 1997 has introduced changes to Section 38 of the Mental Health Act 1983. An interim hospital order (Section 38) can now be made for up to 12 months thereby allowing a longer assessment and trial of treatment before making final recommendations to the court.

Once treatability has been determined there are now a number of new options available at sentencing. The Crime (Sentences) Act 1997 introduced new Sections 45A and 45B to the Mental Health Act 1983. These sections create a power for the Crown Court to attach a hospital direction when imposing a sentence of imprisonment on a defendant with a psychopathic disorder. In effect, the options are now as follows: if the psychiatrist is confident a 'psychopathic' offender is treatable then a recommendation can be made to the court for admission to hospital under Section 37 or Sections 37/41 of the Mental Health Act 1983. If the psychiatrist thinks the offender is not treatable there will be no hospital recommendation (although there could be an informal review of the offender after sentence to reconsider hospitalisation as a transfer from sentence under Sections 47/49 of the MHA 1983). The new 'hospital direction' under Section 45A (colloquially known as a 'hybrid order') is used when the psychiatrist can only say that the offender is probably treatable. The hybrid order requires the doctor to make a recommendation to court for a hospital order (Section 37) and the judge can then decide to make a 'hybrid order' if desired (the recommendation from the doctor is only to be for a hospital order, not the hybrid order itself). The effect of the order is that the defendant receives hospitalisation and a sentence of fixed or indeterminate length at the same time. The defendant will then start the sentence in hospital and may eventually be discharged into the community directly from hospital. However if the defendant becomes untreatable or completes treatment before the sentence expires then transfer can be made back to prison to serve the remaining sentence with eventual release from prison. Use of this new power is currently being audited by the Mental Health Unit of the Home Office. Between October 1997 when the order came into force and September 1998 no hybrid orders were made.

The treatment of adults with psychopathic disorder

The treatment of adults with psychopathic disorder has been very comprehensively reviewed by Dolan and Coid[14] in a study commissioned for the joint Department of Health–Home Office Review of Health and Social Services for Mentally Disordered Offenders and Others Requiring Similar Services, headed by Dr John Reed.[15] This review was undertaken because there is no consensus on the best treatment approach or whether such patients are treatable at all! Some comments that have been made about the poor state of our knowledge on treatment for 'psychopathic disorder' include

'There is, of course, no evidence to demonstrate or to indicate that psychiatry has yet found a therapy that cures or profoundly changes the psychopath'

(Cleckley, 1964)[16]

'One cannot review the literature on treatment of personality disorder without being impressed by how little we know about those conditions'

(Frosch, 1983)[17]

'The state of the treatment literature on anti-social personality disorder is inadequate'

(Quality Assurance Project, 1991)[18]

'It is impossible to review the research literature on treatment of psychopathy without being impressed by two major features: firstly, that research investigations of treatment outcome of psychopathy are few and of poor quality; secondly, and more worryingly, that despite several decades of reviewers commenting to that effect, no obvious improvement has come about to date'

(Dolan and Coid, 1993)[14]

Natural history

Before considering treatment it is important to recognise the natural history of the personality disorders found in the 'psychopath'. There are no firm consistent research based answers to this but it is generally accepted that certain personality disorders tend to improve with age in some individuals; these include borderline, anti-social and histrionic personality disorders. Other disorders are more likely to persist including paranoid, obsessive compulsive, schizoid, avoidant, dependent and passive–aggressive personality disorders. Those cases that improve with time often seem to change from middle age onwards.

Treatment in prison

Historically prisons in many countries have tried various approaches to reform or rehabilitate the recidivist criminal using religious teaching, education, inculcating a work ethic, punitive methods, etc. Psychiatric approaches are typified by the following:

Herstedvester Treatment Centre, Denmark
This centre, opened in the 1930s, was a forerunner of prisons attempting to treat psychopaths by psychotherapeutic means. It was run by a psychiatrist, Dr Sturrup, and based on therapeutic community principles. Originally it relied heavily on the effect of an indeterminate sentence to motivate prisoners to take part so that they could earn their release by improving. The prison claimed to produce long-term improvements in its clients.[19] However, a comparative study, described in the Butler Committee Report,[5] showed that there was no difference in the final reoffending rate of prisoners from Herstedvester compared to similar prisoners from an ordinary prison despite the apparent improvement whilst in treatment.

Grendon Underwood Prison, England
This 200 bed prison, planned in the 1930s, was set up in 1964 in the belief that criminality could be due to a neurosis which could be treated. In practice, the prison was used for the treatment, by group therapy, of those offenders with personality disorders who were able to make use of groups and were already serving a prison sentence. Referral to Grendon Prison is made by the prison medical service after sentencing. The final selection is made by Grendon staff based on the prisoner's intelligence, articulateness, ability and willingness to work in groups and evidence of some personal achievement. The regime at Grendon between 1987–1994 has been described in detail by Genders and Player.[20] Gunn[21] showed that inmates' attitudes and behaviour improved at Grendon compared with that in other prisons but that the beneficial effect of Grendon's regime was counteracted by the environment to which the prisoner returns on release. It was found

that chance factors in the community (e.g. occupation, marriage) after release were as important in the ultimate outcome as the experience of Grendon itself. Overall, after ten years in the community, the re-offending rate of ex-Grendon inmates was the same as that of an equivalent group from ordinary prison[22] although the better motivated and more intelligent may have been have helped more. A further study by Cullen[23] followed the progress over 2 years of 244 fixed sentence inmates released from prison. The men who had stayed at Grendon for under 18 months had a reconviction rate of 40% whereas those who had stayed for over 18 months had a rate of 20%.

It is relevant to note that the inmate population changed between the studies of Gunn and Cullen. Gunn's study contained a higher proportion of younger men serving shorter sentences for acquisitive offences.

C Wing, Parkhurst Prison, England
This wing, which closed in 1995, catered for men with personality disorders characterised by high levels of tension, emotional lability, violence and disturbed behaviour (self-mutilation, impulsive attacks, tension-reducing destruction). Such men are unable to cope with ordinary prison regime and are too disordered (too impulsive or aggressive) to make a success of Grendon Prison. The regime helped these very disordered inmates through their sentence. This was accomplished by being more flexible and giving more attention (medication and counselling) than in ordinary prison. The overall clinical impression was that violent and disruptive incidents were substantially reduced during the inmate's stay in the wing. There has been no study of the long-term effects of the wing. A study of a similar unit in Barlinnie Prison, Scotland (which has now closed) showed a rapid reduction in violent behaviour in the unit and a suggestion of reduced re-offending afterwards.[24]

Treatment in hospital

Conventional hospital
Conventional hospitals tend to admit patients with personality disorder during periods of crises, i.e. during periods of depression, high anxiety or psychosis and this may be useful to prevent harm being done by the patient to himself or those around him. However, most hospitals find that they are unable to treat such patients on a long-term basis because of persistent disruptive, anti-authoritarian behaviour which they are unable to modify. It may be a reflection of this that there has been a reduction in recent years in the number of hospital orders made by the courts on those with psychopathic disorder.

Special hospital
There has been a fall in the rate of admission of patients with psychopathic

disorder to special hospital from approximately 60 a year in 1986–90 to 40 a year in 1991–96. This represents fewer than one in every 2,000 offenders convicted of violent or sexual crimes. The treatment in Broadmoor Hospital consists of psychotherapeutic methods, education, and rehabilitation within the setting of the total institution. The treatment of these patients in high security is a very protracted process and it is not uncommon for patients to become untreatable for periods or sometimes completely so. These 'untreatable psychopaths' can be a particularly disruptive influence, adversely affecting the care of all patients in their particular unit and the hospital.

Medium secure units

Only a small proportion of patients admitted to regional secure units have psychopathic disorder as their principal diagnosis. Most of these patients are admitted from special hospital as part of an attempt to rehabilitate the patient to the community. A few come directly from the courts, prisons and community. The treatment approach is similar to that in special hospital. The extra attention and control which can be provided seems to be effective in reducing disturbed behaviour at least in the institution.

Henderson Hospital, England

This unit in the grounds of the Belmont Hospital, Sutton, was developed in 1947 to treat patients with 'psychopathic disorder' within the National Health Service. It does best with articulate, intelligent, younger psychopaths who had not been very criminal or violent. The unit is most famous for the development, under Maxwell Jones, of its therapeutic community approach. The Henderson Hospital only takes voluntary admissions. It has 29 beds and around half of its residents will have criminal convictions. On the basis of available studies to date the Henderson Hospital appears to produce about the best outcome for 'psychopathically disordered' patients, albeit through a highly selective admission process.[25, 26]

Van der Hoeven Clinic, Utrecht, Holland

This is one of several famous Dutch clinics run by psychiatrists to treat offenders with psychopathic disorder. This particular clinic is a therapeutic community (within a physically secure unit) which employs group psychotherapy in combination with educational rehabilitation and resocialisation programmes. It is supported by a good 'parole' system. The prisoners stay there for about two years. Although the clinic asserts it is successful in producing long-term as well as short-term change, there is a dearth of controlled studies to support this claim.

Management in probation hostels

Probation hostels differ from one another in their ability to improve probationers' behaviour whilst in the hostel. A lesson learned from Sinclair's study[27] was that hostels with a caring but firm atmosphere were the most effective. The least effective were the permissive or negligent and uncaring hostels. Unfortunately, the improvements seen in the behaviour of the probationers during their stay in the hostel were not sustained after leaving. Two or three years later the re-offending rate was the same whatever the original hostel.

Individual psychotherapeutic treatments in the community

The most famous work on this approach was the Cambridge–Somerville Study in the USA.[28] It was an attempt to see if individual counselling would prevent the development of anti-social personality amongst youths at risk. The experiment compared a treated and an untreated group. Treated youths were meant to see the same counsellor on a voluntary basis every week. Unfortunately, the experiment was disrupted by World War II as the counsellors were enlisted. As far as could be worked out in broad terms, however, those who received counselling did no better than those who did not.

Other individual clinical approaches

Psychotherapy with borderline and narcissistic personality disorder has been reviewed by Higgitt and Fonagy.[29] The principal lesson is the need for a long-term commitment to treatment. Workers with each technique claim successes but it is not clear which approach will work in any individual case without a trial.

Reality therapy
This is an attempt to teach social skills in a very practical way to delinquents dealing with here and now problems.

Supportive counselling
This is the backbone of probation and out-patient services. Firmness applied tactfully coupled with acceptance and warmth is probably the most effective style though there is no evidence that it can produce long-term change. Clinically, it seems to be helpful to some subjects in assisting them in staying out of trouble as long as they are receiving the counselling and support.

Dynamic psychotherapies
There have been many sporadic claims of success with dynamic psychotherapies, however there is no consistent supporting evidence. It is

virtually impossible to undertake dynamic psychotherapy with anti-social personality disordered patients although there are reports of some successes in in-patient settings. In general, dynamic psychotherapy is not suitable for the treatment of patients detained on the grounds of psychopathic disorder.

Family therapy

This intervention will expose family dynamics and appears to be a very powerful tool. Empirical studies of effectiveness in personality disordered offenders are lacking.

Group therapy

Group work can be a very useful approach and it is commonly used in institutions where personality disordered subjects are detained.

Cognitive therapies

Where anger and violence present a problem, psychological therapies based on the recognition of automatic thoughts combined with relaxation, general cognition and behavioural modification techniques have achieved some success at modifying the violent behaviour, at least in the short term.[30] This treatment approach will be of help in treating specific aspects of behaviour or attitude in selected patients. The selection criteria are the same as those for psychotherapy in non-'psychopathic' individuals.

Treatment with medication

Medication will not cure personality disorders, but medication may be helpful in some individuals, particularly those with predominant symptoms of tension and anxiety. Patients with borderline personality disorder often seem to be particularly helped by careful use of medication. Those with schizotypal personality disorder and some personality disorders with associated forms of behaviour dyscontrol also seem to benefit. A very comprehensive review of medication effects in patients categorised as suffering from psychopathic disorder was undertaken by Dr Bridget Dolan and Dr Jeremy Coid for the working group on psychopathic disorder for the Reed Report.[1] Dolan and Coid reported their findings in a book published in 1993.[14] Their findings are incorporated into the summaries below.

Benzodiazepines

The available literature on the effect of benzodiazepines on behaviour and personality disorders is not of high quality. However, clinical experience shows that benzodiazepines may be useful in the acute control of severe behaviour or in the short term for periods of anxiety or tension. Caution is needed, however, as reactions have been reported with benzodiazepines leading to disinhibition and rage reactions.[31,32] Generally they should not be used in the treatment of personality disorders, particularly in view of their addictive potential.

Antidepressants

Depression is an integral feature of many personality disorder and it tends to fluctuate irrespective of antidepressant treatment. To date there have not been adequate trials to demonstrate whether patients improving on antidepressants do so because of a pharmacological action or whether any improvement seen is simply due to natural changes in the condition. Nonetheless, patients with personality disorder can become severely depressed, so it is important to use antidepressants when depression is severe. Persistent dysphoric mood and the atypical depression of the borderline state may respond to monoamine oxidase inhibitors (MAOI).[33,34] However, in view of the potential seriousness of side effects and the unreliability of patients with severe personality disorder, a trial of MAOIs may only be appropriate after lithium and carbamazepine have failed.

Maintenance treatment with lithium is a promising development in the treatment of personality disorders.[14] Lithium is particularly indicated in patients with a personality disorder who show impulsiveness, instability of mood, or unpremeditated aggressive outbursts.

Major tranquillisers

Any of the major tranquillisers may be useful in reducing persistent tension – sometimes they seem to work in relatively low doses (e.g. Flupenthixol 20 mg per month or less) but at times of high tension large doses may be required. Low dose therapy may be particularly helpful for patients with schizotypal features and those who suffer from recurrent brief psychotic episodes. Some borderline patients with self-harm, aggressive outbursts and periods of anxiety and depersonalisation also seem to be specifically helped by neuroleptics.

Stimulants

It has long been reported that amphetamines can produce a reduction in feelings of tension in some psychopaths[35,36] but the dangers of abuse and addiction generally outweigh any advantages. There is a great deal of interest in the use of amphetamine compounds in adults who seem to have persistence of childhood attention-deficit hyperactivity disorder. Many such adults in the USA are prescribed amphetamine derivatives with reportedly good effect,[37,38] however, to date in the UK there remains considerable scepticism about this and such prescriptions are rare.

Anticonvulsants

Carbamazepine has been shown to improve overactivity, aggression and poor impulse control.[14] This effect is not restricted to certain personality disorders, rather it seems to be symptom specific so the treatment is probably better used to target symptoms not specific personality diagnoses.

Physical treatments

There have been attempts to treat 'psychopaths' with electro-convulsive therapy and through psychosurgery. However, there is no reliable evidence that either of these treatments is effective for this group.

References

(1) Reed, J. (1994) *Report of The Working Group on Psychopathic Disorder*. Department of Health/Home Office: London.
(2) Department of Health (1999) *Report of the Committee of Inquiry into the Personality Disorder Unit, Ashworth Special Hospital*. Stationery Office: London.
(3) Walker, N. and McCabe, S. (1973) *Crime and Insanity in England, Volume Two: New Solutions and New Problems*. Edinburgh University Press: Edinburgh.
(4) Lewis, A. (1974) Psychopathic disorder: a most elusive category. *Psychological Medicine* **4**, 133–40.
(5) Home Office and Department of Health and Social Security (1975) *Report of the Committee on Mentally Abnormal Offenders* (Butler Report). Cmnd. 6244 HMSO: London.
(6) World Health Organization (1992) *The Tenth Revision of the International Classification of Diseases and Related Health Problems (ICD-10)*. WHO: Geneva.
(7) American Psychiatric Association (1994) *Diagnostic and Statistical Manual of Mental Disorders* (fourth edn) (DSM-IV). APA: Washington, DC.
(8) Coid, J.W. (1992) DSM-III diagnosis in criminal psychopaths: a way forward. *Criminal Behaviour and Mental Health* **2**, 78–94.
(9) Cope, R. (1993) A survey of forensic psychiatrists' views on psychopathic disorder. *Journal of Forensic Psychiatry* **4**, 215–35.
(10) *R* v. *Canons Park Mental Health Review Tribunal Ex parte A*. [1995] Q.B. 60
(11) *Hutchison Reid* v. *Secretary of State for Scotland and Another*. SLR 7.12.1998.
(12) Cleckley, H. (1976) *The Mask of Sanity* (Fifth edition). C.V. Mosby Co: St. Louis.
(13) Coid, J.W. (1993) An affective syndrome in psychopaths with borderline personality disorder? *British Journal of Psychiatry* **162**, 641–50.
(14) Dolan, B. and Coid, J. (1993) *Psychopathic and Antisocial Personality Disorders*. Gaskell: London.
(15) Department of Health and Home Office (1992) *Review of Health & Social*

Services for Mentally Disordered Offenders and Others Requiring Similar Services. Cmnd 2088. HMSO: London.

(16) Cleckley, H. (1964) *The Mask of Sanity* (fourth edn). C. V. Mosby Co: St Louis.

(17) Frosch, J.P. (1983) The treatment of antisocial and borderline personality disorders. *Hospital and Community Psychiatry* **34**, 243–8.

(18) Quality Assurance Project (1991) Treatment outlines for antisocial personality disorder. *Australian and New Zealand Journal of Psychiatry* **25**, 541–7.

(19) Sturrup, G. (1968) *Treating the Untreatable, Chronic Criminals at Herstedvester*. Johns Hopkins University Press: Baltimore.

(20) Genders, E. and Player, E. (1995) *Grendon: A Study of a Therapeutic Prison*. Clarendon Press: Oxford.

(21) Gunn, J., Robertson, G., Dell, S. and Way, C. (1978) *Psychiatric Aspects of Imprisonment*. Academic Press: London.

(22) Robertson, G. and Gunn J. (1987) A ten-year follow-up of men discharged from Grendon Prison. *British Journal of Psychiatry* **151**, 674–8.

(23) Cullen, E. (1993) The Grendon Reconviction Study Part 1. *Prison Service Journal* **90**, 35–7.

(24) Cooke, D.J. (1989) Containing violent prisoners. *British Journal of Criminology* **29**, 129–43.

(25) Dolan, B., Warren, F. and Norton, K. (1997) Change in borderline symptoms one year after therapeutic community treatment for severe personality disorder. *British Journal of Psychiatry*, **171**, 274–9.

(26) Norton, K. and Hinshelwood R.D. (1996) Severe personality disorder. Treatment issues and selection for in-patient psychotherapy. *British Journal of Psychiatry*, **168**, 723–31.

(27) Sinclair, I.A.C. (1971) *Hostels for Probationers*. HMSO: London.

(28) McCord, W. and McCord, J. (1959) *Origins of Crime*. Columbia University Press: New York.

(29) Higgitt, A. and Fonagy, P. (1992) Psychotherapy in borderline and narcissistic personality disorder. *British Journal of Psychiatry* **161**, 23–43.

(30) Levey, S. and Howells, K. (1990) Anger and its management *Journal of Forensic Psychiatry* **1**, 305–27.

(31) Tyrer, P. (1988) *Personality Disorders: Diagnosis, Management and Course*. Wright: London.

(32) Stein, G. (1992) Drug treatment of the personality disorders. *British Journal of Psychiatry* **161**, 167–84.

(33) Cowdry, W.L. and Gardner, D.L. (1988) Pharmacotherapy of borderline personality disorder. *Archives of General Psychiatry* **45**, 111–19.

(34) Markovitz, P.J., Calabrese, J. R., Schulz, S.C. and Meltzer, H.Y. (1991) Fluoxitine in the treatment of borderline and schizotypal personality disorders. *American Journal of Psychiatry* **148**, 1064–7.

(35) Hill, D. (1944) Amphetamine in psychopathic states. *British Journal of Addiction* **44**, 50–4.

(36) Richmond, J.S., Young, J.R. and Groves, J.E. (1978) Violent dyscontrol responsive to d-amphetamine. *American Journal of Psychiatry* **135**, 365–6.

(37) Shaffer, D. (1994) Attention deficit hyperactivity disorder in adults. *American Journal of Psychiatry* **151**(5), 633–8.

(38) Klein, R. (1995) The role of methylphenidate in psychiatry. *Archives of General Psychiatry* **52**, 429–33.

Chapter 11

Learning Disability and Forensic Psychiatry

Introduction

The purpose of this chapter is to discuss the clinical concept of learning disability and its relation to the present legal concept of mental impairment under the Mental Health Act 1983. Next, the degree to which learning disability is associated with offending behaviour and the pattern of particular crimes associated with learning disability will be considered. Case histories are used to describe the interaction between medical and legal systems, and the chapter concludes by examining the facilities available for the learning disabled offender.

Definition

Learning disability is synonymous with the term mental retardation as defined in both ICD-10 and DSM IV. The classification is based on an intelligence quotient (IQ) where 100 is the normal score. Mild learning disability is defined as an IQ of 50–70, moderate learning disability 35–49, severe learning disability 20–34, and profound learning disability below 20. The diagnosis is made by reference to a level of functioning regardless of causation. IQ tests must take account of specific disabilities such as in communication and be validated for the particular culture of the subject. Learning disability is only acceptable as a diagnosis where the disability occurs during the developmental period (under age 18 years).

Where there is additional psychiatric disturbance or evidence of physical disease or injury, then an additional diagnosis must be made. Learning disability does not of itself imply lack of capacity or that the individual is not capable of living independently in the community. The closure of long stay hospitals and the development of community care has shown that many people with mild and moderate learning disability are able to live relatively normal lives with appropriate degrees of support. This development has also led to many more people with learning disabilities coming into contact with the criminal justice system.

Learning disability and the Mental Health Act 1983

Society has traditionally protected those with a learning disability from the full rigour of the law, allowing subnormality of intelligence to be submitted as a mitigating factor, or if severe enough, grounds for a finding of not guilty by reason of insanity. While some people with milder degrees of learning disability can and do cope in prison it is obviously unacceptable to submit those with more severe degrees of disability to ordinary criminal sanctions. Equally, it is generally accepted that learning disability *per se* should not be grounds for committal to hospital unless there is a likelihood of ameliorating the situation. Parker[1] found that over half of those described as subnormal in fact had IQ scores above that of the category in which they had been placed. There is a tendency to ascribe a level of intellectual functioning on the basis of social functioning rather than the more circumscribed criteria of international classification systems.

The Mental Health Act 1983 introduced the new terms *mental impairment* and *severe mental impairment* with the intention of limiting the effects of the law to the few people with learning disability for whom detention in hospital is essential for treatment or for their own protection or the protection of others and where custody is not a viable alternative.[2]

Mental impairment is defined as a state of arrested or incomplete development of mind (not amounting to severe mental impairment) which includes a significant impairment of intelligence and social functioning and is associated with abnormally aggressive or seriously irresponsible conduct. Severe mental impairment is defined as a state of arrested or incomplete development of mind which includes severe impairment of intelligence and social functioning and is associated with abnormally aggressive and seriously irresponsible conduct. Significant and severe are not defined but by common usage are accepted as IQ levels of 60–70, and below 60 respectively. A determination of severe mental impairment is sufficient for a hospital order to be recommended. However, in the case of mental impairment, detention in hospital for treatment must be likely to alleviate or prevent deterioration of the subject's condition.

Of course if a learning disabled offender also suffers from a mental illness then that illness may form the basis of a psychiatric recommendation for compulsory detention.

Learning disability and offending

Studies by West[3] show that IQ is one of the five major factors associated with the development of delinquent behaviour. Subjects with severe learning disability are more likely to be in some form of residential care and so offending in the community is less likely. However, most residential care services now operate a regime of close community integration and so, depending on the degree of supervision, opportunities for community offending are more likely than formerly when most people with this degree of disability were cared for in NHS hospitals. Hospitals were known to absorb offending behaviour by patients and involvement of the police was rare except for the most serious offences. Smaller community homes run by social services, voluntary organisations, and private providers are more likely to involve the police or to seek compulsory admission to hospital by local psychiatric services in the case of offences committed by people in their care. There is considerable reluctance to proceed to formal court proceedings where the accused has a severe disability but court proceedings are often useful to determine the facts of the case and to provide structure to any package of care which may be required.

It should be borne in mind that many people with severe learning disability will be unable to give a true account of their own actions and so many decisions about a response to alleged offending behaviour are taken on the basis of information which lacks the coherence and corroboration which would be needed to secure a criminal conviction.

It follows that a decision not to proceed to a court hearing, while taken for the best possible reasons, may actually deny a person with a learning disability the presumption of innocence until proven otherwise which is the cornerstone of the criminal justice system. It was for this reason that the Criminal Procedure (Insanity and Unfitness to Plead) Act 1991 provided for a trial of the facts requiring the robust burden of proof of 'reasonable doubt' before proceeding to disposal for people who are unfit to plead by reason of disability.

People with milder degrees of learning disability are usually free to move without supervision in the community and so are more likely to come into contact with the criminal justice system if they offend. The full extent of their disability may be obscure, especially for those where a 'social veneer' masks a poor capacity for processing information. In such cases it is important that the subject's ability is properly assessed, as it may have implications for the reliability of his evidence and his ability to stand trial. Offenders with mild degrees of learning disability may often be able to plead and stand trial but where sentence is concerned a variety of community and hospital disposals may be considered as an alternative to sanctions under the criminal law.

A particular problem arises for those with an IQ in the range 70–85. This group is usually described as being in the borderline range of intelligence. Most are capable of living independently but suffer from a range of inadequacies and personality problems which may well predispose to antisocial behaviour. They do not fall within the scope of the mental impairment provisions of the Mental Health Act but may be subject to its provisions in relation to mental illness and psychopathic disorder. Psychosocial assessment and identification of deficiencies of intellect may be important in mitigation and determining an appropriate sentence.

Studies of populations of children show a consistent statistical association between a low IQ and offending.[4] West found that 20% of those with an IQ below 90 become delinquent compared with 9% of those with an IQ of 91–98 and 2% of those above 110. Delinquents on average have an IQ at least 5 points below the population norm. Studies of penal populations show a wide variation (1–45%) in estimates of the incidence of subnormality,[5] though this may reflect the quality of diagnosis, the prisons assessed, the year of assessment, and the quality of the services which might remove the learning disabled from the criminal justice system. Relying on prison studies produces debatable conclusions about the importance of learning disability in criminality.[6] While it may be argued that learning disabled offenders are simply caught more easily, studies such as those by West[3] support the view that people with learning disability do commit more offences. While various criminogenic factors such as large families, low social status and added physical disability may be particularly prevalent amongst the learning disabled, careful matching of samples shows that low IQ is a criminogenic factor in its own right.[3] Low IQ produces behavioural problems before the age of 3 and thus before educational failure.[7] Poor school performance, with its attendant low self-esteem and poor tolerance of frustration may combine with personality traits and inability to learn from experience to produce a greater propensity to react anti-socially when things go wrong.

It is generally asserted that people with learning disability, although capable of any offence, are more likely to commit sex or fire raising offences. This assertion derives largely from clinical practice and a study of the offences committed by learning disabled offenders admitted to hospital,[8] and therefore should be treated with some caution. It is probably the case, however, that people with learning disability who come to the attention of forensic psychiatric services will be accused or convicted of these type of offences. This can be explained by the informal threshold of seriousness observed by social and law enforcement agencies when deciding whether to bring formal proceedings against this group.

Medicolegal assessment of people with a learning disability

An appropriate point of departure in these circumstances is an assessment of intellectual functioning. Specialists in the psychiatry of learning disability are usually able to give a clinical assessment as to whether the subject falls within the ICD-10 classification of learning disability (mental retardation) but where possible this assessment should be confirmed by a formal psychometric assessment carried out by a clinical psychologist with experience of dealing with people with learning disabilities. In addition to an assessment of intellectual functioning it is also necessary to consider the possibility of superimposed mental illness, chromosomal and other genetic abnormalities, acquired brain damage, and specific disability such as autistic spectrum disorders. It is usually necessary to gather as much background information, from reliable informants, as possible. In particular, care should be taken to assess the reliability of the account, given by the subject, of the alleged offence. People with a learning disability are often very keen to comply with people in positions of authority and so may agree to propositions put to them in the course of an interview without realising the implications of their answers. The Police and Criminal Evidence Act 1984 provides for the presence of an appropriate adult during police interviews of persons with a learning disability or mental illness to avoid this possibility.

Issues to be considered

When assessing a subject who is accused of a crime and is believed to have a learning disability, the following matters are relevant.

(1) Does the subject have a learning disability and, if so, of what degree?
(2) Is the subject's behaviour intrinsically linked to his learning disability and does that behaviour fall within the category of abnormally aggressive or seriously irresponsible conduct as provided for in the Mental Health Act 1983?
(3) Is there evidence of mental disorder in addition to learning disability, and if so, does this disorder warrant a recommendation under the Mental Health Act in its own right?
(4) Is the subject fit to plead?
(5) In the case of homicide is diminished responsibility an issue?

Assuming that the subject falls within the categories of mental impairment, severe mental impairment, mental illness, psychopathic disorder, unfit to plead or diminished responsibility then the issue of a recommendation to the court as to disposal must be addressed. Hospital orders under Section 37 of the Mental Health Act 1983 are appropriate where the subject can be classified as mentally impaired or is suffering from another mental disorder and where the therapeutic needs of the individual can best be met in this way. In the case of severe mental impairment the treatability clauses which apply to mental impairment and psychopathic disorder are not a requirement and so this option can be used as an alternative, more humane, form of custodial sentence.

In the great majority of cases detention in hospital will be unnecessary and so a community sanction is more appropriate. The courts are entitled to be satisfied that a community disposal is both therapeutic and robust and that public safety and prevention of re-offending can be adequately addressed. The options for community disposal are:

(1) probation order with a condition of compliance with treatment;
(2) guardianship order under Section 37 of the Mental Health Act 1983;
(3) community supervision order under the provisions of the Criminal Procedure (Insanity and Unfitness to Plead) Act 1991. These disposals allow for complex packages of care to be proposed and allow for a structure whereby they can be monitored and enforced. These packages of care will usually be by multi-agency co-operation and will require a responsible professional to oversee the arrangements.

Case study 3: Sexual aggression and learning disability

Mr A was charged as his third offence (when aged 20 yrs) with the attempted rape of a 12 year old girl. He had induced her into a field where he forced her to undress and was about to rape her when interrupted by passers by. He was duly arrested.

His first offence was of indecently touching a woman in a supermarket for which he received a conditional discharge. His second offence was grabbing the breast of a woman in the street. His demeanour in court led to a psychiatric opinion.

His educational difficulties were well documented and he attended a special school. His IQ was recorded as 65. He had never had gainful employment and he was known to have seriously deficient social skills. He was also known to consort with a delinquent element in his locality. There was evidence of alcohol misuse and this was regarded as having a significant disinhibiting effect on his behaviour. The court accepted a recommendation of psychiatric treatment as a condition of probation. A attended regularly for all appointments but he was difficult to engage therapeutically.

Four months later he was arrested for the attempted rape. At this stage further evaluation revealed that he had been having fantasies of paedophilic rape for many years. He admitted to carrying a knife and fantasising about its use during the course of a rape.

The nature of the index offence and the worrying nature of the fantasies meant that admission to hospital for further evaluation and treatment was deemed essential. The lack of a bed for immediate admission resulted in a custodial sentence but due to his vulnerability in prison arrangements were made for admission to special hospital under Section 47 of the Mental Health Act 1983 with a restriction order under Section 49.

A therapeutic programme offering general and sex education, social skills training, and behavioural therapy with a view to dealing with unwanted sexual impulses was instituted with considerable effect. When his sentence ended his Section 47 order was converted to a notional Section 37 without restriction and he was subsequently discharged to a regional secure unit for further rehabilitation.

Comment

This case illustrates the complex nature of the issues involved in seeking to treat those with a learning disability. Ignorance of sexual matters coupled with poor social skills and a disordered fantasy life can produce, in a learning disabled subject, an individual who poses a serious risk to society and so this aspect must take priority in disposal from court.

However custodial sentences *per se* are unlikely to address the underlying cause of the offence. In this case, although eventually diverted from the criminal justice system, the subject was detained for longer than the original sentence but the package of care and careful rehabilitation is likely to lead to a safer and more productive life in the community in the longer term.

Case study 4: Theft and learning disability

Miss B, aged 21 had a recorded IQ of 67. She was referred to a medium secure unit because of persistent stealing, violence to others and self-injury. Attempts to treat and contain her behaviour in the community and in a local assessment and treatment unit were unsuccessful. She was admitted to the secure unit under Section 3 of the Mental Health Act 1983 on the grounds of mental impairment.

B had a history of developmental delay dating back to infancy. She was educated in the special school system. While there was a long history of behavioural disorder it was reported that the current behaviours became more pronounced after the death of her mother when she was 17 years old. Subsequently she was diagnosed as having an abnormal grief reaction and was treated for depression. She was described as egocentric, manipulative, poorly tolerant of frustration, impulsive and potentially anti-social and aggressive.

Conditions of medium security allowed for a behavioural programme under the direction of a clinical psychologist whereby she was gradually encouraged to take responsibility for her own actions. Such programmes often provoke a temporary exacerbation of behaviour and so the physical boundaries of the unit and the more favourable staffing ratios mean that such a deterioration could be safely contained.

Comment

This case demonstrates how a learning disability can protect a subject from the full rigours of the criminal justice system, in that no one who suffered from her actions had pressed charges. The behaviour outlined above is common to a number of personality disorder syndromes but in this case is likely to be attributable to immaturity of personality in the context of global developmental delay rather than personality disorder *per se*. It also illustrates the particular problem of those with mild learning disability whereby they lack the ability to function at a normal level in society but are able to understand that they compare unfavourably with their peers. This can lead to a degree of frustration and anger which in the context of an immature personality can lead to seriously anti-social behaviour.

Case 5: Theft and borderline learning disability

Mr C was one of 5 children of an intact family where the father suffered from a number of chronic illnesses including epilepsy. There was no history of developmental delay apart from nocturnal enuresis until age 18. He was regarded as a slow learner and left school at 15 with no qualifications. He managed to hold down paid employment for 4 years but failed to get another job.

Mr C came to psychiatric notice as a child due to educational failure and enuresis and his IQ was assessed as 80. As an adult, he was admitted to hospital for recurrent depression, deliberate self-harm, and a fetishistic attachment to ladies' underwear. He was also known to use alcohol to excess. The index offence was in the context of social inadequacy and probable alcohol dependence and as he did not fall within the parameters of mental impairment the court dealt with offences by means of ordinary community sanction.

Comment

This group of people whose IQ falls between 70–85 are increasingly being supported by community teams for people with a learning disability. While they cannot properly be regarded as having a learning disability the skills to support them and offer treatment as necessary are more likely to be found in learning disability services than in adult mental health services. Though of clearly subnormal intelligence they are likely to be treated by the courts as ordinary defendants unless there are particular extenuating circumstances which can be used in mitigation.

Case 6: Violence, depression and learning disability

Miss D was charged with wounding with intent having attacked her mother with a garden ornament causing severe head injury. At the time D falsely believed that she was suffering from a terminal illness and felt it better 'to take her mother with her'.

Her early development was normal apart from intractable school phobia. She was described as backward and she left school at 15 with no qualifications. She was never in regular employment. She was married twice, initially to a man 50 years her senior who died after 10 years of marriage when D was 31. She immediately remarried; again to a man 30 years her senior who died two years later. Following the death of her second husband D became severely depressed and complained of severe abdominal pain for which no organic cause could be found. This was the 'terminal illness' of which she complained at the time of the index offence. Her description of her illness became increasingly bizarre and she was diagnosed as suffering from a major depressive disorder with pronounced nihilistic delusions. On further evaluation she was found to have an IQ of 69. She was admitted to hospital under Section 37 of the Mental Health Act 1983 on the grounds of mental illness and responded well to treatment for her mental illness.

Comment

This case illustrates the co-morbidity often found in cases of people with learning disability who offend. While D undoubtedly had a learning disability, her behaviour was due to her mental illness rather than arrested or incomplete development of mind.

Treatment and management options for the learning disabled offender

Community facilities

Treatment in the community is the mainstay of recommended disposals for people with learning disability who offend or who show seriously challenging behaviour.

The statutory options available are:

(1) probation order with a condition of treatment;
(2) supervision order under the Criminal Procedure (Insanity and Unfitness to Plead) Act 1991;
(3) guardianship under Section 37 of the Mental Health Act 1983;
(4) guardianship under Section 7 of the Mental Health Act 1983.

Regardless of the statutory provision the package of care is likely to be complex and include the following elements:

(1) residential placement with family or in the statutory, voluntary or independent sectors;
(2) educational provision;
(3) structured day activities;
(4) therapeutic intervention by NHS, social services and/or probation service;
(5) monitoring of mental state;
(6) co-ordination and supervision of the overall package of care.

A key element is usually the involvement of a specialist in the psychiatry of learning disability and an appropriate community team.

Local admission facilities

Where a community programme is felt to be inappropriate or where further evaluation is necessary local admission units can provide a structured setting for intervention.

Admission to these units for conditions of greater security may be achieved by detention under Section 3 or 37 of the Mental Health Act 1983. In the case of an order under Section 37 there may be an additional restriction order under Section 41. Since the closure of most of the mental handicap hospitals these admission units function as a support to comprehensive community services rather than as a long-term placement. Accordingly they are used for assessment and trial of therapeutic intervention with a view to establishing a community based programme of care. In particular they can be useful in providing a structured environment in the early stages of behaviour programmes.[9, 10]

Medium secure units

Most general medium secure units will accept only those with the mildest form of learning disability.[11] The need for specialist provision at this level of security was originally identified by the Oxford RHA survey[12] and in the past decade a number of such units within the NHS and the private sector have been commissioned.[13] The main reason for admission to these facilities is that the index behaviour cannot be safely contained in available local facilities. Newer medium secure facilities are developing particular expertise in treating sex offenders and can offer the security and potential length of stay which are no longer available in local facilities.

Special hospitals

At present special hospital facilities for people with learning disability are provided at Rampton and Ashworth Hospitals. These facilities have been reviewed in the light of controversial reports[14, 15] and there is a growing belief that many learning disabled in-patients currently at these units require conditions of less security.[16]

The ongoing review of special hospital provision for all patients is likely to result in smaller purpose built units for the learning disabled group who pose a grave and immediate danger.

The Prison Service

While a proportion of people with learning disability who offend are still likely to be committed to prison, the Prison Service has no specialist provision for this very vulnerable group. Better pre-sentence assessments coupled with the safeguards of the Police and Criminal Evidence Act 1984 and the success of court diversion programmes will, it is hoped, lead to a reduction of inappropriate prison disposals for this group of offenders.

References

(1) Parker, E. (1974) *Survey of Incapacity Associated with Mental Handicap at Rampton and Moss Side Special Hospitals.* Special Hospital Research Unit Publication 11: London.
(2) Jones, R. (1985) *Mental Health Act Manual.* Sweet and Maxwell: London.
(3) West, D.J. (1982) *Delinquency: Its Roots, Careers and Prospects.* Heinemann: London.
(4) Hirschi, T. and Hindelang, M.J. (1977) Intelligence and delinquency: a revisionist review. *American Sociological Review* **42**, 571–87.
(5) Coid, J. (1984) How many psychiatric patients in prison? *British Journal of Psychiatry* **145**, 78–86.

(6) Craft, M. (1983) Low intelligence, mental handicap and criminality. In: *Mentally Abnormal Offenders* (eds M. Craft and A. Craft). Baillière Tindall: Eastbourne.

(7) Rutter, M. and Giller, H. (1983) *Juvenile Delinquency: Trends and Perspectives*. Penguin: London.

(8) Prins, H. (1980) *Offenders, Deviants or Patients? An Introduction to the Study of Socio-Forensic Problems*. Tavistock Publications: London.

(9) Day, K. (1988) A hospital based treatment programme of male mentally handicapped offenders. *British Journal of Psychiatry* **153**, 635–44.

(10) Clarke, D.J. (1989) Antilibidinal drugs and mental retardation: a review. *Medicine, Science and the Law* **29**, 136–46.

(11) Treasaden, I. (1985) Current practice in regional secure units. In: *Secure Provision* (ed. L. Gostin). Tavistock: London.

(12) Department of Psychiatry, University of Oxford (1976) A Survey of the Need for Secure Psychiatric Facilities in the Oxford Region. Oxford Regional Health Authority: Oxford.

(13) Isweran, M.S. and Bardsley, E.M. (1987) Secure facilities for mentally impaired patients. *Bulletin of the Royal College of Psychiatrists* **11**, 52–4.

(14) *Report of the Review of Rampton Hospital* (1980) Cmnd. 8073. HMSO: London.

(15) *Report of the Committee of Inquiry into Complaints about Ashworth Hospital* (1992) Cmnd. 2028. HMSO: London.

(16) Halstead, S.M. and Cassidy, L. (1994) *Assessment of Need for Services for Mentally Disordered Offenders and Others with Similar Needs in South West Thames Regional Health Authority: Learning Disability (Mental Handicap). Survey of Detained Patients by County and by District Health Authority.* St George's Hospital Medical School: London.

Chapter 12

Sexual Offenders – Assessment and Treatment

Introduction

Forensic psychiatrists are interested in the treatment of sexual offenders because they often see the effects of sexual offences on children or adult survivors of childhood sexual abuse.[1] It is hoped that treating sexual offenders will prevent future offences. A second reason is the fact that clinical experience of working with sex offenders demonstrates that they show characteristic cognitions and psychological defence mechanisms. There is evidence to suggest that psychological treatments, particularly cognitive behavioural therapy, can break down these defences and change these distorted cognitions.

The history of treating sex offenders in this country does not date back as far as in the USA. The whole issue of childhood sexual abuse has only been brought to the attention of the public since the late 1980s, with the events in Cleveland. However, as the judge who chaired the Cleveland inquiry has said, 'Child sexual abuse did not begin with Cleveland but stretches back much further into the past'.[2] In the 1960s and 1970s the so-called syndrome of 'baby battering' was first recognised and acknowledged. It later became known as 'non-accidental injury'. However, it was not until the Cleveland investigation that the majority of the public became aware that abuse of children could be sexual as well as physical. It has been recognised for some time that perpetrators of sexual offences often have a history of sexual abuse as children and that the highest risk offenders were all previously sexually abused.[3] Therefore another reason to treat sex offenders is not only to prevent them creating more victims of child sexual abuse but also to prevent those victims going on to become offenders. This idea has been described as the 'cycle of abuse'.[4] Treating sex offenders is one way of breaking this cycle to the extent that it has been suggested that sending sex offenders to prison will not address the problem and it is only through treatment rather than custodial sentences that the rate of sex offending will drop.[5]

Before discussing sexual offenders and their treatment, it is important to recognise that not all forms of sexual disorders are necessarily sexual offences and that not all sex offenders will fit the criteria for a sexual disorder. Some individuals may have a sexual preference for children, but may never commit any sexual offences.

Classification of sexual disorders and gender identity disorders

Classification is usually by the form of behaviour. The *ICD-10 Classification of Mental and Behavioural Disorders*, 10th edition,[6] lists the following forms:

(1) Gender identity disorders (F64)
    F64.0 Transsexualism
    F64.1 Dual role transvestism (wearing clothes of the opposite sex temporarily for enjoyment without the wish for a sex change and without sexual excitement)
    F64.2 Gender disorders of childhood
(2) Disorders of sexual preference (F65)
    F65.0 Fetishism
    F65.1 Fetishistic transvestism (wearing articles of the opposite sex to create the appearance of the opposite sex and for sexual arousal)
    F65.2 Exhibitionism
    F65.3 Voyeurism
    F65.4 Paedophilia
    F65.5 Sadomasochism
    F65.6 Multiple disorders of sexual preference (having more than one disorder)
    F65.8 Other disorders of sexual preference (e.g. making obscene phone calls, frotteurism (rubbing up against others in public places), sexual activity with animals, use of strangulation or anoxia to intensify sexual experience, preference for a partner with an anatomical abnormality).
(3) Psychological and behavioural disorders associated with sexual development and orientation (F66)
    Sexual orientation alone is not to be regarded as a disorder though particular sexual orientations may be problematical for the individual and thus cause distress.
    F66.0 Sexual maturation disorder: uncertainty about sexual orientation leading to anxiety and depression
    F66.1 Egodystonic sexual orientation: distress arising because the subject wishes to be of a different orientation
    F66.2 Sexual relationship disorder: distress arises because of difficulties in forming relationships due to the gender identity or sexual preference.
    F65.9 Disorders of sexual preference unspecified

It is obvious from this classification that some of these behaviours may lead to sexual offending, e.g. exhibitionism and paedophilia, while others may not, e.g. fetishism.

Legal offences

Most sexual offences are indictable offences, the exception being indecent exposure, which is a summary offence. Definitions of indictable and summary offences are given in Chapter 2. Only indictable offences are recorded in the criminal statistics and are referred to as notifiable offences. The notifiable sexual offences are listed in Table 12.1

Table 12.1 Notifiable sexual offences

Buggery	Unlawful sexual intercourse with a girl under 16
Indecent assault on a male	
Indecency between males	Incest
Rape of a female	Procuration
Rape of a male	Abduction
Indecent assault on a female	Bigamy
Unlawful sexual intercourse with a girl under 13	Gross indecency with a child

The offences which are of most relevance to psychiatry include rape, indecent exposure and sexual offences against children.

Rape offences against men

Prior to 1994 rape of a man did not exist in law. These offences were charged as buggery. The Criminal Justice and Public Order Act 1994 introduced the specific offence of rape of a male. In 1997 there were 340 such offences notified to the police, though as with all sexual offences this probably greatly underestimates the true number of these offences.

Rape offences against women

Of all the sexual offences, rape is the one that has been used by feminists as an example of male dominance over women. This has been taken to the extreme view that rape is not a sexual offence but a way in which male dominated society subjugates women; examples of this thinking include 'all men have the capacity to rape'. To a limited extent this latter view has some support from the use of rape in war time.[7] Other support comes from the fact that rapists usually have fewer previous convictions for sexual offences and higher rates of previous violent offending. Attitudinal surveys of men often report wide acceptance of myths about rape.[8] Classifications of rapists have largely failed to describe even a majority of rapists satisfactorily. The most likely reason for this is that rapists differ widely from each other in a much greater way than paedophiles or incest offenders do. Rapists may be more simply classified into those for whom the act of rape is part of a sexual fantasy system which they eventually act out, or those for whom the act of rape is an act of violence against women and the sexual act is the ultimate form of humiliation and subjugation of women.

From 1973 to 1985 there was a 30% increase in rape offences reported to the police. From 1986 to 1996 the number of reported rape offences against women has risen annually from 2,288 to 6,337 in 1997. Rape represents 2% of all offences of violence notified to the police, which in turn represents 7% of all notifiable offences.[9]

Case study 7

A 30 year old man who felt that he had been badly treated by women in a number of relationships decided to get revenge on women by raping them. He committed a series of rapes on women chosen at random from the streets. He wore a mask and threatened the women with a knife. After committing eight of these offences, he was arrested and convicted. He was sentenced to life imprisonment. During his prison sentence, he successfully completed the sex offender treatment programme within the prison system.

Case study 8

A 25 year old man had fantasised about abducting an unknown woman from the street and tying her up and raping her. He had previously committed a number of obscene telephone calls. He masturbated to these fantasies and frequently drove around in his car carrying a mask, rope and a knife. One day, he saw a woman alone in a bus stop and tried to abduct her at knife point. He failed and was arrested and charged with attempted abduction. Although he denied a sexual motive for the offence, because of his previous offences and the items that were found on him, the court concluded that the motive was a sexual one. He received a six year sentence. He was assessed for the sex offender treatment programme and given a penile plesmography test. He was shocked by his own arousal to images of violence and rape. As a result, he was able consciously to accept the true motive for his offending and successfully completed the sex offender treatment programme. On release he was offered further community based treatment as a condition of licence.

However, these two groups represent a minority of rapists. Of increasing recognition in recent years is the so called 'date rape'. The 30% increase in rape convictions between 1973 and 1985 was accounted for by an increase in rape committed by offenders known to the victim, often taking place in the latter's own home. Over the same period of time, there was a decrease in 'stranger rape' and 'gang rapes'. The number of offences against children and older women remained unchanged. A Home Office study in 1989[10] concluded that the increase in rapes by friends and relatives during this period was an apparent increase, in that it was due to increased reporting by the women rather than increased offending. The reason for the increased reporting was felt to be an improvement in the way the police and the courts responded to women reporting rape. Since the 1989 study the number of rapes has increased by 170%, this is still thought to be partly due to increased reporting and recording of this offence.

A study of imprisoned rapists[11] concluded that men who had past convictions for sexual offences were more likely to be serial rapists and commit offences against strangers. The authors clustered their subjects into four groups.

(1) Rapists with substance abuse, who were impulsive and had high rates of previous sexual offending.
(2) Violent rapists, who were more often serial offenders who used gratuitous violence and had a higher rate of paraphilias.
(3) 'Socialised misogynists', 20% of whom committed sexual murder. The offences more often involved buggery and physical humiliation of their victims.
(4) Unsocialised rapists, who had higher incidence of childhood conduct disorder and aggression. They were also likely to be serial offenders (with the second group). One-third of their rape offences had started as burglaries and 42% were sexually dysfunctional during the rape.

Of particular concern are the sadistic rapists and the role that sadistic fantasy plays in their offending. Grubin[12] has suggested that in men who have sadistic sexual fantasies, factors concerned with social and emotional isolation may predict whether they will act out these fantasies. He makes a convincing argument that this isolation results from an underlying disorder of empathy. This has two components, the cognitive, which involves recognising the feelings of others and the emotional response to this recognition. A disorder of either or both might lead to acting out of sadistic sexual fantasies. The possible aetiology of such a disorder could be either organic or developmental.

Indecent exposure

Indecent exposure or exhibitionism is a non-indictable sexual offence. Most men convicted of the offence do not re-offend as it is believed that the court appearance alone has a deterrent effect. If there is a further conviction, then the risk of re-offending increases dramatically.[13] Previously, indecent exposers were classified according to whether the penis was erect or flaccid during the act.[14] However, as with other sexual offences, there is not a satisfactory classification or theory of aetiology for this behaviour. The majority of exposers do so at times of personal stress, are more likely to be married and do not show the characteristics of other sexual offenders.[8] Abel and Rouleau[15] conducted a longitudinal study of 561 male sex offenders. They showed that men reported a number of different paraphilias. Over 80% of exhibitionists showed two or more different paraphilias and one in three had five or more. They also showed that 28% of rapists described a sexual interest in exhibitionism. Treatment of indecent exposers is less likely to be effective if the offender commits a high frequency of offences.

Sexual offences against children

Incest is an offence which is committed if a man has sexual intercourse with a female who is a first degree relative and he is aware of this fact. Because of the fact that sexual intercourse has to occur for an offence to be incest, only 1% of sexual offences against children amounts to incest. The usual offence is indecency with a child or indecent assault. However, this may be an underestimation of the numbers of cases of sexual intercourse with children within the family since very often an offender will plead guilty to a lesser charge rather than not guilty to the more serious offence. In the absence of forensic evidence it may be the word of the child against the defendant. Although the majority of convictions for incest are for father–daughter incest, sexual relationships between brothers and sisters are the commonest.[16] In incest, 65% of relationships involve girls between the ages of 10 and 15 years.[13] In recent years, there has been a much greater recognition of the sexual abuse of children by women, usually mothers abusing their young sons. 20% of such victims are under the age of 4 years and 70% aged from 4 to 10 years of age. The commonest behaviours by women are fondling of the child's genitals and oral sex. Sexual intercourse is the least common, as is the case in male intrafamilial sexual abuse.[17] However, this has to be put in context. In 1993 there were only 12 women imprisoned for sexual offences in the UK.[18]

The number of notifiable offences of incest has decreased from 444 in 1986 to 183 in 1997. The criminal statistics do not record the age of victims of sexual offences except for gross indecency with a child (1,269 in 1997) and unlawful sexual intercourse with a girl under 13 years and under 16 years (148 and 1,112 respectively in 1997). A Home Office study has concluded that the rate of sexual offending against children is much higher than was previously thought.[19]

Previously a distinction was made between intrafamilial offenders against children and extrafamilial offenders. However, because between 20 to 33% of intrafamilial sex offenders show sexual arousal to children, indicating paedophilic attraction, such a distinction is now not thought to be valid[20]. Over 80% of offenders against children are either relatives (13%) or are known to them (68%). One-third of the offenders are adolescents.[19]

The STEP project was commissioned by the Home Office to evaluate the effectiveness of community based treatment programmes for sex offenders.[3] They found that nearly 90%, of the offenders in their analysis were offenders against children. When they described the group as a whole, they found them to be 'isolated, lonely individuals, lacking in self confidence, who were typically under-assertive who could not deal with negative emotions and who were not able to appreciate the emotional distress caused to their victims by their offending behaviour'. They compared intrafamilial offenders with extrafamilial offenders. One difference between the two groups was in the level of emotional congruence with children. This is described in more detail later. Rather than classify offenders against children according to the relationship with their victim, they found that it was more valid to separate all sexual offenders against children into high deviancy and low deviancy groups. The characteristics of the high deviancy group were

(1) They committed offences inside and outside the family.
(2) They offended against both boys and girls.
(3) They were twice as likely to have committed previous sexual offences.
(4) They had a high risk of re-conviction as measured on the Thornton scale (see page 221).
(5) They were much more likely to have been abused as a child.

Rates of offending and recidivism

Almost every researcher and clinician involved in the assessment and treatment of sex offenders recognises that the official figures for convictions represent a very small percentage of the total number of sexual offences committed in one year.[21] The proof for this view is the large disparity between the rates of self reported sexual abuse compared with the number of convictions for sexual offences. Fisher[22] quotes a number of studies of the prevalence of childhood sexual abuse reported to researchers. This varied from 12% of women under the age of 16 reporting abuse to 37% reporting 'contact sexual abuse' before the age of 18 years. Although there is considerable variation in rates of childhood sexual abuse, even the lowest figures put this at 10% and therefore this represents a very significant problem. The official rates for conviction for sexual offences are provided by the Home Office's Annual Criminal Statistics of England and Wales.[9]

In 1996 there were a total of 31,400 sexual offences notifiable to the police, of which one-fifth were rape offences and just over one-half were indecent assaults. In 1997 there were 33,514 sexual offences which was a 6.8% increase on the previous year. This was twice the average increase during the previous ten years. Sexual offences represented 9.6% of all offences of violence in 1997 and 0.77% of all notifiable offences.

A study of the prevalence of convictions for sexual offending followed up a cohort of men who were born in 1953 in England and Wales.[23] This found that 1.1% of these men had been convicted of a notifiable sexual offence (see Table 12.1) by the age of 40 years. Of these offenders, 10% had committed a further sexual offence within five years. It was estimated that 165,000 of the male population of England and Wales in 1993 had a conviction for a notifiable sexual offence.

What then of the re-offending rates of sex offenders? Re-conviction rates for sex offenders are low compared to other groups of offenders, for example, those committing property offences. However, this may not be an accurate description because of the short period of time that is usually used in calculating rates of re-conviction. With most offences the rates are based on a follow-up period of up to five years after previous convictions. However, this may not be a long enough period in the case of sex offenders. Soothill and Gibbens,[24] in a frequently quoted paper, highlighted this fact. They chose one particular group of sexual offenders to study. These were men who had had or attempted to have, sexual intercourse with girls under the age of 13 years. Three separate offences accounted for this behaviour: rape, incest and unlawful sexual intercourse. Men who were convicted of these offences during 1951 or 1961 were followed up until 1974. They calculated the cumulative percentage of offenders who re-offended up until 24 years later. For standard list offences, i.e. all types of indictable offences, 48% of these offenders had re-offended by 22 years of follow up. However, it was more important to discover whether these offenders had committed further sexual or violent offences. They found that 23%, i.e. nearly a quarter, had committed a further sexual or violent offence up to 22 years later. They also showed that these were not trivial offences. Only half of this group of re-offenders had been convicted within five years. Therefore, if the normal length of follow up had been used, there would have been a serious underestimation of the recidivism of sex offenders. Follow up should be for at least ten years before concluding that the offender had not re-offended.

One reason for this finding may have been the fact that the recorded convictions of sexual offences only represents the 'tip of the iceberg'. During the ten year period of follow up, although an offender may not have been convicted, it may be that he was offending, but may simply have not been caught. Support for this comes from a study from the United States.[25] Their community sample of sex offenders admitted to a much greater number of offences, involving many more victims, than the number for which they had been convicted. For example, extrafamilial paedophile offenders each admitted an average of 23 sexual acts with girls and 280 sexual acts with boys. Not surprisingly, the figures for intrafamilial paedophile offenders were lower, these were an average of 81 sexual acts with girls and 62 sexual acts with boys. Rapists admitted an average of seven offences and exhibitionists over 500 offences. However, some caution has to be attached to this study because only a very small number of offenders admitted to a very large number of offences.[18] Recidivism rates vary according to different studies. However, a pattern emerges that re-offending is lowest in intrafamilial offenders against girls, up to 10%, as opposed to up to 30% in extrafamilial abuse of girls. The highest rate of re-offending is extrafamilial offenders against boys where the rate is up to 40%.[26] However, further evidence that these figures may be an under-estimate was demonstrated by Marshall (quoted in Barker and Morgan).[18] He showed that when unofficial records are searched, the true rates of re-offending in sexual offenders were between 2.4 and 2.8 times as high as would be expected from their official criminal records. Other researchers have shown that men who offend against boys outside the family are the highest risk of offending. Grubin and Kennedy[20] interviewed 102 men convicted of sexual offences. They found that one distinct group were the offenders against boys. In this group, the victims were more likely to be strangers, the offenders had higher rates for previous convictions for sexual offences and that they offended against more than one victim. They were also more likely to describe paraphilias other than paedophilia.

A meta-analysis of 61 studies which involved nearly 29,000 sexual offenders recorded recidivism rates amongst different groups of sexual offenders.[27] The recidivism rate for further sexual offences in convicted rapists was 19% and for sexual offenders against children, 13%. The average follow up was for 4–5 years. The recidivism rates for non-sexual violence was significantly higher in rapists compared with sexual offenders against children. These rates are likely to be an underestimate because of the relatively short follow-up period. They attempted to identify predictors of sexual recidivism. Of the demographic variables, only younger age of offending and being single were predictive factors. Anti-social personality disorder and a higher number of previous offences were also predictors. However, the strongest predictors of sexual recidivism were higher levels of sexual deviancy, particularly sexual interest in children as measured by penile plesmography (see page 222). In general, the factors which predicted non-sexual offending were the same as those found in a non-sexual offender population.

Risk assessment in sexual offenders

The task of assessing the risk of sex offenders committing further offences is different from risk assessment in the mentally ill. One obvious difference is that although the mentally ill will not have been convicted of any serious offences, the characteristics of their illness may lead them to be rated at higher risk of harming themselves or other people. In the case of assessing the risk of sexual offences, this is usually needed where a man has already committed at least one sexual offence. It is therefore relatively easy to group known offenders into high and low risk categories. One study[28] showed that re-conviction rates of men with two previous offences was 15 times that of men with only one previous offence. With serious sexual offenders involving severe violence, it would be impossible to say that they would never re-offend even though in reality, the risk of re-offending may be low. In this case, although the risk of an offence occurring is low, the severity of the offence and the consequences would be high.[29] Intrafamilial sexual abusers of children are at lower risk of re-offending than extra-familial abusers of children. But those who offend against both sexes, both prepubertal and post pubertal are at the higher risk. These have been described as the 'polymorphously perverse'.

Marshall[30] analysed the reconviction rate and previous criminal record of a random sample of 13,000 prisoners released from prison during 1987. He found that 402 offenders in the sample (3%) had been in prison for a sexual offence. Within the subgroup of those who also had a previous sexual conviction, 12% had committed further sexual offences within four years of release compared with only 1% of those offenders who had nei-ther a current nor previous sexual conviction. He suggested that a history of sexual offending indicated an increased risk of further offending. Grubin[12] has argued that this type of actuarial prediction of risk, which only uses previous offences, is of limited value. The most important reason for this is that any prediction, if it involves a low frequency event (i.e. less than 1% of all offences), will produce too many false positive results to be accurate. It is obvious that this type of actuarial prediction does not pre-dict which offenders are treatable or which individuals are at higher risk of offending.

Case study 9

Mr B was a 40 year old man, married with two children. In his 20s, his work brought him into contact with young children and on three occasions he sexually assaulted young prepubertal girls. He received a short prison sentence but was not offered any therapy. Thirteen years later, he was convicted of abusing two prepubertal girls who were friends of the family. Following conviction for indecent assault he attended a sex offender treatment group. This was followed up with individual work on sexual fantasies. During the three years of his treat-ment, he disclosed other offences against young girls but denied any sexual attraction to boys. A young boy who was a member of the same family as his female victim, disclosed that he had also been sexually abused by Mr Brown, four years previously. Mr Brown then admitted that he had also been sexually attracted to and offended against young boys. Despite the offer of treatment in the community in a sex offender treatment programme, he was sent to prison for three years. During the three years that Mr B was being treated, both in the group programme and individually, his risk of re-offending was considered significant. However, this risk rose dramatically when it was discovered that he had previously offended against prepubertal boys in addition to girls, even though he had not offended recently. This placed him in the highest risk category. This case demonstrates that risk is not a static concept and information which as it becomes available can significantly alter the level of risk even if the offender does not re-offend.

Risk factors

Any clinician or researcher who has been involved in assessing or treating sexual offenders will have come across the high levels of denial that they demonstrate in the face of incontrovertible evidence. It is not uncommon for a sex offender who has been convicted of an offence, to which he pleaded guilty and served a prison sentence, to later deny that he had committed the offence. Denial in sex offenders is of course, a defence mechanism and it serves to protect offenders from consciously acknowledging the extent of their behaviour and therefore, allows them to re-offend. Denial also exists at varying levels, from absolute denial of the offence, through to denial of the seriousness of the offence or the need for treatment. Another characteristic of sex offenders, which is a risk factor, is their abnormal level of emotional congruence. This is a distorted emotional attachment to children. There are differences according to whether the offenders are fathers or not. Fathers who sexually offend show lower levels of emotional congruence than non-offending fathers. Conversely, offenders who are not fathers show higher levels of emotional congruence compared to non-offenders who are also not fathers. It is suggested that the offenders who are not fathers may have had a developmental disorder in which they became fixed at a child's level of emotional development which accounts for high emotional congruence. This means that they can relate to children in such a way that makes it easier for them to offend against them. In fathers who do not offend, the level of emotional congruence is appropriate and allows them to empathise with their children and understand their emotional needs. Crucially, fathers who offend against children lack these abilities.

As discussed earlier, clinical risk factors based on an understanding of the phenomenonology of sadistic sexual offenders have also been proposed by Grubin.[12] Other risk factors include cognitive distortions, which are described in more detail later.

One assessment scale that is based on an actuarial prediction has been developed by Thornton and employed by, *inter alia*, the Hampshire Constabulary.[31] The assessment involves two initial stages and a third if the offender has undertaken treatment. The scale describes three levels of risk, lower (1 point), medium (2–3 points) and higher (4 and over). One point is scored for each of the following:

(1) If the index offence has a sexual element.
(2) Previous sexual offences.
(3) The index offence includes a non-sexual violent offence.
(4) Previous non-sexual violent offences.
(5) Conviction for sexual offences on more than three occasions in the past.

The second stage involves assessing whether various aggravating factors are present. These include sexual offences with a male victim, non-contact sexual offenders, offences involving a stranger, never having been married, having been in care, substance abuse, a score of 25 or more on the Hare Psychopathy checklist and evidence of deviant arousal measured by penile plesmography. If two or more of these aggravating factors are present, then the risk category is increased by one level. If the offender is in prison then the risk can be increased or decreased depending on his response to treatment, in particular if there is improvement in his risk factors and his behaviour in prison. An analysis of this scale showed that of 162 offenders rated low risk, 9% committed further sexual offences and of 231 offenders rated medium risk, 23% committed further sexual offences. Of the 140 offenders rated high risk, 46% committed further sexual offences.

The STEP report[3] classified offenders into high and low risk. They discovered five factors derived from the psychometric testing, which differentiated between these two groups. High risk offenders were found to have:

(1) higher levels of social inadequacy;
(2) a greater lack of empathy for their victim;
(3) distorted thinking;
(4) higher levels of sexual obsessions;
(5) abnormal emotional congruence.

As with other violent offences, the presence of substance abuse can greatly increase the risk of re-offending. However, the presence of mental disorder does not necessarily predict further re-offending. West[29] has suggested that sexual offending is not characteristic of the mentally ill or the mentally impaired, but the latter may be overrepresented in the criminal justice system because their mental disorder means they are more likely to be caught. Sexual offending in patients with a learning disability is discussed further in Chapter 11.

Penile plesmography (PPG)

This investigative technique aims to measure levels of sexual arousal in men who are subjected to visual and/or auditory depictions of sexual and violent acts. Marshall and Eccles[32] and Howlitt[33] have critically reviewed PPG, including its limitations. It is presently used in five prisons throughout England and Wales as part of the assessment for the sex offender treatment programme. However, the use of the PPG has been criticised by Marshall, who is one of the leading researchers and clinicians working in this field. He stated that if its use was to continue, then at best it is likely to be seen as unscientific (quoted in Turner).[34] Inmates dislike the PPG and the public have difficulty accepting why pornographic material should be shown to sex offenders, even if it is part of their assessment and treatment. Turner[34] states that if its use as part of the assessment for the sex offender treatment programme (SOTP) in prisons is continued, then its limitations must be recognised as well as the fact that consent cannot be truly said to be informed and freely given because refusal to undertake the test could lead to an inmate serving a longer sentence in prison. He suggested that the resources currently used, could instead, be used to assess and treat high risk sexual offenders in prison. But as Case study 8 above demonstrates, it can be useful in challenging denial as part of treatment.

Treatment of sexual offenders

Cognitive behavioural therapy

Behavioural treatment of sex offenders previously focused on changing sexual preferences and was based on the theory of classical conditioning. It was believed that early, often infantile, experiences conditioned the later development of paraphilias such as paedophilia. Behavioural treatment involved reducing deviant arousal, for example by aversion therapy which used adverse stimuli, such as electric shocks or by inducing nausea, which was then paired with the deviant sexual fantasies. The obvious ethical concerns raised by this type of treatment have largely led to them not being used. Some forms of aversion therapy still exist, for example shame aversion therapy in exhibitionists. In this treatment the person exposes to an audience while talking aloud about their thoughts.[8] Instead of attempting to decrease deviant arousal, it has been suggested that it may be more effective to increase non-deviant arousal. This can be achieved using masturbatory reconditioning or covert sensitisation, both of which are described later.

The work of Finkelhor has been particularly influential in the development of cognitive behavioural treatment for sex offenders in both the USA and UK. His four stage model of offending has been described by Fisher.[22]

(1) *Motivation to abuse sexually.* Clinical experience shows that frequently offenders maintain denial of a sexual motive for an offence which they freely admit committing. However, it is believed that their motivation inevitably results from deviant fantasies and arousal which are reinforced by masturbation.
(2) *Overcoming internal inhibitions.* The fact that not everyone who experiences deviant arousal and fantasies goes on to offend, combined

with the knowledge that most sex offenders accept that their behaviour is illegal, suggests that they develop cognitive distortions in order to overcome their own inhibitions to offend. Other disinhibitors include alcohol and drugs.

(3) *Overcoming external inhibitions.* The next stage involves the offender 'setting up' a situation where he is able to offend. For example, a paedophile may offer to babysit.

(4) *Overcoming the resistance of the victim.* The final stage is one where the offender overcomes the victim's own resistance, for example with children by offering gifts as bribes or using threats of violence. It is recognised that some offenders may particularly target vulnerable victims who offer little resistance.

Finkelhor's theory is based on the fact that sex offenders will only commit sexual offences when they have moved through all four stages as described above.

This theory of offending leads naturally to treatment since it suggests therapeutic interventions at all four stages. The essential components of cognitive behavioural therapy for sex offenders, whether this is individually or in a group, have been described by the STEP report.[3] These include the following treatment strategies.

(1) *The offence cycle.* The offender describes in detail the events leading up to the offences. This work should be done early on in treatment since it allows the offender to acknowledge their responsibility and that the offence did not 'just happen' as is a frequent claim. It is at this stage that the various levels and types of denial are most effectively challenged, often by other offenders within the group.

(2) *Challenging distorted thinking.* Psychological defence mechanisms which allow offenders to continue offending include their excuses and justifications (cognitive distortions). For example, paedophiles often claim that they are fulfilling the child's own need for sexual experience. Rapists may believe that a man has the right to have sex with a woman if he takes her out and buys her dinner. Changing this type of thinking is most successfully done in a group setting where other offenders can challenge each other's cognitive distortions.

(3) *Understanding the harm done to victims.* This is often achieved by showing offenders videos of victims of sexual offences describing the effect of the offences on themselves. This can also generate feelings in the offender based on their own experience of sexual abuse earlier in their life. Offenders may also write victims apology letters, which are not sent to the victim, but discussed in the group. The STEP report includes a warning that such work should not be so extensive as to humiliate offenders since this may have a harmful effect and may increase the risk of offending, rather than decrease it. There is also an

issue of undertaking this kind of work with sadistic sexual offenders who will learn that they have caused longer term harm to their victims. This in turn could lead to increased deviant arousal and greater risk of re-offending.

(4) *Fantasy modification*. It is generally accepted that offenders' deviant fantasies are reinforced by masturbating to them. Techniques for changing these fantasies were referred to earlier. One method is covert sensitisation, in which the offender is asked to detail one of their deviant fantasies, following which they are asked to imagine an unpleasant consequence, such as being caught by the police. Another method uses masturbatory reconditioning. This can be done in one of two ways:

  (a) *Thematic shift*, in which deviant fantasies are replaced by non-deviant fantasies during masturbation.

  (b) *Directed masturbation*, when the offender records an audiotape of a preferred non-deviant fantasy and then masturbates to this fantasy to ejaculation.

This work is more appropriately done individually rather than in a group setting. It often takes place after the group work has been completed.

(5) *Social skills and anger control*. It has long been recognised that sex offenders have poor social skills. However, if only this were treated then there would be a danger of producing more socially skilled sex offenders rather than reducing their offending. Anger is also believed to be of relevance, particularly in rape offences.

(6) *Relapse prevention work*. This type of work has developed from relapse prevention work with substance abusers. First, the offender identifies his risk factors for offending. He must then learn to recognise, avoid and cope with situations which are likely to lead to him re-offending. He should recognise that the return of deviant fantasies and arousal could be the first stage of the cycle which may lead to him re-offending. This type of work also involves making the offender aware of high risk situations which he should avoid in future. For example, a paedophile should avoid passing by a children's playground even if it is on the way to work. This has been described as 'seemingly unimportant decisions'. This work is based on the idea that sex offenders may take decisions during their normal day which appear to be unimportant, for example the way that they should walk to work. However, if that decision leads them to a high risk situation such as a children's playground, then they should consciously acknowledge this and take a different route to work, even if this is longer. The basis of relapse prevention work is a conscious recognition by the offender of his own risk of re-offending, the need to change their lifestyle and develop strategies to deal with situations that may increase their risk of re-offending.

Psychoanalytic psychotherapy

Prior to the acceptance of cognitive behavioural therapy as the most effective treatment for sex offenders, group therapy with offenders was often based on psychoanalytic theory. Most of this work has been done in the Portman Clinic which is part of the Tavistock and Portman NHS Trust and has been treating people who suffer from social and sexual deviations with individual and group analytic psychotherapy since the late 1930s. Individual psychoanalytic psychotherapy with sexual offenders has been described by Zachary.[35] As in other psychoanalytic psychotherapy, the issues of transference and counter transference are important. Zachary acknowledges the effect that working with sexual offenders has on the professionals involved which is, of course, the counter transference. Group psychotherapy at the Portman Clinic has been undertaken by treating both victims and perpetrators of incest in the same group setting.[36] Paedophile and incest offenders are not treated in the same group, because of the disruption of group dynamics that this would cause. However, as described earlier, the distinction between intrafamilial and extrafamilial sexual abuse of children may not be as clear as was believed in the past.

Most of the outcome studies of treatment of sexual offenders using psychoanalytic therapy have been undertaken in the USA. At best, the result of treatment of offenders treated with psychoanalytic group or individual therapy has been described as ineffective, but at worst, there is some evidence from the USA that sex offenders treated in psychoanalytic psychotherapy may have higher rates of recidivism than sex offenders who received no treatment at all.[18]

Physical treatment

Other treatments of sexual offenders include physical treatments. This is generally hormonal or what is often called 'chemical castration'. These treatments are based on the hypothesis that there is a direct causal link between sexual offending and circulating levels of testosterone. But no such link has been proved. There is evidence that such treatments do reduce the levels of sexual drive and therefore, it is suggested that they may be more effective in those with a higher sexual drive. However, hormonal treatment does not affect sexual fantasies which are believed to form a crucial part of the cycle of offending. Another problem with this treatment is that all sexual drives, including normal ones are reduced. This would prevent a paedophile having a normal sexual relationship with his wife which may have been encouraged by his therapist. Although the side effects of the treatment are described as not particularly common, the severity of them means that such medication is unsuitable for long-term use. In this country, the most commonly used anti-libidinal drugs are cyproterone acetate and medroxyprogesterone acetate. Both of these act to reduce circulating levels of testosterone. Other drugs which act in other ways which have been used include progesterone, benperidol and goserilin. Although it may appear logical to some to castrate sexual offenders,[37] when this has been done, it has not prevented men from re-offending. Some would only advocate the use of these drugs in extremely rare cases where sexual offending is associated with hypersexuality with high circulating levels of testosterone. But, there are considerable ethical issues in the use of these treatments, especially regarding consent and coercion, in cases where these treatments are made a condition of progress through the prison system or even release on licence.[38]

Effectiveness of treatment

A meta-analysis of 12 different treatment studies investigated the overall effect of treatment on recidivism and which types of treatment were more effective.[39] It found that of those sex offenders who completed treatment, 19% committed further sexual offences compared with 27% of controls who did not receive treatment. Those studies which followed-up offenders for more than five years appeared to show a greater effect of treatment compared with studies with follow-up periods of less than five years. It was suggested that the more effective treatments negated the findings from the study by Soothill and Gibbons[23] referred to earlier, which showed that only 50% of recidivism was evident by five years of follow up. Treatment appeared more effective in community based programmes compared with institutional programmes. Adolescent sex offenders appeared to benefit most of all from treatment. The most effective types of treatment were cognitive behavioural and hormonal. However, up to two-thirds refused hormonal treatment and 50% who began it, subsequently dropped out. This compares with refusal and drop out rates of one-third for cognitive behavioural treatment. Therefore, it is suggested that cognitive behavioural treatment has an advantage over hormonal treatment. This is increased further when the side effects of hormonal treatment are taken into account. Behavioural treatment programmes were not found to be effective.

The effectiveness of cognitive behavioural treatment has been measured in a study of those sex offenders who were referred to one of the seven treatment programmes that were evaluated by the STEP project.[3] Only 5% of the treated sample had committed a further sexual offence at two years follow up, compared to 9% of an untreated sample of sex offenders who had been placed on probation in 1990. The follow-up period is too short to be certain of a treatment effect and the study will be repeated at 5 and 10 years follow up. The study concluded that sexual offending behaviour is affected by treatment that uses the cognitive behavioural model.[40]

Sex offender treatment programmes

Treatment programmes for sex offenders are available in the community, often managed by the local probation service working with other agencies, including social services, the NHS and the voluntary sector. Separate treatment programmes exist within a number of prisons.

Community based treatment programmes

The STEP project[3] analysed a number of community based sex offender treatment programmes running in England as well as one single residential programme. The results of their analysis of the outcomes of treatment showed that over one-half of the offenders who received treatment showed some treatment effect. However, of some concern was the fact that a quarter of the offenders became more inclined to blame their victims. They described a number of different types of treatment programmes which all used the cognitive behavioural model. The shorter term treatment programmes, of up to 60 hours total duration, treated men who were more willing to admit their offences and sexual problems and who showed less justification and distorted thinking. The longer treatment programmes tended to have more of an impact on highly deviant men. One reason why the short-term treatment programme had a good success rate in 60% of men who were treated, may have been because of the fact that they chose a low deviancy population to treat. The men who had been treated in the various programmes were assessed with a number of different scales. These scales measured the following:

(1) the extent to which offenders denied or minimised their offending;
(2) the justifications that they gave for sexual assaults;
(3) the degree to which they demonstrated any empathy towards their victims;
(4) their assertiveness;
(5) their self esteem;
(6) the extent to which offenders blamed external factors, such as the behaviour of their victims, or other problems in their lives, for their offending (often described as the locus of control);
(7) the degree to which offenders were able to develop capacity for intimate relationships with adults; (it is well recognised that 'emotional loneliness' is often deficient in sex offenders);
(8) cognitive distortions;
(9) emotional congruence with children;
(10) whether the offenders had developed strategies of relapse prevention during the course of their treatment;
(11) an attempt to measure whether the sex offender was tending to pro-

vide socially desirable responses rather than admit their true attitudes or beliefs.

The STEP project made a number of important recommendations for the community treatment for sex offenders.

(1) They highlighted the importance of assessment which should be systematic and which should be before, during and after treatment. However they recognised that the scales which they used for this assessment require considerable psychological input.
(2) There should be better training of therapists involved in groups.
(3) Fantasy modification work must be part of any treatment programme.
(4) Offenders must understand the key messages that are given to them during the group and not just learn the jargon.
(5) The goal of treating sex offenders is to decrease offending by reducing denial, reducing their justification and distortion, increasing their empathy for victims and decreasing their deviant arousal and fantasies. Although all the treatment groups recognise this, there was a greater need for offenders to recognise the risk that they might pose in the future and in what particular situations.
(6) The work on victim empathy should only be undertaken with offenders after it is clear that they were able to cope with the acknowledgement of the consequences of what they had done. Since these men have low self-esteem, this could initially become worse during treatment to which they might react defensively and, in anger, blame their victim even more. It was recommended that self-esteem should be enhanced and coping skills taught before the work on victim empathy is undertaken.
(7) There should be more work done with offenders on relapse prevention.
(8) If it was not possible to increase the number of programmes available nationally, then there should be greater selection of appropriate offenders and priority should be given to work on relapse prevention.

Other recommendations concerned the length of programmes and the need for maintenance treatment after attending a programme.

Prison treatment programmes

The sex offender treatment programme (SOTP) was introduced into the Prison Service in England and Wales in 1992. It is based on a cognitive behavioural model of treatment and runs in 25 prisons. The assessment before treatment is based on psychometric testing, clinical interviews and in five prisons, the PPG. The assessment aims to exclude the following groups of sex offenders who it is thought would not benefit from such treatment in prison. This includes the mentally ill, those at high risk of self harm, those with a severe paranoid personality disorder, inmates with an IQ of less than

80 and those where there is evidence of organic brain damage. The sex offender treatment programme consists of four parts:

(1) the core programme.
(2) the thinking skills programme.
(3) the extended programme.
(4) the relapse prevention programme.

The *core programme* is essential for all participants in the SOTP. Its aims are as follows:

(1) to increase the offender's sense of responsibility for the offence and to decrease denial;
(2) to increase the offender's motivation to avoid re-offending;
(3) to increase the degree to which the offender has empathy for his victim;
(4) to help the offender develop skills to avoid re-offending.

The *core programme* consists of 20 blocks with a total of 80 hours of treatment.

The *thinking skills programme* aims to increase the offender's ability to see the consequences of his actions and to help him consider alternative strategies in the future. It is believed that these skills are needed in order that the offender can understand, develop and use strategies of relapse prevention to prevent re-offending in future.

The *extended programme* is a group of shorter related treatment groups which currently includes anger management, stress management, relationship skills and behavioural therapy. This last treatment is on an individual basis and includes work on sexual fantasies, deviant sexual arousal and victimology.

Offenders who have attended the core programme and other parts of the sex offender treatment programme, should also attend a *relapse prevention* group during the year before their release. It is a requirement that they should have successfully completed the other treatment programmes, otherwise attendance at the relapse prevention group is unlikely to be effective. During the group, offenders should produce strategies for relapse prevention which they should be able to practice before their release from prison.

Because of the need for longer term follow up, as explained earlier, the effectiveness of the sex offender treatment programme will not be known until at least the year 2005.[41] However, it has been possible to recognise changes in offenders as demonstrated on the psychometric tests and performance during the groups. There has been some evidence of change in levels of denial, degrees of minimisation and cognitive distortions. Other treatment of sex offenders takes place as part of the therapeutic regime at HMP Grendon.[42]

Legislation affecting sex offenders

During the 1990s, a great deal of legislation has been introduced in response to perceived public concern regarding sex offenders. The first of these was contained in the Criminal Justice Act 1991 and allowed for longer prison sentences for sex offenders.

Criminal Justice Act 1991

The principle that the length of a custodial sentence should be commensurate with the seriousness of the offence was substantially altered under this Act. In the case of violent or sexual offenders, this Act allowed courts to pass a longer than normal sentence if it was 'necessary to protect the public from serious harm from the offender'. Serious harm in this case included psychological as well as physical serious injury. However, the length of sentence was allowed to reflect the perceived risk that violent and sexual offenders might pose in the future. Therefore, an offender could be sent to prison not for what he had actually done but in order to protect the public in the future. The Act also imposed a statutory duty on the court to obtain a psychiatric report where the defendant 'appears to be mentally disordered'. A study of the first 35 cases referred to the Court of Appeal where a longer than normal sentence had been passed showed the significance of these psychiatric reports on the sentencing.[43] It appeared that the Court of Appeal paid particular attention to the psychiatrists' views on personality, the treatability of any disorder and their assessment of the offender's future risk. It was suggested that psychiatric reports were being used to justify an increase in the length of a prison sentence, which was not the purpose for which they were originally commissioned.

The Criminal Justice Act also increased the length of time that a sex offender could be supervised, following release, until the end point of his prison sentence.

Protecting the public

In 1996 the Government published a strategy document entitled *Protecting the Public*.[44] This included chapters on the sentencing and supervision of sex offenders and on automatic life sentences for violent and sexual offenders. The strategy was based on the use of custodial sentences for sex offenders in order to protect the public. It was also recognised that ongoing work with sex offenders was required after their release from prison and that in order to achieve this, an extended period of supervision was necessary. From this document came a number of Acts which in some way aimed to achieve greater control of sex offenders. These include the Crime Sentences Act 1997, the Sex Offenders Act 1997, the Criminal Evidence

(Amendment) Act 1997, the Protection from Harassment Act 1997 and the Sexual Offences (Protected Material) Act 1997.

Crime Sentences Act 1997

As noted above, where a sex offender had been given a prison sentence, the period of statutory supervision after release was increased from three-quarters of the sentence to the end of the sentence by the 1991 Criminal Justice Act. The Crime Sentences Act increased this statutory supervision further, to a minimum of 12 months and a maximum of 10 years, in all but exceptional cases. The length of supervision was to be determined by the sentencing judge, based on the risk to the public from the offender. Additionally, the supervision order on release could contain specific conditions such as attendance at a community based sex offender treatment programme and residence in a probation hostel. It could also include a curfew order which may be enforced by electronic tagging. Failure to comply with these conditions could lead to prosecution and imprisonment if the court believed that that was necessary for the protection of the public.

Sex Offenders Act 1997

This had two parts, the first compelled sex offenders to register with the police and notify them of their address. The second part allowed UK courts to prosecute those people who offended against children in another country. The Act listed the offences to which notification applied. These were essentially the notifiable offences listed in Table 12.1 above. The length of time of notification to the police depended on the length of the prison sentence and varied from a minimum of five years to indefinite. It has been estimated that in 1993 there were 125,000 men who had previously committed offences which were registrable under the Sex Offenders Act.[23]

The Home Office issued a circular[45] which gave guidance on the management of the information acquired under this legislation. This included a requirement that a risk assessment should be carried out by the police before there was disclosure of the information to a third party. It stated that this assessment should take account of:

(1) the nature and pattern of previous offending;
(2) compliance with previous sentences or court orders;
(3) the probability that a further offence will be committed;
(4) the harm such behaviour would cause;
(5) any predatory behaviour which may indicate a likelihood of re-offending;
(6) the potential objects of the harm (and whether they are children or otherwise especially vulnerable);

(7) the potential consequences of disclosure to the offender and their family;
(8) the potential consequences of disclosure in the wider context of law and order.

However, such disclosure should be decided in individual cases and not become the general rule. In a number of high profile cases disclosure has caused sex offenders to leave their homes because of pressure from the public.[46]

Crime and Disorder Act 1998

Included in this Act is a sex offender order which has been in force since 1 December 1998. This is a new civil order which can only be applied for by the police. There are two basic requirements for these orders:

(1) that the person has previously been convicted of or cautioned for a sexual offence; and
(2) he has behaved in such a way as to suggest that this order is necessary to protect the public from the risk of serious harm from him.

The definition of serious harm is the same one that is contained in the Criminal Justice Act 1991 referred to earlier. The application for an order is made to a magistrates' court. The orders will prohibit the offender from certain places in order to protect the public. They should be as specific as possible in time and place, e.g. children's playgrounds within a defined area and at certain times of the day. The offender is also required to register under the Sex Offenders Act 1997. The minimum duration of these orders is five years. They can be applied to any offender who is ten years of age or over and therefore, will include children and adolescents. Breach of the order is a criminal and arrestable offence. The maximum penalty, if convicted, is five years imprisonment.

The draft guidance from the Home Office[47] suggests that when assessing the risk that a sex offender presents, a number of factors should be taken into account. These are essentially the same factors that were described earlier in relation to the Sex Offenders Act 1997, with the addition of an assessment of the accuracy of information regarding the individual and previous compliance with therapeutic help and its outcome. The Home Office recommend that in order to make an accurate assessment of risk, other agencies, including probation, social service departments and health authorities should be involved.

This legislation represents a further change of direction in the management of sex offenders in the community. It is intended to fill a perceived gap in existing provision. Whether it will achieve this will only become apparent if and when these orders are used.

Other legislation

Other acts which are relevant in this field are listed below.

(1) The Criminal Evidence (Amendment) Act 1997 allowed non-intimate samples to be taken for DNA analysis for a variety of violence offences including sexual offences. These would be used to create a national DNA database.
(2) The Sexual Offences (Protected Material) Act 1997 restricted access to victims' statements where the offence was a sexual one.
(3) The Protection from Harassment Act 1997 included the ability to make an injunction to prevent conduct which may be seen as harassment by a potential or actual sexual offender.

The full impact of the recent legislation is yet to be seen. Whether this will fulfil the government's intention to protect the public from sex offenders will not be known for many years.

References

(1) Mullen, P.E., Martin, J.L., Anderson, J.C., Romans, S.E. and Herbison, G.P. (1994) The effect of child sexual abuse on social, interpersonal and sexual function in adult life. *British Journal of Psychiatry* **165**, 35–47.
(2) Butler-Sloss, E. (1997) Post Cleveland: some reflections. In: *Child Sexual Abuse: Myth and Reality* pp 4–5 (ed. S. Hayman). Institute for the Study and Treatment of Delinquency: London.
(3) Beckett, R., Beech, A., Fisher, D. and Fordham, A.S. (1994) *Community Based Treatment for Sex Offenders: An Evaluation of Seven Treatment Programmes*. Home Office: London.
(4) Bailey, S. (1998) Cycles of abuse. *Advances in Psychiatric Treatment* **4**, 64.
(5) Butler-Sloss, E. (1998) Legal perspective. *Advances in Psychiatric Treatment* **4**, 64–5.
(6) World Health Organization. (1992) *The ICD10 Classification of Mental and Behavioural Disorders*. WHO: Geneva.
(7) Mezey, G. (1994) Rape in war. *Journal of Forensic Psychiatry* **5**(3), 583–97.
(8) Blackburn, R. (1993) *The Psychology of Criminal Conduct*. Wiley: Chichester.
(9) Home Office (1998). *Criminal Statistics England and Wales 1997*. Cmnd 4162. The Stationery Office: London.
(10) Lloyd, C. and Walmsley, R. (1989) *Home Office Research Study No 105: Changes in Rape Offences and Sentencing*. HMSO: London.
(11) Grubin, D and Gunn, J. (1990) *The Imprisoned Rapist and Rape*. Home Office: London.
(12) Grubin, D. (1997) Predictors of Risk in Serious Sexual Offenders. *British Journal of Psychiatry* **170** (Supplement 32) 17–21.
(13) Bancroft, J. (1989) *Human Sexuality and its Problems*, second edition, Churchill Livingstone: Edinburgh.

(14) Rooth, F.G. (1971) Indecent exposure and exhibitionism. *British Journal of Hospital Medicine* April, 521–33.

(15) Abel, G.G. and Rouleau, J.L. (1990). The nature and extent of sexual assault. In: *Handbook of Sexual Assault* pp 9–21 (eds W.L. Marshall, D.R. Laws and H.E. Barbaree). Plenum Press: New York.

(16) West, D.J. (1993) Disordered and offensive sexual behaviour. In: *Forensic Psychiatry Clinical, Legal and Ethical Issues* pp 329–372 (eds J. Gunn and P.J. Taylor). Butterworth-Heinemann: London.

(17) Wilkins, R. (1990) Women who sexually abuse children. *British Medical Journal* **300**, 1153–4.

(18) Barker, M. and Morgan R. (1993) *Sex Offenders: A Framework for the Evaluation of Community Based Treatment*. Home Office: London.

(19) Grubin, D. (1999) *Sex Offending Against Children: Understanding the Risk*. Home Office Policing and Reducing Crime Unit: London.

(20) Grubin, D. and Kennedy, H. (1991) A classification of sexual offenders. *Criminal Behaviour and Mental Health* **1**, 123–9.

(21) Mullen, P.E. (1993) Child sexual abuse and mental health: the development of disorder. *Journal of Interpersonal Violence* **8**, 429.

(22) Fisher, D. (1994) Adult sexual offenders. In: *Sexual Offending against Children* pp 1–24 (eds T. Morrison, M. Erooga and R.C. Beckett). Routledge: London.

(23) Marshall, P. (1997) *Research Findings No. 55. The Prevalence of Convictions for Sexual Offending*. Home Office: London.

(24) Soothill, K.L. and Gibbens, T.C.N. (1978) Recidivism of sexual offenders, a reappraisal. *British Journal of Criminology* **18**, 267–76.

(25) Abel, G.G., Becker, J.V., Mittelman, M.S., Cunningham-Rathner, J., Rouleau, J.L. and Murphy, W.D. (1987) Self reported sex crimes of non incarcerated paraphiliacs. *Journal of Interpersonal Violence* **2** (6), 3–25.

(26) Beckett, R. (1994) Assessment of sex offenders. In: *Sexual Offending against Children* pp 55–79 (eds T. Morrison, M. Erooga and R.C. Beckett) Routledge: London.

(27) Hanson, K.R. and Bussiere, M.T. (1998) Predicting relapse: a meta-analysis of sexual offender recidivism studies. *Journal of Consulting and Clinical Psychology*, **66** (2), 348–62.

(28) Phillpotts, G.J.O. and Lancucki, L.B. (1979) *Previous Convictions, Sentence and Reconviction*. HMSO: London.

(29) West, D.J. (1996) Sexual molesters In: *Dangerous People* (ed. N. Walker). Blackstone Press: London.

(30) Marshall, P. (1994) Reconviction of imprisoned sexual offenders. In: *Research Bulletin 36*. Home Office: London.

(31) Hampshire Constabulary (1998) Risk assessment when dealing with dangerous sex offenders. (Unpublished).

(32) Marshall, W.L. and Eccles, A. (1991) Issues in clinical practice with sex offenders. *Journal of Interpersonal Violence* **6**(1), 68–93.

(33) Howlitt, D. (1995) *Paedophiles and Sexual Offences Against Children*. Wiley: Chichester.

(34) Turner, C. (1997) The Prison Service sex offender treatment programme. In: *Treating Sex Offenders in a Custodial Setting* (eds C. Holden and S. Hayman). Institute for the Study and Treatment of Delinquency: London.

(35) Zachary, A. (1998) Individual psychoanalytic psychotherapy with perpetrators of sexual abuse. *Advances in Psychiatric Treatment* **4**, 77–81.

(36) Welldon, E. (1998) Group therapy for victims and perpetrators of incest. *Advances in Psychiatric Treatment* **4**, 82–8.

(37) Cook, D.A.G. (1993) There is a place for surgical castration in the management of recidivist sex offenders. *British Medical Journal* **307**, 79.

(38) Bowden, P. (1991) Treatment: use, abuse and consent. *Criminal Behaviour and Mental Health* **1**, 130–6.

(39) Nagayama-Hall, J.C. (1995) Sexual offender recidivism revisited: A meta-analysis of recent treatment studies. *Journal of Consulting and Clinical Psychology* **63** (5), 802–9.

(40) Hedderman, C. and Sugg, D. (1996) *Does treating sex offenders reduce offending?* Research Findings No. 45, Home Office: London.

(41) Clarke, J. (1997) Sex offender treatment in the Prison Service: an overview. In: *Treating Sex Offenders in a Custodial Setting* (eds C. Holden and S. Hayman). Institute for the Treatment and Study of Delinquency: London pp 9–12.

(42) Genders, E. and Player, E. (1995) *Grendon: A Study of a Therapeutic Prison.* Clarendon Press: Oxford.

(43) Solomka, B. (1996) The role of psychiatric evidence in passing 'longer than normal' sentences. *Journal of Forensic Psychiatry* **7**(2), 239–55.

(44) Home Office (1996) *Protecting the Public.* Cmnd 3190. HMSO: London.

(45) Home Office (1997) *Sex Offenders Act 1997.* Circular 39/1997 Home Office: London.

(46) *The Times*, Saturday January 10th 1998. 'Child sex killer agrees to go to mental hospital'.

(47) Home Office (1998) *The Crime and Disorder Act, Draft Guidance Document.* Home Office: London.

Chapter 13

Women and Juvenile Offenders

Women offenders

Introduction

The purpose of this section is to:

(1) describe the incidence of criminal behaviour in women and of mental abnormality amongst female offenders;
(2) describe relevant aetiological factors associated with criminality in women; and
(3) describe any special types of offences seen in women and any particular medicolegal problems they present.

Incidence of criminal behaviour

The incidence of crime in females, as in males, rises throughout childhood to a peak in adolescence (around 16 years) and then rapidly falls. However, unlike males, who maintain this falling rate throughout their life, there is a small secondary hump in the curve around the mid-40s and mid-50s coinciding with the menopausal period. The pattern of criminal behaviour as measured by official statistics shows that females offend much less than males. Self report studies support the official figures. The extent of the difference varies with age and the extent has also varied over the years. In recent times the female rate has increased so that there is now less difference between male and female rates than there used to be. The overall male to female ratio for offenders convicted or cautioned for indictable offences was 4.67:1 in 1996,[1] compared to 11:1 in 1949. There are 30 times as many males in prison as females which reflects partly the quality of the offending (the females tending to commit lesser offences), and possibly the courts being more lenient to women.[2] However, a study[3] of convicted women in Cambridge showed that the apparent leniency of the courts to women merely reflected the fact that women commit less serious offences and have fewer previous convictions. When this was taken into account there was no sex difference in sentencing.

The pattern of misbehaviour in the two sexes is different. Boys are likely to present primarily with property offences, whereas girls are more likely to come to the attention of the authorities because of being in 'moral danger' from sexual misbehaviour. This may not result in an official offence but may lead to a care order. At a later age, men have a greater chance of being involved in violent offences and major property offences (burglary, robbery). It was said that the most typical adult female offence was shoplifting (though there are reports that males have caught up with females in this area) and offences linked to prostitution.[4] However, it is said that women are increasingly imitating their male counterparts and becoming more violent and criminal as the pattern of offending is changing reflecting, perhaps, female emancipation and social upheaval.

Aetiological factors in female offending

Childhood and family factors
In the case of recidivist female offenders, as in males, there is a strong association with childhood factors, such as bad parenting, criminal fathers, alcoholic parents, large families and lower IQ. Subsidiary factors include physical abnormalities, brain damage, mental illness, bad school records, poverty and mesomorphic build. Cloninger and Guze[5] demonstrated that recidivist female prisoners had a strong family history of psychiatric disorder (as do male offenders). The principal disorders were alcoholism (61%), sociopathy (36%) and drug dependency (14%) in the male relatives and hysteria (34%) in the female relatives. As girls, they showed behaviour disorder at school with a high level of truancy (30%), and expulsion or suspension (30%). They had poor work records with unemployment or frequent changes of jobs and they formed unsatisfactory marriages. The impression was gained, as in other studies,[6] that these factors, though similar to those in the case of boys, were worse in the case of girls. It is as though the girls needed greater stress before they became delinquent and when they did so they were much more likely to be disturbed in other aspects of their life which coincides with the findings that girls may be more resilient in the face of family discord than boys.[7] The possible reasons for girls being less criminal than boys have been summarised by Rutter and Giller.[7] Differences in behavioural disorder between the sexes are culturally linked, e.g. the differences between girls and boys in Afro-Caribbean cultures is less than in Asian cultures (where girls are particularly well behaved). Differences between the sexes has not remained steady with the years; as already noted above, girls are becoming more like boys in their delinquency.

Menstrual cycle and physiological factors
It has been argued that female hormonal changes cause periods of stress which may be associated with offending. The *premenstrual syndrome* has

been defined as the recurrence of symptoms in the premenstruum with absence of symptoms in the postmenstruum. Numerous symptoms have been described including the psychiatric ones of irritability, anxiety, tension, depression, hostility, mood swings, impulsive behaviour and difficulty in concentrating. Dalton[8] claimed that 50% of women prisoners offended in the premenstrual week. Dalton asserted that this coincided with other disturbed behaviour, e.g. infraction of prison rules, poor examination results and motoring offences as well as with symptoms of premenstrual tension. Epps, in Gibbens's study[9] failed to find a link between shoplifting and the menstrual period. However, Hands *et al.*[10] found a regular link between disturbed behaviour and the menstrual period in a small group of women who were showing behaviour disorder in special hospital.

D'Orban and Dalton[11] concluded from a study of women prisoners convicted of violent offences, that the violent behaviour was more likely to occur three days before and two days into the menstrual period rather than in the rest of the menstrual cycle. They also found that the women's awareness of premenstrual symptoms (such as depression or tension) did not correlate with the violent behaviour, i.e. the women might be quite unaware that they had a cyclical behaviour pattern because they did not have the expected symptoms of the premenstrual syndrome at the same time.

It has been asserted that the change in hormone levels during the menopause period was responsible for the increased rate of offending in women aged 45–55. However, closer examination has not always supported this idea, e.g. Gibbens did not find menopausal problems to be more common in the shoplifters of that age group. It has been shown[12] in population studies that there is a vulnerable group of women who have a history of psychiatric complaints in the past for whom the menopausal period is an additional and significant stress. To what extent physiological factors are responsible rather than the psychological stresses which occur at this time is unclear and presumably vary from case to case. The psychological factors which might be significant include the movement of children away from the home, coming to terms with ageing, marital stresses and changes in the role of the woman in the household in the absence of her children.

It has also been reported that violence is associated with blood serotonin levels in males but not females. However, there is no clear explanation for this phenomenon.[13]

Women in prison

There are some 1800 women in prison on any one day in England and Wales (3% of the prison population). They are held in a variety of prisons covering different security requirements. Psychiatric care can be provided in the prison hospitals or on the ordinary wings depending on the severity of the disturbance. There is no equivalent to Grendon Prison for female prisoners.

Arrangements are made for pregnant prisoners to receive antenatal care and for the baby to be delivered in a National Health Service hospital. Two secure prisons and one open one provide basic facilities and allow the mother to keep the baby up to 9 months (secure) and 18 months (open). The policy of then separating mother and child has been criticised (and hostel provision proposed). At any time there are some 30 women with children in prison.

Psychiatric disorder in female offenders

Maden, Swinton and Gunn conducted a case note and interview study of a cross sectional sample comprising 25% of all women serving a prison sentence in England and Wales in 1988 and 1989. A sample of the male sentenced prison population was used for comparison. Diagnoses were made on clinical criteria. The prevalence of psychosis was 2% (similar to the male population) but women had higher rates of learning disability (6% vs 2%), personality disorder (18% vs 10%), neurosis (18% vs 10%) and substance abuse (26% vs 12%).[14] For a more detailed account of this study see Maden.[15]

In an earlier study at Holloway Prison[16] every fourth reception (remand and convicted) was studied to include 638 women. Physical ill health was a major problem in 17% mainly due to genitourinary diseases. Major psychosis occurred in 5%, neurosis in 5%, psychopathy or personality disorder in 21%, alcoholism in 8% and drug dependence in 5%. Thus 44% of female prisoners had some form of psychiatric disorder. One-quarter had a history of psychiatric hospital admissions. A later study of 708 women in Holloway produced similar results.[17]

Cloninger and Guze,[5] in their study of convicted American adult female prisoners, found that the incidence of serious mental illness (e.g. psychosis) was not significantly raised compared to the general population. They found, however, that only 12% had no psychiatric disorder. The principal diagnoses and 26% of the women had both sociopathy (65%) and hysteria (41%). Sociopathy can be equated with anti-social personality and hysteria (Briquet's syndrome) with somatisation disorder (DSM III R) characterised by chronic complaints of multiple body disorders due to neurotic difficulties. These two groups would be covered in the ICD-10 by the dissocial personality disorder (F60.2) and somatisation disorder (F45.0). Alcoholism occurred in 47% and drug dependence in 26%. Other diagnoses included homosexuality (6%), anxiety neurosis (11%), depression (6%), mental deficiency with an IQ less than 60 (6%) and schizophrenia (1.5%).

Other findings are in line with this study. Cowie and Slater[6] studied adolescent girls detained in a classifying centre. This group was less delinquent than the adult prisoners and the level of disturbance less. Nevertheless, 51% of the girls had a psychiatric disorder varying from neurotic symptoms in 20% to seriously disturbed personalities and some serious mental illness in 31%.

These studies illustrate the common finding of a high incidence of psychiatric disorder in serious female offenders. However, the bulk of this disorder is unlikely to lead to a transfer to a psychiatric hospital. Dell and Gibbens[18] found, for example, that only 6% of women remanded for medical reports to Holloway Prison were placed on hospital orders. Of the remainder 80% were released to the community and only 14% imprisoned. Maden, Swinton and Gunn reported that only 5% of their population required transfer to hospital but 22% would benefit from out-patient treatment.[14]

Less serious offenders might be expected to have a lower incidence of psychiatric disorder. This was demonstrated in Gibbens's survey[9] of female shoplifters and the ten year follow up.[19] The majority of the shoplifters (80%) were first offenders and most of them would not re-offend. Of first offenders some 20% and 30% of recidivists had psychiatric disorder at the time of the offence. In the follow up (which was incomplete) 8.5% became in-patients in a mental hospital which is some three times the expected rate. The chance of becoming an in-patient increased with the number of previous offences so that 20% who had both offended before and after the index offence went into hospital. The most common reason for admission was depression and suicide attempts.

Medicolegal aspects of psychiatric disorder

Psychiatric disorder is used in mitigation or as a defence in exactly the same way as in males. There are nevertheless two situations specific to females.

(1) A defence of infanticide following the killing by the mother of her baby (see below and Chapters 3 and 7).
(2) Defences associated with hormone changes particularly the *premenstrual syndrome*, a subject reviewed fully by d'Orban.[20]

There is a long history of women being excused their crime in the belief that disordered menstruation caused a disordered state of mind, e.g. Aurelia Snoswell (1851) was acquitted of the murder of her baby niece on the grounds of insanity due to disordered menstruation. Ann Shepherd (1845) was acquitted of theft on the grounds of 'temporary insanity of the menses'. In a modern court the effect of the premenstrual syndrome was used as the basis for an acquittal against a charge of shoplifting where it was shown that the accused had cyclical episodes of confusion associated with menstruation. The theft was said to have occurred during such an episode. In that case there was clear evidence from the defendant's diary and her husband of the cyclical pattern. There have also been at least two cases of defendants in the English courts using the effects of premenstrual tension successfully to plead diminished responsibility to a charge of murder.

D'Orban concludes that the effects of the premenstrual syndrome may be used in mitigation only in the ways described, i.e. it has to be shown that the syndrome has caused a disturbance of mind of sufficient severity to be a mitigating factor. It would be too simplistic to regard the syndrome as accounting for all the disturbed behaviour shown by the offender. It is usually the final straw in a situation of women with a personality disorder who are already under great stress. Whether or not a plea will be successful will depend in part on the proof that there is a cyclical disorder recognised by the doctors as premenstrual syndrome and the severity of the symptoms.

In making the diagnosis, care has to be taken as histories may be falsified (consciously or unconsciously). On the other hand the cyclical behavioural changes which occur may not coincide with subjective symptoms of depression, tension, etc. as discussed above.

It has been difficult to demonstrate scientifically the success of treatment for premenstrual syndrome though there are plenty of case histories asserting the value of intramuscular progesterone, pyridoxine or oral duphaston.

Offences especially associated with women

Prostitution

Although prostitution *per se* is not an offence there are offences related to it, e.g. soliciting or keeping a brothel. Some 6% of women in prison are serving sentences directly related to prostitution and 25–30% of women remanded to prison are or have been prostitutes. Of these 15% had a history of signs of a mental breakdown,[16] 25% had attempted suicide, 25% were alcoholic, 25% were dependent on drugs and 25% had physical disorders and deformities. Maden reported that of the drug addicted women in his sample of sentenced female prisoners, only 12% had a history of prostitution. Temporary prostitution, particularly in adolescents, may be a depressive act or a psychologically suicidal gesture though economic motives are a common rationalisation.

Child stealing

Child stealing is an offence under the Offences against the Person Act 1861. It applies to the stealing of any child under the age of 14 years with the intent to deprive the parent or guardian. It excludes the abduction of the child by a natural parent which may occur in arguments over access and possession.

Child abduction is a relatively rare offence and of all 'violent offences against the person' recorded by the Home Office, only about 0.08% come under the category of child abduction. It is actually committed more often by males when the motive is usually a sexual one. In the case of women there is a high incidence of psychiatric disorder. Amongst 24 such female offenders d'Orban[21] found 8 cases of schizophrenia, 6 cases of mental retardation (including 2 with a transient psychosis) and 10 cases of personality disorder. Three main motivations were found for the offence.

(1) *Comforting offences:* This group included girls from all the diagnostic groups. They tended to be young girls from a large sibship with a history of parental neglect, a broken home and delinquency. The child stealing was related to feelings of loneliness and deprivation. Many had children of their own taken into care or had become separated from them. The common pattern was to take a child they already knew, perhaps through babysitting, alleging perhaps that the child was being badly looked after or was unwanted. It seemed that this allegation was largely a projection of their own feelings of rejection.

(2) *Manipulative offences:* The four subjects in this group were of hysterical personality. Only one had a delinquent history and one had a psychiatric history. The child was stolen (often after considerable planning) in order to control a particular situation and to manipulate their partner. Typically, they might steal a baby and claim it was theirs in order to deceive their partner. Most of this group received penal sentences.

(3) *Impulsive psychotic offences:* This contained a schizophrenic patient and transiently psychotic subnormal patients. All had a history of previous psychiatric treatment. The offences seemed bizarre and impulsive. Sometimes the act was understandable in terms of their delusional ideas, in some the act was inexplicable and in others the stealing seemed to be a comforting action to a psychotic subject whose own children had been taken into care.

Appleby[22] expressed concern about the lack of understanding of these offences leading to inappropriate sentencing.

In these cases the courts, whilst sympathetic to the mentally ill or subnormal offender, are very concerned for the safety of the public. D'Orban reported a repetition of child stealing in 3 of his 24 cases. The children stolen in d'Orban's series were well cared for except for one who was killed by a psychotic offender.

Homicide by women

Women commit homicide five times less than men. When they do the victim is, in 80–90% of cases, a family member (50% a child, 34% a spouse) whereas only 40% of victims of males are family members. In two-thirds of cases the women are found to be mentally disturbed compared to one-third of men.[23]

Spouse murder

In many cases the women kill in retaliation for years of abuse, physical violence and emotional stress. The killing is often precipitated by the victim starting the physical confrontation, the violence commonly occurring in the kitchen. The charge is generally manslaughter (due to lack of intent) though a defence of self-defence is sometimes successful. More recently, the defence of provocation has been successful in the well publicised cases of Thornton and Ahluwalia. For a full description, see Mackay.[24] The courts generally deal sympathetically with such cases.

In a minority of cases the killing will arise from criminal motives such as revenge or greed (for financial gain) and occasionally a third party may be hired to do the killing.

Murder of parents (parricide)

This seems to be rare[25] i.e. 3.5% of all killings. Daughters commit parricide much less often than sons. Of 17 parricides by women, gathered from prison and psychiatric hospital, 14 were matricides and the others patricides. The matricides were committed by middle aged women with psychoses (11 cases), personality disorder (2 cases) or alcoholism (1 case). The women were living in a hostile-dependent relationship with their mothers and the killing was precipitated by the mother's deteriorating physical and mental condition. Two patricides were committed by younger women in retaliation for chronic abuse and violence by the father.

Infanticide and child killing

In the cases of these two offences 25% of all homicide victims are under 16 years and 80% of these children are killed by their parents. In children under 1 year, 60% are killed by their mother.

It is useful to consider three groups:

(1) *Neonaticide:* killing the child within 24 hours;
(2) *Filicide:*
    (a) killing the child within the first year for which the defence of infanticide (see Chapter 3) is possible as it is for neonaticide;
    (b) killing of the child after the first year.

Scott describes a variety of motives for killing children[26] which was reviewed by d'Orban.[27] In a series of 89 women charged with the killing or attempted murder of their children, there were six distinctive groups.

(1) *Battering mothers* (40% of cases): These are cases of fatal non-accidental injury often occurring impulsively. Women who commit such offences may have a variety of psychiatric problems including personality disorder, depressive disorder and low intelligence. They may also have social problems and histories of maltreatment in childhood.

(2) *The mentally ill* (27% of cases): This group includes women with depressive disorder associated with attempted suicide, personality disorder and psychotic illness. Women falling into this category often contemplate simultaneous suicide. Psychosis was diagnosed in two-thirds of these cases, half of which were suffering from puerperal psychosis.

(3) *Neonaticides* (12% of cases): These are women who kill their children within 24 hours of birth (see below).

(4) *Retaliating mothers* (10% of cases): In these cases, it is believed that the aggression directed against the spouse is displaced on the child. These women tend to have serious personality disorders with histories of frequent psychiatric hospital admissions.

(5) *Women who kill unwanted children* (9% of cases): Two groups of women are described in these cases – those who are impulsive with histories of delinquency and drug abuse who kill their children deliberately and those who are immature and passive who kill their child by neglect.

(6) *Mercy killing:* These cases are very rare and occur in cases of children with illness.

Consecutive filicide

This is thought to be rare but cases are described of mothers killing babies serially. They are usually found to have severe personality disorders.[28]

Neonaticide

The commonest reason for neonaticide is because the baby is unwanted (80%). Methods of killing include suffocation, strangulation, head trauma, drowning, exposure and stabbing. Drowning is commonly in toilets where the child may be born. Suffocation usually occurs after the first cry. After the death an attempt is often made to hide the body. The offender is almost always an unmarried mother who is usually under the age of 25 years. The majority of the offenders are passive young women who have become pregnant and wish to get rid of the unwanted child because of shame and fear. Most are otherwise totally law abiding and indeed it is their degree of conformity which inhibits their seeking an abortion or coming to terms with the pregnancy. They usually ignore the pregnancy and carry on their life as if nothing had happened, hiding their pregnancy completely from the family. Whilst there are a very small number of women with little ethical restraint who may repeat the offence, the majority of the group will not. Whilst this accounts for the majority of cases Resnick[29] and others have also described neonaticide as a result of an acute psychosis where the motive was delusional, altruistic killing for the child's sake in cases of deformed children, and cases of child battering.

Killing within the first year

This has been well reviewed by Marks.[30, 31] D'Orban's series[27] showed the two causes which were equally common were 'battering' (see Chapter 7) and mental illness which between them account for 80% of the deaths. The mental illnesses included psychotic illness, acute reactive depression associated with a suicide attempt and severe depressive symptoms in mothers with marked personality disorders. However, puerperal psychosis was not as common as would be expected. Some two-thirds of women who kill their child commit suicide before trial. The battering cases were sudden impulsive acts with loss of temper precipitated by the baby's behaviour. There were also some cases of killing to get rid of an unwanted child, one case of a mercy killing of a deformed child and cases of women killing the child to make their spouse suffer (the Medea complex – Medea killed her children, when her spouse Jason left her, in order to punish him).

It has been suggested that some killings by suffocation escape detection and are mistaken for 'sudden infant death syndrome'.[31] It has been suggested that up to 10% of registered 'cot deaths' may be homicides.

Killing after the first year

As the children get older the chances of being killed by the mother decrease markedly largely due to the fact that battering, as the cause of death, falls rapidly by the fourth year. By this time the children are mobile and are able to recognise their parents' tension and avoid provoking parental wrath. It is also found that mercy killing did not occur after the first year. However, mental illness remained an important cause.

Legal outcome after child killing

The defence of infanticide is discussed in Chapter 3.

Neonaticide

The courts are sympathetic to this group of offenders. Generally a plea of infanticide is successful despite the infrequency of gross psychiatric illness in this group. The Infanticide Act 1938 required only that there should be a disturbance of the balance of mind. There is no doubt that at the time of the killing the women are in a disturbed emotional state. In actual practice the degree of disturbance acceptable to the court seems much less than that required had the defence been one of diminished responsibility. In these cases the sentence after the finding has usually been a probation order with or without psychiatric supervision.

Killing within and after the first year

A verdict of murder is rare. In d'Orban's series there were only two cases of murder and in both older children had been killed in retaliation against a spouse. There seems to have been little connection otherwise between the motivations of the homicides and the verdicts and sentences of the court. In the cases of homicide by battering, for example, the main verdicts were manslaughter due to lack of intent to kill, manslaughter due to diminished responsibility and infanticide. The sentences varied between hospital orders, probation and imprisonment. A similar variety of verdicts and sentences occurred in each group. This great variety reflects how any particular motivation may occur with any mental states for which there are a variety of appropriate disposals.

Münchausen Syndrome by Proxy

The term, also known as factitious illness by proxy, covers the syndrome of mothers deliberately creating an impression that their child is ill.[32, 33] Bools has fully reviewed the subject.[34] Information may be falsified (either verbally or by tampering with specimens and charts). Alternatively, the child may have medicines withheld, be repeatedly suffocated (to resemble blackouts), poisoned or gassed. Cases of fabrication of psychiatric disorders have also been reported. There have also been cases of factitious disorders in pregnancy leading on to Münchausen Syndrome by Proxy after birth. Diagnosis may require admission and secret observation of the mother with the child including the use of a video. The false illness may start within the first two years and the child may be taught to lie to and cheat doctors. However, it may present in children who do have genuine underlying illness. Excessive investigations may be carried out, the child may be kept from school and treatments may be given. Death may result where abuse occurs. Such mothers seem to be inadequate people who enjoy the status and contact with hospital staff, perhaps escaping from domestic problems. It has been suggested that they have overinvolved relationships with their child. There may also be considerable hostility towards the child particularly where there is physical abuse. It has been reported that mothers have high incidence of somatoform disorders, along with alcohol abuse, eating disorders and self harm. There have been very few examples of Münchausen Syndrome by Proxy associated with psychotic illness. Management (including involvement of social services and police) will depend on the extent of the danger to the child.

Young offenders

Introduction

The purpose of this section is to complete the information about young offenders. The courts and the law in relation to young offenders are discussed in Chapter 2. Rutter and Giller[7] discuss in detail the interventions which have been tried with juvenile delinquents. Bailey gives an overview of the management of adolescent offenders.[35]

Aetiology of juvenile offending

Anti-social behaviour is normal in young people but is mostly confined to adolescence and is short lived. The rates of offending in young people are high and this has led to an increase in public concern particularly following a number of highly publicised cases. In 1996 44,300 juveniles (aged 10–17) were sentenced for indictable offences compared to 73,700 adults. This represented an increase of approximately 5% from the previous year whereas the adult rate had fallen by 1%.[1] However the rates of grave offences committed by young people, especially homicide, do not appear to have increased significantly over the years.

There have been numerous theories about the roots of juvenile offending. These are reviewed by Kolvin[36] and Bailey.[37] Most research points to three main risk areas, child centred, family centred and contextual which all interact. Child centred factors include learning disabilities, genetic factors and psychiatric morbidity. Family centred factors would include parenting abilities, abuse and family criminality. The contextual factors include substance abuse, peer groups, employment and opportunity for criminal activity. It has been reported that juvenile offending can be prevented by addressing a number of these risk factors, particularly with early family support and education. Persistent delinquent behaviour in childhood and adolescence is an indicator of persisting anti-social behaviour in adult life.

Interventions

Modern surveys have resulted in pessimistic conclusions about the efficacy of interventions with juvenile offenders. At best there is some evidence that some treatment programmes can be effective with some subpopulations, at least in the short term. The problems involved in research in this field are immense. The main ones may be listed as follows.

(1) Ascertaining exactly what intervention was carried out and whether it was done competently and persistently (e.g. was the group therapy

given by trained and sensitive personnel or by untrained, poorly motivated staff?)

(2) Being sure that other interventions (not measured by the research) were not also being used, e.g. punitive measures or greater supervision as well as the 'psychotherapy' being studied.

(3) Being sure that the treatment group is as expected (and not altered during the course of the study) and that the matching group is truly like the treatment group. This is often extremely difficult to do, particularly when dealing with small numbers.

(4) Being sure of the validity and sensitivity of outcome measures, e.g. being a member of a treatment group may bias whether official action is taken after an offence and thus the treatment group may appear to have a different outcome to the comparison group. Simple offence counting may ignore a change in quality of the offending.

(5) Being sure that the follow up period was long enough. It is frequently found that the improvement obtained in the institution is gradually dissipated over the next three years.

The features of succesful interventions which lead to more positive outcomes are

(1) targeting the treatment programme to the appropriate adolescent group;

(2) having a focused and structured programme;

(3) using a programme with cognitive components that focus on attitudes, values and beliefs;

(4) programmes based in the community tend to have better outcomes than residential programmes.

The principal interventions which have been tried with young offenders are set out below

Behavioural modification programmes

These clearly produce changes in behaviour in the short term whilst treatment is being carried out but there is uncertainty about the longer term benefits. They are carried out both in the community and the family.

Counselling and psychotherapy

Overall studies have not demonstrated improved outcome results but there is evidence that some (the neurotic or willing) may do better with psychotherapy whilst others (the aggressive or non-amenable) do worse. Similarly, it seems that matching the supervising officer to the personality of the offender may affect the results. There have been reports of the use of art therapy in young offenders, particularly the younger age group, to enable them to communicate about their offending behaviour. Treatment programmes have been established for juvenile sex offenders run on cognitive behavioural lines. Other similar cognitive behavioural programmes have been developed to address anger management and problem solving.[38]

Therapeutic institutional regimes
These have not been shown to be convincingly superior to traditional institutional regimes in terms of reconviction rates, both traditional and therapeutic regimes having reconviction rates about 60–70%. However, studies of individual institutions show that in some institutions the delinquents improve whilst they are there and in others they get worse.[39] This seems to reflect the quality of the 'parenting' by the staff providing good role models, with good staff–adolescent relationships, firm expectations, discipline, higher standards and a harmonious, warm atmosphere producing the best result. Paying attention to recreation and work programmes and adolescent–adolescent relationships is also important. Unfortunately the beneficial effects of the institutions do not persist beyond three years follow up. What is not clear is whether a custodial approach is better or worse than a non-custodial one. There are a number of studies suggesting overall that a non-custodial approach is, at least, as effective as a custodial one but there may be some delinquents who do better after a period of custody probably because it provides time for cognitive and emotional development.

Facilities available for the management of young offenders

Introduction

This topic has been reviewed by Sheldrick.[40] Prior to the nineteenth century juvenile offenders were dealt with in the same way as adults. Throughout the next century there was a gradual development of measures to deal specifically with juvenile offenders as it was thought that they could be rehabilitated. Special institutions and legislation have been developed and refined. In recent years there has been an increasing emphasis on keeping young offenders out of the legal system and in the community because of the failure to demonstrate the efficacy of any institutional interventions. There is a fear of doing harm to the young people in institutions either by their picking up criminal ways or being subject to brutalisation which is so often a feature of such places. However in the last decade there has been a growing concern about younger offenders and the leniency of the courts. It has also been felt that there was a lack of secure placements and the authorities were unable to deal with persistent offending. Thus police are encouraged to caution first offenders rather than prosecute (depending on the offence) though it remains to be conclusively proven that this is a more effective way of dealing with delinquents. This has led to two changes in legislation, the Criminal Justice and Public Order Act 1994 and the Crime and Disorder Act 1998.

The first of these Acts introduced secure training orders (see Chapter 2). The second has completely reviewed youth justice. It has introduced the Youth Justice Board for England and Wales. This will be responsible for all secure facilities for young offenders. The Act has recognised the need for a co-ordinated multi-agency approach to youth justice by developing the Youth Justice Service which will consist of representatives from local authorities, probation and police to develop strategies for tackling juvenile offending. There will also be Youth Offending Teams operating at a local level, and which will include members from probation, social services, police, education, local authorities and health authorities to co-ordinate crime prevention and response to youth crime.

Custodial facilities

These facilities fall into those organised by the local authority or Department of Health and those organised by the Home Office. Education departments are responsible for schools for maladjusted pupils (both residential and non-residential).

Local authority and Department of Health facilities

Observation and assessment centres
These are places in which juveniles can be detained whilst observations are made on the offender and background information collected. They may be single or mixed sex institutions. They provide facilities for education, exercise and hobbies. They may have a secure wing or access to such security in another centre. The secure wings are physically secure areas designed to prevent absconding. Children cannot be held in them, however, for more than 72 hours without a youth court's permission. In the observation and assessment centres, psychiatrists will be involved in providing psychiatric reports in relevant cases.

Community homes
This term covers a variety of local authority run homes for juveniles who are usually on care orders. They may also be used where a residence requirement has been placed on a juvenile offender who is under a supervision order. The homes may provide education on the premises or make use of local schools. The degree of security varies considerably but most are not secure establishments. The home, besides providing care and training, can provide counselling through its own staff and social workers. Psychological and psychiatric expertise may also be available. Within the same system are secure establishments which are able to look after those juveniles who have shown dangerous behaviour. The secure establishments

are otherwise run on the same principles as the open ones. These include the Aycliffe Centre and Red Bank School in the north of England.

Youth treatment centres

At the time of writing (1999) there are two such centres serving the country, Glenthorne, near Birmingham and St Charles at Brentwood, Essex.[41] They are secure treatment units managed by the Department of Health. The staff are drawn from social work, nursing and education. Psychologists and psychiatrists attend on a sessional basis. The clients are a heterogeneous group of psychologically disordered juveniles of both sexes between the ages of 12 and 18 years, though the younger ones are preferred as having a greater chance of benefiting. They will have behaved very dangerously or have been very difficult or persistent absconders elsewhere. An account of the Glenthorne centre where a behavioural approach is adopted is given by Reid.[42] A psychotherapeutic community approach is adopted at St Charles.

Psychiatric services

There is increasing recognition of the need for specialist forensic adolescent psychiatric services. Young people in institutions show a high level of mental health problems including suicidal behaviour. Adolescents released from custody also have higher rates of psychiatric morbidity than those in the community. There is also evidence of high rates of co-morbid mental illness in young people with conduct disorder, particularly affective disorder. A study in 1996 that gained information from all agencies dealing with young offenders confirms the overall view that they are a highly disturbed group who may be a danger to themselves or others, who present to a number of the agencies but whose mental health needs are neither well recognised nor met.[42] Adolescent forensic psychiatry services are presently limited and it is therefore a speciality that will continue to expand and develop.

At present most juvenile offenders who are suspected of having a mental disorder which is treatable are referred to either child or adolescent psychiatric services. Occasionally referrals will be seen by the adult forensic psychiatric services. Some may be assessed in the observation and assessment centres. In-patient care can be offered in children's psychiatric wards or an adolescent unit. Secure psychiatric adolescent facilities and adolescent forensic psychiatric services are continuing to develop. There are two in-patient adolescent regional secure units within the NHS in Newcastle and Manchester and one based at St Andrew's Hospital in the private sector.

Age is no bar to the use of hospital orders and therefore, where appropriate, juveniles can be admitted on all the sections of the Mental Health Act. They can also be detained in an adolescent psychiatric secure facility under Section 53 of the Children and Young Persons Act 1933.

Special hospitals have, in the past, accepted juveniles but as far as possible they are not now admitted. There are services for young men within maximum security but the patients tend to be 17 years or more.

Home Office facilities

Remand centres

These centres take young adults on remand. Although these centres may be geographically adjacent to adult prisons they are designed to keep these offenders away from adult offenders. The remand centre should provide appropriate work and recreation. Whereas the age group is normally 18–21, in rare cases very difficult boys of 15 years or more can be admitted if a certificate of unruliness can be obtained from the court. This practice is discouraged and it is expected that the secure facilities in observation and assessment centres should contain these boys. Remand centres will make use of prison medical staff and visiting psychiatrists to prepare psychiatric reports for the courts and to provide treatment for the mentally disordered offenders as appropriate.

Young offenders' institutions

This term from the 1988 Criminal Justice Act covers a variety of institutions set up under the 1988 Criminal Justice Act. It encompasses the old detention centres and youth custody centres (previously borstals). The aim is to develop a positive regime through activities and staff relationships in order to encourage self-discipline, a sense of responsibility and personal development. Each offender has an individual officer who takes a special interest. Links with families are encouraged as is through-care with probation.

The institutions vary in security and are divided into those for juvenile males (15–17), those for short-term young adult males (18–20), those for long-term young adults (18–20) and those for females. The regime for the juvenile and short-term older males is brisk and busy with a very structured day and an emphasis on education. The longer term inmate will have an emphasis on work skills and education. Some contain on the same campus a remand centre alongside the areas for the convicted.

Psychiatrists are attached to a number of young offender institutes to offer an assessment and treatment service as required. Feltham Young Offenders' Institution and Glen Parva Young Offenders' Institution have full time medical staff specialising in the care of offenders with psychiatric problems.

The institutions have been criticised for sometimes failing to separate satisfactorily the different categories of offender, and for failing to provide satisfactory regimes or single accommodation.

Secure training centres

These were introduced in the Criminal Justice and Public Order Act 1994. However the first of them did not open until 1998.

Children as witnesses

Children may give evidence in court. If the court judges that a child does not understand the oath, evidence may be received anyway if the court judges that the child is sufficiently intelligent and understands the duty of speaking the truth (Section 38(i), Children and Young Persons Act 1933). Furthermore, since 1988 this evidence does not have to be supported by independent evidence. Video connection with the court and the child is permitted to save the child having to appear in court. Arrangements can also be made for a child in court to be shielded from seeing the offender in appropriate cases (e.g. sexual assault). At the time of writing it is unclear whether courts will accept as evidence a videotaped recording of an interview with a child (e.g. an interview between a psychiatrist and an abused child). It is not resolved whether the lack of opportunity to cross examine the child would bar the use of such evidence. The jury would be expected to bear in mind the child's age and maturity in making a decision about the evidence.

References

(1) Home Office (1992) *Criminal Statistics. England and Wales 1991*. Cmnd. 2134. HMSO: London.
(2) Walker, N. (1965) *Crime and Punishment in Britain*. Edinburgh University Press: Edinburgh.
(3) Farrington, D.P. and Morris, A.M. (1983) Sex, sentencing and reconviction. *British Journal of Criminology* **23**, 229–47.
(4) d'Orban, P.T. (1971) Social and psychiatric aspects of female crime. *Medicine, Science and the Law* **11**, 275–81.
(5) Cloninger, R.C. and Guze, S.B. (1970) Female criminals: their personal, familial and social backgrounds. *Archives of General Psychiatry* **23**, 554–8.
(6) Cowie, J., Cowie, V. and Slater, E. (1968) *Delinquency in Girls*. Heinemann: London.
(7) Rutter, M. and Giller, H. (1983) *Juvenile Delinquency, Trends and Perspectives*. Penguin Books: Harmondsworth.
(8) Dalton, K. (1961) Menstruation and crime. *British Medical Journal* **2**, 1752–3.
(9) Gibbens, T.C.N. and Prince, J. (1962) *Shoplifting*. Institute for the Study and Treatment of Delinquency: London.
(10) Hands, J., Herbert, V. and Tennant, G. (1974) Menstruation and behaviour in a special hospital. *Medicine, Science and the Law* **14**, 32–5.
(11) d'Orban, P.T. and Dalton, J. (1980) Violent crime and the menstrual cycle. *Psychological Medicine* **10**, 353–9.
(12) Ballinger, C.B. (1976) Psychiatric morbidity and the menopause: clinical features. *British Medical Journal* **2**, 1183–5.
(13) Moffitt, T.E., Brammer, G.L., Caspi, A., Fawcett, J.P., Raleigh, M., Ywiler, A. and Silva, P. (1998) Whole blood serotonin relates to violence in an epidemiological study. *Biological Psychiatry*, **43**(6) 446–57.
(14) Maden, A., Swinton, M. and Gunn, J. (1994) A criminological and psychiatric

survey of women serving a prison sentence. *British Journal of Criminology* **34** (2), 172–91.

(15) Maden, A. (1996) *Women, Prisons and Psychiatry: Mental Disorder Behind Bars*. Butterworth and Heinemann: London.

(16) Gibbens, T.C.N. (1971) Female offenders. *British Journal of Hospital Medicine* **6**, 279–86.

(17) Turner, T.H. and Tofler, D.S. (1986) Indicators of psychiatric disorder among women admitted to prison. *British Medical Journal* **292**, 651–3.

(18) Dell, S. and Gibbens, T.C.N. (1971) Remands of women offenders for medical reports. *Medicine, Science and the Law* **11**, 117–27.

(19) Gibbens, T.C.N., Palmer, C. and Prince, J. (1971) Mental health aspects of shoplifting. *British Medical Journal* **3**, 113–30.

(20) d'Orban, P.T. (1983) Medicolegal aspects of the premenstrual syndrome. *British Journal of Hospital Medicine* **30**, 404–9.

(21) d'Orban, P.T. (1976) Child stealing: a typology of female offenders. *British Journal of Criminology* **16**, 275–81.

(22) Appleby, L. and Maden, A. (1991) Baby stealing. *British Medical Journal* **302**, 1480–1.

(23) d'Orban P.T. (1990) Female homicide. *Irish Journal of Psychological Medicine* **7**, 64–70.

(24) MacKay, R.D. (1995) *Mental Condition Defences in the Criminal Law*. Clarendon Press: Oxford.

(25) d'Orban P.T. and O'Connor A. (1989) Women who kill their parents. *British Journal of Psychiatry* **154**, 27–33.

(26) Scott, P.D. (1973) Parents who kill their children. *Medicine, Science and the Law* **13**, 120–6.

(27) d'Orban, P.T. (1979) Women who kill their children. *British Journal of Psychiatry* **134**, 560–71.

(28) d'Orban, P.T. (1990) A commentary on consecutive filicide. *Journal of Forensic Psychiatry* **1**, 260–5.

(29) Resnick, P.J. (1970) Murder of the newborn: a psychiatric review of neonaticide. *American Journal of Psychiatry* **126**, 1414–9.

(30) Marks, M. and Kumar, R. (1993) Infanticide in England and Wales. *Medicine, Science and the Law* **33**(4), 329–39.

(31) Marks, M. (1996) Characteristics and causes of infanticide in Britain. *International Review of Psychiatry* **8**, 99–106.

(32) Meadows, R. (1989) Suffocation. *British Medical Journal* **298**, 1572–3.

(33) Meadows, R. (1989) Münchausen syndrome by proxy. *British Medical Journal* **299**, 248.

(34) Bools, C. (1996) Factitious illness by proxy. Münchausen syndrome by proxy. *British Journal of Psychiatry* **169**(3), 268–75.

(35) Bailey S. (1996) Current perspectives on young offenders: aliens or alienated. *Journal of Clinical Forensic Medicine* **3**, 1–7.

(36) Kolvin, I. and Kolvin, P. (1990) Young offenders. In: *Principles and Practices of Forensic Psychiatry* (eds R. Bluglass and P. Bowden). Churchill Livingstone: Edinburgh.

(37) Bailey, S. (1997) Adolescent offenders. *Current Opinions* **10**, 445–8.

(38) Hollin, C. (1993) Advances in the psychological treatment of delinquent behaviour. *Criminal Behaviour and Mental Health* **3**, 142–57.

(39) Sinclair, I. and Clarke, R. (1982) Predicting, treating and explaining delinquency: the lessons from research on institutions. In: *Developments in the Study of Criminal Behaviour*, Vol. I, *The Prevention and Control of Offending* (ed. P. Feldman). John Wiley and Sons Ltd: Chichester.

(40) Sheldrick, C. (1990) Approaches to treatment and facilities available. In: *Principles and Practice of Forensic Psychiatry* (eds R. Bluglass and P. Bowden). Churchill Livingstone: Edinburgh.

(41) Parker, E. (1985) The development of secure provision. In: *Secure Provision* (ed. L. Gostin). Tavistock Publications: London and New York.

(42) Reid, I. (1982) The development and maintenance of a behavioural regime in a secure youth treatment centre. In: *Developments in the Study of Criminal Behaviour*. Vol. I, *The Prevention and Control of Offending* (ed. P. Feldman). John Wiley and Sons Ltd: Chichester.

Chapter 14

Dangerousness, Risk Assessment and Risk Management

Introduction

The forensic psychiatrist is frequently expected to comment on risk. The request for this opinion will come from the court in relation to the sentencing of mentally disordered offenders; from the Mental Health Review Tribunal in relation to patients being discharged into the community; the Home Office in relation to patients detained under restriction orders being considered for discharge into the community; and from the managers of the hospital in relation to the detention of a patient under the Mental Health Act 1983. In addition, within the prison service, an opinion on risk may be requested by the Parole Board for inmates serving long or life sentences. There is also now an increasing trend for forensic psychiatrists to be asked to comment on risks posed by patients under the care of general psychiatrists. The risks posed by patients are in the forefront of the mind of a psychiatrist on a day to day basis in relation to management, degree of security and observation required, progress of the underlying disorder, the reaction of the offender to stress, safety in the community and various possible provoking situations. This chapter will deal first with definitions of dangerousness, harm, risk assessment and risk management, before considering the process of risk assessment and the estimation of risk through the application of the evidence base, and will conclude with a discussion on reducing and managing risks.

Definitions

In recent years the concept of dangerousness has been joined by concepts of risk assessment, risk management and the prevention of harm.

Dangerousness

There is no agreed definition of dangerousness. The Butler Committee[1] equated 'dangerousness' '... with a propensity to cause serious physical injury or lasting psychological harm'. Scott[2] defined dangerousness as 'an unpredictable and untreatable tendency to inflict or risk irreversible injury or destruction'.

The broad definition within American criminal justice is 'risk of harmful behaviour to others'.[3]

The following vignette illustrates the use of the concept of 'dangerousness'.

> Mr Smith suffers from schizophrenia. He used to be an animal welfare officer and still has an interest and skill in this. Unfortunately despite a good premorbid personality he attacked his wife with a large kitchen knife because he was ill and he believed she was a witch melting down dogs and babies for candle making. The incident was precipitated by a severe argument with his wife about an unpaid debt although during this he didn't disclose his abnormal ideas. He believed he had to kill her as he was next for the rendering process. He is now improved but ambivalent about the need for medication. How dangerous is he?

This demonstrates the limitation of the concept of dangerousness. Mr Smith was certainly very dangerous to his wife when he was ill and untreated. He is now less dangerous and when he is discharged he will be potentially dangerous depending on the course of his illness. He is probably not dangerous at all to animals. As can be seen dangerousness requires qualification to be meaningful and as will be seen this is where risk assessment and risk management are helpful.

Danger and harm

Danger is the exposure to risk of harm. Mrs Smith was in danger when she was in the house with her husband because she was exposed to his intent to kill her. Harm however may be physical or psychological. Mrs Smith was stabbed so she suffered physical harm, however, the whole scenario was extremely distressing and she now has flashbacks, anxiety and nightmares so has therefore suffered psychological harm too.

Risk

This is the likelihood that harm will occur. In fact risk can refer to the likelihood of both a negative outcome, i.e. harm or a positive outcome, i.e. a benefit. When Mr Smith was a lot better he wanted to walk in the hospital grounds alone with his wife. The doctor decided there was a risk Mr Smith still had deep seated delusional ideas about his wife and was concerned, however, this was considered quite unlikely, i.e. the risk of there being deep seated delusions was low. Mrs Smith felt she needed some time alone with her husband as they had been apart for so long now. The team decided that after the therapy they had both received to date the risk of them benefiting by being together outweighed the risk of harm so they had walks alone.

Although risk can and probably should be seen to refer to both harms and benefits in everyday practice risk it is almost always used solely to refer to harm 'It's a risky situation', 'she likes to take risks', 'what's the risk?'.

Risk assessment

This is the assessment of the likelihood (risk) of harm occurring in different circumstances. It would be better understood if it were termed the 'assessment of risk of harm' but in common usage it is shortened to risk assessment. Risk assessment should really be looking at and balancing harms and benefits but in practice it almost always only looks at harms. *Risk management* is the process of reducing the likelihood of specific harms occurring.

Risk assessment – the process
A thorough risk assessment can be a very complicated and lengthy proce-dure taking many weeks. A risk assessment can, however, range from a judgement made by a single person without any documentation of the process, e.g. the nurse asks the ward doctor 'can Mr Smith and his wife stay out in the hospital grounds for an extra ten minutes today?', to a multi-disciplinary/multi-agency in-depth review and documentation of years of behaviour with a description and assessment of the risks of a wide range of harms. There is no magical, or special sophisticated approach to risk assessment that can be used for all occasions. However, the systematic collection and processing of information with the application of the best available knowledge and evidence base can improve predictions.

The assessment
To understand the process it will be best to start with a simple risk assessment. The first question to be asked is: 'What risk is being assessed?' In Mr Smith's case it needs to be decided whether a risk assessment will determine the risk he will stab his wife again, or the risk he will stab her again if he becomes non-compliant with medication, or the risk he will become non-compliant, or the risk he will go to her house if he absconds from the grounds, the risk he will stab a priest, a postman, or next time shoot a work colleague – which risk is being assessed? Let us assume we want to know the risk that he will shoot a work colleague if he becomes ill again.

The assessment can now take several forms. It can be made on the grounds of clinical judgement alone or it can be subject to an actuarial assessment using a validated rating scale. Studies of most rating scales and clinical judgement alone show a fairly poor predictive ability. This is not surprising as many of the factors which influence the risk of harm being assessed are usually difficult if not impossible to control (later this will be seen to be a part of risk management) e.g. the risk of Mr Smith shooting a colleague depends not only on his mental illness and his access to guns etc. but also on his level of stress —'so an argument may make an incident more likely as might a loss of something valuable etc.

Risk prediction instruments

There are many instruments available for attempting to predict future harmful behaviour in offenders. There are however very few validated instruments for use in mentally disordered offenders. When using an instrument, care must be taken to understand the sample population on which the instrument has been validated: for example it would be of no help in predicting repeat arson to use an instrument designed for predicting reconviction of sex offenders and neither would it be of much help to use an instrument validated on rapists for predicting repeat indecent exposure. Instruments therefore tend to have either a narrow application (which is likely to increase their predictive power) or else they are so general that they are unhelpful. Consideration must always be given to the potential harm for the offender in being unfairly judged as dangerous, e.g. the clinical team may have to take a decision to advise that a patient is rehabilitated away from potential victims.

The process

The risk assessment will be better as more information is known. It is clear that prediction of future harm can be no better than the information it is based upon, e.g. if you only have (or are only using) 10% of the relevant information about a case you cannot expect (except by chance) to make a prediction which is any more than 10% accurate. In practice a range of risks will all be assessed together so the best way to produce a high quality assessment will be to assign a person on the team to collate information and then to begin information gathering. It is important to recognise the difference between risk information and risk assessment. The collection of good risk information is vital, it informs the assessment but it is not the assessment itself. It is important to know where to look for information and the sources below are all very useful.

(1) *Interviews with the patient* which will need to be repeated as the patient's condition improves and may also include information gathered through therapy sessions.
(2) *Interviews with informants* including relatives for historical information and friends/colleagues for more up to date information. Previous professionals involved in a case often have very helpful information either as undocumented facts or helpful opinions or knowledge of further sources.
(3) *GP records* can give useful clues to unreported behaviour.
(4) *Hospital records.* Be careful to make sure all information is accessed. Often the most helpful detailed day-to-day observations are in the

nursing notes (which may be very lengthy after a stay of several years) and when the patient is discharged these bulky notes may be removed from the main file and stored separately, so often specific mention is needed to obtain them. Many hospitals still do not have a single multidisciplinary record so archived and current records are likely to be found in different departments e.g. Psychology, Occupational therapy, Music therapy, Social work, Community teams etc. and a specific request would be needed to obtain these. Unfortunately, a simple request for a patient's 'old notes' from another hospital will usually be met with the medical file alone (containing a few typed reports from other disciplines) or increasingly frequently a refusal to send original notes so photocopies are sent instead. Regrettably hospital files tend to be poorly organised and very useful information all too commonly seems to end up in a miscellaneous section stuffed loosely into the pouch at the back of the file (this is a good source for letters to and from patients and other personal information with no other logical place for it to be filed but it is not usually photocopied when only copies are sent). When extracting information from reports etc. always try to go back to the original description of a behaviour as over time when descriptions are replicated from report to report information tends to become distorted and lost. Hospital records are usually kept for a patient's lifetime.

(5) *Social services records* are not kept indefinitely but if available can be a source of very useful information about childhood and formative experiences.

(6) *School records* can sometimes be obtained from schools, from relatives or the patient themselves. Alternatively for younger patients it is sometimes possible to speak on the telephone to old teachers/headmasters.

(7) *Probation records* are often consulted, particularly as the probation service has a specific remit to reduce the risk of harm to the public. When an assessment of dangerous behaviour is being undertaken records are usually supplied without difficulty.

(8) *Court documents* – when a patient has been convicted of a crime or is facing charges for one it should be possible to obtain witness statements and a transcript of the police taped interview with the defendant. The patient may already have a copy or copies can be requested from the patient's solicitor or after conviction the probation service may be able to supply them. If the tape transcript is poor the actual tapes can usually be requested and listened to. In the case of significant crimes in the past where no documents can be obtained it can be valuable to contact the principal police officer in the case, as he or she may still be available and may have both documents and other useful information that was never documented.

(9) *A list of previous convictions* can be obtained either if a court case is

underway or from the probation service, otherwise it can be hard to obtain. The police and central criminal records office will usually consider the information confidential (under the Data Protection Act) and not for disclosure.

(10) *Prison records* are rather like hospital records with a variety of sources to access. A knowledge of the best terminology helps. The files can only be read in the prison. All prisoners have an inmate medical record (known as the IMR). Security information, e.g. assaults, escapes, drug dealing etc. can be accessed either in the general prison file (known as the 20/50) or sometimes in a separate file kept in the security department – access can usually be gained with the help of the prison medical officer. Longer term prisoners will have a parole file with a large amount of helpful risk information in it. Life sentence prisoners will have a parole file and a life sentence plan. Separate records will be held by the prison psychology and prison probation departments. Some prisons with specialised programmes e.g. sex offender treatment programmes, and HMP Grendon Underwood will also have files about the therapeutic programmes.

Whenever checking for information be careful to check under pseudonyms if known.

Processing the information
The ultimate would be a document in which all risk information is gathered together for easy access, with the risk areas clearly identified and a statement about forms of harm of which there appears to be no risk. After documenting all the known risk behaviour/harms and their context as well as possible antecedents, behaviour and consequences, an attempt can be made to describe the factors which would increase and decrease the risks of the harms occurring. As with all reports it is important to document the source of the information, the purpose of the report etc. A single document describing risk behaviour allows entry into a more dynamic risk assessment process. The statement 'If Mr Smith absconds he is unlikely to harm his wife' is only valid at the time it was made. It cannot take into account changes in his mental state etc. A single document kept on disk can be updated, it can contain information about where further information can be collected when time allows, it can allow repeated assessments over time as often the volume of information to be sifted through if not in a single document can be so large that to keep rereading it for assessments can be impractical . Most importantly a single document allows not only the author to be abreast of the relevant information but other members of the team can now access it and perform more efficiently and effectively.

If time does not allow the above then the next best procedure would at least be to document what can be recalled about a patient at the time a risk assessment is made.

Clearly it would be impractical to investigate and document risk information in detail for all patients but the exercise will pay dividends for the most dangerous cases, those where long-term management is needed and those cases which are difficult and the team or different agencies are not in agreement about the risks and their management.

The estimation of risk

It is likely that predictions about harmful behaviours will be more accurate in the short term than the longer term as the likelihood of a significant uncontrollable event having happened such as a bereavement, accidents, non-compliance etc. will increase with time. It is also likely that prediction of a more frequent behaviour, for instance repeated minor assaults will be better than prediction of a less frequent one, e.g. an attempt to enucleate the eye of a future victim. Nevertheless it is often asserted that clinicians have, in fact, very little ability to predict harm in the longer term and that doctors grossly overpredict it.

The belief that clinicians have a special ability to gauge the future risk of harm posed by mentally disordered offenders was shaken by the findings in the 1970s by Steadman *et al.*,[4] on the follow up of patients released from the Dannemora State Hospital for Insane Criminals in the USA. Baxstrom, a prisoner, who was declared insane and dangerous by psychiatrists was detained beyond the tariff of his sentence in the above hospital for treatment. His appeal, based on the lack of a judicial court hearing to determine his dangerousness, was successful and his detention was declared unconstitutional. He and 967 similarly unfairly detained patients were therefore transferred to a civil hospital, although they had all been previously judged to be dangerous. At four years follow up 20% of the men and 26% of the women had assaulted someone, although the majority of these assaults were minor. On the other hand, it was estimated that some 50% of the original 967 ended up living in the community without being reconvicted. The others stayed in or were returned to ordinary psychiatric hospital. In short, over 75% of the original 967 patients appear to have been detained unnecessarily in the secure hospital on the grounds of 'dangerousness'. Similar findings occurred in other hospitals in the United States.

So, although it seems that the risks were overpredicted is it the case that doctors are really no better than anyone else at gauging risks? Kozol *et al.*[5] studied a group of sexual offenders whom they believed were dangerous and had been detained. A subgroup of these patients was released as 'safe' by a tribunal against the doctors' advice. Another group was released after treatment when the doctors considered them to be safe. The doctors' group had a recidivism rate of 6.1% whilst the tribunal's group had a recidivism rate of 34.7%, strongly suggesting that the doctors were better at assessing the risks than the tribunal. This finding was echoed by Acres[6] in his study of patients discharged from Broadmoor Hospital by doctors or by tribunals. Nevertheless, it is also clear that whilst one-third of the tribunal group re-offended, two-thirds would nevertheless have been detained unnecessarily.

On the other hand, whilst Kozol *et al.* showed that doctors were better than the tribunal at assessing dangerousness, Harding *et al.*[7] found in an experimental situation that doctors did not achieve a higher level of agreement about dangerousness and psychiatrists tended to rate a patient as more dangerous than did non-psychiatrists. They concluded that there should be better training for psychiatrists based on operational definitions of dangerousness in order to get better inter-rater reliability but the problem of predicted accuracy would remain. There are two reactions to this dilemma. The libertarian view, outlined by Bottoms,[8] argues that because of the poor prediction rate and the tendency of the psychiatrist to be over-cautious, only those offenders with a history of, say, three previous offences should be subject to this judgement. In such a subgroup of offenders the chances of a successful prediction would be about 66%, much higher than in the general population. Bottoms argues that the current system of locking up three people in order to prevent one offending is unjust. The protectionist view is outlined by Walker.[9, 10] He argues that the detention of three offenders to prevent one offending is justified to prevent harm to the innocent victim. Simply because we cannot prevent the majority of cases of violence does not mean we should give up trying to prevent a few cases. At the present time the protectionist view is the one adopted by society and the courts and is the one most psychiatrists are identified with.

The application of the evidence base

In practice the best risk assessment is likely to be gained from a process of gaining some anchor points/starting levels for the future risk of a behaviour based on research evidence and then to use what else is known about a patient to scale the risks up or down. At present the evidence base is widely scattered. The reader can consult further for partial analyses of the evidence base but a full analysis is not yet available. This chapter only aims to give the general trends apparent to date.

Monahan and Steadman[3] have described a very useful and usable framework for considering risk factors in clinical practice as follows: Risk factors for violence in the mentally disordered can be of four types, those related to

(1) dispositional factors;
(2) clinical factors;
(3) historical factors;
(4) contextual factors.

Dispositional risk factors

These are factors that reflect the individual person's characteristics, traits, tendencies and styles of interacting. There are many possible characteristics within this domain that may be related to violence, but those which are mostly strongly related are probably anger, impulsivity and psychopathy.

Anger

Anger is a normal emotion. Not all people who become angry will be violent and on the converse some people will be violent without being angry. Anger, however, is associated with violence and loss of control. It is likely that anger leads to aggression or violence through three main mechanisms, angry thoughts, angry feelings and the context of the situation. The thoughts encountered in this emotional state will vary but it is not uncommon for individuals to experience fantasies of retribution which can sometimes be severe and very compelling. The emotional state involves increased arousal with features of the fight/flight reaction. The adrenalin surge of anger can lead to a feeling of increased energy, anxiety and agitation. The threshold for loss of control will be lowered. The contextual component relates to the circumstances causing the anger. Violence/ aggression is much more likely when a person is in direct interpersonal conflict than when the person is feeling angry but is alone. The relevance of anger for those with mental disorder is that many psychiatric conditions are characterised by pathological changes in emotional states and this includes pathological anger, e.g. feeling angry when there is no provocation or other reason for it as might be found in depression and mania, or experiencing anger which develops rapidly and severely in response to minimal stimulation as might be found in borderline personality disorder.

Impulsivity

The degree to which we are impulsive varies from person to person. High levels of impulsivity are likely to be associated with an increase in risky behaviours including getting into situations which lead to violence or other harmful outcomes, such as arson, sexual assault. The trait of impulsivity is important for psychiatrists because it is positively associated with a number of mental health problems, including brain damage, alcohol intoxication and some personality disorders.

Psychopathy

The concept of psychopathy referred to here is the description of individuals as found in Hare's *Psychopathy Checklist*.[11] The cluster of traits which

Hare describes as the syndrome of psychopathy include those which will lead to an increased risk of harm. The traits include lack of empathy, dominance, forcefulness, lack of anxiety, lack of guilt, impulsivity, sensation seeking, and a tendency to violate social norms. The degree to which 'psychopathy' is present in the mentally disordered will be highly relevant to their future risk of causing harm.

Clinical risk factors

These are the various psychiatric disorders that have been demonstrated to be associated with increased risk of harming others. Full descriptions of individual disorders and their association with harm will be found in separate chapters in this book. Areas to consider within this domain are substance abuse, personality disorders, schizophrenia, delusions, hallucinations and mood disorders. It should be noted that despite a consensus in the past that there was no link between mental illness and crime it has now been adequately demonstrated that links do exist.[12] Schizophrenia is associated with an increased risk of violence and there seems to be a relatively high incidence of depression in those who commit homicide. In trying to understand the links for use in risk assessment however, it is more useful to concentrate on the effect of symptoms on future risk behaviour than it is to try to link diagnoses to the risks.

Delusions

Any delusional system might lead to harmful behaviour, but the strongest links seem to be between persecutory ideas that others wish to harm the patient, and delusions of infidelity.

The link between hallucinations and risk of harm is mostly common sense. In general there is more risk of harm associated with command hallucinations to behave dangerously than those to behave in benign ways and the risk is also greater if a patient is showing evidence of responding to the hallucinations rather than ignoring them. Despite this most patients with hallucinations do not behave dangerously as a result of them. Care must be taken to differentiate between true hallucinations and those which are 'voices' reported by personality disordered patients where attention must be paid to dynamic and personality factors rather than concentrating too much on the voices which may even be reported to be giving homicidal instructions.

Mood disorders

Depression can lead to harmful behaviour but the relationship is complex. Irritability can cause repeated minor confrontations, whereas delusional ideas can lead to serious violence for example in the mother who kills her children to save them from the AIDS infection she falsely believes she has given them. In mania elation and grandiosity alone do not usually lead to significant planned harm although the reckless behaviour that ensues may cause harm, e.g. buying and driving a high performance car, however when irritability is prominent or when the manic patient is detained, then the risks increase considerably. Other causes of irritability and disinhibition, such as substance misuse will increase the risk of harm, whereas some symptoms of illness may reduce the risks, for instance negative symptoms of schizophrenia, profound depression.

Historical and contextual risk factors

These are events that have been experienced in the past that may predispose to violence and aspects in the current environment that may be conducive to the occurrence of violent behaviour.

As far as is known most of these factors are of the same general significance for the mentally well as the mentally disordered. Relevant factors include an increased risk of offending with a strong family history of criminality, a probable link with deficient child rearing, an increase in some types of offending with a history of childhood sexual abuse. Unstable work and educational histories are more frequent in offenders.

Past history of violence

In both the mentally well and the mentally abnormal, past behaviour predicts future behaviour in general terms. In the mentally ill however, specific attention should be paid to the behaviour when the person was unwell since it is this rather than the behaviour in-between time which is most likely to predict future behaviour if the person becomes unwell again. For both mentally ill and well individuals a particularly malignant behaviour to be on the alert for is an escalation of harmful behaviour. This may reflect some deteriorating factor, e.g. increasingly bad illness, increasing drug addiction or most worryingly it may be the result of a planned course of action in performing increasingly daring acts for self gratification at the expense of victims.

Family supports and social network

A lack of family support and social network may lead to a deterioration in the patient's condition and an increase in risk as a result, whereas close family contact may lead to family members or social supports becoming targets for harmful behaviour.

Age

The peak age of offending in the general population is in the mid- to late adolescent years with an eventual decline by middle age. Mentally disordered offenders tend to commit their first offence at a later age and the decline in offending with age is less marked.

Sex

Men commit far more crime than women, although these differences vary for different crimes. In mentally disordered offenders whilst males still present with more harmful behaviour the preponderance of males over females is less marked.

Race

Any differences between the mentally abnormal and the general population are as yet difficult to interpret.

Socio-economic status

The lower socio-economic groups are over-represented amongst offenders and particularly in non-fatal crimes of violence. In the mentally disordered however, whilst at the time of committing an offence homelessness and poverty are common, the background of the person appears to show a wider diversity of classes before the drift down the socio-economic scale.

Marital status

A past history of a stable marriage is likely to indicate a lower risk for the future in both the mentally well and the mentally disordered, however in the latter illness factors may have negated the benefit if the personality has deteriorated.

Personality

This is a large topic. In general it appears that the best general predictor of behaviour in the personality disordered is their past behaviour.[13] Traits likely to be linked to particularly harmful behaviour include high levels of jealousy, suspicion, sadistic fantasy and guiltlessness. A tendency to impulsivity and poor anger control will increase the risk of harmful behaviour in the mentally well and unwell alike.

Neurobiological factors

Some forms of brain damage and disease increase the likelihood of harm e.g. frontal lobe damage causing disinhibition and irritability. Although research suggests that there might eventually be neurobiological markers (e.g. serotonin measurements), that can assist with the prediction of harmful behaviour, at present no such facility exists. Stature and physical size can in some individuals make them more dangerous although this can be deceptive and small people too can be physically dangerous. There is no specific relationship to mental disorder.

Intellectual function

There is an overrepresentation of people with lower IQ in those arrested, although whether this reflects increased crime or more likelihood of being caught is unclear. The general pattern of harmful behaviour is not known to be any different with respect to intelligence whether a person is mentally disordered or mentally well.

Miscellaneous

The presence or absence of employment or meaningful daily activities can also have differing effects in different patients with different conditions. In some it may produce particular stresses whereas for others the activities may be protective. The availability of weapons, drugs and alcohol will have obvious bearing on the risks. The hobbies and interests of patients may produce peculiar modifications to the risk equation, e.g. a morbid interest in butchery or a special skill at martial arts.

Reducing and managing risks

Reducing and managing risks is commonly known as 'risk management'. Risk management can be of two very different types. First, there is the blind 'keep your fingers crossed' approach whereby risks are taken with little real background assessment e.g. with incomplete information a patient who has now 'settled' is given increasing leave in the community on the basis that they have been incident free so far, so it is hoped that this will remain the case. Second, there is the approach based on a full assessment of risk then and in the light of a thorough management plan the risks are monitored and reduced as the patient moves forward in rehabilitation, e.g. a patient begins increasing leave off the unit having discussed with therapist and learnt about early warning signs for feeling angry and having practised ways of dealing with the feelings should they occur.

In forensic psychiatric practice it is common to undertake a full risk assessment and then the factors which increase or decrease priority risk areas will receive attention. This is likely to involve the patient in many hours of therapy gaining an understanding of how and why risk behaviours have been occurring, e.g. understanding the role of stress, anxiety, anger and other emotions in precipitating harmful behaviour. Patients will then learn the early warning signs of these and strategies to de-escalate the emotion if it starts. Patients will also learn ways of living to avoid situations that are likely to precipitate the emotions. Early warning signs of illness will be learnt along with strategies to seek help. Social and living skills will be maximised. Relatives and carers will be appraised of the same information as the patient with regard to risk factors and their management. When the stakes are high change will be effected gradually. On discharge there will be close follow up by staff who were involved in the in-patient care (who know the patient well). A final and most helpful aspect in forensic practice is the frequent independent assessment of cases by clinical and lay persons not otherwise managing the case. This occurs through the process of Mental Health Review Tribunals and Home Office scrutiny of cases and can result in continual new insights into the risk factors to be attended to.

References

(1) Home Office and DHSS (1975) *Report of the Committee on Mentally Abnormal Offenders* (Butler Committee). Cmnd 6244. HMSO: London.
(2) Scott, P.D. (1977) Assessing dangerousness in criminals. *British Journal of Psychiatry* **131**, 127–42.
(3) Monahan, J. and Steadman, H.J. (1994) *Violence and Mental Disorder Development in Risk Assessment*. University of Chicago Press: London.
(4) Steadman, H.J. and Keveles, G. (1972) The community adjustment and criminal activity of the Baxstrom patients 1966–1970. *American Journal of Psychiatry* **129**, 304–10.
(5) Kozol, H.L., Boucher, R.J. and Garofalo, R.F. (1972) The diagnosis and treatment of dangerousness. *Journal of Crime and Delinquency* **18**, 371–92.
(6) Acres, D.I. (1975) The after care of special hospital patients. Appendix 3 in Home Office and DHSS *Report of the Committee on Mentally Abnormal Offenders*. Cmnd. 6244. HMSO: London.
(7) Harding, T. and Montandon, C. (1982) Does dangerousness travel well? In: *Dangerousness: Psychiatric Assessment and Management* (eds J.R. Hamilton and H. Freeman). Gaskell for the Royal College of Psychiatrists: London.
(8) Bottoms, A.E. (1982) Selected issues in the dangerousness debate In: *Dangerousness: Psychiatric Assessment and Management*. Gaskell for the Royal College of Psychiatrists: London.
(9) Walker, N. (1982) Ethical aspects of detaining dangerous people. In: *Dangerousness: Psychiatric Assessment and Management* (eds J.R. Hamilton and H. Freeman). Gaskell for the Royal College of Psychiatrists: London.

(10) Walker, N. (1991) Dangerous mistakes. *British Journal of Psychiatry* **158**, 752–7.

(11) Hare, R.D., Harpur, T.J., Hakstian, A.R., Forth, A.E., Hart, S.D. and Newman, J.P. (1990) The revised psychopathy checklist: descriptive statistics, reliability, and factor structure. *Psychological Assessment: A Journal of Consulting and Clinical Psychology* **2**, 338–41.

(12) Robins, L.N. and Reiger, D.A. (eds) (1991) *Psychiatric Disorders in America: The Epidemiological Catchment Area Study*. Free Press: New York.

(13) Mullen, P.E. (1997) Assessing risk of interpersonal violence in the mentally ill. *Advances in Psychiatric Treatment* **3**, 166–73.

Chapter 15

Writing a Report

Introduction

This chapter will concentrate on report writing for detained patients and offenders. It will not cover report writing for child care and civil litigation cases. For a good review of report writing in child care cases see Tufnell *et al.*[1]

In forensic psychiatry reports may be requested by:

(1) courts and solicitors
(2) Mental Health Review Tribunals
(3) managers of hospitals in relation to detention in hospital
(4) the Home Office in relation to patients detained under a restriction order
(5) prison doctors for
    (a) advice on diagnosis and treatment
    (b) advice to the parole and lifer boards on the mental state of offenders suspected of having an abnormality
(6) consultant psychiatrists in non-forensic psychiatric settings for advice on cases with 'forensic' problems or management problem presenting a risk to others
(7) the Mental Health Act Commission when requesting a second opinion
(8) social services when offenders are involved in child care proceedings
(9) miscellaneous other sources, e.g. the Department of Education on teachers who have offended.

In addition to the above, reports will be prepared as admission and discharge summaries, reports for case conferences, risk assessments etc.

A good background to report writing for the criminal courts has been given by Bluglass.[2] A psychiatric report may have far reaching effects as Scott[3] has pointed out. It may play a large part in the decision to deprive a patient of his liberty for years in hospital, or it may delay his return to the community. As well as doing good, a report can do harm. As will become apparent, the relationship of a psychiatrist to a person whom he as an expert witness is assessing is not the same as that which normally exists between a doctor and a patient. The psychiatrist considers not only the patient's needs and wishes but is obliged to balance this against the estimated risks posed by the patient.

In preparing any report, especially when acting as an expert witness, the psychiatrist must be as accurate, independent and as fair as possible. The report must be free of emotion and prejudice, moral judgements and exasperation. At the same time it should appear to be prepared by a doctor, one who is impartial yet genuinely concerned with the welfare of the offender.[2]

Reports on a subject appearing in court

The request for the report

Requests for psychiatric reports on offenders are made relatively rarely. The request may come from the court, or from the Crown Prosecution Service or defending solicitor.

The reasons for asking for a report include:

(1) disturbed behaviour in court
(2) a bizarre offence
(3) a history of mental disorder
(4) an offence which is out of character
(5) the nature of the offence, e.g. homicide, repeated sexual offences, arson.

Before undertaking an assessment, the psychiatrist should be clear what questions are to be answered. This may require correspondence or a telephone conversation with whoever has asked for the report.

Before submitting the report, it is important to discuss the contents with any relevant professionals such as probation officers or other psychiatrists in order to check its accuracy and importantly to check that any recommendations being made that may impact on other professionals are known by them in advance. A copy of a report requested by the court should be sent to the probation officer. When the report is requested by the subject's solicitor it is important to obtain permission before sending copies elsewhere. It is not uncommon for the doctors employed by the defence and prosecution to be in contact and make their opinions known to each other before the hearing. This does have the advantage that there is an opportunity for a sharing of information.

The crucial questions

The psychiatrist may need to consider the following questions.

(1) Whether the defendant is fit to plead and stand trial.
(2) Whether he was capable of forming intent at the time of the offence.

(3) Whether there are grounds for specific defences, e.g. automatism, diminished responsibility, provocation.
(4) Whether the defendant suffered or suffers from any form of mental disorder particularly a form subject to a treatment order.
(5) If so, whether he is in need of treatment.
(6) If so, where and by whom should this treatment be given.
(7) Whether it should be as an in-patient or out-patient, and which category.
(8) The prognosis.

Background information

Before seeing the defendant the psychiatrist should obtain and study background information.

In practice the background information supplied by magistrates' courts is usually extremely sparse and it is often necessary to request further information. Solicitors usually supply more background information but contact with other agencies may still be needed.

Information to consider requesting include:

(1) witness statements;
(2) transcripts of police taped interviews (when a defendant's case is moved from the magistrates' court to the Crown Court 1 and 2 are bound together and then known as the *committal file* or *depositions*);
(3) presentence probation reports;
(4) a list of previous convictions;
(5) the defendant's proof of evidence;
(6) certain exhibits of relevance, e.g. writing/letters that may suggest mental illness, albums of indecent photographs in sex offence cases etc.;
(7) other background information, e.g. GP files, old psychiatric notes, social work reports, school reports etc.

The interview

The interview in a remand prison is usually held in the prison hospital. It is necessary to contact the hospital beforehand to arrange the interview. The times available will normally be on weekdays between 9–11.45 am and 2–4 pm, though prisons are trying to be more flexible and sometimes interviews are allowed out of these hours. If the subject is on bail, the interview can be arranged at a suitable out-patient clinic. If the subject is in a hostel (e.g. a bail hostel) it may be more useful to go there which will have the advantage of allowing you to obtain the staff's observations.

At the interview the psychiatrist should first check that the person before him is the person he wants to see. There can be numerous Smiths in a prison. After normal introductions the psychiatrist should explain who requested the report and for what reason, and who will see the report and the lack of confidentiality (see Chapter 16 on the ethics of reports). A report requested by the court will be disclosed in open court to both defence and prosecution. A defence report, on the other hand, may be retained by the solicitor if it does not help his client. It is proper to explain to the subject what information the psychiatrist has already had. An explanation to the subject of the way the interview will be conducted is often very helpful. The procedure can then be that of a standard psychiatric interview covering basic information (although for medicolegal reports you should make sure you ascertain the court dealing with the case, the stage of the proceedings, e.g. pretrial, presentence and whether a probation officer has been allocated and if so who it is), family history, personal history, sexual history, occupational history, personality development, medical and psychiatric history, the events and mental state associated with the offence and any symptoms of illness at the time of interview. Physical examination should be carried out if indicated although it is very rare for this to be necessary.

From the history it may become clear that other interviews or clinical investigations may be needed. Some investigations may be difficult to arrange if the subject is in custody and it will be necessary to contact the prison medical officer.

The subject may refuse to cooperate with the interview even though it is requested by his solicitor or ordered by the court. In the case of a subject remanded on bail he may simply refuse or fail to attend. In that case the referring agent should be informed. In the case of a court request the subject may then be remanded in custody for the report. When an offender attends but proves hostile and difficult this too can be reported as well as any other observations. The subject's hostility may arise from a mental abnormality such as paranoid delusions which involve the court and the psychiatrist. Where such an abnormality is suspected it may be appropriate to recommend further observation in hospital under Section 35 but enough information may have been gathered to allow a diagnosis to be made.

The recommendations

If the interviewee is found to have a mental disorder the following arrangements must be considered:

(1) *Treatment order* (Section 37): The psychiatrist must assure the court that there is a hospital willing to take the patient within 28 days of the order being made. The referring agent must ensure that a second doctor has interviewed the patient and also prepared a report in accordance with the Mental Health Act (see Chapter 3). Where there is no hospital bed available for the patient then the psychiatrist should contact the appropriate purchasing authority with details of the case and his

recommendations. The authority is then in a position to discharge its responsibilities.

(2) *Guardianship order* (Section 37): Here the psychiatrist must be sure that the local social services are willing to receive the patient into guardianship. Again a second doctor is required (see Chapter 3).

(3) *Probation order:* The psychiatrist must be sure that the probation officer agrees to the order and that the subject is willing to accept it. If psychiatric care is to be recommended then specific provision for such care must be made.

(4) *Orders under Sections 35, 38 and 36:* in these cases the psychiatrist who accepts the patient is likely to be the one who prepares the report. He must be sure that facilities are available to allow the court to make the orders within the legally prescribed times (see Chapter 3). If facilities cannot be made available within the appropriate time a request for a further remand should be made.

(5) *Hospital and limitation direction* (colloquially known as a hybrid order) (Section 45A): This is only available for psychopathic disorder and requires the same medical recommendations as a hospital order under Section 37 (see Chapter 3 for more details).

Style of the report

The report to the court will be read by laymen and must be given in non-technical language. If a technical term is used then a phrase explaining it should be added either in the report or in an appendix at the back.

Psychodynamic and psychoanalytical terms are notoriously difficult for the layman. Repression, dissociation, etc. should be expressed in ordinary language, e.g. 'he pushed the memory to the back of his mind', 'he ignored the reality of the situation'. Other words which give trouble are 'personality disorder', 'EEG', 'schizoid', etc. Terms like 'immature' or 'unstable' should be qualified to explain their meaning. Intelligence expressed in terms of mental age or IQ can be very misleading without explanation to put the figures into perspective.

Length and form of report

There are certain general principles which must be remembered when preparing any report, whether it is a report for a case conference, for the Parole Board or the High Court. These principles are now commonly used as a framework for courses on report writing.

Your report must be able to stand alone, i.e. there must be sufficient information in it for its purpose and conclusions to be understood without any special knowledge of the patient/defendant. In England reports are usually four to six sides long, although some favour longer reports, especially in complex cases. Very brief reports (one or two paragraphs) are unlikely to have sufficient information in them to win the court's confidence.

Make sure each page is numbered and has a header or footer with the patient/defendant's name on it and also possibly the date of preparation of the report and its purpose, e.g. Report on Mr X for the Mental Health Review Tribunal or *R* v. *Mr X*. Consider, especially for medicolegal reports using $1\frac{1}{2}$ spacing and at least $1\frac{1}{2}$ inch margins as readers of your report will often make notes on it. Paragraphs should be numbered for easy reference. If a report is long, e.g. over 15 pages consider a contents page. Consider a statement of confidentiality and whether the report may be copied. Lastly remember that your report will last a long time, consider its contents carefully, it may outlive your own professional career and it may come back to haunt you.

A model example of an expert witness report (for any expert witness e.g. psychiatrist, surgeon, handwriting specialist, engineer, architect etc.) has been produced by the Judiciary Committee of The British Academy of Experts. This body has recommended a standard format for all experts with the aim of trying to aid ease of reading for courts and judges and also to make sure experts concentrate on relevant matters, e.g. making clear which evidence in a report is fact as opposed to hearsay etc. This model example/template is not yet being used by psychiatrists.

There are various ways of writing a report. The following is an example on which reports may be based. The main part of the report must be factual. Opinions should be restricted to the final section. It is useful to use sub-headings as illustrated below.

Introduction

The introductory paragraph should include who has requested the report, what the report is to be used for, what issue is at stake (this can include the offences being considered and the reason the report has been requested), where and when the defendant was seen, which papers were examined, which people were spoken to. Also consider confirming that the defendant has understood the limits of confidentiality of the report and has consented to its preparation.

Psychiatrists differ widely in their manner of referring to the subject of the report (e.g. Smith, Mr Smith, John Smith, John, the defendant, the patient, your client etc.). There is no right or wrong way to go about this but the full name may be the best option as it will help to avoid confusion between, for example, Mr (Paul) Smith, the father and Mr (John) Smith, the son, as the use of both names is more likely to accurately identify a person than the use of single names. Try to keep informal comments out of your report. If you wish to pass on informal observations, thank anyone for commissioning a report from you, charge a fee or anything else then put this information in a separate covering letter; do not include it in the report, it is surprising how many experts do.

Family history

This should draw out the main positive and negative events which help in the understanding of the case. Tact is required if facts turn up of which the subject was unaware, e.g. illegitimacy. The court can be warned in the report that the subject does not know it or it should be left out if not relevant. Mention the nature of the family relationships, and any history of mental disorder or delinquency in the family if relevant.

Personal history

This section deals with birth, physical and emotional development, experiences of separation, evidence and chronology of behaviour disorder (running away, lying, stealing, firesetting, violence, school behaviour and truancy) or neurotic behaviour (phobias, nightmares, anxieties, depressions etc.). The development of relationships with peers, teachers and school performance should be covered. Occupational and marital history will come in this section. Some subjects will show disturbance in many areas from an early age and this should be documented.

Sexual history

This section deals with sexual orientation, the onset of puberty, sexual relationships, fantasy life, and any manifestation of sexual deviation. Care has to be taken that no more is described than is required for the particular case. Clearly where sexual offending is the problem this section will be fuller. However, it is otherwise enough to assure the court that it is not an area that gives rise to public concern.

Personality

This section will be better described if information can be gained from an informant, such as a friend or relative.

Previous medical and psychiatric history

It is important to enquire specifically about head injuries and any associated change of character. The past psychiatric history should be described in detail.

Drug and alcohol history

This is a very important section and should be described fully. You should include a description of the effect that any drugs or alcohol have on the defendant.

Mental state at the time of the offence

This section deals with the subject's behaviour just before and at the time of the offence. Deciding what criminal act happened at the time is the province of the court and the subject is best avoided. Particularly avoid giving the defendant's account to the court. The psychiatrist's job is to throw light on the mental state at the time. Was there a psychiatric disorder, if so what was it and how would it affect the defendant's behaviour?

Current mental state

This describes the patient when interviewed and lists the important features, both positive and negative. Include a comment on the defendant's apparent sincerity or lack of it. Also give an estimate of intelligence (e.g. below average, within the average range).

Opinions and recommendations

This section will give the doctor's opinion as to whether the patient is mentally disordered or not, the nature of the disorder, and what should be done about it. Where there is doubt about diagnosis or management this should be stated (e.g. 'It is difficult to be certain in this case as the symptoms are vague, but nevertheless, on balance, I believe that the defendant has the mental illness of depression and requires psychiatric treatment'). Opinions must also be given addressing other specific issues of importance in the case, e.g. fitness to plead, abnormality of mind. You should make sure that you back up your opinions with reasoning as to why you have arrived at your particular opinion.

Recommendations should be expressed with proper respect for the court, realising that the court has to find a balance. The court may be offered other opinions which are diametrically opposed to the report and it may have before it evidence which makes the psychiatric recommendation inappropriate.

If in conclusion you have no psychiatric recommendation you should say so. If you are concerned about the defendant's mental state you could recommend that a copy of your report is passed on to the Prison Medical Service should the defendant receive a custodial sentence. The court is not obliged to follow your recommendations, the judge can decide on any action he or she wishes and unfortunately mentally ill patients are sometimes imprisoned even when psychiatrists recommend hospitalisation, although this is rare.

Oral evidence

In the majority of cases a written report is sufficient. However, the psychiatrist may have to appear in court to be cross-examined on a report in several situations including:

(1) When the defence and prosecution have reports with opposing views.
(2) When the prosecution is unwilling to accept a psychiatric defence. Peter Sutcliffe, the so-called 'Yorkshire Ripper', was charged with multiple murder. His defence of diminished responsibility rested on all the

psychiatrists asserting that he suffered from the mental illness of schizophrenia. The prosecution refused to accept this and cross-examined every psychiatric witness about their examination (how carefully had they examined the case), the reliability of their findings (could the defendant be imitating illness), and their interpretation (how certain can one be that these are signs of illness).

(3) When a judge wishes to make a restriction order he or she is obliged to take oral evidence from one of the psychiatrists who saw the patient, but may disregard the psychiatrist's view. The judge may enquire about risk of harm to the public, the prognosis and whether the arrangements the psychiatrist has made will protect the public.

(4) Oral evidence is required for a jury to consider the question of fitness to plead.

When giving oral evidence to support his report and opinion the psychiatrist is an expert witness. He may attend the trial from the beginning to hear all the evidence to make sure that none had escaped him. He should have his psychiatric notes with him and can consult them as needed. The psychiatrist will have little difficulty if he has followed Scott's golden rule[3] of reading his finished report and asking the question, 'Could I substantiate all the facts mentioned if I were to be cross-examined upon them and is the whole report strictly fair to the offender?'

The psychiatrist, when giving oral evidence, will be asked about his findings, which he can affirm, explain or enlarge on if necessary and describe how he obtained them. He will also be asked about his conclusions. He should stick to his original conclusion unless some conflicting facts (sufficient to make him change his mind) appear with which he was previously unacquainted. It is perfectly understandable to a court that two experts, seeing the same facts, will reach different opinions. The barrister may want to test the psychiatrist's views, 'Is it not the case, doctor, that the offender showed no signs of illness when seen by Dr. X?' or, 'Is it not the case, doctor, that the offender may have learned the symptoms of this illness and may be deceiving you?' The psychiatrist is well advised to admit to the possibility of such a suggestion but to assert firmly his own opinion that he believes his view to be the more probable, 'It is possible that a person can imitate mental illness and deceive a doctor but in this case, taking all the evidence [which can be listed if necessary], it is my opinion that the offender is suffering from mental illness and is not deceiving me'. The psychiatrist's view in the end may not be accepted by the court who may have the very difficult job of balancing conflicting and powerful arguments.

In the court the clerk of the court (a lawyer) and the usher organise the proceedings. On arriving at court the doctor should introduce himself to them. They will show him where he can sit. When the magistrate or judge enters the court the usher orders the people in the court to stand and the magistrate or judge exchanges a bow with the body of the court before all sit. The clerk of the court, sitting below the bench, informs the bench of the case to be heard. The defendant is then called to the dock to answer the charges put to him. When the doctor is called to give evidence he will be asked to swear on the Bible to tell the truth. He may choose alternatively to affirm (without the Bible). Questions will be directed first by the barrister (or solicitor) who called him and then he may be cross-examined by the other side. In simple cases the questions are merely a way of getting the doctor to affirm the statements in his report. The magistrates or judge may also ask questions for clarification.

A coroner is addressed as 'Sir', a magistrate as 'Your Worship', county court judges, recorders and circuit judges in Crown Courts as 'Your Honour', a judge of the Central Criminal Court or High Court (who may preside in a Crown Court), Court of Appeal or House of Lords as 'My Lord'. Presidents of Tribunals are addressed as 'Sir' or Madam'.

In court speak clearly and audibly to the bench and the barrister with sufficient pauses to allow the statements to be written down. It is normal practice to dress conservatively for the court.

Who sees psychiatric reports for the court?

Psychiatric reports requested by the court or prosecution are in no sense confidential. The court will send a copy to the prosecution and defence solicitor. It should be expected that the offender will at least be told the main points by the court or the defence solicitor and may even be given a copy of the report. The report is also likely to be given to the probation officer. If the offender is sent to prison or hospital it is quite possible that the report will be sent with him or follow him. The report will often then be passed on to other psychiatrists, psychologists, nurses, Mental Health Review Tribunal doctors, prison medical doctors, parole boards, etc. Finally, the report may appear at future court appearances.

Psychiatric reports to Mental Health Review Tribunals

The request for the report

The tribunal will ask the responsible medical officer for an up to date report. In cases on restriction orders requests also come from the Home Office to the responsible medical officer who can send the Home Office a copy of his tribunal report. The Home Office, who may disagree with the responsible medical officer, will then send their comments about the report to the Tribunal. The detained patient's solicitor may ask an independent psychiatrist to provide a psychiatric report. The Mental Health Act states that this doctor should be given every facility to examine the case.

The crucial questions

These are outlined in Chapter 4. They include:

(1) Is the patient still suffering from a mental disorder?
(2) Is it of such a nature that detention in hospital continues to be required?

Sources of information

The information will principally be in the records of the patient's treatment and progress (the clinical notes). Discussing the case directly with staff looking after the patient will be valuable.

Arrangements for aftercare

Where a responsible medical officer or independent doctor is recommending discharge or transfer then it clearly gives the tribunal the maximum chance of accepting the recommendation if the necessary aftercare arrangements have been made.

The style of the report

It can be assumed that the tribunal is relatively sophisticated in psychiatric terminology and common technical terms will be understood.

The form of the report

Your report should include a very detailed history, similar to a psychiatric court report and of similar length. The main differences will be that for the purposes of the tribunal details of the offence can be discussed and progress in hospital must be covered. The tribunal will be interested in understanding the patient's motivation for what he did (discussed under mental state at time of the offence) and his subsequent reaction to it (was there insight and remorse). Similarly, his previous convictions can be openly discussed (usefully in the section on personality) and the bearing this has on the risks he now poses. These previous convictions can be listed with, if appropriate, details to describe exactly what happened (a simple charge of actual bodily harm may conceal an abortive serious offence). The tribunal will be interested in the treatment the patient has received (give details) and the patient's response with particular attention to current mental state and prognosis. An analysis of the risks the patient presents is required (see Chapter 4). The list of questions set by the Home Office for restricted patients (see below) is a useful guide.

The opinion aims to answer the tribunal's crucial questions. It is good practice for the responsible medical officer to discuss his reasons and recommendations with the patient before the tribunal. The responsible medical officer is normally expected to attend the whole tribunal to be ready to be cross-examined by the patient or his solicitor or by the tribunal members (see Chapter 4).

Who will see the report?

The tribunal will pass the report to the client's solicitor who will show it to and discuss it with the client unless the psychiatrist has convinced the tribunal that it would do harm to do so. The report will become part of the tribunal's file as well as part of the patient's notes and will therefore be read in the future. For patients detained under a restriction order the Home Office will also keep a copy to which it will refer in future years.

Psychiatric report to the managers of a hospital

The request for the report

The managers (see Chapter 4) request a brief report when the responsible medical officer proposes renewing the detention of a patient.

The crucial questions

These are presented on the appropriate form

(1) Does the patient suffer from mental illness or severe mental impairment and is his mental disorder of a nature or degree which makes it appropriate for him to receive medical treatment in a hospital; and *either,*
   (a) such treatment is likely to alleviate or prevent a deterioration in his condition, or
   (b) the patient, if discharged, is unlikely to care for himself, to obtain the care which he/she needs, or to guard him/herself against serious exploitation?
(2) Does he/she suffer from psychopathic disorder or mental impairment, and is his/her mental disorder of a nature or degree which makes it appropriate for him/her to receive medical treatment in a hospital and is such treatment likely to alleviate or prevent a deterioration in his condition?
(3) Finally is it necessary,
   (a) for the patient's health or safety, and/or
   (b) for the protection of other persons
   that the patient should receive treatment and it cannot be provided unless he/she continues to be detained under the Act?

The source of information

The answers will be derived from the knowledge of the responsible medical officer.

Making arrangements

It is only necessary to be sure that the patient can continue to be looked after in the hospital. The patient must be informed that the renewal is being considered and that he has a right to speak to the managers.

The style of the report

The report will be read by the lay managers of the hospital who may only have a very basic understanding of psychiatric terms, therefore non-technical language should be used.

The form of the report

The report is usually made on a standard form (form 30). The psychiatrist has to indicate whether other methods of treatment are available, e.g. out-patient treatment, and why such alternative treatment is not appropriate and why informal admission is not appropriate.

The written report is read by the managers who expect to meet the doctor at the time of the hearing in order that the very brief written report can be enlarged on if necessary. The Mental Health Act Commission has suggested that the renewal should become a more formal procedure in which the managers meet the patient, doctor, social worker and a relative.

Who will see the report?

The report is usually held in the medical records department with a copy in the clinical file too. Under current practice the patient does not see it. The report may be produced at future renewals.

Psychiatric report to the Home Office in relation to patients detained under a Restriction Order (Sections 37/41)

The request

The Home Office, on behalf of the Minister responsible for restricted patients, requires:

(1) Regular reports on the progress of restricted patients (the Annual Statutory Report (ASR))

(2) A further report about a patient if the responsible medical officer is proposing a change in the leave status of the patient or a transfer to another hospital either fully or on trial leave. A restricted patient can be granted leave within the hospital or grounds at the responsible medical officer's discretion but cannot leave the grounds or be transferred elsewhere without the Minister's permission. The patient's return to the community is normally accomplished in stages. The Home Office requires a full report about each patient when an application is made by the responsible medical officer to accomplish one of these stages.

The crucial questions

The Home Office has recently renewed their checklist of points which should be covered in the Annual Statutory Report. It is sensible to also think through these points when making a request for leave or transfer. It can be useful to telephone the appropriate officer at the Home Office to discuss any leave/transfer proposals and the type of letter required. The checklist of points and guidance is reproduced below:

> 'A report is required to be submitted annually on the anniversary of the detention order. It should contain information about the progress of the patient over the previous year and about the multidisciplinary team's future treatment plans. The attached check list offers guidance on the sort of issues which the report should cover. All members of the patient's multidisciplinary team should be asked for views on the patient's progress, and those contributions should be included in the report to the Home Office. Documents prepared for other purposes (e.g. MHRT reports, Case Conference reports) may be submitted as an Annual Statutory Report as long as they are no longer than three months old. Please indicate if such a report is to be regarded as an ASR.'

Checklist of points considered by the Home Office in examining cases of restricted patients

The role of the Home Office in the management of restricted patients is to protect the public from serious harm. To carry this out effectively, the Home Office needs to know

(1) why a patient has been dangerous in the past;

(2) whether they are still dangerous (if so, why; if not, why not and in what circumstances they might be dangerous again), and

(3) what the treatment plan is.

The following list is not exhaustive, but is intended to cover some of the points which may need to be addressed when reporting to the Home Office.

Not all points will apply to all patients; but all sections (not just that covering the main diagnosis) that apply to a particular patient should be completed. Attaching relevant reports is always encouraged.

Reports to the Home Office should reflect the views of the multi-disciplinary team. Please indicate whether the team has been consulted.

For all patients
(1) Should the patient still be detained and for what reasons?
(2) If yes, which level of security does the patient need?
(3) What is the team's current understanding of the factors underpinning the index offence and previous dangerous behaviour?
(4) What change has taken place in respect of those factors (i.e. to affect the perceived level of dangerousness)?
(5) What are the potential risk factors in the future (e.g. compliance with medication, substance abuse, potential future circumstances, etc.)
(6) What are the patient's current attitudes to the index offence, other dangerous behaviour and any previous victims?
(7) What is the outward evidence of change (i.e. behaviour in hospital, on leave, attitudes towards staff and patients and potential victim groups)? How has the patient responded to stressful situations? Describe any physical violence or verbal aggression.
(8) Have alcohol or illicit drugs affected the patient in the past and did either contribute to the offending behaviour? If so, is this still a problem in hospital and what are the patient's current attitudes to drugs and alcohol? What specific therapeutic approaches have there been towards substance abuse?
(9) Which issues still need to be addressed, and what are the short- and long-term treatment plans?
(10) What is known about circumstances of the victim, or victim's family?

Patients with mental illness
(11) How is the patient's dangerous behaviour related to their mental illness?
(12) Which symptoms of mental illness remain?
(13) Has stability been maintained under differing circumstances? Under what circumstances might stability be threatened?
(14) Has medication helped and how important is it in maintaining the patient's stability?
(15) To what extent does the patient have insight into their illness and the need for medication?
(16) Does the patient comply with medication in hospital? Is there any reluctance? Would they be likely to comply outside?

Patients with psychopathy
(17) What are the individual characteristics of the personality disorder?

(18) What have been the treatment approaches to specific problem areas?
(19) Is the patient now more mature, predictable and concerned about others? Please give evidence.
(20) Are they more tolerant of frustration and stress? Please give evidence.
(21) Does the patient now take into account the consequences of their actions and learn from experience? Please give evidence.

Patients with mental impairment
(22) How has the patient benefited from treatment/training?
(23) Is their behaviour more acceptable? Please give evidence.
(24) Is the patient's behaviour explosive or impulsive? Please give evidence.
(25) Does the patient now learn from experience and take into account the consequences of their actions? Please give evidence.

Patients with dangerous sexual behaviour (all forms of mental disorder)
(26) Does the patient still show undesirable interest in the victim type?
(27) Describe any access to the victim type and the patient's attitude towards this group?
(28) What form has sexual activity in hospital taken?
(29) What do psychological tests or other evaluation indicate?
(30) What is the current content of fantasy material?

Patients who set fires (all forms of mental disorder)
(31) What interest does the patient still have in fires?
(32) Have they set fires in hospital?
(33) What access do they have to a lighter or matches?
(34) In what way do fires appear in current fantasy material?
(35) Does the patient have insight into previous fire setting behaviour?

And, finally
(36) Please give any other relevant information which would be useful to the Home Office.

Sources of information

Clearly the information is contained in all the documents relating to the patient, particularly the medical, nursing, psychological and social reports. A copy of the original witness statements relating to the index offence should be obtained in order that the offence is properly understood.

Making arrangements

Provisional arrangements appropriate to the stage of leave or transfer requested should be made and described along with the request. The Home

Office has to consider the safety of the public and therefore arrangements should be thorough and commensurate with the risks posed by the patient in that situation. Whilst it might be too risky to send a particular deluded patient suffering from paranoid schizophrenia unaccompanied and un-supervised on leave in the community, it might be perfectly safe for him to go shopping in the local village accompanied by staff. When the proposals are for the patient to live in the community and leave the hospital (either on trial leave or conditional discharge) a detailed plan of provisional arrangements should be made, a social worker identified to be the super-visor and a doctor to be the responsible medical officer. These people should know the patient's case well and know how to elicit crucial points e.g. the state of the patient's delusions, his sexual drive, etc.

The style of the report

Home Office officials may have become familiar with psychiatric terms but they have no formal training in it nor has the Minister. It is better therefore to stick to non-technical language with explanations of technical terms.

The form of the report

The report is usually in the form of a letter which may begin (or end) with a recommendation or request by the responsible medical officer. This is then supported by a detailed report on the patient covering the relevant points required by the Home Office in order to show the request is reasonable. At the end the proposed arrangements should be explained in detail to reas-sure the Minister that the proposal is a safe and sensible one. The letter will therefore usually run to about one and a half sides. A telephone call to support the letter can be useful. The Home Office may take several weeks to reply to the letter and may require further information before giving a decision. In the end the request may be rejected or modified arrangements proposed.

Who sees the report?

The report becomes the property of Home Office officials and the Minister. It will remain on the Home Office file and will be referred to in future and may influence later judgements.

Psychiatric reports in relation to applications for a subject to be admitted to special hospital

The request for the report

The local admission panels of each special hospital (see Chapter 1) require a psychiatric report to accompany a request for a bed within special hospital for a patient. The report will usually be prepared by the doctor who is currently responsible for the patient. The responsible medical officer will ask for an opinion from a special hospital consultant before submitting a report, in which case both will write to the local admission panel.

The crucial questions

It must be shown the subject fulfils the criteria for detention under the Mental Health Act. It is also necessary to demonstrate that the subject is a grave and immediate danger to others in any setting other than a special hospital. This may be because of

(1) being a persistent absconding risk, even from a regional secure unit, coupled with behaviour which makes him a grave and immediate danger to the public; or
(2) that although he is not an absconder (or his absconding is controlled) his behaviour in the hospital represents a grave danger to staff and patients and cannot be controlled even within a regional secure unit.

In short, what must be asked is whether, after all reasonable measures have been taken, is it the case that unless the patient is moved to a special hospital someone is likely to be seriously injured?

Sources of information

The medical and nursing notes including incident sheets, witness statements in the case of offenders, the prison notes in the case of convicted prisoners, contain the essential information. A careful search must be made to discover all the relevant risk information and the factors which surround it.

The arrangements

It is expected that alternatives for the patient have been excluded, e.g. transfer to an intensive care ward or regional secure unit.

The style of the report

Knowledge of psychiatric terms can be assumed. However, it is necessary to be particularly accurate, detailed, thorough and clear with a good analysis of the risks involved.

The form of the report

The report and request usually are put in a letter beginning or ending with the request. The report will follow the lines of a court report which not only shows which psychiatric disorder the patient suffers from but will give particular attention to the behaviour which is causing anxiety. A list should be included in the discussion of all violent or dangerous incidents, giving dates and a brief description of what he did, what he was trying to do and any injuries sustained. In this way a very clear picture can be built up of the development of the present situation and why it is so worrying. It is also important to report what measures have been taken and with what results. The current legal situation should be discussed. The subject may be detained in hospital already on a section or may be awaiting trial and it may be hoped to recommend to the court that a hospital order be made.

The report may be the sole basis for discussion by the admission panel who makes the decision as to whether a special hospital bed can be offered. As they may have no other information, the importance of clarity and a high level of detailed information cannot be underestimated.

Who sees the report?

The report will become part of the special hospital files if the patient is accepted as well as remaining in the local hospital file. It will be examined by many people in the future when judgements have to be made about release. It could turn up at a Mental Health Review Tribunal, at which time it could be seen by the patient.

Psychiatric report to the prison doctor

The request

The prison doctor may request a report for:

(1) An opinion on the need for transfer out of prison to a hospital.
(2) A body such as the Parole Board or its Discretionary Life Panel (for which oral evidence may also be required as in a Mental Health Review Tribunal).

The crucial questions

Where an opinion on the need for transfer out of prison is required the questions will be:

(1) What is the diagnosis?
(2) What treatment should be given?
(3) Where should the treatment be given?

It may be that the subject will accept treatment in prison and his psychiatric condition is such that it can be easily managed there or it may be that psychiatric hospital care will be required. The prison doctor hopes to make use of the psychiatrist's experience, both of the disorder and of the psychiatric facilities.

Where the opinion is required for a body such as a Parole Board or the Discretionary Life Panel the reason for the request must be clarified. It may be that there is a hope that the psychiatrist can contribute to the estimation of risk of re-offending or it may be that the board or panel wish to know what psychiatric facilities could be made available for supervision of the subject once he returns to the community.

Source of information

The main document to consider is the Inmate Medical Records (known colloquially as the IMR). Security and risk information may also be found in the general prison discipline file kept in the prison general office. You can usually obtain this file, although it may need authority from the prison senior medical officer – the file is known colloquially as the 20/50. Other useful records may also be found in the hospital nursing documentation, prison psychology files and the prison probation files, although you will need special permission from the psychologist or probation officer to access these. You should, of course, discuss the case with prison staff as well as interviewing the inmate. For parole reports you should read the parole file (usually kept in the general office) and for lifer reports the life sentence plan (kept in the general office). In some prisons there are also special programmes, e.g. sex offender treatment programme, reasoning and rehabilitation courses, armed robbers courses, so there will also be further records and reports if there are special programmes in the prison you are visiting.

The arrangements

Normally any special arrangements will be made by the prison doctor unless it is clearly more sensible for the visiting psychiatrist to do so.

The style of the report

The report for the Parole Board or Discretionary Life Panel will be read by lay people and therefore psychiatric terms should be explained and technical terms avoided as far as possible.

Form of the report

This should be similar to that of a court report so that the opinion can be seen to follow from the history. If a return to the community is being considered then the report must describe accurately what facilities are available.

Who sees the report?

The report will go into the prison medical file and where appropriate to the Parole Board. It must be assumed, therefore, that it will have fairly general circulation. The prisoner will receive a copy of any report prepared for the Parole Board or Discretionary Life Panel.

Psychiatric reports for other psychiatrists in ordinary settings

The report

The consultant in a catchment area hospital may request a second opinion from a forensic psychiatrist in order to advise on a forensic problem.

The crucial questions

These will depend on the reason for referral which must be clarified. Usually the consultant wants help to manage dangerous or difficult patients and is hoping to make use of the forensic psychiatrist's experience in this field or of the secure facilities. The questions will be:

(1) What is the diagnosis and can the patient be detained if necessary under the Mental Health Act, or should he be discharged from hospital?
(2) Is the optimal treatment being given already?
(3) Is it safe to leave the patient where he is or should he be transferred to a more secure unit and, if so, which one?

Sources of information

This will be contained in all the previous clinical notes. If there has been violence or an offence then objective accounts (witness statements, incident forms) should be obtained if possible. A full psychiatric history must be obtained including all forensic details.

The arrangements

The referring consultant will usually be grateful for any help about legal aspects with which he may be unfamiliar, such as advising on how to use court disposals to best effect. It will often help if the forensic psychiatrist plays an active part in affecting a transfer to a more secure environment.

Style of the report

Clearly in this case the report can be in ordinary technical language.

Form of the report

It may be sent as a letter or as a report with a covering letter. The latter has the advantage that it can be used as a supporting report should it be required. The report will cover the history in the same way as a court report but will also deal with the questions brought up by the referring doctor. The opinion should be addressed to these questions. Clear advice which recognises the anxieties in the original referral will be welcome.

Who will see the report?

The report will become part of the psychiatric notes of the patient. If used to apply for a transfer or for a report to the court it will be fairly generally distributed. It will be read in the future and may affect judgments. It is possible that it could turn up at the Mental Health Review Tribunal and be seen by the subject.

References

(1) Tufnell, G., Cottrell, D. and Georgiades, D. (1996) 'Good practice' for expert witnesses. *Clinical Child Psychology and Psychiatry* **1** (3), 365–83.
(2) Bluglass, R. (1979) The psychiatric court report. *Medicine, Science and the Law* **19**, 121–9.
(3) Scott, P.D. (1953) Psychiatric reports for magistrates' courts. *British Journal of Delinquency* **4**, 82–97.

Chapter 16

Ethics and Forensic Psychiatry

Introduction

Ethics are defined in the Oxford English Dictionary as 'the rules of conduct recognised in certain limited departments of human life'. Since the late 1970s there has been an increasing interest in medical ethics particularly in psychiatry, by many bodies interested in the rights of patients. In the field of forensic psychiatry this has led to a close examination of the relationship between the patient, the psychiatrist and the state.[1] The ethics of working with prisoners and other detained people have been addressed in a United Nations declaration of 1981, the World Medical Association 1975 'Declaration of Tokyo' and 'Declaration of Geneva', the World Psychiatric Association 1996 'Declaration of Madrid', BMA guidance for doctors in prisons, Royal College of Psychiatrists' guidance on ethical issues in psychiatric practice in prisons[2] and most recently the Council of Europe's recommendations on the ethical and organisational aspects of health care in prisons.[3] All practising psychiatrists should be familiar with the General Medical Council's guidance: *Good Medical Practice*,[4] *Maintaining Good Medical Practice*[5] and *Confidentiality*.[6]

Essentially a doctor must offer in prison (or other place where people are detained) the same standard of care as outside. The doctor must not partake in any activities involving torture or inhuman and degrading treatment or punishment. Medical skills should not be used for non-medical purposes. Where they are used for investigative purposes such as in forensic psychiatry, the situation must be fully explained to the prisoner. The prisoner's rights and dignity must not be overridden.

The British Medical Association (BMA) in their handbook of medical ethics[7] draw together the ethical position of doctors in the United Kingdom. The handbook deals with many situations met generally in medicine as well as certain specific situations in psychiatry. It recognises that a doctor may have either a therapeutic collaborative relationship with a patient or a relationship where the doctor acts as an impartial examiner (in order to provide a report at the request of a third party). In a traditional therapeutic relationship the patient is free to choose his doctor, the patient gives informed, free consent to any treatment and the doctor is responsible to the patient. It will be immediately obvious that this traditional therapeutic relationship rarely obtains in forensic psychiatry where patients do not have a right to choose their doctor when in prison or detained in hospital and where the doctor may feel a duty to the institution. This chapter will deal with the following matters:

(1) the ethics of the expert psychiatric report;
(2) the ethics of risk assessment;
(3) the ethics of assessing the defendant's responsibility;
(4) the ethics of the treatment and management of detained patients.

The ethics of the expert psychiatric report

The Royal College of Psychiatrists considers it unethical for a psychiatric report to be prepared by doctors other than by consultant psychiatrists or trainees under their supervision. The present arrangements in England and Wales do not always meet this standard.

When the defence or Crown Prosecution Service require a psychiatric report they will ask a psychiatrist to provide one. Ideally such an expert will not be professionally connected with the case but would give an opinion or interpret facts, using specialised knowledge and experience. In practice the defendant's own psychiatrist is also usually asked to give an expert opinion. The court, Crown Prosecution Service or defence may legitimately wish to have an independent report instead of or in addition to one by the patient's own psychiatrist. They will commonly refer a request for a report to a collection of doctors, e.g. the team of prison medical officers or the team of forensic psychiatrists who decide amongst themselves who will write the report.

When the court orders a report the defendant is expected to co-operate with the doctor. If he refuses or fails to attend whilst on bail, for example, the court may order a remand in custody for an examination by the prison doctors. Generally, if the defence is asking for a report the defendant will have been consulted. However, it is possible (e.g. when a patient is so disordered as to be unfit to plead) for the defence to ask for a report without being able to obtain consent from the defendant. Nevertheless, whatever the court orders nothing can force the defendant to give either a frank or a full history.

The psychiatrist will obtain information from the documents in the case that he will incorporate into the report which may lead to conclusions which the defendant may prefer to avoid. The opinion of the psychiatrist will be primarily addressed to the questions raised by the person or body who requested the report. It is therefore proper that the psychiatrist makes all this clear to the subject at the start of the interview. It is good practice after normal introductions to tell the subject:

(1) Who invited the doctor to see him.
(2) What the doctor does professionally (i.e. that he is a psychiatrist).
(3) The purpose of the examination (e.g. to prepare a report for the court or the solicitor on the mental state of the defendant with particular attention to its relationship to the offence).
(4) What information the doctor has already been given (e.g. statements, social enquiry report).
(5) That this is not a normal medical interview and what is learned and is relevant to the report may not be regarded as confidential between patient and doctor.
(6) How the report may be used in the sentencing (e.g. to allow the court to consider the possibility of making a hospital order or that the psychiatrist's risk assessment may influence sentencing).
(7) What rights the patient has to refuse to co-operate.

The ethical dilemmas facing psychiatrists in their dual role as the agent of the court and on behalf of the patient are brought into sharp focus when medical evidence is given to court when the court is considering a discretionary life sentence.[8] The court clearly sees a role for medical evidence when considering a discretionary life sentence (*R* v. *Hodgson* (1968) 52 Cr App R 113). The three conditions laid down in *R* v. *Hodgson* have been accepted by the courts and they are

(1) that the offences are grave enough to require a very long sentence;
(2) that the person may be of 'unstable character'; and
(3) if further offences are committed, the consequences to others may be specially injurious. The Court of Appeal in interpreting *R* v. *Hodgson* has stated that establishing that the offender is a person of 'unstable character' should be based on medical evidence. Mental conditions that have been accepted by courts have included mental illness, personality disorder, and sexual deviancy. Where medical evidence is presented on personality disorder, such evidence may indicate serious risk of future offending coupled with the conclusion that the condition is untreatable, in most cases leading to the judge imposing a discretionary life sentence. When giving such evidence the psychiatrist is largely acting as an agent of the court and society.

In the USA the ethical dilemmas involved are partly resolved by separation of forensic examiner and treating psychiatrist. In the UK the psychiatrist giving forensic evidence may be the catchment area forensic psychiatrist or visiting prison psychiatrist responsible for the defendant and will therefore be responsible both for giving evidence to the court and for providing treatment. There is no ultimate resolution to the ethical problems involved. They can be partially addressed by clearly informing the patient/prisoner on the purpose and likely consequences of a psychiatric report; confining evidence to assessment of mental disorder and the likely future consequences of that disorder and keeping in mind that ultimately it is the judge considering all the evidence, including the medical evidence, who determines whether a discretionary life sentence is appropriate or not.[8]

Sometimes an ill defendant will refuse or be unable to co-operate. The reasons for this vary from the effect of a paranoid psychosis that renders the defendant hostile and suspicious, to an inability to concentrate or think logically due to severe mental illness. In these situations the psychiatrist will report the unwillingness or inability of the subject to co-operate. There is here a possible ethical dilemma, for the BMA advises[7] that a doctor may properly choose to refuse to examine a subject who does not wish to be examined. Disclosure will need to be justified either in the patient's best interests, where GMC guidance advises that the patient is informed of disclosure, or in the 'public interest' where 'failure to disclose information may expose the patient or others to risk of death or serious harm'.[6] There is a fuller discussion of the issues of disclosure later in this chapter. Where a prisoner is in need of medical treatment, disclosure to court will usually be justified. This situation has clear affinities to making a recommendation for detention for treatment, though in this case the court is acting as the 'applicant' for purposes of the Mental Health Act. The principle to be adhered to at all times is whether the threshold for breach of confidentiality on the various grounds a breach can be made (see below) is reached. This principle applies to the rare case where a patient will allow some but not all information to be disclosed to the court. If such information is essential to the psychiatric opinion then either the psychiatrist should decline to provide a report or disclose according to the principle above. In difficult cases it would be prudent for the psychiatrist to discuss the case with their defence body.

In approaching the defendant the psychiatrist must always maintain that consideration for the defendant which is part of the medical ethic and his report should be clearly seen to be the report of a doctor brought in to give an objective account. In the report care must be taken to distinguish between those things which are supported by objective evidence and those which are not. The psychiatrist's opinion must be clearly separated from his findings (see Chapter 15). The report once completed is sent to the party requesting it. The party may be willing to allow copies of the report to be sent by the psychiatrist to other interested people, e.g. a probation officer or the prison doctor. This permission is usually assumed if the court requests the report as it is normally in everyone's interest that this is done. On the other hand once the report is sent to a third person the psychiatrist has no control on who else will see it. The General Medical Council[4] advises that where patients are seen without referral from the patient's general practitioner, that the general practitioner be informed. It should therefore be good practice to inform the patient's general practitioner if findings arise from the report which merit ongoing assessment or treatment. However, such information cannot be passed to the patient's general practitioner unless the patient agrees. The report is the property of the referring agent but they will usually consent to information being passed to the patient's general practitioner or own psychiatrist (if it is in the patient's best interest).

Joseph[9] discusses the ethical problems of bias of expert witnesses when they appear for prosecution or defence. He argues that bias is inevitable where expert witnesses provide reports for courts, and they are generally weighted towards the side that instructs them. Expert witnesses should always be on the lookout for unwitting bias and strive to avoid it. Court appointed experts have been advocated as the solution to this inbuilt bias. However, in a field like psychiatry where there is no consensus on contentious issues such as the treatability of personality disorder, bias is perhaps unavoidable even with court appointed experts. Joseph[9] concludes that the adversarial system still remains the best system for avoiding bias.

The ethics of risk assessment

Psychiatrists inevitably become caught up in the process of giving an opinion on the degree of risk posed to others (see Chapter 14). The psychiatrist will be asked directly about risk in the following instances:

(1) the application of a restriction order by a court;
(2) applications to the hospital managers for the renewal of detention;
(3) the proceedings of Mental Health Review Tribunal when considering discharge;
(4) reports to the Home Office on patients detained on a restriction order;
(5) when commenting about the degree of hospital security required;
(6) when making a recommendation for an order for detention in hospital under Sections 2, 3, 4 and 5;
(7) courts or the Crown Prosecution Service may ask directly for a risk assessment to be carried out to assist the court in sentencing (see above for discussion of discretionary life sentences);
(8) when reporting to the parole board and lifers board.

The imperfections in the psychiatrist's ability to make accurate predictions has already been noted (Chapter 14). A psychiatrist's comments on risk may lead to the prolonged detention of a defendant or detained patient in hospital.[8] This has been subject to criticism and considered unethical because of the lack of data confirming the psychiatrist's alleged skills as a predictor of risk. Nevertheless, despite these criticisms and in the absence of a better system, it remains normal practice to continue to give such advice. The BMA does not comment on this specialised area. Currently, the Mental Health Act requires psychiatrists to continue to take on the task and it is clearly still regarded as ethical to do so by the profession as a whole.

The ethics of assessing responsibility

Psychiatrists, in providing a psychiatric report dealing with the question of responsibility (intent, disordered mental states, diminished responsibility, insanity, etc.) enter an area in which, it may be argued, the psychiatrist is being taken beyond the boundaries of his expertise. The law employs its own definitions and concepts of mental disorder which often differ substantially from standard medical understanding of abnormal mental states (see Chapter 3). In the case of diminished responsibility, for example, the psychiatrist will be asked not only to describe the defendant's mental state at the time of the offence (a reasonable question to be asked of an expert) but also the extent to which this impaired his responsibility – a question really for the jury. Chapter 3 outlines the three limbs of a diminished responsibility defence. Courts and lawyers will expect the psychiatrist to comment on the third limb, namely how 'substantially' responsibility is diminished. The psychiatrist is entitled to refuse to give such an opinion on the grounds that they have no expertise in this area but the court is likely to find that stance unhelpful. The psychiatrist might provide the jury with their opinion on which factors are relevant in considering responsibility but state firmly that it is ultimately a matter for the jury.

Psychiatrists should be especially careful in compiling pretrial reports (fitness to plead, insanity, diminished responsibility) where the defendant denies the charge.[10] The psychiatrist is best advised[10] to avoid discussion of the offence and issues relevant to sentencing where the charge is denied.

The General Medical Council[4] insists that doctors in providing care must recognise and work within the limitations of their professional competence. Psychiatrists who provide an opinion in issues of competence should therefore ensure that they have sufficient knowledge and training in assessing medicolegal aspects of mental responsibility when asked to give an opinion in such matters.

The ethics of the care of the detained patient

The ethics of detaining patients

The decision about which categories of mental disorder allow detention, and under what conditions, is made by parliament and incorporated into the Mental Health Act 1983. The right not to be detained unnecessarily has to be weighed against the right to be detained when necessary. Mental health law differs in different countries, for example in certain states in the United States of America, such as California, detention procedures are judicial. It is reported that the effects of this are that many seriously mentally ill people are not treated but live a disordered life in urban squalor and find themselves sooner or later transferred to the criminal justice system. There is a growing feeling that the pendulum has swung too far in such cases.[11]

The ethics of consent

Normally, it is illegal to give treatment without the patient's consent except in certain special circumstances, e.g. emergencies when capacity to consent is affected (e.g. by unconsciousness, confusion or the undue influence of others) and when the conditions in Part 4 of the Mental Health Act 1983 are met (see Chapter 4). In the case of detained patients, consent should be sought if at all possible. For consent to be genuine it should be uninfluenced by coercion or by misdirection and it must be based on sufficient information. The doctor must decide what a reasonable doctor would give as information as well as providing information about alternative treatment. The Department of Health recommends (following Court of Appeal rulings) that where treatment carries substantial or unusual risks the patient should be so advised. The doctor should give reasons for his own choice. The doctor has a duty to use reasonable care and skill in this matter.

Successive legal judgements on consent to treatment have resulted in the 'three stage test' of competency to give consent to treatment. The three-stage test states that the patient must be

(1) able to comprehend and retain relevant information;
(2) believe it;
(3) weigh it in the balance so as to arrive at a choice.

Courts have stated that the patient's capacity must be 'commensurate with the gravity of the decision'. Thus abnormalities in the patient's mental state may interfere with the ability to 'weigh in the balance' information required to make an informed choice about treatment. Lady Justice Butler-Sloss in the Court of Appeal, when examining the case of a woman with a needle phobia stated that 'if a compulsive disorder or phobia from which the patient suffers stifles belief in the information presented to her, then the decision may not be a true one'. She also stated in the same case 'a decision to refuse medical treatment by a patient capable of making the decision does not have to be sensible, rational or well conceived'. Thus the three-stage test does not require the patient to come to a wise decision but does require that the patient can 'believe' and 'weigh' the information. For a comprehensive discussion of these issues see Kennedy and Grubb[12] on which this section is based. Case law continues to refine the law on consent. In complicated cases the clinician will need to consult appropriate legal advice.

The problem arises of the patient, detained or not detained, who is permanently unable to consent (e.g. a severely subnormal patient) to treatments not covered by the Mental Health Act. The House of Lords has ruled[13] that the doctors have a common law duty to act in the best possible interests of the patient. This would cover routine accepted physical treatments.

It can be argued that no patient detained against his will can give free consent because he is always aware that the doctor in charge of his detention will be influenced by whether or not he complies with treatment. He may feel that he will only get out if he takes the treatment. The Mental Health Act and accompanying Code of Practice[14] set out the legal framework of what to do when consent is not obtained (see Chapter 4). The Mental Health Act Commission and procedure of second opinion ensures that the rights of detained patients are addressed. The Code of Practice[14] gives guidance on recognising whether a patient has the mental capacity to give consent. The matter is one for clinical judgement in the light of the law and the Code's guidelines. To be capable of giving consent the patient should fulfil the three-stage test described above as for any other competent patient. The patient should also be able to understand the nature of the proposed treatment, its consequences (and the consequence of not having it) and its risks (expressed in broad terms). The patient has a right to be given all relevant information and the right to choose if possible. When it is necessary to obtain consent then the psychiatrist has to judge if real consent has been given, if not then he must seek a formal second opinion from the Mental Health Act Commission. Successive legal judgments have defined which treatments constitute 'medical treatment given to him [the patient] from which he is suffering' (Section 63 Mental Health Act). Kennedy and Grubb[12] define it as

> 'treatment which, taken as a whole, is calculated to alleviate or prevent deterioration of the mental disorder from which the patient is suffering, and includes a range of acts ancillary to the core treatment, including those which prevent the patient from harming himself or which alleviate the symptoms of the disorder.'

Case law[12] has accepted forcible feeding for the treatment of anorexia nervosa and other psychiatric illnesses (including forms of personality disorder), or use of restraint or reasonable force in a case of a pregnant woman, suffering from schizophrenia, requiring a caesarean section.

Confidentiality and the detained patient

The ideal ethical position for all patients is that a doctor must protect information acquired in the course of a doctor–patient relationship. The BMA[7] and GMC[6] set high value on medical confidentiality. There are, however, a number of exceptions when information is not kept confidential. The following list is based on the GMC guidance on confidentiality,[6] which should be read by all practising psychiatrists.

(1) The patient gives consent.
(2) The information is given to a relative or carer where, on medical

grounds it is undesirable to seek the patient's consent (where this would reveal damaging medical facts to the patient) or the patient is unable to give consent and the carer needs to know (e.g. a psychotic patient).
(3) The information is required to be revealed through due legal process.
(4) Where the doctor has an overriding duty to society to reveal the confidence (e.g. knowledge of a serious crime, terrorism, information in relation to the patient's incapacity to drive) or to prevent a serious risk to public health (e.g. a patient with a serious infective disease refusing to take precautions against its spread).
(5) For medical research in certain circumstances.
(6) Where a committee of the GMC is investigating a doctor's fitness to practise and requires such information but as in all cases of disclosure the consent of the patient should be obtained if possible.

Where the patient refuses consent to disclosure the patient's wishes must be respected. However, in the case of detained patients there are further situations where information is disclosed without the patient's consent. These are

(1) for a Mental Health Review Tribunal;
(2) to the hospital managers on recommending renewal of detention;
(3) to the Home Office who require information on restricted patients;
(4) information to the advisory board to the Home Office;
(5) to the Mental Health Act Commission.

Some of these situations are discussed below in more detail and follow closely GMC guidance on confidentiality.[6]

Consent to disclosure

Information that a patient gives to a doctor remains the property of the patient and should not be disclosed without permission, with the exception of the necessary sharing of information with other persons concerned with the clinical care of the patient. Permission to disclose is valid only if the patient fully understands the nature and consequences of the disclosure.

Information to a relative or carer

It is regarded as ethical to disclose relevant information to a relative or other appropriate persons when it is thought undesirable for patients to be told the full implications of their condition or the patient is incapable of giving consent. A difficult situation can arise when an abused person asks that information about the abuse be kept confidential. Sometimes disclosure is justified in the victim's interest in order to prevent further harm, particularly in the case of children or the incapacitated.

Information required by due legal processes

This may happen either because

(1) there is a statute requiring certain information to be given to particular bodies, e.g. the reporting of certain infectious diseases;
(2) an order is made by a court of law that the doctor discloses information.

In this country, unlike some, information given by a patient is not regarded as privileged in law, i.e. protected from disclosure in all circumstances. A refusal by the doctor to comply may be regarded as contempt of court. Such a court order is likely to be issued in cases of personal litigation. Legal advice should be sought if there are doubts. The court may order the medical records to be disclosed to

- the subject
- his legal adviser
- a medical adviser to the subject
- a combination of the second and third points.

The court may hear the evidence in camera if convinced that the evidence would be damaging to the patient.

Duty to society

It is regarded as ethical (but not in all countries) for the doctor's duty to society to override his duty to maintain his patient's confidence in limited circumstances. In forensic psychiatry practice this may occur when a patient reveals that he has committed or is about to commit a grave crime. GMC guidance[6] states

> 'disclosures may be necessary where a failure to disclose may expose the patient, or others, to risk of death or serious harm. In such circumstances you may disclose information promptly to an appropriate person or authority.'[11]

The police may, for example, ask for access to personal medical information that will help them with their enquiries. In general the doctor should seek, if possible, to persuade the patient to disclose or give permission for the information to be released. Failing this the doctor must decide if disclosure is justified in the public interest. Sometimes a patient will ask whether the doctor will treat information about a crime confidentially. No absolute assurance can be given.

The leading case is that of *R* v. *Edgell* (*W* v. *Edgell* (1989) Court of Appeal 8.11.89). Dr Edgell was commissioned by solicitors to prepare a report for a Mental Health Tribunal. Dr H. Edgell became aware, during an interview with the patient at a special hospital, of information indicating dangerousness. This information was not available to the Mental Health Review Tribunal. Against the wishes of the patient and the patient's solicitor Dr Edgell sent this information to the Home Office who in turn disclosed it to the MHRT. The Court of Appeal ruled that Dr Edgell was right to do so.

This case is discussed in detail by Kennedy and Grubb.[12] A number of questions remain unanswered in relation to the law's attitude to disclosure in the public interest. First, it is not clear what risks of harm would be sufficient to justify disclosure of confidential information in the public interest. Second, it is unclear whether the doctor merely has to believe a risk exists or whether there needs to be objective proof that a real risk of physical harm exists. The General Medical Council recognises that disclosure against the patient's wishes can be justified where there is a risk of death or serious harm to the patient and where disclosure is necessary for the prevention or detection of a serious crime. It is for the individual doctors to decide how to interpret the word 'serious' and it would be prudent to seek advice from a defence body in difficult cases. Kennedy and Grubb[12] point out that the court is not obliged to follow GMC guidance and there may therefore be tension between the legal and professional obligations of confidentiality and hence disclosure in the public interest. The GMC's[6] last word on this area should be borne in mind namely 'Doctors who decide to disclose confidential information must be prepared to explain and justify their decisions'.

In America an important rule was established by the Tarasoff decision.[15] A patient told his therapist of a plan to kill his former girlfriend. The therapist, realising the dangerousness of the situation, consulted colleagues, recommended involuntary detention and asked the police to detain the patient if they came across him. The police did interview him but then released him as he appeared rational and promised to stay away from the intended victim. The patient then broke off treatment. Two months later he murdered her. The relatives sued the therapist and the police, claiming that the victim should have been warned of the danger. The suit was initially dismissed but upheld on appeal to the Californian Supreme Court. The ruling, initially that the therapist had a duty to protect a potential victim (i.e. a duty to warn) was later modified to place a duty on the therapist to use reasonable care to protect the victim, e.g. by simply hospitalising the patient. Versions of the ruling were adopted in several states. As yet there is no such ruling in Britain. All sorts of problems arise from such a ruling. How is the therapist to judge which threats are real threats and must be acted on and what effect will all this have on the patient's readiness to confide in his therapist?

For the purposes of medical research

Information about a patient may be used in research approved by a research ethics committee. Whether it is appropriate to seek consent from the patient depends on the nature of the research; e.g. a simple account of the outcome of treatment might not require the consent of the patient. On the other hand, special enquiries taken directly from the patient for research purposes would require consent, as would an experimental trial of treatment. The Royal College of Psychiatrists[16] urges that great care be taken with detained patients and 'incompetent' patients. Detention may affect the patient's ability to give free consent. There should be no suggestion, for example, that compliance will lead to release. The patient should be allowed a period of time to quietly consider the carefully explained and discussed proposal. Similar arrangements should stand for prisoners. Where the subject has no capacity to give consent, research is still possible if the patient does not resist inclusion and relatives have been informed and have given consent. If there are no relatives a suitable independent person who knows the patient should be consulted. A judgement has to be made as to whether the patient would be likely to consent if he had the capacity. When information in the form of a case history is published in a scientific paper it is normal not to obtain consent but to disguise details to hide the identity of the patient.

Research in prisons is particularly sensitive because of the prisoner's detention. There is a national ethics committee especially set up to judge the ethical issues in prison research.

Information for the Mental Health Review Tribunal

Tribunals must be held by law at certain stated intervals on each detained patient (see Chapter 4). The responsible medical officer must give, even without the patient's consent, a report which will disclose details obtained in the therapeutic relationship. Furthermore the case notes will be made available to the tribunal members (normally only the medical member). The doctor is not only expected to act as a professional witness and give an account of his patient but also as an expert witness in the sense of giving an opinion. The report of the doctor will normally be made available to the patient through his solicitor unless the doctor has some quite outstanding reason, which convinces the tribunal that it would be harmful for the patient to see the report. It is good practice therefore for the doctor to discuss his report with the patient beforehand, indicating what his views to the tribunal will be and the reasons for them.

Information to the hospital managers

On renewal of a section, at present, the managers, after seeing the responsible medical officer and receiving his reason for continuing detention, do not consult the patient except at the patient's request. The information given to the managers (who are usually three lay persons) will have been obtained within the doctor–patient relationship but will be confined to essentials. The patient's consent is not required. The Mental Health Act

Commission recommends that the renewal be a thorough procedure with the patient being seen automatically. It is good practice to explain matters to the patient at the time of the renewal.

Information to the Home Office on restricted patients

The Home Office expects regular reports on restricted patients and full reports when the requests are made to alter conditions relating to the restriction order. In this situation it is normal not to obtain a patient's consent before sending these reports but it must remain good practice to explain to the patient what has been said and the reasons for any opinion. There is no doubt that this situation can be a difficult one because a patient may have no insight into his condition and may therefore not appreciate the doctor's reasons for failing to support the patient's wish to be released.

Information to the advisory board to the Home Office

The members of the advisory board (see Chapter 4) expect, on visiting a patient, to have full access to the medical records although they may be lay-men. They need to do this in order to prepare a report for the Home Office on restricted patients who have been nominated as patients of particular dangerousness who need the consideration of the board. It is not normal for the patient's consent to be obtained for this information to be revealed. Furthermore, the report of the committee is not made available either to the responsible medical officer or to the patient.

Information to the Mental Health Act Commission

The Mental Health Act Commissioners are entitled to review case records and may do so without the patient's consent, from time to time, when a visit is made to a hospital to check on the care of detained patients, even though the commissioners may not be medically qualified. When a problem of consent to treatment arises with a detained patient, the Mental Health Act Commission sends an approved practitioner to give a second opinion. That doctor will expect to have access to the medical notes. The consent of the patient would not be required.

The ethics of the control of detained patients

In looking after detained patients there are various situations in which staff may be obliged to physically hold or contain a patient, e.g. during a violent outburst or during a determined attempt to abscond. Clearly the rights of staff in this situation must be understood as well as there being a code of behaviour for the staff to follow.

Rights of staff

Staff receive legal protection from a charge of assault when in the course of their duty they have to do such things as use physical force, give injections without consent, seclude or prevent a patient absconding. Both common law and the Mental Health Act protect them. The common law allows the imposition of treatment without consent when given to prevent a criminal act occurring or to save life or prevent a serious harm (e.g. treating an unconscious patient). No civil proceedings may be brought without leave of the High Court, and no criminal proceedings except by or with the consent of the Director of Public Prosecutions in respect of an act purporting to be done as part of the duty arising out of the Mental Health Act 1983 (Section 139). For such proceedings to succeed the court must be satisfied that the person accused acted in bad faith or without reasonable care. Jones[17] in his annotation of Section 139 states that the House of Lords held that treatment may necessarily involve the exercise of discipline and control.

The ethics of physical control

Guidelines are needed to indicate when physical control should be used, including seclusion, lest it be used arbitrarily. The Mental Health Act Code of Practice[14] outlines a number of situations where seclusion may be justified including behaviour that is threatening or dangerous. It outlines ways to minimise the use of seclusion – keeping patients informed and attending to their complaints, having defined personal space for patients, ensuring open space and access to facilities such as a telephone, structured and energetic activities, and having trained staff.

All psychiatric units should have clear policies on the use of restraint. Physical restraint should be used as a last resort, in an emergency to prevent significant harm being done. Staff who restrain patients should be skilled in safe methods of physical restraint. 'Control and restraint' methods originally developed in the prison system have been adapted for use in hospitals. These methods must be taught by properly trained instructors to ensure proper use of potentially dangerous methods of control. They should always be employed in an overall framework of de-escalation techniques for controlling potentially dangerous situations. There must be careful monitoring of the use of physical restraint to ensure that it is not being abused and is always reasonable in the circumstances. The Code states that a senior manager should be informed if restraint lasts for more than two hours and that a review procedure should be available for such cases.[14]

Seclusion is defined as the supervised confinement of a patient alone in a locked room. Seclusion should be used as little as possible. It is only indicated as a last resort to contain severely disturbed behaviour that is likely to cause harm to others. It should never be used to control the suicidal or merely because equipment is being damaged. It can be minimised in secure units, if suitable levels of staffing, training and facilities are provided, i.e. a small ward or area given over to the very intensive care of the very disturbed. Units employing seclusion must have a policy that lays down minimum standards for the review of seclusion within the guidance set out in the Code of Practice,[14] which must be adhered to. The secure room should be properly heated, lit, ventilated and safe. Continuous observation should be possible whilst offering privacy from other patients.

Treatment by programmes of behaviour modification

The term behaviour modification is used to refer to programmes in which attempts were made to apply to practical issues, management and treatment, the principles and techniques which have been developed from systematic and experimental studies on human and animal behaviour. The problems of using such techniques on detained patients include the risk of abuse, either by excessive zeal or ignorance of untrained staff. There may be a loss of flexibility, loss of compassion and loss of respect for the rights of patients. This problem (and the problem of 'time out' and other psychological treatments) has been addressed in the Code of Practice.[14] No treatment should deprive a patient of food, shelter, water, warmth, a comfortable environment, confidentiality or reasonable privacy. Managers have a responsibility to see that behaviour modification programmes are clearly set out and understandable. A person with sufficient skills should monitor the programme and the patient. A programme must be part of an agreed treatment plan and not a sudden reaction to unwanted behaviour. Patients and relatives must be fully informed. A patient's consent should be sought if possible. However if consent cannot or is not obtained the treatment can be used if the RMO consults with a suitably trained person who is not part of the team responsible for the patient. If the treatment then goes ahead the RMO should notify the management. The RMO is responsible for seeing that the staff involved in the therapy have the necessary skills.

Duty of care

When a doctor has accepted responsibility for treating a patient he takes on a duty of care which is shared by his team. The BMA[7] point out that the doctor has a responsibility for continuing care until the patient is handed on to another doctor.

The ethics of medical care in prison

Ethical problems can arise in the case of all prisoners but particularly with the mentally abnormal offender.

The Health Advisory Committee to the Prison Service[18] advises that equivalence of care should be central to the provision of mental health care in prisons. Citizens, on entering prison, do not lose their right to comprehensive health care. Policies on health care apply equally to prisoners and to the base population. A poor standard of health care does not form part of the punishment element of imprisonment. Problems arise in the application of this principle of equivalence because health care has to be, of necessity, provided separately to prisoners through dedicated services within prisons, as they cannot usually go out to normal NHS treatment facilities. The Chief Inspector of Prisons[19] has criticised the separation of health care in prisons from that of the NHS because of the perceived gap in policy of services provided in the Prison Health Service and the NHS. The practical problem of providing adequate medical care in prisons is discussed in Chapter 1.

As well as the general concern about lack of equivalence between health care and prisons and the NHS, the following points have caused particular concern.

(1) Prisoners cannot choose their own doctor. It is particularly important therefore that the prison medical officers accept the responsibility of providing a professional relationship with their patient which shall be as good as that of a doctor working outside prison. Access to a second opinion should be easy.

(2) The conditions and standard of care (reflecting different skills and staffing levels) in prison health care centres for the care of the mentally ill may fall far below that in psychiatric hospitals.[18, 19] Health care policy is for those prisoners requiring in-patient psychiatric care to receive that care in a NHS hospital. Health care centres in prisons are not expected to provide full in-patient care. The shortcomings of prison health care centres may therefore be the result of failure on the part of the NHS to provide adequate facilities to meet the needs of those prisoners requiring in-patient treatment.

(3) The prison doctor has a duty to the patient, but he also has a duty to the institution. This could cause a conflict of interests[20] but as Gunn[21] points out, the doctor's first responsibility must always be the welfare of the patient within the framework of the institution. The BMA supports the view that prison doctor should not have to fulfil both functions.

(4) The prison doctor may be required to comment on the prisoner's fitness to face disciplinary charges in prison and to state whether a mental disturbance accounts for offending behaviour. If the prisoner is mentally unfit it is normal to be excused punishment and for the doctor to take over his care. Gunn[21] points out that this activity is no different from psychiatrists assessing offenders for the court.

(5) The prison doctor may be required to comment on a prisoner's fitness for punishment. Prison doctors in England restrict themselves to commenting on the inmate's fitness for adjudication. The United Nations standard minimum rules for the punishment of prisoners allows close confinement and reduction of diet, providing it is not calculated to damage health. The BMA advice is that doctors should not be associated with any dietary restriction (or other punishment) which would damage health. The doctor therefore has a role in deciding if a procedure is excessive or dangerous to the prisoner's health. If it is, then the doctor should make a written report and refuse to be further associated with the procedure. The doctor should not be associated with corporal punishment or incarceration in a dark cell. Some have argued that a doctor should have nothing to do with any punishment. However, trying to excuse sick people from adjudication for such punishment rather than by refusing to examine them at all[21] may better preserve medical integrity.

(6) The prison doctor may prescribe drugs but this has to be with the prisoner's consent, as prison hospitals are not covered by the Mental Health Act. However, in cases of emergency, under common law, medication may be given without consent to save life, to restrain a violent prisoner who is violent because of his clinical condition, or to prevent irretrievable deterioration.

(7) There may be a clash between the need to keep people safely in custody and the duties of the Prison Health Service, to provide treatment to prisoners as defined by the GMC which places considerable weight on respecting patients' dignity and privacy and ensuring that care of patients remains the doctor's first concern. This is most starkly illustrated by the ethical concerns raised by many doctors about the shackling of prisoners when visiting hospitals outside the prison and most particularly when women are giving birth to children.

(8) Good care in prisons is not subject to outside scrutiny in the same way as treatment to detained patients in the NHS is through the Mental Health Act Commission. Procedures which attract guidance in the Mental Health Act Code of Practice, such as seclusion and use of restraint, are used in prisons but are not subject to the same scrutiny. Health care facilities, practice and resources are commented on by the Chief Inspector of Prisons in reports on individual prisons and in thematic reviews of care. The Health Advisory Committee for the Prison Service provides independent advice to ministers on health care in prisons. In recent years the Prison Health Directorate has issued standards for health care which are open to audit. Such health care standards will now be included in the prison auditing process. Health care in prisons is thus becoming more open and accountable.

Doctors and torture

Torture is the deliberate infliction of severe and excruciating pain in hatred, revenge or for extortion or control, etc. A doctor should have nothing to do with it.

It is agreed that, despite the extreme dangers, the doctor has a duty to expose torture, especially when his own patients are victims. The doctor may also come across torture directly or from seeing injured patients. The perpetrators may be acting for the state or on their own.

Britain is a signatory to the European Convention of Human Rights of which Article 3 says that no one shall be subjected to 'inhuman and degrading treatment or punishment'.[22] Inspectors from the convention will make *ad hoc* visits to places where people are detained, e.g. prisons, police cells, psychiatric hospitals and nursing homes. The purpose is to expose deficiencies and bad practice and bring them to the notice of governments in the expectation that they will be corrected. The findings will clarify and modify ethics in this area. If the corrections do not occur the findings will be published.

References

(1) Appelbaum, P. (1997) A theory of ethics for forensic psychiatry. *Journal of the American Academy of Psychiatry Law* **25**, 233–47.
(2) Royal College of Psychiatrists (1992) *Ethical Issues in Psychiatric Practice in Prisons*. Council Report CR15. Royal College of Psychiatrists: London.
(3) Council of Europe (1998) *Recommendations of the Committee of Ministers to Member States Concerning the Ethical and Organisational Aspects of Health Care in Prisons*. CM(97)79. Council of Europe: Strasbourg.
(4) General Medical Council. *Good Medical Practice*. General Medical Council: London.
(5) General Medical Council. *Maintaining Good Medical Practice*. General Medical Council: London.
(6) General Medical Council. *Confidentiality*. General Medical Council: London.
(7) British Medical Association (1993) *Medical Ethics Today: Its Practice and Philosophy*. British Medical Journal Publishing Group: London.
(8) Smith, A. (1998) Psychiatric evidence and discretionary life sentences. *Journal of Forensic Psychiatry* **9**(1), 17–38.
(9) Joseph, P. (1998) He who pays the piper. *Journal of Forensic Psychiatry* **9** (3), 509–12.
(10) Richard, W.M. and Buchanan, A. (1998) Ethical problems in forensic psychiatry. *Current Opinion in Psychiatry* **11**, 695–702.
(11) Campbell, R.J. (1985) Lessons for the future drawn from United States legislation and experience In: *Psychiatry, Human Rights and the Law* (eds M. Roth and R. Bluglass). Cambridge University Press: Cambridge.
(12) Kennedy, I. and Grubb, A. (1998) *Principles of Medical Law*. Oxford University Press: Oxford.

(13) Legal Correspondent (1984) Consent to treatment: the medical standard reaffirmed. *British Medical Journal* **288**, 802–3.

(14) Department of Health and Welsh Office (1993) *Code of Practice: Mental Health Act 1983*. HMSO: London.

(15) Roth, L.H. and Meisel, A. (1977) Dangerousness, confidentiality, and the duty to warn. *American Journal of Psychiatry* **134**, 508–11.

(16) Royal College of Psychiatrists (1990) Guidelines for research ethics committees on psychiatric research involving human subjects. *Psychiatric Bulletin* **14**, 48–61.

(17) Jones, R.M. (1996) *Mental Health Act Manual*, fifth edition. Sweet and Maxwell: London.

(18) Health Advisory Committee for the Prison Service (1997) *The Provision of Mental Health Care in Prisons*. Home Office: London.

(19) HM Inspectorate of Prisons (1996) *Patient or Prisoner? A New Strategy for Health Care in Prisons*. Home Office: London.

(20) Bowden, P. (1976) Medical practise: defendants and prisoners. *Journal of Medical Ethics* **2**, 163–72.

(21) Gunn, J. (1985) Psychiatry and the prison medical service. In: *Secure Provision* (ed. L. Gostin). Tavistock Publications: London and New York.

(22) Harding, T.W. (1989) The application of the European Convention of Human Rights to the field of psychiatry. *International Journal of Law and Psychiatry* **12**, 245–62.

Index